Lecture Notes in Computer Science

Commenced Publication in 1973
Founding and Former Series Editors:
Gerhard Goos, Juris Hartmanis, and Jan van Leeuwen

Ted Herman   Sébastien Tixeuil (Eds.)

Self-Stabilizing Systems

7th International Symposium, SSS 2005
Barcelona, Spain, October 26-27, 2005
Proceedings

 Springer

Volume Editors

Ted Herman
University of Iowa
Department of Computer Science
Iowa City, IA 52242, USA
E-mail: herman@cs.uiowa.edu

Sébastien Tixeuil
Université Paris-Sud
LRI
Bâtiment 490, 91405 Orsay Cedex, France
E-mail: tixeuil@lri.fr

Library of Congress Control Number: 2005934787

CR Subject Classification (1998): C.2.4, C.2, C.3, F.1, F.2.2, K.6

ISSN   0302-9743
ISBN-10   3-540-29814-2 Springer Berlin Heidelberg New York
ISBN-13   978-3-540-29814-4 Springer Berlin Heidelberg New York

Springer is a part of Springer Science+Business Media

springeronline.com

© Springer-Verlag Berlin Heidelberg 2005
Printed in Germany

Typesetting: Camera-ready by author, data conversion by Scientific Publishing Services, Chennai, India
Printed on acid-free paper   SPIN: 11577324   06/3142   5 4 3 2 1 0

Preface

Self-stabilization is an established principle of modern distributed system design. The advantages of systems that self-recover from transient failures, temporary security attacks, and spontaneous reconfiguration are obvious. Less obvious is how the ambitious goal of recovering from the most general case of a transient fault, namely that of an arbitrary initial state, can lead to a simpler system design than dealing with particular cases of failures. In the area of mathematical problem-solving, Pólya gave the term "the inventors paradox" to such situations, where generalizing the problem may simplify the solution. The dramatic growth of distributed systems, peer-to-peer distribution networks, and large grid computing environments confronts designers with serious difficulties of complexity and has motivated the call for systems that self-recover, self-tune, and self-manage. The principles of self-stabilization can be useful for these goals of autonomous system behavior.

The Symposium on Self-Stabilizing Systems (SSS) is the main forum for research in the area of self-stabilization. Previous Workshops on Self-Stabilizing Systems (WSS) were held in 1989, 1995, 1997, 1999, and 2001. The previous Symposium on Self-Stabilizing Systems (SSS) took place in 2003. Thirty-three papers were submitted to SSS 2005 by authors from Europe (16), North America (8), Asia (4), and elsewhere (5). From the submissions, the program committee selected 15 for inclusion in these proceedings. In addition to the presentation of these papers, the symposium event included a poster session with brief presentations of recent work on self-stabilization.

The technical contributions to the symposium this year showed that the area has matured deeply since its first mathematical definition more than thirty years ago. Although there remains a core of four "classical" self-stabilization papers (that close gaps and open problems), the main part of the proceedings is dedicated to either extensions of self-stabilization (six contributions, dealing with snap-stabilization, code stabilization, self-stabilization with either dynamic, faulty or Byzantine components) or to applications of self-stabilization (five contributions, related to operating systems, security, or mobile and *ad hoc* networks).

The symposium of 2005 was one of the events of MANWEEK 2005, which also included the International Conference on Management of Multimedia Networks and Services (MMNS 2005), the International Workshop on IP Operations and Management (IPOM 2005), and the IEEE/IFIP International Workshop on Autonomic Grid Networking and Management (AGNM 2005). The site for the symposium and the other conferences was the Universitat Politècnica de Catalunya, in Barcelona. The SSS 2005 sessions were held on October 26 and 27.

We thank the organizers of MANWEEK 2005, especially Joan Serrat of the Universitat Politècnica de Catalunya, for making local arrangements.

August 2005

Ted Herman
Sébastien Tixeuil

Organization

Steering Committee

Anish Arora, The Ohio State University
Ajoy K. Datta, University of Nevada at Las Vegas
Shlomi Dolev, Ben-Gurion University of the Negev
Sukumar Ghosh, University of Iowa
Mohamed G. Gouda, University of Texas at Austin
Ted Herman, University of Iowa
Shing-Tsaan Huang, National Central University, Taiwan
Vincent Villain, Université de Picardie

Program Committee

Jorge Cobb, University of Texas at Dallas
Pascal Felber, Université de Neuchâtel
Roy Friedman, Technion
Felix Gärtner, RWTH Aachen
Maria Gradinariu, IRISA / INRIA Rennes
Ted Herman (Chair), University of Iowa
Jaap-Henk Hoepman, Radboud University Nijmegen
Hirotsugu Kakugawa, Hiroshima University
Mikhail Nesterenko, Kent State University
Marina Papatriantafilou, Chalmers University
Manish Parashar, Rutgers University
Franck Petit, Université de Picardie
Srikanta Tirthapura, Iowa State University
Sébastien Tixeuil, Université Paris-Sud

Additional Reviewers

Doina Bein	Christian Boulinier	Praveen Danturi
Ken Calvert	Thomas Clouser	Murat Demirbas
Bertrand Ducourthial	Ajoy Datta	Martin Gairing
Stéphane Devismes	Shlomi Dolev	Yinnon Haviv
Sukumar Ghosh	Mohamed Gouda	Sayaka Kamei
Lisa Higham	Shing-Tsaan Huang	Boris Koldehofe
Ronen Kat	Yoshiaki Katayama	Xiaolin Li
Sandeep Kulkarni	Mikel Larrea	Stephane Messika
Toshimitsu Masuzawa	Vincent Matossian	Phillipe Raipin Parvedy
Yoshihiro Nakaminami	Rajesh Patel	Laurent Rosaz
Sriram Pemmaraju	Michel de Rougemont	Philippas Tsigas
Nir Tzachar	Oliver Theel	Chen Zhang
Vincent Villain	Antonino Virgillito	
Guangsen Zhang	Anat Bremler-Bar	

Table of Contents

Snap-Stabilizing Optimal Binary Search Tree

Doina Bein[1], Ajoy K. Datta[1], and Vincent Villain[2]

[1] School of Computer Science, University of Nevada, Las Vegas
{siona, datta}@cs.unlv.edu
[2] LaRIA,Université de Picardie Jules Verne, France
villain@laria.u-picardie.fr

Abstract. We present the first snap-stabilizing distributed *binary search tree* (BST) algorithm. A *snap-stabilizing* algorithm guarantees that the system always behaves according to its specification provided some processor initiated the protocol. The maximum number of items that can be stored at any time at any processor is constant (independent of the size (n) of the network). Under this space constraint, we show a lower bound of $\Omega(n)$ on the time complexity for the BST problem. We then prove that starting from an arbitrary configuration where the nodes have distinct internal values drawn from an arbitrary set, our algorithm arranges them in a BST order in $O(n)$ rounds. Therefore, our solution is asymptotically optimal in time and takes $O(n)$ rounds. A processor i requires $O(\log s_i)$ bits of space where s_i is the size of the subtree rooted at i. So, the root uses $O(\log n)$ bits. The proposed algorithm uses a *heap* algorithm as a preprocessing step. This is also the first snap-stabilizing distributed solution to the heap problem. The heap construction spends $O(h)$ (where h is the height of the tree) rounds. Its space requirement is constant (independent of n). We then exploit the heap in the next phase of the protocol. The root collects values in decreasing order and delivers them to each node in the tree in $O(n)$ rounds following a pipelined delivery order of sorted values in decreasing order.

Keywords: Binary search tree, heap, self-stabilization, snap-stabilization.

1 Introduction

Given a binary tree where every node holds one key (value) drawn from an arbitrary set of real values, we design a snap-stabilizing distributed algorithm to arrange the values in the tree to obtain a binary search tree. A self-stabilizing [5,6] system, regardless of the initial states of the processors and initial messages in the links, is guaranteed to converge to the intended behavior in finite time. A *snap-stabilizing* [2,4] algorithm guarantees that it always behaves according to its specification. In other words, a snap-stabilizing algorithm is also a self-stabilizing algorithm which stabilizes in 0 steps.

The BST construction works as follows. First, the values in the tree are re-arranged as a heap (we implement a MaxHeap but a MinHeap is equally possible). Based on the heap arrangement, the root collects values in decreasing

T. Herman and S. Tixeuil (Eds.): SSS 2005, LNCS 3764, pp. 1–17, 2005.

order and delivers them to each node in the tree (a sequential, pipelined delivery of sorted values in decreasing order). The tree structure is not modified by our algorithm.

Related Work: A heap construction that supports insert and delete operations in arbitrary states over a variant of the standard binary heap [3] with the maximum capacity of K items is proposed in [8]. It takes $O(m \log K)$ heap operations to stabilize (m is the initial number of items in the heap). The space complexity per node i is $O(h_i)$ where h_i is the height of the subtree T_i in the binary heap rooted at node i. Stabilizing search 2-3 trees are investigated in [9]. The stabilization time is $O(n \log n)$ rounds where n is the number of nodes in the initial state and the space complexity per node i is $O(d_i)$ where d_i is the distance from the root to node i.

Contributions: This paper has two major contributions. It includes the first snap-stabilizing binary search tree (BST) and the first snap-stabilizing heap algorithm. Being snap-stabilizing gives our algorithms a unique feature — they *always* behave as expected by their specifications. It should be noted that a self-stabilizing algorithm is guaranteed to satisfy the desired specification *only* in a finite time. In the context of the BST problem, in a self-stabilizing BST solution, if the root initiates a BST computation, it is not guaranteed that the tree will become a BST when the computation terminates. If the computation is repeated (a bounded but unknown number of times), the self-stabilizing algorithm guarantees that eventually, the tree will become a BST. The proposed snap-stabilizing solution achieves a much better solution than the above. It ensures that when a BST computation initiated by the root terminates, the tree is a BST. Thus, we do not need to repeat the computation unless the application program demands repeated sorting of the values in the tree.

A key feature of our solution is that the maximum number of items that can be stored at any time at any processor is constant (independent of the size (n) of the network). Under this space constraint, our solution is asymptotically optimal in time and takes $O(n)$ rounds. A processor i requires $O(\log s_i)$ bits where s_i is the size of the subtree rooted at i. So, the root uses $O(\log n)$ bits. The proposed algorithm uses a snap-stabilizing heap algorithm as a preprocessing step. This is also the first snap-stabilizing distributed solution to the heap problem. The cost of the heap construction is $O(h)$ rounds and constant (independent of n) space.

Outline of the Paper: In Section 2, we present the computational model, snap-stabilization, and the specification of the BST problem. We present the solution (the detail code of the algorithm) in Section 3. Due to lack of space, the detail code of the predicates and macros are omitted. They are available in the technical report [1]. We give a sketch of the correctness proof in Section 4, while the detail proof is available in [1]. We finish the paper with some concluding remarks in Section 5.

2 Preliminaries

Distributed System: We consider an asynchronous binary tree network of n processors with distinct ID's. The root is denoted by r. We will use nodes and processors interchangeably. The processors communicate using bi-directional links. We assume the local shared memory model of communication. The program of every processor consists of a set of *shared variables* and a finite set of actions. A processor can only write to its own variables, and read its own variables and variables owned by the neighboring processors. Each action is of the following form: $< label > < guard > \longrightarrow < statement >$. The guard of an action in the program of any process p is a boolean expression involving the variables of p and its neighbors. The statement of an action of p updates one or more variables of p. An action can be executed only if its guard evaluates to true. We assume that the actions are atomically executed, meaning, the evaluation of a guard and the execution of the corresponding statement of an action, if executed, are done in one atomic step.

The *state* of a processor is defined by the value of its variables. The *state* of a system is the product of the states of all processors. We will refer to the state of a processor and system as a *(local) state* and *(global) configuration*, respectively. A processor p is said to be *enabled* in a configuration γ if there exists at least an action A such that the guard of A is true in γ. We consider that any processor p executed a *disabling action* in the computation step $\gamma_i \mapsto \gamma_{i+1}$ if p was enabled in γ_i and not enabled in γ_{i+1}, but did not execute any action between these two configurations. (The disabling action represents the following situation: At least one neighbor of p changed its state between γ_i and γ_{i+1}, and this change effectively made the guard of all actions of p false.) Similarly, an action A is said to be enabled (in γ) at p if the guard of A is true at p (in γ). We assume an *unfair and distributed daemon*. The *unfairness* means that a processor p may never be chosen by the daemon to execute an action even if it is continuously enabled unless it is the only enabled processor.

A *computation step* is a transition between two configurations where the transition contains at least one action and at most one action per processor. The *distributed* daemon implies that during a computation step, if one or more processors are enabled, then the daemon chooses at least one (possibly more) of these enabled processors to execute an action.

In order to compute the time complexity measure, we use the definition of *round* [7]. This definition captures the execution rate of the slowest processor in any computation. Given a computation e, the *first round* of e (let us call it e') is the minimal prefix of e containing the execution of one action (an action of the protocol or the disable action) of every continuously enabled processor from the first configuration. Let e'' be the suffix of e, i.e., $e = e'e''$. Then *second round* of e is the first round of e'', and so on.

Snap-Stabilization: We assume that in a normal execution, at least one processor (called, the *initiator*) initiates the protocol upon an external (w.r.t. the protocol) request by executing a special type of action, called an *initialization action*.

Definition 1 (Snap-Stabilization). *Let P be a protocol designed to solve a task T. P is called* snap-stabilizing *if and only if, starting from any configuration, any execution E of P always satisfies the specification of T.*

Specification 21 (BST Problem). *A protocol P is considered as a BST algorithm, if and only if the following conditions are true: (i) Any computation initiated by the root terminates in finite time. (ii) When the computation terminates, the values in the tree satisfy the BST property.*

Remark 1. To prove that a BST algorithm is snap-stabilizing, we have to show that every execution of the protocol satisfies the following two properties: (i) starting from any configuration, the root eventually executes an initialization action. (ii) Any execution, starting from this action, satisfies Specification 21.

The time needed to reach the configuration where the initialization action is enabled is called the *delay* of the protocol.

3   Binary Search Tree Algorithm

In this section, we describe the data structures used, followed by a detailed explanation of how the algorithm works when the initiator (the root process) starts the algorithm until the values are arranged in the tree such that it becomes a BST. We divide the algorithm code in two parts: module $Heap$ (Subsection 3.1) and module $Sort$ (Subsection 3.2).

A node i holds four *constants*. The constants are not changed by the BST algorithm. The constants are: the value $V.i$ that needs to be sorted in the tree, the parent ID $p.i$, the left child ID $left.i$, and the right child ID $right.i$. If i does not have any of the above three neighbors, the corresponding constant's value is represented as $\perp$. For example, for the root node r, $p.r = \perp$, and for the leaf nodes, $left.i = right.i = \perp$. We denote the set of neighbors and set of children of i by $N.i$ and $D.i$, respectively. We assume that the tree has n nodes and has a height of h. Let T_i be the subtree rooted at i. Then s_i and h_i denote the number of nodes and height, respectively, of T_i.

Our BST construction is transparent to the changes (addition or removal of notes) in the tree structure. If such changes occur, then the algorithm will incorporate the changes "on the fly" by nodes either entering an abnormal situation with respect to their new neighbors, or by completing the current cycle and restarting a new cycle with added/deleted values. We assume that after the add/remove operations/queries are executed, our algorithm will be initiated by the root and a new BST tree will be constructed in $O(n)$ rounds. This makes the lower bound of $\Omega(n)$ under the constraints considered in this work higher than that of the usual functions (e.g., find, insert, and delete) for a non-stabilizing BST.

The basic idea of the algorithm is as follows: The algorithm runs in two phases. The root initiates the BST computation by starting a heapify process (shown as Module $Heap$ in the algorithm) to create a maxheap of the tree. Then the root initiates the second phase (shown as *Sort* module). During this phase, the values are placed in the nodes in the BST order, placing the highest value first, the second highest value next, and so on. As the maxheap has been created in the previous phase, the root holds the maximum value of the tree. This highest value is sent to the rightmost node (say, i) of the tree. The destination of the second highest value (say, *second*) is dependent on if i is a leaf or an internal node. If i is a leaf node, then *second* is sent to the parent of i (say, j). Then the third highest value (say, *third*) will be sent to the left child of j (if present) or to the parent of j. If i is an internal node, then *second* goes to the left child of i. Thus, values are placed in the tree following a right-parent-left order.

The algorithm will be similar if we have constructed a minheap instead of the maxheap. In that case, in the second phase, the values will be placed following a left-parent-right order. From now on, heap will imply maxheap. If a node i satisfies the maxheap property with respect to its parent and children, we say i is in heap order or in HO in short.

Some of the variables used by a node i are described below. The rest of the variables will be defined in the informal explanations in the next two subsections. The sorted value $SV.i$ will contain the final sorted value at the end of the algorithm. $tSV.i$ is used to store a temporary sorted value. The heap value $HV.i$ is the result of the first phase (*Heap* module). The module *Sort* needs to maintain the size of the subtrees rooted at each node. This size variable $s.i$ for node i is computed in *Heap* and used in *Sort*.

A node may use at most seven states (see Figure 1 below). Module *Heap* uses six states: C (cleaning state), B (ready to start the heapify process), M, M^{left}, M^{right} (the states corresponding to if the maximum heap value HV is based on its own heap value, the maximum heap value of its left child, the maximum heap value of its right child, respectively), P (the *Heap* phase finished at this node, and the *Sort* phase is ready to start at this node). Module *Sort* uses C, P, and T (the algorithm is terminated).

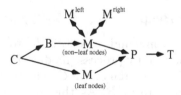

Fig. 1. The seven states used by the algorithm

A configuration in which the root is in state C is called a *clean configuration*. Starting from such a configuration, all other nodes in the tree will eventually reach C state. If all nodes are in C state, then the corresponding configuration is termed as a *normal starting configuration*. Any configuration reachable from a normal starting configuration by executing the algorithm guards is called a *normal configuration*. All other configurations are considered to be *abnormal*.

Some abnormal configurations can be locally detected by the processors. This local detection is implemented using the *abnormal* predicates in Algorithms 3.1 and 3.2. These predicates are used as guards of correction actions in order to avoid possible deadlocks and to speed up the protocol. Unfortunately, some problems of abnormal configurations cannot be locally detected. For example, the initial configuration may contain some sorted values (in tSV) that do not match any V values. The correction actions can remove the locally detectable problems in $O(h)$ rounds even before the root executes its initialization action. The other problems are eventually removed during the suffix of the protocol starting from the initialization action of the root.

Starting from an abnormal configuration, an execution not necessarily will bring the system to a normal starting configuration, but to a normal configuration. When a node has an abnormal predicate enabled, it will change its state to C, and all the nodes in its subtree will enter C state, but not necessarily its parent (e.g. if the parent state is B).

Starting from a normal configuration where the root is able to execute the initialization action with no delay, the tree will become a BST in $O(n)$ rounds. In general, the worst delay is $O(n)$ rounds because the worst initial configuration is the one where no node has any of the abnormal predicates enabled, but there is a node with an incorrect tSV value (that does not match any V values). Thus, the abnormal configurations do not increase the asymptotic time bound. So, starting from any configuration, the tree will become a BST in $O(n)$ rounds.

The interface between the two layers (application and BST) at a node i is implemented by two variables: input value to the sorting protocol $V.i$ and the final or output sorted value $SV.i$. However, every time the BST protocol runs, we do not want to disturb the application layer by writing (or overwriting) the value of $SV.i$ unless the value has changed. So, when the BST protocol terminates, i's sorted value is first placed in $tSV.i$. Then $tSV.i$ and $SV.i$ are compared. The value of $tSV.i$ is copied into $SV.i$ only if the values are different (see Actions $rP3$, $iP3$, and $lP1\&3$ of module *Sort*).

3.1   Constructing the Heap

Upon receiving an external command to sort, if the root is enabled to start the BST protocol, it starts the heapify process (module $Heap$). The root is enabled to initiate if it is in C and its children are in C. The root broadcasts the heapify command by changing its state to B. As this message (wave) goes down the tree, all internal nodes change their state from C to B. When this broadcast wave reaches the leaf nodes, they change their state from C to M to initiate the heapify process (or wave). During this upward wave, the nodes compute two things: the heap value (the maximum value in their subtrees) and the size of their subtrees. When this wave reaches the root, the root changes its state to M and the heap is created. The root then initiates another top-down wave by changing its state from M to P. The next phase, i.e., the BST construction phase starts from the P state. We now describe the heap construction in more detail by referring Algorithm 3.1.

1. *(Start building a Heap)* If the root is in C, its children will change to C in at most one round. Either Action aCm or aCb is enabled, and since it is the only enabled action, it is eventually executed in at most one round. When its children change to C, the root changes its state from C to B and sets HV to its internal value V (Action CB). An internal node changes its state from C to B when its parent is in B and its children are in C. An internal node also initializes its heap value HV with its input (or initial) value V (Action CB).

Figure 2(a) shows the clean configuration for a 11-node binary tree. After B wave is executed top-down, the tree state is shown in Figure 2(b). We show only the node's internal value V, state S, and heap value HV. Symbol * means that the value is not important.

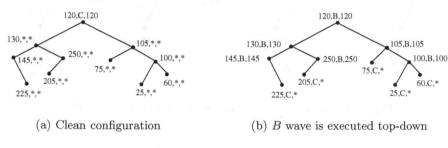

(a) Clean configuration   (b) B wave is executed top-down

Fig. 2. Initial stage of constructing the heap

2. *(Calculating Heap and s.i Values)* A leaf node i changes its state from C to M and executes macro $init(i)$ (Action CM). In the macro $init(i)$, the node i sets the size of its subtree, $s.i$ to 1 and sets the heap values of its left (lHV) and right (rHV) subtrees to $\bot$ (indicating a non-existent value).

When a parent of a leaf node detects that all its children are in state M (Action BM^* is enabled), it executes macro $init(i)$, change from B to M, and executes macro $set\_HVs(i)$. If the (parent) node holds a value smaller than any of the heap values of its children, it chooses as its heap value the larger heap value $(lHV$ or $rHV)$ among its children and pushes its own heap value (HV) toward the child that was holding the larger heap value. This heapification process goes up the tree until it reaches the root.

Predicate $update\_HVs(i)$ is *true* when due to the heapification process at the parent of i, i's heap value became smaller than the values of its children. So, $HV.i$ needs to be swapped with that of one of its children. Predicate $h\_order(i)$ is true if i satisfies the heap property with respect to its children.
For a non-leaf node i that is about to execute the macro $set\_HVs(i)$, we consider three cases.

Case 1). $HV.i$ is larger than the heap values of its children. So, heap order is maintained at i. Then the macro $set\_HVs(i)$ does not change the variables $S.i$ (remains M) and $HV.i$.

Case 2). Assume that the heap value of one of the children (say, the right child *right.i*) of i is higher than both $HV.i$ and that of the left child of i. The macro *set_HVs(i)* selects $dir.i = right$ and sets $S.i = M^{right}$. So, node i will push its old heap value (now in variable *down.i*) to its right child. Assume that *down.i* is larger than the heap values of the children of *right.i*. So, *down.i* (the old value of i) needs to be pushed only one level down the tree where it becomes the new heap value of *right.i* in at most two rounds: First Action lrM is performed at *right.i*, then Action $M^{lr}M$ is executed at node i (i changes its state back to M). Figure 3 shows a part of a binary tree to illustrate this case. For each node we show the variable s, the state S, lHV, HV, rHV, and *down*. Symbol b means ⊥. The check mark symbol marks an enabled node.

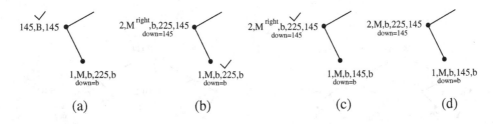

Fig. 3. Macro *set_HVs* executed at the node with $V = 145$

Case 3). Similar to Case 2 except that *down.i* is smaller than the heap value of one of the children of *right.i*. So, the old value of i (now in *down.i* needs to be pushed at least two levels down the tree before it finds a node j where *down.i* becomes the heap value of j. In Figure 4, the value 130 is pushed down two levels. For each node we show the variable s, the state S, lHV, HV, rHV, and *down*. Symbol b means ⊥. The check mark symbol marks an enabled node.

Smaller values may be pushed to a node i from its ancestor. When that happens, i changes its state from M to M^{left}/M^{right}. When the wave (changing

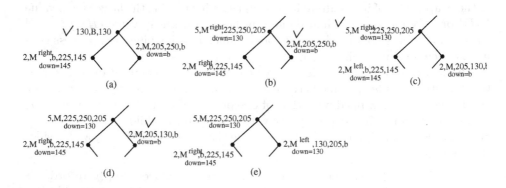

Fig. 4. Macro *set_HVs* executed at node with $V = 130$

state from B to M) reaches the root, the root changes its state from B to M. Then the root may change to state M^{left} or M^{right} if it needs to push its heap value (which is its internal value and now in $down.r$) down the tree. Then it pushes $down.r$ to either M^{left} or M^{right}. When the corresponding child of the root receives the value $down$, the root goes back to M and stays in M since it has no ancestors.

    3. *(Finishing the Heap Construction)* Predicate $consistency(i)$ is *true* when the heap values of the children of i stored at i are the same as the heap values stored at the corresponding children. When the root and its children are in state M and $consistency(r)$ is *true*, the root changes its state to P and executes macro $init\_P(r)$ (Action MP). Eventually, every node changes its state from M to P. This P wave eventually reaches the leaves. The root initiates the BST construction when the root and its children are in P, i.e., the root can start the next phase even if note all nodes of the tree are in P state.

    Starting from the clean configuration presented in Figure $2(a)$, after executing the *Heap* module when the root and its children are in state M, a possible configuration is given in Figure $5(a)$. The root, when surrounded by M state children, changes its state to P (Figure $5(b)$). For each node we show the variable s, the state S, lHV, HV, rHV, and $down$. Symbol b means $\perp$.

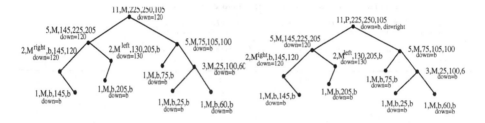

   (a) Root and its children are done   (b) P wave starts from the root

Fig. 5. The root and its children are done executing Module Heap

    We defined various *abnormal* predicates to characterize different types of local inconsistencies at a node during the heap construction. If any of these predicates is *true* at a node, then the only enabled action at that node will be aCm. This action when executed changes the state of the node to C.

3.2   Constructing the BST

At the end of the heap construction, every node changes it state from M to P and executes the macro $init\_P(i)$. In this macro, every non-leaf node i sets the variable $dir.i$ to point to the child that will receive the sorted value from the root. Recall that the sorted values are placed in right-parent-left order.

    Every node (including the root) will receive a sorted value from the root and send its heap value to the root. These two actions are executed concurrently.

Algorithm 3.1. *Module Heap*

Predicates

abnormal_B(i) :: is true when the node, in state B, is in abnormal situation with some neighbor (parent or child).
abnormal_M*(i) :: is true when the node, in state M, either has some variables with abnormal values or is in abnormal situation with some neighbor (parent or child).
consistency(i) :: is true when the nodes stores in $rHV.i$ and $lHV.i$ the heap values of its children (if any).
h_order(i) :: is true when the node has the MaxHeap property.
update_HVs(i) :: is true when the node needs to update its heap value since some child has a bigger heap value than itself.

Macros

init(i) :: is executed when changing from B/C to M state.
init_P(i) :: is executed when changing from M to P state to prepare the node for BST construction.
set_HVs(i) :: selects the child $dir \in \{left, right\}$ that has the maximum heap value by comparing $lHV.i$ and $rHV.i$.

{Program for the root node r}

CB $S.r = C \wedge \forall_{j \in D.r} S.j = C \longrightarrow S.r = B;\ HV.r = V.r$

BM^* $\neg abnormal\_B(r) \wedge S.r = B \wedge \forall_{j \in D.r} S.j \in \{M, M^{left}, M^{right}\} \longrightarrow init(r);\ S.r = M;\ set\_HVs(r)$

$M^{lr}M$ $\neg abnormal\_M^*(r) \wedge \exists_{j \in \{left, right\}} (S.r = M^j \wedge j.r \neq \bot \wedge HV.j.r = down.r) \longrightarrow S.r = M$

MP $\neg abnormal\_M^*(r) \wedge S.r = M \wedge \forall_{j \in D.r} S.j = M \wedge consistency(r) \longrightarrow S.r = P;\ init\_P(r)$

aCm $(S.r = B \wedge abnormal\_B(r)) \vee (S.r \in \{M, M^{left}, M^{right}\} \wedge abnormal\_M^*(r)) \longrightarrow S.r = C$

{Program for an internal node i, which is the d child of its parent, $d \in \{left, right\}$}

CB $S.i = C \wedge S.p.i = B \wedge \forall_{j \in D.i} S.j = C \longrightarrow S.i = B;\ HV.i = V.i$

BM^* $\neg abnormal\_B(i) \wedge S.i = B \wedge S.p.i = B \wedge \forall_{j \in D.i} S.j \in \{M, M^{left}, M^{right}\} \longrightarrow$
        $init(i);\ S.i = M;\ set\_HVs(i)$

$M^{lr}M$ $\neg abnormal\_M^*(i) \wedge \exists_{j \in \{left, right\}} (S.i = M^j \wedge j.i \neq \bot \wedge HV.j.i = down) \longrightarrow S.i = M$

lrM $\neg abnormal\_M^*(i) \wedge S.i = M \wedge S.p.i = M^d \wedge h\_order(i) \longrightarrow HV.i = down.p.i$

MM^* $\neg abnormal\_M^*(i) \wedge S.i = M \wedge update\_HVs(i) \longrightarrow set\_HVs(i)$

MP $\neg abnormal\_M^*(i) \wedge S.i = M \wedge S.p.i = P \wedge \forall_{j \in D.i} S.j = M \wedge consistency(i) \longrightarrow S.i = P;\ init\_P(i)$

aCm $(S.i = B \wedge abnormal\_B(i)) \vee (S.i \in \{M, M^{left}, M^{right}\} \wedge abnormal\_M^*(i)) \longrightarrow S.i = C$

{Program for a leaf node i, which is the d child of its parent, $d \in \{left, right\}$}

CM $S.i = C \wedge S.p.i = B \longrightarrow HV.i = V.i;\ init(i);\ S.i = M;$

lrM $\neg abnormal\_M^*(i) \wedge S.i = M \wedge S.p.i = M^d \longrightarrow HV.i = down.p.i$

MP $\neg abnormal\_M^*(i) \wedge S.i = M \wedge S.p.i = P \longrightarrow S.i = P;\ init\_P(i)$

aCm $(S.i = M \wedge abnormal\_M^*(i)) \vee S.i \in \{B, M^{left}, M^{right}\} \longrightarrow S.i = C$

Upon completion of the heap, the root holds the maximum (heap) value of the entire tree, its children hold the maximum (heap) values of their subtrees, and so on. The above heap property is exploited in the BST construction. The root first sends out its own heap value to the rightmost place in the tree. The root then gets the second highest value of the tree easily (in constant steps) from one of its children. So, the concurrency of the two main tasks — sending the sorted value to the proper place and moving the heap values upward toward the root — are achieved by using the heap property. That is the reason of using the heap phase as a pre-processing phase of the BST construction.

When a sorted value sent to a node belongs to that node (i.e., it is the node's sorted value), it is stored in tSV. A node is done sorting if all nodes in its subtree (including itself) received their final sorted values. This is checked in the predicate *done*. When a node is done, it changes its state to T. Obviously, this wave of state change from P to T starts from the leaves and ends at the root. When the root changes its state to T, the algorithm terminates. In the following, we describe a normal execution of module *Sort*:

4. *(Select Sorted Values for all Nodes)* Predicate *new_sorted()* is *true* if the root still has values to sort: $HV.r \neq \bot$, either it just started or the previous sorted value has been delivered ($down.r = \perp$), there are nodes that need more sorted values ($s.r > 0$), and it has consistency with its children ($consistency(r) = true$).

If the root is in P and Predicate $new\_sorted()$ is $true$, the only enabled action is Action $rP1$. So, it will eventually be executed. The current $HV.r$ value is moved into $down.r$, $s.r$ is decremented, and $HV.r$ becomes $\perp$. Then the larger of the heap values of one of its children is moved in $HV.r$ by executing the macro $move\_HVs(r)$. That will enable Action $rP1$ again.

5. *(Receive Sorted Value and/or Collect Heap Value)* Although these two actions are executed concurrently, we present them separately below:

5.1 *(Receive Sorted Value)* We first define a *target node* for some node. For some node i, if the condition $s.i > 0 \vee (s.i = 0 \wedge (left.i \neq \perp \wedge s.left.i = 1)$ is *true*, then there exists a unique node j to which $down.i \neq \perp$ will be delivered (either $j = i$ or j is one of the children of i). We call node j the *current target* of node i. $dir.i$ holds the value j.

We use the following predicates in this part of the algorithm:

Predicate $sent\_sorted(i)$ is $true$ if the non-root node i has previously received another value from its parent $p.i$ and it has already delivered it.

Predicate $my\_turn(i)$ is $true$ if it is the turn of node i to collect its sorted value. Node i has no current sorted value ($tSV.i \neq \perp$), either it has no right subtree ($right.i = \perp$) or is full ($s.right.i = 0$), and has a value ($down.i \neq \perp$) that was not taken by any of the children of node i (Predicate $sent\_sorted(i)$ is *false*).

Predicate $get\_sorted(j)$ is $true$ if j, the $d \in \{left, right\}$ child of its parent i, is allowed to copy in $down.i$ the value stored at its parent, j still needs sorted values ($s.j > 0$), it is the current target of node i ($dir.i = d$), and the sorted value held by i is a new one ($down.i \neq down.j$).

During the BST construction, if Predicate $my\_turn(i)$ is $true$, the target of node i is i itself. Otherwise, for a non-leaf node i, the target j of node i is one of the children of i that is allowed to copy into $down.j$ the value stored at $down.i$ if either Action $iP1$ or $lP1\&3$ is enabled and executed. We now consider the three types of target node j of node i (root, internal, and leaf) below:

[Root]) The target node is the root itself ($i = j = r$). Then $my\_turn(r)$ is $true$ and the only enabled action is Action $rP3$. The root moves $down.r$ into $tSV.r$, updates $SV.r$ if necessary, and selects its left child (if exists) as its current target (by changing $dir.r$ to $left$), and sets $down.r$ to $\perp$.

[Internal] The target node j is an internal node. We have two cases for j:

I1) If $my\_turn(j)$ is $true$, then the only enabled action for j is Action $iP3$ which is similar to Action $rP3$.

I2) If $my\_turn(j)$ is $false$, then the only possible enabled action for j is Action $iP1$. $iP1$ is enabled if $get\_sorted(j)$ is $true$ and the condition $down.j = \perp \vee sent\_sorted(j)$ are $true$.

Condition $down.j = \perp \vee sent\_sorted(j)$ is $true$ if either j has never received a value from i ($down.j = \perp$), or has previously received another value from i and has already delivered it ($sent\_sorted(j)$ is $true$).

When Action $iP1$ is performed, $down.i$ is copied into $down.j$, $s.j$ is decremented, and j checks if it has to give up its heap value to its parent (Predicate $moveup\_hv(j)$ is explained below).

[Leaf] The target node j is a leaf node. Since the only value the leaf is allowed to receive is its own sorted value, the target of j is j itself. If $get\_sorted(i)$ is *true*, the only action enabled at j is $lP1\&3$, so it eventually gets executed.

5.2 *(Collect Heap Value)* Predicate $moveup\_hv(i)$ is *true* for some node i if i's heap value ($HV.i \neq \bot$) was taken by $p.i$ as its heap value. In that case, i selects the larger of the heap values of its children as its next heap value. Variable $dhv.i$ indicates which child (heap value) will be selected. We now need to distinguish three cases.

Case 1 [$HV.i = \bot$]. i waits until $done(i)$ becomes *true* so that it can change to state T.

Case 2 [$HV.i \neq \bot \wedge lHV.i = \bot \wedge rHV.i = \bot$]. If node i is the root node r, then it has to wait until Action $rP1$ becomes enabled and gets executed. Then $HV.i$ becomes $\bot$ and *Case 1* becomes applicable.

If i is a non-root node, then when $moveup\_hv(i)$ is *true*, the heap value $HV.i \neq \bot$ is moved up the tree from node i to its parent $p.i$ (action $iP1$, $iP4$, $lP1\&3$, or $lP4$ is enabled and executed). $HV.i$ becomes $\bot$ and *Case 1* becomes applicable.

Case 3 [$HV.i \neq \bot \wedge (lHV.i \neq \bot \vee rHV.i \neq \bot)$]. Node i is a non-leaf node, and there exists a unique node j (decided in macro $move\_HVs(i)$) that will move its heap value to i's heap value when one of Actions $rP1$, $iP1$, $iP4$, $lP1\&3$, and $lP4$ is executed. Node j is one of the children of i and is called the *current sink* of node i.

If node i is the root node r, then it has to wait until Action $rP1$ becomes enabled and gets executed. Then macro $move\_HVs(r)$ is executed and $HV.i$ receives the larger of the heap value of its children. Either *Case 2* or *Case 3* becomes applicable then.

If i is a non-root node, then if $moveup\_hv(i)$ is *true*, the heap value $HV.i \neq \bot$ is moved up the tree from node i to its parent $p.i$ and i executes macro $move\_HVs(i)$ (Action $iP1$ or $iP4$ is enabled and executed). Either *Case 2* or *Case 3* becomes enabled.

For example, starting from a configuration where the root and its children are in state P, after executing the action $rP1$, we obtain the configuration shown in Figure 6(a). Now its right child has to execute $iP1$ before the root is able to move again and execute $rP2$. Also its left child has to execute $iP4$ before the root can execute $rP1$. Once both children execute, we obtain the configuration as shown in Figure 6(b). For each node, we show the variable s, the state S, lHV, HV, rHV, $down$, and dir. Symbol b means $\bot$.

6. *(Sets its Own Sorted Value and Adjusts the Direction for the Future Sorted Values)* If $my\_turn(i)$ is *true*, i collects its sorted value and adjusts the direction of sorted values toward its left subtree, if it exists. Otherwise, $dir.i$ is set to $\bot$.

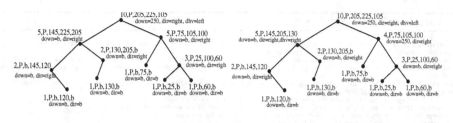

(a) Root generates a sorted value
(Action $rP1$)

(b) Right node gets the value,
left node changes its HV

Fig. 6. Some state ending the execution of *Heap* module by root and its children

7. *(Terminating the BST)* Predicate $done(i)$ is *true* when node i has $HV.i = \perp$, does not need more sorted values from the root, and has its currently sorted value $tSV.i \neq \perp$.

When a leaf node i is done receiving the sorted values ($done(i)$ is *true*), it changes its state from P to T. When a non-leaf node i is done receiving its sorted values (predicate $done(i)$ is *true*) and all its children are in state T, i changes its state from P to T (Action PT is enabled).

We defined various *abnormal* predicates to characterize different types of local inconsistencies at a node during the BST construction. If any of these predicates is *true* at a node, then the only enabled action at that node will be aCb. This action when executed changes the state of the node to C.

4 Proof of Correctness

Due to lack of space, we give a brief summary of the correctness proof, while details are available in [1].

We first present the proof of correctness assuming the weakly fair daemon. (A daemon is *weakly fair* if a continuously enabled process will be eventually chosen by the daemon.) Later in Section 4.2, we show that the algorithm works under the unfair daemon as well. The time and space complexity of the algorithm are discussed in Section 4.1.

We first show a lower bound of $\Omega(n)$ on the time complexity for the BST problem under the constraint as discussed earlier (Lemma 1).

Next, we show how the algorithm corrects any abnormal configuration into a normal configuration in finite number of rounds. Considering faulty networks, the system may start in an *abnormal configuration* where there exists at least one *abnormal processor*. We prove that if some node i is abnormal, then $S.i$ becomes C in at most one round. Using this result, we show that if $S.i = C$, all the nodes in the subtree rooted at i, T_i change to C in $O(h_i)$ rounds. Then in $O(h)$ rounds the system reaches a configuration which does not contain any local problem and the behavior of the protocol is now almost as the normal behavior (the result is in Lemma 4. We conclude that the *delay* (the time needed for

Algorithm 3.2. *ModuleSort*

Predicates

abnormal_P(i, d) :: is true when the node, in state P, either has some variables with abnormal values or is in abnormal situation with some neighbor (parent or child).

s_consistent(i) :: is true when $s.i$ is consistent with the variables s of its children (either the node and its children need no more sorted values, or if it needs, then the number of values needed suffices the node and the children needs).

abnormal_T(i) :: when the node, in state T, either has some variables with abnormal values or is in abnormal situation with some neighbor (parent or child).

done(i) :: is true when the node is done executing the current BST cycle.

get_sorted(i) :: is true when the node is ready to receive a sorted value from its parent.

moveup_hv(i) :: is true when the node heap value was taken by its parent.

new_sorted() :: is true when the root has generated a new sorted value.

my_turn(i) :: is true when it is the node turn to store its sorted value (currently stored in $down.i$).

sent_sorted(i) $\equiv$ is true when the node has sent the sorted value it held to one of its children (to its target node).

Macro move_HVs(i) :: selects the child $dhv \in \{left, right\}$ that has the maximum heap value.

{Program for the root node r}

$rP1$ $\neg abnormal\_P(r, \perp) \land S.r = P \land new\_sorted() \longrightarrow$
        $down.r = HV.r;\ s.r = s.r - 1;\ HV.r = \perp$
        if $(lHV.i \neq \perp \lor rHV.i \neq \perp)$ then $move\_HVs(r)$

$rP2$ $\neg abnormal\_P(r, \perp) \land S.r = P \land sent\_sorted(r) \land \neg my\_turn(r) \longrightarrow down.r = \perp$

$rP3$ $\neg abnormal\_P(r, \perp) \land S.r = P \land my\_turn(r) \longrightarrow$
        $tSV.r = down.r$
        if $SV.r \neq tSV.r$ then $SV.r = tSV.r$
        if $left.r \neq \perp$ then $dir.r = left$ else $dir.r = \perp$
        $down.r = \perp$

PT $\neg abnormal\_P(r, \perp) \land S.r = P \land done(r) \land \forall_{j \in D.r} S.j = T \longrightarrow S.r = T$

aCb $(S.r = P \land abnormal\_P(r, \perp)) \lor (S.r = T \land abnormal\_T(r)) \longrightarrow S.r = C$

{Program for an internal node i that is the d child of its parent, $d \in \{left, right\}$}

$iP1$ $\neg abnormal\_P(i) \land S.i = P \land get\_sorted(i) \land (down.i = \perp \lor sent\_sorted(i)) \longrightarrow$
        $down.i = down.p.i;\ s.i = s.i - 1$
        if $moveup\_hv(i)$ then $HV.i = \perp$
           if $(lHV.i \neq \perp \lor rHV.i \neq \perp)$ then $move\_HVs(i)$

$iP3$ $\neg abnormal\_P(i) \land S.i = P \land my\_turn(i) \longrightarrow$
        $tSV.i = down.i$
        if $SV.i \neq tSV.i$ then $SV.i = tSV.i$
        if $left.i \neq \perp$ then $dir.i = left$ else $dir.i = \perp$

$iP4$ $\neg abnormal\_P(i) \land S.i = P \land \neg(get\_sorted(i) \land sent\_sorted(i)) \land \neg my\_turn(i) \land moveup\_hv(i) \longrightarrow$
        $HV.i = \perp$
        if $(lHV.i \neq \perp \lor rHV.i \neq \perp)$ then $move\_HVs(i)$

PT $\neg abnormal\_P(i, d) \land S.i = P \land done(i) \land \forall_{j \in D.i} S.j = T \longrightarrow S.i = T$

aCb $(S.i = P \land abnormal\_P(i, d)) \lor (S.i = T \land abnormal\_T(i)) \longrightarrow S.i = C$

{Program for a leaf node i that is the d child of its parent, $d \in \{left, right\}$}

$lP1\&3$ $\neg abnormal\_P(i) \land S.i = P \land get\_sorted(i) \land down.i = \perp \longrightarrow$
        $down.i = down.p.i;\ s.i = 0$
        if $moveup\_hv(i)$ then $HV.i = \perp$
        $tSV.i = down.i$
        if $SV.i \neq tSV.i$ then $SV.i = tSV.i$

$lP4$ $\neg abnormal\_P(i) \land S.i = P \land \neg get\_sorted(i) \land moveup\_hv(i) \longrightarrow HV.i = \perp$

PT $\neg abnormal\_P(i, d) \land S.i = P \land done(i) \longrightarrow S.i = T$

aCb $(S.i = P \land abnormal\_P(i, d)) \lor (S.i = T \land abnormal\_T(i)) \longrightarrow S.i = C$

the root to execute the initialization action) of our algorithm is $O(n)$ rounds (Lemma 2).

Once we establish the finite round delay (as above), our remaining obligation is to show that starting from a normal starting configuration, the tree will satisfy the BST property in finite rounds.

We prove that starting from a normal starting configuration, the state of every node eventually becomes B (for non-leaf nodes) or M (for leaf nodes). Any internal node i sets its heap value and changes its state from B to $M/M^{left}/M^{right}$. When the root r is in M state, then $HV.r$, $lHV.r$, and $rHV.r$ hold the maximum value in the entire tree, in its left subtree, and in its right subtree, respectively. We conclude that, starting from a normal starting configuration, in at most $4h + 3$ rounds, the tree will satisfy the heap property and all nodes will be in state P (Lemma 3).

Note that the guarded actions of Module $Sort$ for each process (root, internal, and leaf node) are mutually exclusive. So, at any time during the BST construction, at most one of the root actions is enabled, at most one of any internal node actions is enabled, and at most one of any leaf node actions is enabled. This was done to implement a sequential, pipelined delivery of sorted values in decreasing order.

The root will continue sending the sorted values (via $down.r$) in descending order as long as there exists a target node for a value ($new\_sorted()$ will be $true$ as long as $s.r > 0$). The value of $down.r$ follows a path of current target nodes, starting from the root and ending at some node in the tree. When the root takes the heap value of its sink node to make it a sorted value, in at most one round, the child adjust its heap value to one of its children. In at most n rounds, the root is done generating sorted values, and in at most additional h rounds every node in the system receives its sorted value (Lemma 4), and enters state T. Once the root enters T state, the BST construction is done.

Finally, we prove that starting from an arbitrary configuration where the nodes have distinct internal values drawn from an arbitrary set, our algorithm arranges them in a BST order in $O(n)$ rounds (Theorem 1).

Theorem 1 and Lemma 1 imply that the proposed BST algorithm is time optimal.

Lemma 1. *Under the space constraint that the maximum number of items that can be stored at any time at any processor is constant (i.e., independent of n), the lower bound on the time complexity for arranging n values in a given tree in a distributed manner such that the tree becomes a binary search tree (BST) is $\Omega(n)$.*

Proof. Assume that all the values larger (respectively, smaller) than the root's value are currently in the left (respectively, right) subtree of the root. Then $n-1$ values have to pass by the root to move to their right place in the BST. As the root has a constant memory, it will require the root to execute at least n actions to move those values.

Lemma 2. *The delay is in $O(n)$ rounds.*

Lemma 3. *Starting from a normal starting configuration, it takes at most $4h+3$ rounds to heapify the tree.*

Lemma 4. *Starting from a normal configuration, where the root and its children are in state P, in at most $n + h$ rounds, every node in the system receives its sorted value and changes its state to T.*

Theorem 1. *Starting from an arbitrary configuration where n values are arranged in a binary tree, each node holding a single key value, Algorithm 3.2 arranges those n values such that the tree becomes a BST in $O(n)$ rounds and requires $O(\log n)$ space.*

4.1   Complexity

All the variables used by a node i except one ($s.i$) require $O(1)$ space complexity. Variable $s.i$ requires $O(\log s_i)$ bits where s_i represents the total number of nodes in the subtree T_i rooted at i. In the worst case, (for the root node) the space complexity is $O(\log(n))$. The heap construction does not use this variable, it is needed only for the BST construction. But, just for better presentation, we included the the computation of $s.i$ in Module Heap. Therefore, we claim that the heap construction uses $O(1)$ space. The BST construction requires $O(\log n)$ space in the worst case.

Both the time complexity and delay of the proposed algorithm is $O(n)$ rounds.

Starting from a normal starting configuration, the time to arrange the values as a heap is $O(h)$ (at most $4h + 3$ rounds)(Lemma 3).

Starting from an arbitrary configuration, the time to arrange the values such that the tree is a BST order is $O(n)$ rounds (Theorem 1).

4.2   Unfair Daemon

In any round, the total number of actions executed by all processes is bounded. Since any execution of our algorithm has a bounded complexity in terms of steps (or actions), the total number of actions executed in a normal execution is bounded. Thus, the duration of a round cannot be extended forever by ignoring some enabled processes for an indefinite period of time.

5   Conclusion

We present the first snap-stabilizing distributed *binary search tree* (BST) algorithm and the first snap-stabilizing heap algorithm. A key feature of both the solutions is that the maximum number of items that can be stored at any time at any processor is constant — independent of the size (n) of the network.

The proposed snap-stabilizing distributed BST solution ensures that when a BST computation initiated by the root terminates, the tree is a BST. Under the space constraint, our BST solution is asymptotically optimal in time and takes $O(n)$ rounds. A processor i requires $O(\log s_i)$ bits of space where s_i is the size of the subtree rooted at i. So, the root uses $O(\log n)$ bits.

The heap construction spends $O(h)$ rounds where h is the height of the tree. Its space requirement is constant, independent of n.

If the space complexity of the heap solution is asymptotically optimal, it is an open problem to show that it is possible to design a BST protocol with a space complexity of $O(1)$ while keeping a time complexity of $O(n)$.

Our BST construction is transparent to changes in the tree structure (by adding/removing nodes). If such changes occur, then the algorithm will incorporate the changes "on the fly" by nodes either entering an abnormal situation with their new neighbors, or by completing the current cycle and restarting a new cycle with added/deleted values. Since the performance of the usual functions on the tree (as find, insert, delete) is directly related to the structure of the tree (height, balanced or unbalanced property etc.) and as we have mentioned before, our algorithm does not alter the tree structure, we do not address this issue of performance here.

Also, the usual operations on the tree make sense if the tree has the BST property. Since the BST property is guaranteed when the algorithm terminates, and for stabilization purposes the algorithm is an infinite cycles of complete BST construction, these functions insert, find, delete can be applied to the output values.

References

1. D Bein, AK Datta, and V Villain. Self-stabilizing Optimal Binary Search Tree. *Tech Report*, www.cs.unlv.edu/ siona/Research/SS/tech05a.pdf, 2005.
2. A Bui, AK Datta, F Petit, and V Villain. State-optimal snap-stabilizing PIF in tree networks. In *Proceedings of the Third Workshop on Self-Stabilizing Systems*, pages 78–85. IEEE Computer Society, 1999.
3. T. Cormen, C. Leiserson, and R. Rivest. *Introduction to Algorithms*. The MIT Press, 1992.
4. A Cournier, AK Datta, F Petit, and V Villain. Enabling snap-stabilization. In *Proceedings of the Twentythird International Conference on Distributed Computing Systems*, pages 78–85. IEEE Computer Society, 2003.
5. EW Dijkstra. Self-stabilizing systems in spite of distributed control. In *EWD 391, In Selected Writings on Computing: A Personal Perspective*, pages 41–46, 1973.
6. S Dolev. *Self-Stabilization*. MIT Press, Cambridge, MA, 2000.
7. S Dolev, A Israeli, and S Moran. Uniform dynamic self-stabilizing leader election. *IEEE Transactions on Parallel and Distributed Systems*, 8(4):424–440, 1997.
8. T. Herman and T. Masuzawa. Available stabilizing heaps. *Information Processing Letters*, 77:115–121, 2001.
9. T. Herman and T. Masuzawa. A stabilizing search tree with availability properties. *Fifth International Symposium on Autonomous Decentralized Systems (ISADS 2001)*, pages 398–405, 2001.

Synchronous vs. Asynchronous Unison

Christian Boulinier, Franck Petit, and Vincent Villain

LaRIA, CNRS FRE 2733,
Université de Picardie Jules Verne, France

Abstract. This paper considers the self-stabilizing unison problem. The contribution of this paper is threefold. First, we establish that when any self-stabilizing asynchronous unison protocol runs in synchronous systems, it converges to synchronous unison if the size of the clock K is greater than C_G, C_G being the length of the maximal cycle of the shortest maximal cycle basis if the graph contains cycles, 2 otherwise (tree networks). The second result demonstrates that the asynchronous unison in [3] provides a universal self-stabilizing synchronous unison for trees which is optimal in memory space. It works with any $K \geq 3$, without any extra state, and stabilizes within $2D$ rounds, where D is the diameter of the network. This protocol gives a positive answer to the question whether there exists or not a universal self-stabilizing synchronous unison for tree networks with a state requirement independant of local or global information of the tree. If $K = 3$, then the stabilization time of this protocol is equal to D only, i.e., it reaches the optimal performance of [8]. The third result of this paper is a self-stabilizing unison for general synchronous systems. It requires $K \geq 2$ only, at least $K + D$ states per process, and its stabilization time is $2D$ only. This is the best solution for general synchronous systems, both for the state requirement and the stabilization time.

1 Introduction

We consider the problem of *phase synchronization* [9] in self-stabilizing [5] uniform distributed systems. Phase synchronization consists in designing a synchronization mechanism devoted to a distributed protocol made of a sequence of phases $0, 1, \ldots$ such that no process starts to execute its phase $i + 1$ before all processes have completed their phase i. It is also required that no process will be permanently blocked from executing its phase $i + 1$ if all processes have completed their phase i. This mechanism induces a global abstract device called *phase clock* to maintain the current phase number, incremented each time a phase completes. In a distributed environment, each process maintains its own copy of the phase clock. Therefore, the problem consists in the design of a protocol insuring that all the phase clocks are in phase. The phrase "in phase" has a natural meaning in *synchronous* systems. In such systems, a global signal is assumed to simultaneously increment all clock variables. So, the clocks are in phase if the values of all clock variables are identical. The (*synchronous*) *unison* [7] problem consists in the design of a protocol to keep all clocks in phase, i.e., to insure identical time on all clocks and increment in unison.

T. Herman and S. Tixeuil (Eds.): SSS 2005, LNCS 3764, pp. 18–32, 2005.

In *asynchronous* systems, there is no global signal. So, one can at most ensure that no process starts to execute its phase $i + 1$ before all processes have completed their phase i. But this kind of synchronization needs $O(D)$ rounds between two phases. So, in general, the synchronization requirement is relaxed as follows: the clock are in phase if the values of two neighboring processes do not differ by no more than 1, and the clock value of each process is incremented by 1 infinitely often. The *asynchronous unison* [4] deals with this criteria.

Related Works. Numerous works in the area of self-stabilization deals with the phase synchronization problem. In this paper, we focus on deterministic solutions for uniform systems only. Moreover, we limit our discussion to tree and general networks. In the rest of this section, K is the size of the clock, S is the number of states the processes are required to have, D is the diameter of the network, n the number of processes, and Δ is the maximum degree of a process.

Self-stabilizing Synchronous Unison. The first self-stabilizing synchronous unison is given in [7]. It works on a general graph but it requires unbounded clocks. The first protocol with a bounded memory space is proposed in [1]. It needs $K \geq 2\Delta D$, and stabilizes in $3\Delta D$ steps. As it is noticed in [8], the Δ factor is due to the model: It is assumed that a process cannot read more than the state of one neighbor at a time. From now on, all the protocols we discuss will be assumed to work on a model where every process can read the state of all its neighbors at a time. In this model, the solution in [1] needs $K \geq 2D$ ($S = K$) and stabilizes in at most $3D$ steps only. To our knowledge, this is the only deterministic synchronous unison for general uniform networks (according to our restrictions).

A solution for tree networks is proposed in [8]. It requires $K = 3^m$ ($m > 0$), $S = K$, and stabilizes in $(D \times (K - 1))/2$ steps. Note that the stabilization time is equal to D only for $m = 1$ ($K = 3$), but is greater than $2D$ when $m \geq 2$. Thus, in the case $3^m \geq 2D$, the solution in [1] is better. In terms of stabilization time, the best solution on trees is proposed in [11]. It stabilizes in at most D steps only. Moreover, this protocol is *"universal"*, meaning that K can take any value greater than or equal to 2 and the state requirement does not need any global information like either n or D. It depends on Δ only: $S = (\Delta + 1)K$.

Self-stabilizing Asynchronous Unison. The self-stabilizing asynchronous unison was introduced in [4]. Two deterministic protocols are proposed. The former works assuming unbounded clock, the latter needs $K \geq n^2$ (according to our model) ($S = K$). In [3], the authors show the lower bound for K. K must be greater than C_G, where C_G is the length of the maximal cycle of the shortest maximal cycle basis if the graph contains cycles, 2 otherwise (tree networks). They also show that S, the amount of space, must be greater than $K + T_G - 2$, where T_G is the length of the longest chordless cycle (0 in tree networks). In the same paper, they present an algorithm reaching these bounds. This protocol is optimal in terms of state requirement. One can notice that C_G and T_G are bounded by n. So, even if C_G and T_G are unknown, we can choose $K \geq n + 1$ and $S = K + n - 2 \geq 2n - 1$. The protocol is still better than [4].

Contribution. The contribution of this paper is threefold. We first show that there exists a strong connection between the asynchronous and synchronous unisons: when any self-stabilizing asynchronous unison protocol runs in synchronous systems, it converges to synchronous unison if $K > C_G$. The first result of this surprising connection is that the solutions in [4] and [3] are also self-stabilizing for the synchronous unison in synchronous systems.

The second result is that [3] provides a universal self-stabilizing synchronous unison for trees which is optimal in memory space. It works with any $K \geq 3$, $S = K$, and stabilizes within $2D$ rounds. This protocol gives a positive answer to the question in [10]: "*Does there exist a universal self-stabilizing synchronous unison protocol for tree networks with a state requirement independant of local or global information of the tree (e.g. n, D, or Δ)?*" We can also remark that for $K = 3$, the stabilization time is equal to D only, i.e., that reaches the optimal performance of [8]. It is really surprising that a general protocol written for asynchronous unison solves the synchronous with such performances.

However, these good results do not hold for general synchronous systems. In this case, as claimed previously, the protocol needs $K > C_G$ and $S = K + T_G - 2$, which is, in general, worst than $2D$ [1], and stabilizes in $CP_G + T_G + D$—CP_G is the lenght of the longest elementary chordless path of G, which is also worst than $3D$ [1] in general. The third result of this paper is a new universal solution which takes advantages of both approaches in [1,3]. This protocol, called *SS-MinSU*, requires $K \geq 2$ only, $S \geq K + D$, and its stabilization time is $2D$ only. This is the best solution for general synchronous systems, both for the state requirement and the stabilization time.

Paper Outline. In the next section (Section 2), we describe the distributed system and the model we consider in this paper. In the same section, we also state what it means for a protocol to be self-stabilizing and give formal statements of finite incrementing systems. In Section 3, we state the problems considered in this paper, and establish that any self-stabilizing asynchronous unison executed in a synchronous system also solves the synchronous unison if $K > C_G$. In the same section, we discuss performance issues of the protocol in [3] executed in synchronous settings. Algorithm *SS-MinSU* and its correctness are presented in Section 4. Finally, we make some concluding remarks in Section 5.

2   Preliminaries

In this section, we define the distributed systems and programs considered in this paper, and state what it means for a protocol to be self-stabilizing. Next, we present the notions of finite incrementing system and reset.

Distributed System. A *distributed system* is an undirected connected graph, $G = (V, E)$, where V is a set of nodes—$|V| = n$, $n \geq 2$—and E is the set of edges. Nodes represent *processes*, and edges represent *bidirectional communication links*. A communication link (p, q) exists iff p and q are neighbors. The set of neighbors of every process p is denoted as $\mathcal{N}_p$. The *degree* of p is the number of neighbors of p, i.e., equal to $|\mathcal{N}_p|$.

The program of a process consists of a set of registers (also referred as variables) and a finite set of guarded actions of the following form: $<label>:: <guard> \longrightarrow <statement>$. Each process can only write to its own registers, and read its own registers and registers owned by the neighboring processes. The guard of an action in the program of p is a boolean expression involving the registers that p can read. An action can be executed only if its guard evaluates to true. The actions are atomically executed, meaning, the evaluation of a guard and the execution of the corresponding statement of an action, if executed, are done in one atomic step.

The *state* of a process is defined by the values of its registers. The *configuration* of a system is the product of the states of all processes. Let a distributed protocol $\mathcal{P}$ be a collection of binary transition relations denoted by $\mapsto$, on $\mathcal{C}$, the set of all possible configurations of the system. $\mathcal{P}$ describes an oriented graph $\Gamma = (\mathcal{C}, \mapsto)$, called the *transition graph* of $\mathcal{P}$. A sequence $e = \gamma_0, \gamma_1, \ldots, \gamma_i, \gamma_{i+1}, \ldots$, $\forall i \geq 0, \gamma_i \in \mathcal{C}$, is called an *execution* of $\mathcal{P}$ iff $\forall i \geq 0, \gamma_i \mapsto \gamma_{i+1}$. A process p is said to be *enabled* in a configuration γ ($\gamma \in \mathcal{C}$) if there exists an action A such that the guard of A is true in γ. (When there is no ambiguity, we will omit γ.) Similarly, an action A is said to be enabled (in γ) at p if the guard of A is true at p (in γ). We assume that each transition from a configuration to another is driven by a *distributed scheduler* called *daemon*. In this paper, we consider two types of distributed daemons: (1) the *asynchronous daemon* chooses any nonempty set of enabled processes to execute an action in each computation step, and (2) the *synchronous daemon* chooses all enabled processes to execute an action in each computation step. The asynchronous daemon can be assumed to be fair. *Fairness* means that in all executions, every process executes an action infinitely often. Otherwise, the daemon is said to be *unfair*.

The distributed systems considered in this paper are assumed to be uniform. A distributed protocol is *uniform* if every process with the same degree executes the same program. In particular, we do not assume unique process identifier or some consistent orientation of links in the network such that any dynamic election of a master clock can be feasible.

Self-stabilization. Let $\mathcal{X}$ be a set. A *predicate* P is a function that has a Boolean value—true or false—for each $x \in \mathcal{X}$. A predicate P is *closed* for a transition graph Γ iff every state of an execution e that starts in a state satisfying P also satisfies P. A predicat Q is an attractor of the predicat P, denoted by $P \rhd Q$, iff Q is closed for Γ and for every execution e of Γ, begining by a state satisfying P, there exists a configuration of e for which Q is true. A transition graph Γ is *self-stabilizing* for a predicate P iff true $\rhd P$.

Finite Incrementing System and Reset. Let $\mathbb{Z}$ be the set of integers and K be a strictly positive integer. Two integers a and b are said to be *congruent modulo K*, denoted by $a \equiv b[K]$ iff $\exists \lambda \in \mathbb{Z}$, $b = a + \lambda K$. We denote $\bar{a}$ the unique element in $[0, K-1]$ such that $a \equiv \bar{a}[K]$. The *distance* $d_K(a, b) = \inf(\overline{a-b}, \overline{b-a})$. In the following, we assume $K \geq 3$.

Two integers a and b are said to be *locally comparable* iff $d_K(a, b) \leq 1$. We then define the *local order relation* $\leq_l$ as follows: $a \leq_l b \overset{\text{def}}{\Leftrightarrow} 0 \leq \overline{b-a} \leq 1$. Given two locally comparable integers a and b, $b \ominus_l a \overset{\text{def}}{=} \overline{b-a}$ if $a \leq_l b$, $b \ominus_l a \overset{\text{def}}{=} \overline{-a-b}$ otherwise ($b \leq_l a$). Note that $b \ominus_l a \equiv b - a[K]$. So, if $a_0, a_1, a_2, \ldots a_{p-1}, a_p$ is a sequence of integers such that $\forall i \in \{0, \ldots, p-1\}$, a_i is locally comparable to a_{i+1}, then we define the local variation of this sequence as follows: $S = \sum_{i=0}^{p-1} (a_{i+1} \ominus_l a_i)$.

Clearly, $S \equiv a_p - a_0[K]$ and $S \equiv 0[K] \Leftrightarrow a_p - a_0 \equiv 0[K]$.

We define $\mathcal{X} = \{-\alpha, \ldots, 0, \ldots, K-1\}$, where α is a positive integer. Let φ be the function from $\mathcal{X}$ to $\mathcal{X}$ defined by $\varphi(x) = \overline{x+1}$ if $x \geq 0$, $\varphi(x) = x + 1$ otherwise ($x < 0$). The pair $(\mathcal{X}, \varphi)$ is called a *finite incrementing system*. K is called the *period* of $(\mathcal{X}, \varphi)$. Let $tail_\varphi = \{-\alpha, \ldots, 0\}$ and $stab_\varphi = \{0, \ldots, K-1\}$ be the sets of "extra" values and "expected" values, respectively. The set $tail_\varphi^*$ is equal to $tail_\varphi \setminus \{0\}$. We denote by $\leq_{tail}$ the natural total order on $tail_\varphi$, and $\leq$ the natural order on $\mathcal{X}$. A *reset* on $\mathcal{X}$ consists on enforcing any value of $\mathcal{X} \setminus \{-\alpha\}$ to $-\alpha$ without using φ.

3   Distributed Unison

In this section, we first state the problems considered in this paper. Next, we recall some definitions and results established in [3]. Then, we show that any self-stabilizing asynchronous unison also solves the synchronous unison when it is executed on a synchronous system if $K > C_G$. Finally, we discuss performance issues of the protocol in [3] executed in synchronous settings.

3.1   Problem Definition

We assume that each process p maintains a clock register r_p with an incrementing system $(\mathcal{X}, \varphi)$, i.e., the only applicable operation on r_p is φ, algorithmically defined as follows:

$$Cond \longrightarrow r_p := \varphi(r_p)$$

Our responsability is to define $Cond$ such that the specifications discussed below are verified. Let SU and WU be two predicates—SU and WU stand for *strong unison* and *weak unison*, respectively. Let γ be a system configuration, we define the two following predicates:

$$SU(\gamma) \overset{\text{def}}{\equiv} \forall p \in V, \ \forall q \in \mathcal{N}_p : (d_K(r_p, r_q) = 0) \text{ in } \gamma$$

$$WU(\gamma) \overset{\text{def}}{\equiv} \forall p \in V, \forall q \in \mathcal{N}_p : (r_p \in stab_\varphi) \wedge (d_K(r_p, r_q) \leq 1) \text{ in } \gamma$$

In the remainder, we will abuse notation, referring to the corresponding set of configurations simply by SU (resp. WU).

The *synchronous* (*distributed*) *unison* problem is specified as follows:

Unison (Safety): *SU* is closed;
No Lockout (Liveness): In *SU*, every process p increments its clock variable infinitely often.

With a synchronous daemon, the problem is trivialy solved by $Cond \equiv \mathbf{true}$.

The *asynchronous* (*distributed*) *unison* problem is to design a uniform protocol so that the following properties are true in every execution:

Unison (Safety): *WU* is closed;
Synchronization: In *WU*, a process can increment its clock r_p only if the value of r_p is lower than or equal to the clock value of all its neighbors;
No Lockout (Liveness): In *WU*, every process p increments its clock r_p infinitely often.

Note that the asynchronous distributed unison problem is usually specified in the literature in terms of safety and liveness only—refer to [4,6]. These two specifications are not sufficient for $K = 3$. Actually, since $\forall p \in V, \ r_p \in \{0, 1, 2\}$, $\forall p, q \in V, \ d_K(r_p, r_q) \leq 1$ in every configuration. So, clearly, the above trivial guarded action satisfies the safety property. The liveness property is guaranteed by the fairness of the daemon. However, any process may execute the action a finite number of times before any of its neighbors execute the action once. Obviously, such a behavior is not the expected behavior. That shows the significance of the synchronization property.

Remark 1. *If $K \geq 4$ and the safety is satisfied, then the synchronization is satisfied.*

Lemma 1. *If a uniform distributed protocol $\mathcal{P}$ solves the asynchronous distributed unison problem, then $Cond \equiv \forall q \in \mathcal{N}_p : (r_q = r_p) \vee (r_q = \varphi(r_p))$.*

Proof. From the Synchronization property, $Cond \Rightarrow \forall q \in \mathcal{N}_p : (r_q = r_p) \vee (r_q = \varphi(r_p))$. Assume that there exists an execution of $\mathcal{P}$ leading in a configuration γ such that there exists a process p satisfying $\forall q \in \mathcal{N}_p : (r_q = r_p) \vee (r_q = \varphi(r_p))$ and $Cond$ is false in γ. Let Δ_p be the number of neighbors of p. Denote Δ_p^γ, the number of neighbors q of p such that $r_q = \varphi(r_p)$ in γ. Consider now the clique with $n = \Delta_p + 1$ processes. The clock value of $n - \Delta_p^\gamma$ processes is equal to r_p, whereas the clock value of Δ_p^γ processes is equal to $\varphi(r_p)$. In such a configuration, $Cond$ being false, the system is at a deadlock. This contradicts the "No Lockout" property. $\square$

In the remainder, we will show that, if $K > C_G$—the cyclomatic characteristic of G, formally defined in Definition 3 below—, then the above guarded action solves the asynchronous unison problem. If $K \leq C_G$, then there is a possibility of deadlocks [3]. Obviously, we obtain a kind of unicity: a distributed asynchronous system depends on the choice of the incrementing system $(\mathcal{X}, \varphi)$ only. Therefore, the only interesting problem is to stabilize these protocols, i.e., to solve the above problems with the extra global specification: $\mathbf{true} \triangleright SU$ (respectively, $\mathbf{true} \triangleright WU$).

3.2   Path Delay and Properties in WU

In this subsection, we consider configurations in WU only. So, the clock values of neighboring processes are locally comparable. Let us recall the notion of path delay and some of its properties established in [3].

Definition 1 (Path Delay). *The delay of a path* $\mu = p_0 p_1 \ldots p_k$, *denoted by* Δ_μ, *is the local variation of the sequence* $r_{p_0}, r_{p_1}, \ldots, r_{p_k}$, *i.e,*

$$\Delta_\mu = \sum_{i=0}^{k-1} \left(r_{p_{i+1}} \ominus_l r_{p_i} \right) \text{ if } k > 0, \ 0 \text{ otherwise } (k = 0).$$

The path delay is an algebraic notion. Obviously, $\Delta_\mu = -\Delta_{\tilde{\mu}}$, where $\tilde{\mu}$ designates the reverse path of μ. Let $\mu_1 = p_0 p_1 \ldots p_j$ and $\mu_2 = p_j \ldots p_{k-1}$ be two paths. By the Chasle relation: $\Delta_{\mu_1 \mu_2} = \Delta_{\mu_1} + \Delta_{\mu_2}$.

Consider two neighboring processes p and q. In any configuration in WU, if p or q is enabled, then there are only three possible cases:

1. q is enabled. In this case, $r_p \ominus \varphi(r_q) = r_p \ominus r_q - 1$.
2. Both p and q are enabled. Then, $\varphi(r_p) \ominus \varphi(r_q) = r_p \ominus r_q$.
3. p is enabled. Then, $\varphi(r_p) \ominus r_q = r_p \ominus r_q + 1$.

From this fact, we obtain by induction the following lemma:

Lemma 2. *Let* μ *be a path* $p_0 p_1 \ldots p_k$. *Consider any system transition* $\gamma \mapsto \gamma'$. *Let* Δ (Δ', *respectively*) *be the delay on the path* μ *at the state* γ (γ', *resp.*). *During* $\gamma \mapsto \gamma'$:

1. *If* p_0 *is incremented and* p_k *is not, then* $\Delta' = \Delta - 1$.
2. *If both* p_0 *and* p_k *are incremented or none is incremented, then* $\Delta' = \Delta$.
3. *If* p_k *is incremented and* p_0 *is not, then* $\Delta' = \Delta + 1$.

Definition 2 (Intrinsic Delay). *The delay between two processes* p *and* q *is* pq-*intrinsic if it is independent of the choice of the path from* p *to* q. *The delay is intrinsic iff it is* pq-*intrinsic for every* p *and* q *in* V.

From Lemma 2, if a path $\mu = p_0 p_1 \ldots p_0$ is a cycle, then the delay on μ is an invariant for any execution of any asynchronous unison. The absolute value of this invariant is called the *residual* of μ. In [3], we showed that the delay is intrinsic if and only if all the residuals are equal to 0. In particular, the path delay is intrinsic on a tree.

Let us define Predicate WU_0 which is true for a system configuration γ iff γ satisfy WU and the delay is intrinsic in γ. Since the residuals are invariant, we can claim the following theorem:

Theorem 2 ([3]). WU *and* WU_0 *are closed for any execution of an asynchronous unison. Moreover, for any execution starting from a configuration in* WU_0, *the no lockout property is guaranteed.*

The delay being intrinsic iff it is equal to 0 on every cycle, by linearity, a path delay is intrinsic iff it is equal to 0 on a cycle basis [2]. We borrow the following definition from [3]:

Definition 3 (Cyclomatic Characteristic). *If G is an acyclic graph, then its cyclomatic characteristic C_G is equal to 2. Otherwise (G contains cycles), let Λ be a cycle basis. Denote $\lambda(\Lambda)$ the length of the longest cycle in Λ. The cyclomatic characteristic of G, C_G, is equal to the lowest $\lambda(\Lambda)$ among cycle bases.*

Theorem 3 ([3]). *For any asynchronous unison, $K > C_G \Leftrightarrow WU = WU_0$.*

3.3   From Asynchronous to Synchronous Unison

We assume that all the executions considered in this subsection start from a configuration $\gamma \in WU_0$. Denote Δ_{pq} the common value of delays on paths from p to q. We say that p *"precedes"* q in a configuration γ iff $\Delta_{pq} \leq 0$. Similarly, p and q are *"γ-synchronous"* if $\Delta_{pq} = 0$ in γ. Denote the γ-synchronization relation by $\equiv_\gamma$. Since the network is connected, the precedence relation is a preorder, and the γ-synchronization relation is the related equivalence relation. According to precedence relation, the minimal processes (maximal processes, respectively) are γ-synchronous. The set of minimal processes (resp. maximal processes) is never empty because the network is finite. Moreover, every minimal process is obviously enabled. We denote by V_0 the set of minimal processes at each state.

The quotient of the *precedence* relation by the equivalence γ-synchronous relation defines a total order on V, denoted by $\leq_\gamma$. Note that $\frac{V}{\equiv_\gamma}$ is a singleton if and only if γ satisfies SU. Moreover, $\frac{V}{\equiv_\gamma}$ is a finite set totaly ordered by $\leq_\gamma$. This quotient can be modified in each transition.

Let $\gamma \in WU_0$. Let k be the number of equivalent classes in $\frac{V}{\equiv_\gamma}$. The equivalence classes are denoted by $V_0, V_1, \ldots, V_{k-1}$ with $V_0 <_\gamma V_1 <_\gamma \ldots <_\gamma V_{k-1}$.

Obviously, $\forall p, q \in V$, $p \in V_i$, $q \in V_j \Rightarrow \Delta_{pq} = j - i$. We are now able to define the map Σ on the configuration set WU_0 by: $\Sigma(\gamma) = (V_0, V_1, \ldots, V_{k-1})$. Note that $\Sigma(\gamma) = (V) \Leftrightarrow \gamma \in SU$.

Lemma 3. *Let $\gamma \in WU_0$. For every transition $\gamma \mapsto \gamma'$ scheduled by the synchronous daemon: if $p \in V_0$ in γ then $p \in V_0$ in γ'.*

Proof.   Let p, q be two processes such that $p \neq q$, and $p \in V_0$ in γ. Since $p \in V_0$ in γ, p is enabled. Denote by ρ the value of Δ_{pq} in γ. There are two cases:

1. $q \in V_0$ in γ. Then, q is also enabled in γ and $\Delta_{pq} = 0$ in γ'.
2. $q \notin V_0$ in γ. Then, $\rho > 0$ and from Lemma 2, $\Delta_{pq} \in \{\rho - 1, \rho\}$ in γ'.

In both cases, q precedes p in γ'. Thus, p is minimal in γ'. $\square$

The distance between two processes p and q, denoted by $d(p, q)$ is the length of the shortest path between p and q. Let $p \in V$. We denote δ_p as $\max_{q \in V} d(p, q)$. Let k be a positive integer. Define $B(p, k)$ as the set of processes such that $d(p, q) \leq k$. Note that the diameter D of the network is equal to $\max_{p \in V} \max_{q \in V} d(p, q)$.

Theorem 4 ($WU_0 \triangleright SU$). *For every execution starting from any $\gamma \in WU_0$ and scheduled by the synchronous daemon, SU is an attractor for WU_0. The time of convergence from WU_0 to SU is upper bounded by D, and this bound is optimal.*

Proof. Consider an infinite executions $e = \gamma_{t_0}, \gamma_{t_1}, \ldots$ such that $\gamma_{t_0} \in WU_0$. Let $k_t = |\frac{V}{\equiv_{\gamma_t}}|$. We denote $\Sigma(\gamma_t)$ by $(V_0^t, V_1^t, \ldots, V_{k_t-1}^t)$. Let p be an element of $V_0^{t_0}$ with the lowest $\delta_p = w$. Of course, we have $k_{t_0} - 1 \leq w$. We will prove by induction that: $\forall i \in \mathbb{N}, B(p, i) \subseteq V_0^{t_0+i}$. This will prove that for $i = w$, $V_0^{t_0+i} = V$. Hence, the time convergence is less than or equal to w, which is less than or equal to D.

If $i = 0$, then $B(p, 0) = \{p\} \subseteq V_0^{t_0}$. Assume that $i \geq 0$ and $B(p, i) \subseteq V_0^{t_0+i}$. Let $q \in B(p, i + 1)$. Then, q is a neighbor of an element q' of $B(p, i)$. There are two cases:

1. $q \in V_0^{t_0+i}$. By Lemma 3, $q \in V_0^{t_0+i+1}$.
2. $q \notin V_0^{t_0+i}$. Then, $r_q = \varphi(r_{q'})$. So, q is not enabled in γ_{t_0+i}. It follows that $q \in V_0^{t_0+i+1}$.

In both cases, $q \in V_0^{t_0+i+1}$. We deduce $B(p, i+1) \subseteq V_0^{t_0+i+1}$. And by induction $\forall i \in \mathbb{N}, B(p, i) \subseteq V_0^{t_0+i}$. The first part of the theorem follows.

Let p be one extremity on a diameter of G ($\delta_p = \max_{q \in V} \delta_q$). Assume that $r_p = 0$ in γ_0. We define for each q such that $d(q, p) = k$ ($k \in 1, \ldots, D$), $r_q = \overline{k}$. This configuration is clearly in WU_0 because the residuals are equal to 0. Starting from such a configuration γ_0, SU is reached in at least D steps. We showed that D can be reached. This proves the second part of the theorem. □

Note that at the beginning of this section, we made the assumption that the delay is intrinsic—Theorem 4 holds only under this assumption. If the delay is not intrinsic, by Theorem 3, there is a residual which is not equal to 0. The residuals are (1) invariants during the execution of the protocol and (2) equal to 0 in SU. Therefore, if the delay is not intrinsic, the system may not converge to SU. In Figure 1, all the configurations are in WU, but they are not in WU_0. However, starting from Configuration (i), the system will never converge to SU— Configurations (i) and (iv) are identical.

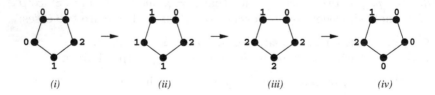

(i) (ii) (iii) (iv)

Fig. 1. A counter-example with $K = 3$ and $C_G = 5$

From Theorems 4 and 3 follows :

Theorem 5. *If $K > C_G$, then any self-stabilizing asynchronous unison $\mathcal{P}$ designed for the asynchronous daemon solves the self-stabilizing synchronous unison if $\mathcal{P}$ is driven by the synchronous daemon.*

The bounded memory unisons for asynchronous settings in [4,6] satisfy $K > C_G$ because $K \geq n^2$. In [3], we proposed an algorithm called $SSAU$. In the same paper, we showed that Algorithm $SSAU$ solves the self-stabilizing asynchronous unison if $K > C_G$. It follows:

Corollary 1. *If $K > C_G$, then driven by the synchronous daemon, the self-stabilizing asynchronous unisons in [3,4,6] are self-stabilizing synchronous unisons.*

3.4 Performances of Algorithm $SSAU$

We will discuss the performances of the protocol (for asynchronous systems) proposed in [3], in the remainder referred as Algorithm $SSAU$—recalled in Algorithm 1. Theorem 5 shows that if an asynchronous unison designed for asynchronous systems is self-stabilizing, then it is also a self-stabilizing synchronous unison in a synchronous environment. However, the stabilization time still depends of the algorithm. We will now compute an upper bound of the stabilization time of Algorithm $SSAU$ in a general synchronous system. Next, we show its performances in synchronous trees.

Algorithm 1. $(SSAU)$ General Self-Stabilizing Asynchronous Unison

Constants and variables:
   $\mathcal{N}_p$: the set of neighbors of process p; $r_p \in \chi$;
Boolean Functions:
   $ConvergStep_p \equiv r_p \in tail_\varphi^* \wedge (\forall q \in \mathcal{N}_p : (r_q \in tail_\varphi) \wedge (r_p \leq_{tail_\varphi} r_q))$;
   $LocCorrect_p \quad \equiv r_p \in stab_\varphi \wedge$
$\qquad\qquad\qquad (\forall q \in \mathcal{N}_p, r_q \in stab_\varphi \wedge ((r_p = r_q) \vee (r_p = \varphi(r_q)) \vee (\varphi(r_p) = r_q)))$;
   $NormalStep_p \equiv r_p \in stab_\varphi \wedge (\forall q \in \mathcal{N}_p : (r_p = r_q) \vee (r_q = \varphi(r_p)))$;
Actions:
   $NA : NormalStep_p \vee ConvergStep_p \longrightarrow r_p := \varphi(r_p)$;
   $RA : \neg LocCorrect_p \wedge (r_p \notin tail_\varphi) \quad \longrightarrow r_p := -\alpha$; (* Reset *)

Let $e = \gamma_0 \gamma_1 \ldots \gamma_k \ldots$ be a maximal execution of Algorithm $SSAU$. A reset is a pair (p, t) where p is a process and $t > 0$ such that p executes Reset Action in the transition $\gamma_{t-1} \mapsto \gamma_t$, $r_p \neq -\alpha$ in γ_{t-1} and $r_p = -\alpha$ in γ_t. We say that p is reset (to $-\alpha$) in the configuration γ_t (or at time t).

Let (p_1, t_1) and (p_2, t_2) be two resets. We say that (p_1, t_1) *generates* (p_2, t_2), notation $(p_1, t_1) \overset{r}{\rightsquigarrow} (p_2, t_2)$ if and only if the following three conditions hold:

1. $t_1 < t_2$
2. $p_2 \in \mathcal{N}_{p_1}$ and $\forall t \in [t_1, t_2 - 1] : r_{p_2} \notin tail_\varphi$
3. $r_{p_2} = -\alpha$ in γ_{t_2} (p_2 is reset at time t_2)

Since we are considering synchronous executions, $(p_1, t_1) \overset{r}{\rightsquigarrow} (p_2, t_2)$ implies that $t_2 = t_1 + 1$. The relation $\overset{r}{\rightsquigarrow}$ defines a Directed Acyclic Graph (DAG), called *reset DAG*. If (p_1, t_1) is not generated by an other reset, we say that (p_1, t_1) is an *initial reset*. In [3], we showed that in any execution (synchronous or not), given one process p, there exists at most one t such that (p, t) is an initial reset. Clearly, $t = 1$ for any synchronous execution.

A *hole* in a graph is a chordless cycle. A reset DAG is *hole-transitive* iff $(p_1, t_1) \overset{r}{\rightsquigarrow} (p_2, t_2) \overset{r}{\rightsquigarrow} \ldots \overset{r}{\rightsquigarrow} (p_i, t_i)$ and $p_1 p_2 \ldots p_i p_1$ is a hole, then $(p_1, t_1) \overset{r}{\rightsquigarrow} (p_i, t_i)$. A *stutter* is every path of the following forms: $(p_0, t_0)(p_1, t_1)(p_0, t_2)$.

Definition 4. *Let T_G be a constant such that T_G is either equal to 2 if G is a tree network or equal to the length of the longuest hole of the network otherwise.*

In [3], we showed that the reset DAG contains no stutter and is hole-transitive, and Algorithm $SSAU$ is self-stabilizing with respect to WU if $\alpha \geq T_G - 2$, or if $T_G = 3$ and $\alpha = 0$. So, under the above condition, the hole-transitivity property and the absence of stutter imply that the projection of $p_0, p_1, \ldots, p_k$ on G of any path $(p_0, t_0), (p_1, t_0 + 1) \ldots (p_k, t_0 + k)$ on reset DAG is an elementary chordless path. Since every initial reset begins at time $t = 1$ implying two neighboring processes:

Lemma 4. *If $\alpha \geq T_G - 2$, the depth of the reset DAG is at most CP_G, where CP_G is the length of the longest elementary chordless path of G.*

So, under the above conditions ($\alpha \geq T_G - 2$), the propagation time of resets is at most CP_G. Clearly, the back up time on the tail is bounded by α, and by Theorem 5, the time of convergence to SU is less than or equal to D. Therefore:

Theorem 6. *Driven by the synchronous daemon, the self-stabilization time of Algorithm $SSAU$ is upper bounded by $CP_G + \alpha + D$. If the topology is a tree, since $CP_G = D$, if $\alpha = 0$, then the self-stabilization time of Algorithm $SSAU$ is upper bounded by $2D$.*

Note that it is easy to build an example showing that the bound CP_G can be reached. One could think that the reset propagation could be done in $O(D)$ steps. Unfortunately, the resets may not be propagated linearly in the network. This is due to the fact that a register may be equal to 0. In that case, the 0 values behave as barriers which must be bypassed by reset propagations—a 0 value is not reset. Figure 2 shows an example of a system with such behavior—the clock of p being equal to 0 prevents the reset initiated by q to be "directly" propagated from the left to the right part of the network.

Theorem 6 provides a positive answer to the question in [10] whether there exists or not a universal self-stabilizing synchronous unison for tree networks with a state requirement independant of local or global information of the tree—e.g. n, D, or Δ.

Corollary 2. *If $\alpha = 0$, Algorithm $SSAU$ is a universal self-stabilizing synchronous unison for tree networks with K ($K \geq 3$) states per process, which stabilizes in at most $2D$ steps.*

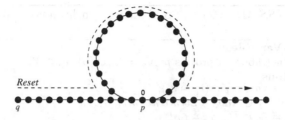

Fig. 2. An example showing why a reset may not be propagated in $O(D)$ steps

Another consequence of Theorem 6 is that if we take $K = 3$ on a tree, we are always in $WU = WU_0$. So, there is no reset. Algorithm $SSAU$ is then equivalent to the one guarded action protocol in Algorithm 2, which simply implements the "natural" clock incrementation.

Algorithm 2. Optimal Self-Stabilizing Synchronous Unison in Trees $(K = 3)$

Constants and variables:
  $\mathcal{N}_p$: the set of neighbors of process p; $r_p \in \{0, 1, 2\}$;
Action:
  $NA : \forall q \in \mathcal{N}_p : (r_p = r_q) \vee (r_q = \varphi(r_p)) \longrightarrow r_p := \varphi(r_p);$

Theorem 7. *If $\alpha = 0$ and $K = 3$, then Algorithm $SSAU$ is a self-stabilizing synchronous protocol for tree networks which is optimal in both the stabilization time—D steps, and number of states per process—3 states.*

4   Efficient Synchronous Unison for General Networks

In the previous section, we showed that the stabilization time of Algorithm $SSAU$ is upper bounded by $CP_G + \alpha + D$. It is not very efficient in a general graph. We now propose a self-stabilizing synchronous unison for general connected graph, called Algorithm SS-$MinSU$. It is shown in Algorithm 3. Algorithm SS-$MinSU$ improves the stabilization time of Algorithm $SSAU$.

It is also based on an incrementing system, but the resets are managed by the two following mechanisms:

1. A process p resets its clock to $-\alpha$ only if the clock values of p and all its neighbors are in $stab_\varphi$, but not in phase—Action RA;
2. If the clock value of p or one of its neighbors is in $tail_\varphi$, then p sets its clock to 1, plus the minimum values in $\{p\} \cup \mathcal{N}_p$—Action TA.

If a system configuration is in $WU \setminus SU$, a reset is enable. So this algorithm has no trade with the constant C_G. In other words, Algorithm 3 requires the period $K \geq 2$ only. The number of states per process is equal to $\alpha + K$ with $\alpha \geq D$. So, it works with only $D + K$ states per process. The stabilization time is at most $3D$ steps.

Algorithm 3. (*SS-MinSU*) Self-Stabilizing Synchronous Unison in General Graphs

---

Constants and Variables:

$\mathcal{N}_p$: the set of neighbors of process p; $\overline{\mathcal{N}_p} = \mathcal{N}_p \cup \{p\}$; $r_p \in \mathcal{X}$;

Boolean Functions:

$LocalUnison_p \equiv \forall q \in \mathcal{N}_p : (r_p = r_q)$;

$NormalStep_p \equiv r_p \in stab_\varphi \wedge LocalUnison_p$;

$TailStep_p \quad \equiv \exists q \in \overline{\mathcal{N}_p},\ r_q \in tail_\varphi^*$;

$ResetInit_p \quad \equiv (\forall q \in \overline{\mathcal{N}_p},\ r_q \in stab_\varphi) \wedge \neg LocalUnison_p$

Actions:

$NA : NormalStep_p \longrightarrow r_p := \varphi(r_p)$;

$TA : TailStep_p \quad \longrightarrow r_p := \varphi(min\{r_q, q \in \overline{\mathcal{N}_p}\})$;

$RA : ResetInit_p \quad \longrightarrow r_p := -\alpha$; (* Reset *)

Correctness Proof and Performance Analysis

Definition 5 (convergence state). *Let* $e = \gamma_0 \gamma_1 \ldots \gamma_i \ldots$ *be a maximal execution of Algorithm SS-MinSU. A convergent state is a pair* (p, i) *where* p *is a process and* $i \geq 0$ *such that in* γ_i, *either* $r_p \in tail_\varphi^*$ *or* $i > 0$, $r_p = 0$, *and there exists* $q \in \overline{\mathcal{N}_p}$ *such that* $r_q = -1$ *in* γ_{i-1}.

In the remainder, when it is necessary, we denote the value of r_p in γ_i by $\gamma_i.r_p$. Let (p_1, i_1) and (p_2, i_2) be two convergent states. We say that (p_1, i_1) *generates* (p_2, i_2), denoted by $(p_1, i_1) \overset{cs}{\rightsquigarrow} (p_2, t_2)$, iff the following three conditions hold: (1) $i_2 = i_1 + 1$; (2) $p_2 \in \overline{\mathcal{N}_{p_1}}$; (3) $r_{p_2} = -\alpha$ in γ_{i_2} and $r_{p_1} = 0$ in γ_{i_1} or $r_{p_2} = 0$ in γ_{i_2} and $r_{p_1} = -1$ in γ_{i_1} or $r_{p_2} \in tail_\varphi - \{0, -\alpha\}$ in γ_{i_2} and $\gamma_{i_2}.r_{p_2} = \varphi(\gamma_{i_1}.r_{p_1})$. Relation $\overset{cs}{\rightsquigarrow}$ defines a Directed Acyclic Graph (DAG), called *convergent DAG*. If (p_0, t_1) is not generated by an other convergent state, (p_1, t_1) is an *initial convergent state*.

Due to the lack of space, some formal proofs are omitted. We first prove the No Lockout property. Next, we give a condition for which the convergent DAG is finite and the system stabilizes for SU. The idea behind the finitude proof of the convergent DAG is to show that every path in the reset DAG is a path where registers are incremented in each step at most $\alpha + 1$ times. Then, we show that if $\alpha > D$, $-\alpha$ does not appears twice in a same path. Since every path starts at time 0 or 1, we deduce that at time $2D$ all convergent states disappeared, and the system is stabilized.

Theorem 8 (No lockout property). *The No Lockout Property is garanteed.*

Sketch of Proof. Let $e = \gamma_0 \gamma_1 \ldots \gamma_i \ldots (i \geq 0)$ be a maximum execution. There are two cases:

1. For every $i > 0$, there is no convergent state. Then, we show that for any maximal execution e, initial convergent states are possible only if $i \in \{0, 1\}$. Moreover, if for every $i > 0$ there exists no convergent state, then the system is in SU. So, the system is in SU and the No Lockout property is garanteed.

2. There exists $i > 0$ with a convergent state. Let p be a process among processes in convergent state such that r_p contains a minimal value in r_p. Assume that $r_p \neq 0$ in γ_i. Then, p is enabled (Action TA). Assume that $r_p = 0$ in γ_i. Then, if $r_p = -\alpha$ in γ_{i+1}, p is enabled (Action RA) in γ_i. Otherwise, since r_p contains the minimal value in $tail_\varphi$, $\forall q \in \overline{\mathcal{N}_p}$, $r_q = 0$ in γ_i. So, p is enabled in γ_i. $\square$

Theorem 9. *If $\alpha \geq D$, then Algorithm SS-MinSU is self-stabilizing with respect to SU, it stabilizes in at most $D + \alpha$ steps, and there is no reset for $t > D$.*

Sketch of Proof.   For every $e = \gamma_0 \gamma_1 \ldots \gamma_i \ldots$ $(i \geq 0)$, every path μ of the convergent DAG having a maximal length starts in γ_0 or in γ_1. If μ starts with a reset in either γ_0 or γ_1, then its length is at most α. Assume that the first convergent state $(p, 0)$ is not a reset. We show that if $r_p \leq -D$, then its length is at most $|r_p|$. Otherwise $(r_p > -D)$, its length is at most $D + \alpha$, and it there is a reset, it is at time $|r_p| + 1 \leq D$. $\square$

Clearly, from Theorem 9, if $\alpha = D$, then the system stabilizes in $2D$ steps. Following the same reasonning as the proof of Theorem 5, we can easily show the following corollary:

Corollary 3. *If $\alpha \geq D$, then Algorithm SS-MinSU is self-stabilizing with respect to SU, and it stabilizes in at most $2D$ steps.*

Note that the synchronous unison can be reached while the clock values are still in the tail. In any case, we can always insert between SS-$MinSU$ and the user application, the map Ψ from $\mathcal{X}$ to $stab_\varphi$ such that:

$$\Psi : r_p \rightarrow \overline{r_p}[K]$$

5   Concluding Remarks

We have discussed in this paper the self-stabilizing unison problem. We establish that when any self-stabilizing asynchronous unison protocol runs in synchronous

Table 1. Performances of Self-Stabilizing Unisons in Synchronous Trees

	Number of Clock Values (K)	Number of States per Process (S)	Stabilization Time (worst case)
Specific Algorithms			
[8]	$K = 3^m (m > 0)$	$S = K$	$\frac{D \times (K-1)}{2}$
	$K = 3$	$S = 3$	D
General Algorithms			
[1]	$K \geq 2D$	$S = K$	$3D$
Algorithm $SSAU$	$K > 3$	$S = K$	$2D$
Algorithm $SSAU$	$K = 3$	$S = 3$	D
Algorithm SS-$MinSU$	$K \geq 2$	$S = K + D$	$2D$

Table 2. Performances of Self-Stabilizing Unisons in Synchronous General Graphs

	Number of Clock Values (K)	Number of States per Process (S)	Stabilization Time (worst case)
[1]	$K \geq 2D$	$S = K$	$3D$
[4]	$K \geq n^2$	$S = K$	$\Omega(n^2)$
Algorithm $SSAU$	$K \geq C_G + 1$	$S \geq K + T_G - 2$	$CP_G + T_G + D$
Algorithm $SS\text{-}MinSU$	$K \geq 2$	$S \geq K + D$	$2D$

systems, it converges to synchronous unison if the size of the clock $K > C_G$. We have also shown that the asynchronous unison in [3] provides a universal self-stabilizing synchronous unison for trees which is optimal in memory space. Finally, We designed a self-stabilizing unison for general synchronous systems requiring $K \geq 2$ only, $K + D$ states per process, and its stabilization time is $2D$ only. Comparaisons of the results of this paper are presented in Tables 1 and 2 for tree and generals synchronous networks, respectively.

References

1. A Arora, S Dolev, and MG Gouda. Maintaining digital clocks in step. *Parallel Processing Letters*, 1:11–18, 1991.
2. C Berge. *Graphs and hypergraphs*. Elsevier Science Publishers B.V. (North-Holland), 1989.
3. C Boulinier, F Petit, and V Villain. When graph theory helps self-stabilization. In *PODC '04: Proceedings of the twenty-third annual ACM symposium on Principles of distributed computing*, pages 150–159, 2004.
4. JM Couvreur, N Francez, and M Gouda. Asynchronous unison. In *Proceedings of the 12th IEEE International Conference on Distributed Computing Systems (ICDCS'92)*, pages 486–493, 1992.
5. EW Dijkstra. Self stabilizing systems in spite of distributed control. *Communications of the Association of the Computing Machinery*, 17:643–644, 1974.
6. S Dolev. *Self-Stabilization*. The MIT Press, 2000.
7. MG Gouda and T Herman. Stabilizing unison. *Information Processing Letters*, 35:171–175, 1990.
8. T Herman and S Ghosh. Stabilizing phase-clocks. *Information Processing Letters*, 54:259–265, 1995.
9. J Misra. Phase synchronization. *Information Processing Letters*, 38(2):101–105, 1991.
10. F Nolot. *Self-stabilizing phase clock in distributed systems*. PhD thesis, LaRIA, Université de Picardie Jules Verne, Amiens, France, 2002. Dissertation in French.
11. F Nolot and V Villain. Universal self-stabilizing phase clock protocol with bounded memory. In *IPCCC '01, 20th IEEE International Performance, Computing, and Communications Conference*, pages 228–235, 2001.

A Snap-Stabilizing DFS with a Lower Space Requirement*

Alain Cournier, Stéphane Devismes, and Vincent Villain

LaRIA, CNRS FRE 2733,
Université de Picardie Jules Verne, Amiens (France)
{cournier, devismes, villain}@laria.u-picardie.fr

Abstract. A *snap-stabilizing protocol*, starting from any arbitrary initial configuration, always behaves according to its specification. In [4], we presented the first snap-stabilizing depth-first search (*DFS*) wave protocol for arbitrary rooted networks working under an unfair daemon. However, this protocol needs $O(N^N)$ states per processors (where N is the number of processors) and needs ids on processors. In this paper, we propose an original snap-stabilizing solution for this problem with a strongly enhanced space complexity, i.e., $O(\Delta^2 \times N)$ states where Δ is the degree of the network. Furthermore, this new protocol does not need a completely identified network: only the root needs to be identified, i.e., the network is *semi-anonymous*.

1 Introduction

In an arbitrary rooted network, a Depth-First Search (*DFS*) Wave is initiated by the root. In this wave, all the processors are sequentially visited in depth-first search order. This scheme has many applications in distributed systems. For example, the solution of this problem can be used for solving mutual exclusion, spanning tree computation, constraint programming, routing, or synchronization.

The concept of *self-stabilization* [7] is the most general technique to design a system tolerating arbitrary transient faults. A self-stabilizing system, regardless of the initial states of the processors and messages initially in the links, is guaranteed to converge to the intended behavior in finite time. *Snap-stabilization* was introduced in [2]. A *snap-stabilizing* protocol guaranteed that it always behaves according to its specification. In other words, a snap-stabilizing protocol is also a self-stabilizing protocol which stabilizes in 0 time unit. Obviously, a *snap-stabilizing* protocol is optimal in stabilization time.

Related Works. Several self-stabilizing (but not snap-stabilizing) wave protocols based on the *depth-first token circulation (DFTC)* have been proposed for arbitrary rooted networks, e.g., [9,11,10,6]. All these papers have a stabilization

---

* A full version of this paper is available at www.laria.u-picardie.fr/~devismes/ tr2005-05.pdf

T. Herman and S. Tixeuil (Eds.): SSS 2005, LNCS 3764, pp. 33–47, 2005.
© Springer-Verlag Berlin Heidelberg 2005

time in $O(D \times N)$ rounds where N is the number of processors and D is the diameter of the network. The protocols proposed in [11,10,6] attempted to reduce the memory requirement from $O(\Delta \times N)$ [9] to $O(\Delta)$ states per processor where Δ is the degree of the network. However, the correctness of all the above protocols is proven assuming a (weakly) fair daemon. Roughly speaking, a daemon is considered as an adversary which tries to prevent the protocol to behave as expected, and fairness means that the daemon cannot prevent forever a processor to execute an enabled action.

The first snap-stabilizing $DFTC$ has been proposed in [12] for tree networks. In arbitrary networks, a *universal transformer* providing a snap-stabilizing version of any (neither self- nor snap-) protocol is given in [3]. Obviously, combining this protocol with any $DFTC$ protocol, we obtain a snap-stabilizing $DFTC$ protocol for arbitrary networks. However, the resulting protocol works assuming a weakly fair daemon only. Indeed, it generates an infinite number of snapshots, independently of the token progress. Therefore, the number of steps per wave cannot be bounded. Finally, we propose in [4] the first snap-stabilizing DFS protocol for arbitrary rooted network assuming an unfair daemon, i.e., the weakest scheduling assumption. In contrast with the previous solutions, the time complexity of each wave of the protocol can now be bounded in terms of steps.

Contribution. The protocol of [4] works on identified networks and needs $O(N^N)$ states per processor. In this paper, we reduce this space complexity to $O(\Delta^2 \times N)$ states per processor using a method similar to that in [1]. This new solution also works assuming an unfair daemon. Moreover, our protocol does not need a completely identified network: only the root needs to be identified, i.e., the network is *semi-anonymous*. Unfortunately, the time complexities of our protocol are greater than those in [4]: a complete DFS Wave needs $O(N^2)$ rounds and $O(N^3)$ steps instead of $O(N)$ rounds and $O(N^2)$ steps. Nevertheless, the gain of space requirement is such that the worst time complexities are a minor drawback.

Outline of the Paper. The rest of the paper is organized as follows: in Section 2, we describe the model in which our protocol is written. Moreover, in the same section, we give a formal statement of the Depth-First Search Wave Protocol solved in this paper. In Section 3, we present the protocol and the intuitive ideas of its correctness (due to the lack of space, the proof of correctness has been omitted). Finally, we make concluding remarks in Section 4.

2   Preliminaries

Network. We consider a *network* as an undirected connected graph $G = (V, E)$ where V is a set of *processors* ($|V| = N$) and E is the set of *bidirectional communication links*. We consider networks which are *asynchronous* and *rooted*, i.e., among the processors, we distinguish a particular processor called *root*. We denote the root processor by r. A communication link (p, q) exists if and only if p and q are neighbors. Every processor p can distinguish all its links. To simplify the presentation, we refer to a link (p, q) of a processor p by the *label* q. We assume that the labels of p, stored in the set $Neig_p$, are locally ordered by $\prec_p$. We assume that $Neig_p$ is a constant and shown as an input from the system.

Computational Model. In our model, each processor executes the same program except r. We consider the local shared memory model of computation. The program of every processor consists in a set of *shared variables* (henceforth, referred to as variables) and a finite set of *actions*. A processor can write to its own variable only, and read its own variables and that of its neighbors. Each action is constituted as follows: $< label > :: < guard > \rightarrow < statement >$. The guard of an action in the program of p is a boolean expression involving variables of p and its neighbors. The statement of an action of p updates one or more variables of p. An action can be executed only if its guard is satisfied. We assume that the actions are atomically executed, i.e., the evaluation of a guard and the execution of the corresponding statement, if executed, are done in one atomic step.

The *state* of a processor is defined by the value of its variables. The *state* of a system is the product of the states of all processors. We will refer to the state of a processor and the system as a *(local) state* and *(global) configuration*, respectively. We note $\mathcal{C}$ the set of all possible configuration of the system. Let $\gamma \in \mathcal{C}$ and A an action of p $(p \in V)$. A is said *enabled* in γ if the guard of A is satisfied in γ. Processor p is said to be *enabled* in γ if it has an enabled action in γ.

Let a distributed protocol $\mathcal{P}$ be a collection of binary transition relations denoted by $\mapsto$, on $\mathcal{C}$. A *computation* of a protocol $\mathcal{P}$ is a *maximal* sequence of configurations $e = (\gamma_0, \gamma_1, ..., \gamma_i, \gamma_{i+1}, ...)$, such that for $i \geq 0$, $\gamma_i \mapsto \gamma_{i+1}$ (called a *step*) if γ_{i+1} exists, else γ_i is a terminal configuration. *Maximality* means that the sequence is either finite (and no action of $\mathcal{P}$ is enabled in the terminal configuration) or infinite. All computations considered in this paper are assumed to be maximal. The set of all possible computations of $\mathcal{P}$ is denoted by $\mathcal{E}$.

As we have already said, each execution is decomposed into steps. Each step is shared into three sequential phases atomically executed: (i) every processor evaluates its guard, (ii) a *daemon* (also called *scheduler*) chooses some enabled processors, and (ii) the chosen processors execute some of their enabled actions. When these three phases are done, the next step begins.

A *daemon* can be defined in terms of *fairness* and *distributivity*. In this paper, we use the notion of *weakly fairness*: if a daemon is *weakly fair*, then every continuously enabled processor is eventually chosen (by the daemon) to execute an action. We also use the notion of *unfairness*: the *unfair* daemon can forever prevent a processor to execute an action except if it is the only enabled processor. Concerning the *distributivity*, we assume that the daemon is *distributed* meaning that, at each step, if one or more processor are enabled, then the daemon chooses at least one (possibly more) of these processors to execute actions.

We consider that any processor p executed a *disabling action* in the computation step $\gamma_i \mapsto \gamma_{i+1}$ if p was *enabled* in γ_i and not enabled in γ_{i+1}, but did not execute any action between these two configurations. (The disabling action represents the following situation: at least one neighbor of p changes its state between γ_i and γ_{i+1}, and this change effectively made the guard of all actions of p false.)

To compute the time complexity, we use the definition of *round* [8]. This definition captures the execution rate of the slowest processor in any computation. Given a computation e ($e \in \mathcal{E}$), the *first round* of e (let us call it e') is the minimal prefix of e containing the execution of one action (an action of the protocol or the disabling action) of every enabled processor from the first configuration. Let e'' be the suffix of e such that $e = e'e''$. The *second round* of e is the first round of e'', and so on.

In order to make our protocol more readable, we design it as a *composition* of four algorithms. In this composition, if a processor p is enabled for k of the combined algorithms, then, if the daemon chooses it, p executes an enabled action of each of the k algorithms, in the same step. Variables, predicates, or macros of Algorithm A used by Algorithm B are shown as inputs in Algorithm B.

Snap-Stabilizing Systems. Snap-stabilization [2] is a general concept which can be apply to several kinds of distributed protocol. However, the protocol presented in this paper is a *wave protocol* as defined by Tel in [13]. So, we now propose a simpler definition of snap-stabilization holding for wave protocols:

Definition 1. *[Snap-stabilization for Wave Protocols] Let $\mathcal{T}$ be a task, and $\mathcal{SP_T}$ a specification of $\mathcal{T}$. A wave protocol $\mathcal{P}$ is snap-stabilizing for $\mathcal{SP_T}$ if and only if: (i) at least one processor eventually executes a particular action of $\mathcal{P}$, and (ii) the result obtained with $\mathcal{P}$ from this particular action always satisfies $\mathcal{SP_T}$.*

Specification of the Depth-First Search Wave Protocol.

Specification 1. *Let* Visited *be a set of processors. A finite computation $e \in \mathcal{E}$ is called a DFS Wave if and only if: (i) r initiates the DFS Wave by initializing* Visited *with r, (ii) all other processors are then sequentially included in* Visited *in DFS order, and (iii) r eventually detects the termination of the process.*

Remark 1. So, in the practice, to prove that our protocol is snap-stabilizing we have to show that every execution of the protocol satisfies: (i) r eventually initiates a *DFS* Wave, and (ii) thereafter, the execution satisfies Specification 1.

3 Algorithm

We now present an informal description of our DFS Wave protocol (see Algorithms 1 to 8 for the formal description). Along this description, we will give the main keys to understand why our protocol is snap-stabilizing. For a sake of clarity, we divided our protocol, referred to as Algorithm $\mathcal{DFS}$, into four phases:

1. The *visiting phase* (Algorithms 1 and 2) sequentially visits the processors in depth-first search order: Starting from r, the visit progresses as deeply as possible in the network. When the visit cannot progress anymore (i.e., the

visit reaches a processor with a completely visited neighbourhood), the visit backtracks to the latest visited processor having some non-visited neighbors, if any. The visit terminates when it backtracks to r and r has a completely visited neighbourhood.

2. The *cleaning phase* (Algorithms 3 and 4) cleans the trace of the last visiting phase so that the root is eventually ready to initiate another visiting phase again. The cleaning phase is initiated only when the visiting phase is entirely done.

3. The *confirmation phase* (Algorithms 5 and 6) prevents to forgot some processors in the visiting phase initiated by the root (especially when the system contains some erroneous behaviors). The confirmation phase is performed each time the protocol needs to be sure that all the neighbors of the latest visited processor have been visited by the *normal* visiting phase, i.e., the visiting phase from the root. Indeed, since the system starts from any configuration, some visiting phases can be rooted at another processor than r, i.e., the *abnormal* visiting phases.

4. The *abnormal trees' deletion* (Algorithms 7 and 8) erases all the *abnormal* visiting phases.

In order to more precisely describe this four phases, we first present how to implement a non self-stabilizing DFS protocol (visiting phase and cleaning phase). We then explain the problems appearing when we use this protocol in a self-stabilizing[1] context and how to solve them (abnormal trees' deletion, confirmation phase, ...). In particular, we will present some tools used for insuring the snap-stabilization of our protocol, i.e., the optimality of our protocol in terms of stabilization time.

Algorithm 1. *Visiting Phase* for $p = r$

Inputs:
on read: $Neig_p$: set of neighbors (locally ordered);
       $Child_p$: macro of the *abnormal trees' deletion*;
on read/write: Que_p: variable of the *confirmation phase*;

Constants: $L_p = 0$; $Par_p = \bot$;

Variable: $S_p \in Neig_p \cup \{idle, rdone\}$;

Macro:
$Next_p$ $= (q = \min_{\prec_p}\{q' \in Neig_p :: S_{q'} = idle\})$ if q **exists**, $rdone$ **otherwise**;
$RealChild_p = \{q \in Child_p :: E_q \neq E_p \Rightarrow E_p = B\}$;   /* valid for $S_p \neq idle$ only */
Predicates:
$End(p)$ $\equiv (\forall q \in Neig_p :: S_q \neq idle \Rightarrow Par_q \neq p)$
$AnswerOK(p) \equiv (Que_p = A) \wedge (\forall q \in Neig_p :: S_q \neq idle \Rightarrow Que_q = A)$
$Forward(p)$ $\equiv (S_p = idle) \wedge (\forall q \in Neig_p :: S_p = idle)$
$Backward(p)$ $\equiv (\exists q \in Neig_p :: S_p = q \wedge Par_q = p \wedge S_q = done)$
         $\wedge [AnswerOK(p) \vee (\exists q \in Neig_p :: S_q = idle)]$

Actions:
$F\text{-}action :: Forward(p)$ $\rightarrow$ $S_p := Next_p$; $Que_p := Q$;
$B\text{-}action :: Backward(p)$ $\rightarrow$ $S_p := Next_p$;

---

[1] Remember that our snap-stabilizing protocol is a self-stabilizing protocol which stabilizes in 0 time unit.

Visiting Phase. In our non self-stabilizing protocol, each processor p maintains two variables to implement this phase[2]:

- $\forall p \in V$, $S_p \in Neig_p \cup \{idle,\ done\}$ if $p \neq r$ and $S_p \in Neig_p \cup \{idle,\ rdone\}$ if $p = r$. $S_p = idle$ means that p is ready to be visited. $S_p = q$ such that $q \in Neig_p$ means that p participates to a visiting phase and its *successor* in the visit is its neighbor q (respectively, p is called the *predecessor* of q). Finally, S_p is set to *done* (resp. *rdone* if $p = r$) when the visit locally terminates at p.
- $\forall p \in V$, Par_p is used for keeping a mark of the DFS spanning tree computed by the protocol. Indeed, Par_p designates the *parent* of p in the traversal: when p is visited for the first time, it designates its predecessor with Par_p. Obviously, r never has any parent. So, we state that Par_r is the constant $\perp$.

Since our protocol is non self-stabilizing, any execution must start from particular configurations. We call these configurations the *normal initial configurations*. Here, there is only one normal initial configuration for our protocol and it is defined as follows: $\forall p \in V$, $S_p = idle$. In this configuration, the root r initiates a visiting phase by pointing out using S_r to its minimal neighbor p in the local order $\prec_r$ (*F-action*). By this action, r becomes the only *visited* processor. Then, at each step, exactly one processor p is enabled and two cases are possible:

a) $S_p = idle$ and $\exists q \in Neig_p$ such that $S_q = p$. In this case, $p \neq r$ and p executes *F-action* to be visited for the first time. First, p points out to q (its predecessor) using Par_p. Then, p computes S_p as follows:
   - **If** p has still some non-visited neighbors, i.e., $\exists p' \in Neig_p$ such that $S_{p'} = idle$, then p chooses its minimal non-visited neighbor by $\prec_p$ as its successor in the traversal.
   - **Otherwise** p sets S_p to *done*.
b) $S_p = q$ ($q \in Neig_p$) and $S_q = done$, i.e., the visiting phase backtracks to p because the visit from q is terminated. In this case p executes *B-action*:
   - **If** p has still some non-visited neighbors, then it updates S_p by pointing out to a new successor (its minimal non-visited neighbor by $\prec_p$).
   - **Otherwise** it sets S_p to *done* (resp. *rdone* if $p = r$).

Therefore, step by step, the visiting phase dynamically built a spanning tree of the network rooted at r (w.r.t. the Par variable), noted $Tree(r)$. It is easy to see that this phase follows a DFS order and the number of steps required for the phase is $2N - 1$. Moreover, since the behavior is sequential, the number of rounds is the same. Finally, S_r is eventually set to *rdone* meaning that the visiting phase is terminated for all processors. By this latter action, r initiates the cleaning phase.

Cleaning Phase. The aim of the cleaning phase is to erase the trace of the last visiting phase in order to bring the system in the normal initial configuration

---

[2] This phase does not exactly correspond to Algorithms 1 and 2. Indeed, we will see later that this phase must be modified in order to run correctly in a self-stabilizing context.

Algorithm 2. *Visiting Phase* for $p \neq r$

Inputs:
on read: $Neig_p$: set of neighbors (locally ordered);
  $Child_p$: macro of the *abnormal trees' deletion*;
on read/write: Que_p: variable of the *confirmation phase*;
  E_p: variable of the *abnormal trees' deletion*;
Variables: $S_p \in Neig_p \cup \{idle, wait, done, rdone\}$; $Par_p \in Neig_p$; $L_p \in \mathbb{N}$;

Macros:
$WaitOrDone_p = wait$ **if** $(S_p = idle)$, $done$ **otherwise**;
$Next_p \qquad\quad = (q = \min_{\prec_p} \{q' \in Neig_p :: S_{q'} = idle\})$ **if** q **exists**, $WaitOrDone_p$ **otherwise**;
$Pred_p \qquad\quad = \{q \in Neig_p :: S_q = p \wedge E_q = C\}$;
$RealChild_p \quad = \{q \in Child_p :: E_q \neq E_p \Rightarrow E_p = B\}$;   /* valid for $S_p \neq idle$ only */
Predicates:
$End(p) \qquad\qquad \equiv (\forall q \in Neig_p :: S_q \neq idle \Rightarrow Par_q \neq p)$
$AnswerOK(p) \equiv (Que_p = A) \wedge (\forall q \in Neig_p :: S_q \neq idle \Rightarrow Que_q = A)$
$Forward(p) \quad\;\; \equiv (S_p = idle) \wedge (|Pred_p| = 1) \wedge End(p)$
$WaitOk(p) \qquad \equiv Normal(p) \wedge (S_p = Wait) \wedge [AnswerOK(p) \vee (\exists q \in Neig_p :: S_q = idle)]$
$Backward(p) \quad \equiv Normal(p) \wedge (\exists q \in Neig_p :: S_p = q \wedge Par_q = p \wedge S_q = done)$
$\qquad\qquad\qquad\quad \wedge [AnswerOK(p) \vee (\exists q \in Neig_p :: S_q = idle)]$
$BadSucc(p) \qquad \equiv Normal(p) \wedge AnswerOk(p)$
$\qquad\qquad\qquad\quad \wedge (\exists q \in Neig_p :: S_p = q \wedge q \notin RealChild_p \wedge S_q \neq idle)$
Actions:
$F\text{-}action \quad\;\; :: Forward(p) \quad\rightarrow Par_p := (q \in Pred_p); S_p := Next_p;$
$\qquad\qquad\qquad\qquad\qquad\qquad Que_p := Q; L_p := L_{Par_p} + 1; E_p := C;$
$Fbis\text{-}action :: WaitOk(p) \quad\rightarrow S_p := Next_p;$
$B\text{-}action \quad\;\; :: Backward(p) \rightarrow S_p := Next_p;$
$IE\text{-}action \quad :: BadSucc(p) \;\;\rightarrow S_p := Next_p;$

Algorithm 3. *Cleaning Phase* for $p = r$

Inputs:
on read: $Neig_p$: set of neighbors (locally ordered);
  $End(p)$: predicate of the *visiting phase*;
on read/write: S_p: variable of the *visiting phase*;

Predicate:
$Clean(p) \equiv (S_p = rdone) \wedge End(p) \wedge (\forall q \in Neig_p :: S_q \in \{idle, rdone\})$

Action:
$C\text{-}action :: Clean(p) \rightarrow S_p := idle;$

---

again ($\forall p \in V$, $S_p = idle$). Only the root can detect if the visiting phase is entirely done: when r sets S_r to $rdone$. Since the root detects the end of the visiting phase, the $rdone$ value is propagated toward the leaves of $Tree(r)$ following the Par variables ($RD\text{-}action$) to inform all processors of this termination (to that goal, we add the state $rdone$ into the definition of S_p, $\forall p \in V \setminus \{r\}$). Then, each leaf of $Tree(r)$ successively cleans itself by setting its S variable to $idle$ ($C\text{-}action$). Therefore, the system eventually reaches the normal initial configuration again. This phase adds $2N - 1$ steps and the number of additional rounds is $2H + 1$ where H is the height of the tree computed during the visiting phase (n.b., H is bounded by $N - 1$).

We presented a non self-stabilizing DFS protocol. Of course, in the context of self-stabilization, this protocol does not work correctly. So, we must modify its existing actions as well as we must add some other actions. In particular, we introduce the *confirmation phase* to guarantee that a visiting phase initiated by the root eventually visits **all** processors. This latter point is crucial to obtain a snap-stabilizing protocol.

Algorithm 4. *Cleaning Phase* for $p \neq r$

Inputs:
on read: $Neig_p$: set of neighbors (locally ordered);
$\qquad\qquad Par_p$: variable of the *visiting phase*;
$\qquad\qquad End(p)$: predicate of the *visiting phase*;
$\qquad\qquad Normal(p)$: predicate of the *abnormal trees' deletion*;
on read/write: S_p: variable of the *visiting phase*;

Predicates:
$RdonePar(p) \equiv Normal(p) \wedge (S_p = done) \wedge (S_{Par_p} = rdone)$
$Clean(p) \qquad \equiv Normal(p) \wedge (S_p = rdone) \wedge End(p) \wedge (\forall q \in Neig_p :: S_q \in \{idle, rdone\})$

Actions:
$RD\text{-}action :: RdonePar(p) \rightarrow S_p := rdone;$
$C\text{-}action \quad :: Clean(p) \qquad \rightarrow S_p := idle;$

Modifying the Existing Actions. Starting from any arbitrary configuration, the system may contain successors' cycles. We detect this error by using a new variable L for each processor. For the root, L_r is the constant 0. Each other processor p dynamically computes its L variable each time it executes $F\text{-}action$: $L_p := L_q + 1$ where q is the predecessor of p (n.b., p does not execute $F\text{-}action$ if it has several predecessors). Typically, L_p contains the length of the path from the root r to p w.r.t. the variable Par. Obviously, in a cycle of successors, at least one processor p satisfies $L_p \neq L_{Par_p} + 1$.

In the visiting phase, we have shown that a visited processor p sets S_p to *done* (resp. *rdone* if $p = r$) when all its neighbors have been visited. In the non self-stabilizing context, p can easily detect when all neighbors are visited: when $\forall p' \in Neig_p$, $S_{p'} \neq idle$. However, in a self-stabilizing scheme, since some neighbors of p may belong to abnormal visiting phases, this condition is not sufficient. So, in order to guarantee that every neighbor of p is visited, we introduce a new phase, the *confirmation phase*. The aim of this phase is to insure that a processor p, participating to a visiting phase initiated by r, sets S_p to *done* (resp. *rdone* if $p = r$) only when its neighbourhood is completely visited by the visiting phase from r. To apply this concept, we add the state *wait* into the definition of S_p, $\forall p \in V \setminus \{r\}$ and we change $F\text{-}action$ of the initial protocol: when a processor $p \neq r$ receives a visiting phase ($F\text{-}action$) and satisfies $\forall p' \in Neig_p$, $S_{p'} \neq idle$, it now sets S_p to *wait* instead of *done* (see Macros $Next_p$ and $WaitOrDone_p$). This action initiates the *confirmation phase*. We now describe in details the *confirmation phase*.

Confirmation Phase. To implement this phase, we introduce a new variable Que_p for each processor p: $Que_p \in \{Q, R, W, A\}$ if $p \neq r$ and $Que_p \in \{Q, R, A\}$ if $p = r$. The Q and R value are used for resetting the part of the network which is concerned by the confirmation phase. The W value corresponds to the request of a processor: "Have I terminated my visiting phase?". The A value corresponds to the answer sending by the root (n.b., the root is the only processor able to generate a A value). We now explain how this phase works.

The confirmation phase concerns processors such that $S \neq idle$ only. Variable Que_p of a processor p is initialized by $F\text{-}action$ of the visiting phase: $Que_p := Q$. This value forces all its neighbors satisfying $S \neq idle$ to execute $Que := R$ ($R\text{-}action$). When all the neighbors of p have reset, p also executes $Que_p := R$. Then, the R values are propagated up as far as possible following the Par variable (R-action). By this mechanism, the A values are deleted in the Par paths of p and its neighbors (in particular, the A values present since the initial configuration). Thus, from now on, when a A value reaches a requesting processor, this value cannot come from anyone but r and the processor obviously belongs to the normal visiting phase. Now, as we have seen before, a processor q ($q \neq r$) eventually waits a confirmation from the root that all its neighbors are visited ($S_q = wait$). In this case, q and its neighbors satisfying $S = done$ execute W-action[3], i.e., $Que := W$ meaning that they are now waiting for an answer from r. W value is propagated toward the root if possible (a processor p propagates the W value when all its children satisfies $Que \notin \{Q, R\}$). When the W value reaches the children of r, r executes its A-action: it sends an answer (A) to its children and so on. So, if q and its neighbors receive this answer (A), q is sure that it and all its neighbors belong to $Tree(r)$. In this case, q satisfies $AnswerOk(q)$ and executes $Fbis$-action to set S_q to $done$ meaning that the visiting phase from it is now terminated and so on.

We now explain why a visited processor needs to initiate the *confirmation phase* only once: when it executes F-action. Assume that a processor of the visiting phase initiated by r, p, has a neighbor q such that q belongs to an abnormal visiting phase. We have already seen that, when p is visited for the first time (F-action), it also executes $Que_p := Q$. This action initiates the *confirmation phase* and forces q to execute $Que_q := R$ (R-action). This value erases all A values in the Par path of q. Since only r can generate a A value, q never receives any A. Thus, p cannot satisfy $AnswerOk(p)$ while q belongs to an abnormal visiting phase. As a consequence, p cannot set S_p to $done$ (resp. $rdone$ if $p = r$) while one of its neighbor belongs to an abnormal visiting phase (see $Fbis$-action and B-action).

Unfortunately, starting from the normal initial configuration, this phase strongly slows down the initial protocol, nevertheless, it does not generate any deadlock. The worst case (starting from the normal initial configuration) is obtained with a computed tree of height in $O(N)$ with a number of leaves also in $O(N)$ at a distance in $O(N)$ of the root. In that case, $\Theta(N)$ W-actions are initiated by these leaves. So, the complexity is in $\Theta(N^2)$ steps. Due to the sequentiality along the path from a requesting leaf to the root, the complexity in terms of rounds is also in $\Theta(N^2)$.

Of course, we have now to deal with abnormal configurations. We first introduce a new action in the visiting phase to remove some deadlock due to the variables' initial configurations of the visiting phase itself.

IE-Action. To prevent the system from any deadlock, we add IE-action to solve a case which can only appear in the initial configuration: The active end of $Tree(r)$ (i.e., the only processor $p \in Tree(r)$ such that $End(p) \wedge S_p \notin \{done,$

---

[3] Starting from an arbitrary configuration, the neighbors of q satisfying $S = done$ can belong to $Tree(r)$, so, they must also receive an acknowledgment from r so that q knows that they are not in an abnormal visiting phase.

Algorithm 5. *Confirmation Phase* for $p = r$

Inputs:
on read: $Neig_p$: set of neighbors (locally ordered);
  S_p: variable of the *visiting phase*;
  $RealChild_p$: predicate of the *visiting phase*;
Variable: $Que_p \in \{Q, R, A\}$;

Predicates:
$Require(p) \equiv (S_p \neq idle) \wedge [[Que_p = Q \wedge (\forall q \in Neig_p :: S_q \neq idle \Rightarrow Que_q \in \{Q, R\})]$
  $\vee [Que_p = A \wedge (\exists q \in Neig_p :: (S_q \neq idle \wedge Que_q = Q)$
  $\vee (q \in RealChild_p \wedge Que_q = R))]]$
$Answer(p) \equiv (S_p \neq idle) \wedge (Que_p = R) \wedge (\forall q \in RealChild_p :: Que_q \in \{W, A\})$
  $\wedge (\forall q \in Neig_p :: S_q \neq idle \Rightarrow Que_q \neq Q)$

Actions:
$R\text{-}action :: Require(p) \rightarrow Que_p := R;$
$A\text{-}action :: Answer(p) \rightarrow Que_p := A;$

Algorithm 6. *Confirmation Phase* for $p \neq r$

Inputs:
on read: $Neig_p$: set of neighbors (locally ordered);
  S_p, Par_p: variables of the *visiting phase*;
  $RealChild_p$: macro of the *visiting phase*;
  $End(p)$: predicate of the *visiting phase*;
  $Normal(p)$: predicate of the *abnormal trees' deletion*;
Variable: $Que_p \in \{Q, R, W, A\}$;

Predicates:
$Require(p) \quad \equiv Normal(p) \wedge (S_p \neq idle)$
  $\wedge [[Que_p = Q \wedge (\forall q \in Neig_p :: S_q \neq idle \Rightarrow Que_q \in \{Q,R\})]$
  $\vee [Que_p \in \{W,A\} \wedge (\exists q \in Neig_p :: (S_q \neq idle \wedge Que_q = Q)$
  $\vee (q \in RealChild_p \wedge Que_q = R))]]$
$WaitAnswer(p) \equiv Normal(p) \wedge (S_p \neq idle) \wedge (Que_p = R) \wedge (Que_{Par_p} = R)$
  $\wedge (\forall q \in Neig_p :: S_q \neq idle \Rightarrow Que_q \neq Q)$
  $\wedge [End(p) \Rightarrow (S_p \neq rdone \wedge (S_p \in Neig_p \Rightarrow S_{S_p} \neq idle))]$
  $\wedge [\neg End(p) \Rightarrow (\forall q \in RealChild_p :: Que_q \in \{W,A\})]$
$Answer(p) \quad \equiv Normal(p) \wedge (S_p \neq idle) \wedge (Que_p = W) \wedge (Que_{Par_p} = A)$
  $\wedge (\forall q \in RealChild_p :: Que_q \in \{W, A\})$
  $\wedge (\forall q \in Neig_p :: S_q \neq idle \Rightarrow Que_q \neq Q)$

Actions:
$R\text{-}action \ :: Require(p) \quad \rightarrow Que_p := R;$
$W\text{-}action :: WaitAnswer(p) \rightarrow Que_p := W;$
$A\text{-}action \ :: Answer(p) \qquad \rightarrow Que_p := A;$

$rdone\}$) can designate as successor a processor q (i.e., $S_p = q$) such that q belongs to $Tree(r)$. Now, thanks to the confirmation phase, p eventually knows that it does not designate a "good" successor because p and q receives an acknowledgment (A) from r. So, p eventually changes its successor by $IE\text{-}action$. In the following, $IE\text{-}action$ is considered as an action of the visiting phase. This action is enough to break the deadlock of the visiting phase rooted at r. This action (and the confirmation phase associated) does not add a significant cost.

We need now to deal with abnormal visiting phases, i.e., visiting phases rooted at another processor than r. The *abnormal trees' deletion* we now introduce erases these abnormal visiting phases.

Abnormal Trees' Deletion. We first explain how to detect the abnormal visiting phases. In a normal visiting phase, each non-root processor p must maintain some properties based on the value of its variables and that of its parent. We list these conditions below:

1. If p is involved in the DFS Wave ($S_p \neq idle$) and p is designated as successor by its parent ($S_{Par_p} = p$) then S_p must be different of the *rdone* value. Indeed, the *rdone* value is generated by the root only and is propagated down in the spanning tree.

2. If p is involved in the DFS Wave and p is not designated as successor by its parent ($S_{Par_p} \neq p$) then the visiting phase from p is terminated, i.e., $S_p \in \{done, rdone\}$.
   - If $S_p = rdone$ then its parent, Par_p, must satisfy $S_{Par_p} = rdone$. Indeed, the *rdone* value is propagated from the root to the leaves of $Tree(r)$ after the end of the visiting phase.
   - If $S_p = done$ then, as $S_{Par_p} \neq p$, the visiting phase has backtracked to Par_p (by *B-action*). So, either Par_p points out to another successor, i.e., $S_{Par_p} \in Neig_{Par_p} \setminus \{p\}$; or the visiting phase from Par_p is also terminated, i.e., $S_{Par_p} \in \{done, rdone\}$. More simply, if $S_{Par_p} \neq p$ and $S_p = done$ then, $S_{Par_p} \notin \{idle, wait\}$.

3. Finally, if p is involved in the DFS Wave and p satisfies 1. and 2. (Predicate $GoodPar(p)$) then its level L_p must be equal to one plus the level of its parent (Predicate $GoodLevel(p)$).

If one of these conditions is not satisfied by p then $AbRoot(p)$ is *true*. Now, starting from any configuration, p may satisfy $AbRoot$. We can then remark that the abnormal visiting phase from p shapes an abnormal tree noted $Tree(p)$: $\forall q \in V$, $q \in Tree(p)$ if and only if there exists a sequence of nodes ($p_0 = p$), ..., p_i, ..., p_k such that, $\forall i \in [1...k]$, $p_i \in Child_{p_{i-1}}$ (among the neighbors designating p_{i-1} with Par, only those satisfying $S \neq idle \wedge \neg AbRoot$ are considered as p_{i-1} children).

We now explain how the protocol cleans these abnormal trees. In order to clean the abnormal tree $Tree(p)$, we cannot simply set S_p to *idle*. Since some processors in the visiting phase can be in $Tree(p)$. If we simply set S_p to *idle*, then p can participate again to the visiting phase of the tree of which it was the root. As we do not assume the knowledge of any bound on the L values (we may assume that the maximum value of L is any upper bound of N), this scheme can progress infinitely often, and the system contains an abnormal tree which can prevent the progression of the tree of the normal visiting phase ($Tree(r)$). We solve this problem by paralyzing the progress of any abnormal tree before removing it. First, a processor p can be visited from its neighbor q only if q satisfies $S_q = p$ and $E_q = C$ (see $Pred_p$). Then, if p hooks on to $Tree(q)$ (*F-action*), it also executes $E_p := C$. If q is an abnormal root, then it sets its variable E_q to B and broadcasts this value in its tree (and only in its tree). When q receives an acknowledgment of all its children (Value F of Variable E), it knows that all the processors p of its tree have $E_p = F$ and no processor can now participate in the visiting phase from any p. So, q can leave its tree (*EC-action*) and it will be no more visited by this abnormal visit. Thus, by this mechanism, all the abnormal trees eventually disappear.

The management of the E variables adds new kind of errors. Indeed, $\forall p, q \in V$ such that $S_p \neq idle \wedge S_q \neq idle \wedge Par_q = p \wedge \neg AbRoot(q)$, p and

---

Algorithm 7. *Abnormal trees' Deletion* for $p = r$

Inputs:
on read: $Neig_p$: set of neighbors (locally ordered);
          S_p, Par_p, L_p: variables of the *visiting phase*;
Constant: $E_p = C$;

Macros:
$Child_p = \{q \in Neig_p :: Par_q = p \wedge S_q \neq idle \wedge L_q = L_p + 1$ /* valid for $S_p \neq idle$ only */
          $\wedge \; (S_p = q \Rightarrow S_q \neq rdone) \wedge [[S_p \neq q] \Rightarrow [(S_q = rdone \wedge S_p = rdone) \vee (S_q = done)]]\}$;

---

q must satisfy $(E_p, E_q) \in \{(B,C), (B,B), (B,F), (F,F), (C,C)\}$. Predicates $FCorrection(p)$, $BCorrection(p)$, and $CCorrection(p)$ allows to detect if this condition is not satisfied by p and q. Now, we can remark that these kinds of error are local and can only appear in the initial configuration. So, we simply correct it by executing $S_q := idle$ and $E_q := C$ (*EC-action*).

To remove an abnormal tree, any processor in the tree has at most three actions to execute. So, the additional cost of this phase is in $\Theta(N)$ by tree for both steps and rounds. So, in the worst case ($\Theta(N)$ abnormal trees), the cost is in $\Theta(N^2)$ steps but is still in $\Theta(N)$ rounds because trees are removed in parallel.

Nevertheless, the presence of abnormal trees in the system involves an over-cost in terms of steps for the visiting, cleaning, and confirmation phases, respectively (the overcost in terms of rounds is not significant because the abnormal trees are removed in $\Theta(N)$ rounds). Indeed, each time a processor p initiates a question (in the confirmation phase), this question can be propagated to (in the worst case) all the processors of the network. So, the overcost is $O(N)$ steps for each processor ($O(N)$) of each tree ($O(N)$), i.e., $O(N^3)$ steps. Concerning now the visiting phase, a processor p such that $p \neq r$ can execute an action of the visiting phase while it is in an abnormal tree (because of the initial configuration) or can hook on to abnormal tree by *F-action*. But, in both cases, a confirmation phase will be initiated (by p or one of its descendants) before p executes another action of the visiting phase. As explained before, this phase will lock the visiting phase for p until it leaves its tree. In the same way, p may execute its cleaning phase once (*RD-action* and *C-action*) to leave its tree but the next time it hook on to an abnormal tree, it will be lock by the confirmation phase and will execute no action of the cleaning phase until it leaves the tree by the abnormal trees' deletion. So, the overcost is $O(1)$ steps for each processor ($O(N)$) of each tree ($O(N)$), i.e., $O(N^2)$ steps. Hence, globally, the presence of abnormal trees in the system involves an overcost in terms of steps which is significant for the confirmation phase only: $O(N^3)$ steps.

Snap-stabilization of the Protocol. From the previous discussion, we know that, from normal configurations (i.e., configurations containing no abnormal trees), a traversal rooted at r is completely performed (i.e., visiting, cleaning, and confirmation phases) in $O(N^2)$ steps. Also, we know that the presence of abnormal trees in the system involves an overcost of $O(N^3)$ steps (mainly due to the confirmation phase). Finally, these abnormal trees are removed from the systems in $O(N^2)$ actions of the abnormal trees' deletion. So, despite the daemon (weakly

---

Algorithm 8. *Abnormal trees' Deletion for $p \neq r$*

Inputs:
on read: $Neig_p$: set of neighbors (locally ordered);
$\quad\quad\quad$ Par_p, L_p: variables of the *visiting phase*;
on read/write: S_p: variable of the *visiting phase*;

Variable: $\quad$ $E_p \in \{B, F, C\}$;

Macros:
$Child_p = \{q \in Neig_p :: Par_q = p \land S_q \neq idle \land L_q = L_p + 1 \quad$ /* valid for $S_p \neq idle$ only */
$\quad\quad\quad \land \ (S_p = q \Rightarrow S_q \neq rdone)$
$\quad\quad\quad \land \ [[S_p \neq q] \Rightarrow [(S_q = rdone \land S_p = rdone) \lor (S_q = done \land S_p \notin \{idle, wait\})]]\}$;

Predicates:
$GoodLevel(p) \quad \equiv (S_p \neq idle) \Rightarrow (L_p = L_{Par_p} + 1)$
$GoodPar(p) \quad\quad \equiv (S_p \neq idle) \Rightarrow [[S_{Par_p} = p \Rightarrow S_p \neq rdone]$
$\quad\quad\quad\quad\quad\quad \land \ [(S_{Par_p} \neq p) \Rightarrow ((S_p = rdone \land S_{Par_p} = rdone)$
$\quad\quad\quad\quad\quad\quad \lor (S_p = done \land S_{Par_p} \notin \{idle, wait\}))]]$
$AbRoot(p) \quad\quad \equiv GoodPar(p) \Rightarrow \neg GoodLevel(p)$
$FreeError(p) \quad \equiv (S_p \neq idle) \Rightarrow (E_p = C)$
$BadC(p) \quad\quad\quad \equiv (S_p \neq idle \land E_p = C \land E_{Par_p} = F)$
$Normal(p) \quad\quad \equiv \neg AbRoot(p) \land FreeError(p) \land \neg BadC(p)$
$BError(p) \quad\quad \equiv (S_p \neq idle) \land (E_p = C) \land [\neg AbRoot(p) \Rightarrow (E_{Par_p} = B)]$
$\quad\quad\quad\quad\quad\quad \land \ (\forall q \in Child_p :: E_q = C)$
$FError(p) \quad\quad \equiv (S_p \neq idle) \land (E_p = B) \land [\neg AbRoot(p) \Rightarrow (E_{Par_p} = B)]$
$\quad\quad\quad\quad\quad\quad \land \ (\forall q \in Child_p :: E_q = F)$
$FAbRoot(p) \quad\quad \equiv (E_p = F) \land AbRoot(p)$
$BCorrection(p) \equiv (S_p \neq idle) \land (E_p = B) \land \neg AbRoot(p) \land (E_{Par_p} \neq B)$
$FCorrection(p) \equiv (S_p \neq idle) \land (E_p = F) \land \neg AbRoot(p) \land (E_{Par_p} = C)$
$CCorrection(p) \equiv (S_p \neq idle) \land (E_p = C) \land \neg AbRoot(p) \land (E_{Par_p} = F)$
$CError(p) \quad\quad \equiv FAbRoot(p) \lor BCorrection(p) \lor FCorrection(p) \lor CCorrection(p)$
Actions:
$EB\text{-}action :: BError(p) \rightarrow E_p := B;$
$EF\text{-}action :: FError(p) \rightarrow E_p := F;$
$EC\text{-}action :: CError(p) \rightarrow E_p := C; \ S_p := idle;$

---

fair or unfair), the abnormal trees cannot prevent forever the progression of the visiting phase rooted at r. Then, the normal visiting phase terminates at r in a finite number of steps ($O(N^3)$). After this termination, the trace of the visiting phase are erased by the cleaning phase in $\Theta(N)$ steps. So, it is easy to see that, in the worst case, if the daemon tries to prevent r to initiate a new visiting phase, the system eventually reaches the normal initial configuration. In this configuration, r is the only enabled processor and $F\text{-}action$ is the only enabled action at r. So, r executes $F\text{-}action$ in the next step and we obtain a contradiction. Hence, from any configuration, the visiting phase starts at r after $O(N^3)$ steps.

Since r executes $F\text{-}action$, the visiting phase (rooted at r) sequentially progresses as deeply as possible in the network. When the visit cannot progress any more, the visit backtracks to the latest visited processor having some non-visited neighbors, if any. The visit terminates when it backtracks to r and r considers that its neighbourhood is completely visited. Obviously, to be DFS, the traversal performed by the visiting phase must not backtrack too earlier, i.e., the traversal must backtrack from p only when $\forall q \in Neig_p, q \in Tree(r)$. Now, this property is guaranteed by the confirmation phase. Indeed, since p hooks on to the normal tree ($Tree(r)$) by $F\text{-}action$, the confirmation phase insures p will executes $S_p = done$ (resp. $rdone$ if $p = r$) only when $\forall q \in Neig_p, q \in Tree(r)$. Finally, we have already seen that the visiting phase rooted at r is executed in $O(N^3)$ steps.

Hence, by Definition 1, it is easy to see that Algorithm $\mathcal{DFS}$ is snap-stabilizing for Specification 1 under an unfair daemon (see [5] for a detailed proof).

Complexity Issues. From the previous explanations, we can deduce that the delay to start a DFS Wave is $O(N^3)$ steps and $O(N^2)$ rounds, respectively. Similarly, a complete DFS Wave is executed in $O(N^3)$ steps and $O(N^2)$ rounds, respectively. Consider now the space requirement. We do not make any bound on the value of the L variable but it is easy to see that Algorithm $\mathcal{DFS}$ remains valid if we bound the maximal value of L by N. So, by taking account of the other variables, we can deduce that Algorithm $\mathcal{DFS}$ is in $O(\Delta^2 \times N)$ states.

4   Conclusion

We proposed in [4] the first snap-stabilizing DFS wave protocol for arbitrary rooted networks assuming an unfair daemon. Until this paper, it was the only snap-stabilizing protocol solving this problem. Like in [4], the snap-stabilizing DFS wave protocol presented in this paper does not use any pre-constructed spanning tree and does not need to know the size of the network. Moreover, it is also proven assuming an unfair daemon. However, using this protocol, a complete DFS Wave is executed in $O(N^2)$ rounds and $O(N^3)$ steps while we obtain $O(N)$ rounds and $O(N^2)$ steps in [4] for the same task. But, our new solution brings some strong enhancements. In one hand, the new protocol works on a *semi-anonymous* network instead of a completely identified network. In the other hand, it requires $O(\Delta^2 \times N)$ states per processor instead of $O(N^N)$.

References

1. L Blin, A Cournier, and V Villain. An improved snap-stabilizing pif algorithm. In *DSN SSS'03 Workshop: Sixth Symposium on Self-Stabilizing Systems (SSS'03)*, pages 199–214. LNCS 2704, 2003.
2. A Bui, AK Datta, F Petit, and V Villain. State-optimal snap-stabilizing PIF in tree networks. In *Proceedings of the Fourth Workshop on Self-Stabilizing Systems*, pages 78–85, Austin, Texas, USA, June 1999. IEEE Computer Society Press.
3. A Cournier, AK Datta, F Petit, and V Villain. Enabling snap-stabilization. In *23th International Conference on Distributed Computing Systems (ICDCS 2003)*, pages 12–19, Providence, Rhode Island USA, May 19-22 2003. IEEE Computer Society Press.
4. A Cournier, S Devismes, F Petit, and V Villain. Snap-stabilizing depth-first search on arbitrary networks. In *OPODIS'04, International Conference On Principles Of Distributed Systems Proceedings*, pages 267–282. LNCS, 2004.
5. A Cournier, S Devismes, and V Villain. A snap-stabilizing dfs with a lower space requirement. Technical Report 2005-05, LaRIA, CNRS FRE 2733, 2004.
6. AK Datta, C Johnen, F Petit, and V Villain. Self-stabilizing depth-first token circulation in arbitrary rooted networks. *Distributed Computing*, 13(4):207–218, 2000.

7. EW Dijkstra. Self stabilizing systems in spite of distributed control. *Communications of the Association of the Computing Machinery*, 17:643–644, 1974.
8. S Dolev, A Israeli, and S Moran. Uniform dynamic self-stabilizing leader election. *IEEE Transactions on Parallel and Distributed Systems*, 8(4):424–440, 1997.
9. ST Huang and NS Chen. Self-stabilizing depth-first token circulation on networks. *Distributed Computing*, 7:61–66, 1993.
10. C Johnen, C Alari, J Beauquier, and AK Datta. Self-stabilizing depth-first token passing on rooted networks. In *WDAG97 Distributed Algorithms 11th International Workshop Proceedings, Springer-Verlag LNCS:1320*, pages 260–274, Saarbrücken, Germany, September 24-26 1997. Springer-Verlag.
11. C Johnen and J Beauquier. Space-efficient distributed self-stabilizing depth-first token circulation. In *Proceedings of the Second Workshop on Self-Stabilizing Systems*, pages 4.1–4.15, Las Vegas (UNLV), USA, May 28-29 1995. Chicago Journal of Theoretical Computer Science.
12. F Petit and V Villain. Time and space optimality of distributed depth-first token circulation algorithms. In *Proceedings of DIMACS Workshop on Distributed Data and Structures*, pages 91–106, Princeton, USA, May 10-11 1999. Carleton University Press.
13. G Tel. *Introduction to distributed algorithms*. Cambridge University Press, Cambridge, UK, Second edition 2001.

Self-stabilization of Byzantine Protocols

Ariel Daliot and Danny Dolev

School of Engineering and Computer Science,
The Hebrew University of Jerusalem, Israel
{adaliot, dolev}@cs.huji.ac.il

Abstract. Awareness of the need for robustness in distributed systems increases as distributed systems become integral parts of day-to-day systems. Self-stabilizing while tolerating ongoing Byzantine faults are wishful properties of a distributed system. Many distributed tasks (e.g. clock synchronization) possess efficient non-stabilizing solutions tolerating Byzantine faults or conversely non-Byzantine but self-stabilizing solutions. In contrast, designing algorithms that self-stabilize while at the same time tolerating an eventual fraction of permanent Byzantine failures present a special challenge due to the "ambition" of malicious nodes to hamper stabilization if the systems tries to recover from a corrupted state. This difficulty might be indicated by the remarkably few algorithms that are resilient to both fault models. We present the first scheme that takes a Byzantine distributed algorithm and produces its self-stabilizing Byzantine counterpart, while having a relatively low overhead of $O(f')$ communication rounds, where f' is the number of actual faults. Our protocol is based on a tight Byzantine self-stabilizing pulse synchronization procedure. The synchronized pulses are used as events for initializing Byzantine agreement on every node's local state. The set of local states is used for global predicate detection. Should the global state represent an illegal system state then the target algorithm is reset.

1 Introduction

On-going faults whose nature is not predictable or that express complex behavior are most suitably addressed in the Byzantine fault model. It is the preferred fault model in order to seal off unexpected behavior within limitations on the number of concurrent faults. Most distributed tasks require the number of concurrent Byzantine faults, f, to abide by the ratio of $3f < n$, where n is the network size. See [13] for impossibility results on several consensus related problems such as clock synchronization. Additionally, it makes sense to require systems to resume operation after a major failure without the need for an outside intervention and/or a restart of the system from scratch. E.g. systems may occasionally experience short periods in which more than a third of the nodes are faulty or messages sent by all nodes may be lost for some time due to a network failure.

Such transient violations of the basic fault assumptions may leave the system in an arbitrary state from which the protocol is required to resume in realizing its task. Typically, Byzantine algorithms do not ensure convergence in such cases,

T. Herman and S. Tixeuil (Eds.): SSS 2005, LNCS 3764, pp. 48–67, 2005.
© Springer-Verlag Berlin Heidelberg 2005

as strong assumptions are usually made on the initial state and thus merely focus on preventing Byzantine faults from notably shifting the system state away from the goal. A *self-stabilizing* algorithm bypasses this limitation by being designed to converge within finite time to a desired state from any initial state. Thus, even if the system loses its consistency due to a transient violation of the basic fault assumptions (e.g. more than a third of the nodes being faulty, network disconnected, etc.), then once the system becomes coherent again the protocol will successfully realize the task, irrespective of the resumed state of the system. In trying to combine both fault models, Byzantine failures present a special challenge for designing stabilizing algorithms due to the "ambition" of malicious nodes to incessantly hamper stabilization, as might be indicated by the remarkably few algorithms resilient to both fault models.

We present an algorithm for transforming any Byzantine protocol to its self-stabilizing semi-synchronous counterpart, which is to the best of our knowledge, the first general scheme to do so for arbitrary protocols in the Byzantine fault model. Our result operates in the semi-synchronous network model typical of Byzantine protocols, though our scheme will also transform any asynchronous algorithm into its self-stabilizing semi-synchronous counterpart. Transient failures can practically be equivalent to the existence of an unbounded number of concurrent Byzantine failures. No distributed algorithm can reach its goal deterministically, in the face of permanent unbounded Byzantine failures, unless digital signatures are used. In a self-stabilizing paradigm, using digital signatures to counter Byzantine nodes exposes the protocols to "replay-attack" which might empty its usefulness.

Thus, deterministic protocols that tolerate permanent unbounded Byzantine failures by using digital signatures do not guarantee operation from arbitrary states and are thus not self-stabilizing. Hence, in order to self-stabilize and tolerate unbounded Byzantine failures it is essential to assume that eventually the bound on the permanent number of Byzantine failures is less than a third of the network. From this arbitrary state our protocol causes the user's target algorithm to converge efficiently. Therefore our result is stronger than just resilience to permanent unbounded Byzantine faults.

The algorithm assumes the existence of a module that delivers synchronized pulses to all the nodes. The function of the pulse synchronization is to align the activities of the participating nodes in a self-stabilizing and fault-tolerant manner. The use of an external pulse module subjects the protocol to a single point of failure. This necessitates an internal pulse mechanism in order to guarantee continuous function of the system at times that the external pulse is missing, which obliterates the benefit of circumventing any internal mechanisms with external ones. The only distributed internal protocols that delivers periodic synchronized pulses in a self-stabilizing manner tolerant to Byzantine faults are [7,9].

The idea of the algorithm, in a bird's-eye view, is to run at each node, in the background, the self-stabilizing Byzantine protocol that periodically invokes tightly synchronized pulses. Subsequent to a pulse, the node initiates Byzantine agreement on its local application state. This ensures that following some bounded time there is consensus on the local state of every node (inclusive of faulty nodes). All correct nodes then evaluate whether this global application snapshot corresponds to a legal state of the basic program and, if required, collectively reset it at the next pulse.

The overhead of our protocol is $O(f')$ communication rounds, where f' is the actual number of permanent faults, in addition to the time complexity of the transformed non-stabilizing algorithm. We utilize a Byzantine Agreement protocol that works in a time-driven manner that we have presented in [6], which makes the agreement procedure progress as a function of the actual message transmission times and not the upper bound on the message transmission times. Consequently, the additional overhead can in effect be very low.

We postulate that the semi-synchronous network model is a very realistic and ubiquitous model that is essentially the underlying setting of overlay networks and even the internet. Our result implies that the semi-synchronous network model allows for a very extensive treatment of different models of fault tolerance.

2   Related Work

There are very few specific protocols that tolerate both transient failures as well as permanent Byzantine faults. In this section we survey most of them. Towards the end of the section we describe a few general schemes that aim at stabilizing arbitrary asynchronous non fault tolerant algorithms. To the best of our knowledge our result is the only general scheme that transforms an arbitrary Byzantine algorithm into a multitolerant program that is self-stabilizing in the presence of permanent Byzantine failures.

The concept of *multitolerance* is coined by Kulkarni and Arora [2,17] to describe the property of a system to tolerate multiple fault-classes. They present a component based method for designing multitolerant programs. It is shown how to step-wise add tolerance to the different fault-classes separately. They design as an example a repetitive agreement protocol tolerant to Byzantine failures and to transient failures. Similarly, mutual exclusions for transient and permanent (non Byzantine) faults is designed. In [16] a multitolerant program for distributed reset is designed that tolerates transient and permanent crash failures. It is not shown how the method can be utilized for designing arbitrary algorithms, rather, particular problems are addressed and protocols are specifically designed for these problems using the method.

Nesterenko and Arora [20] define and formalize the notion of *local tolerance* in a multitolerant fault model of unbounded Byzantine faults that eventually comply with the $3f < n$ ratio. Local tolerance refers to the property of faults being contained within a certain distance of the faulty nodes so that nodes outside this containment radius are able to eventually attain correct behavior. They present two locally tolerant Byzantine self-stabilizing protocols for the particular problems of graph coloring and the dining philosophers problem.

Other examples are the two randomized self-stabilizing Byzantine clock synchronization algorithms presented by Dolev and Welch [12]. Both protocols have exponential convergence time. Our deterministic self-stabilizing Byzantine clock synchronization algorithm in [8] converges in linear time[1].

Many papers have been published that seek to find a universal technique to convert an arbitrary asynchronous protocol into a self-stabilizing equivalent. Thus these works have very limited handling of faults besides the transient faults. The concept of a *self-stabilizing extension* of a non-stabilizing protocol is brought by Katz and Perry [15]. They show how to compile an arbitrary asynchronous protocol into a self-stabilizing equivalent by centralized predicate evaluation. A self-stabilizing version of Chandy-Lamport snapshots that is recurrently executed is developed. The snapshot is evaluated for a global inconsistency and a distributed reset is done if necessary. This is improved by the local checking method of Awerbuch et al., [4]. Kutten and Patt-Shamir [18] present a time-adaptive transformer which stabilizes any non-stabilizing protocol in $O(f')$ time but on the expense of the space and communication complexities. A stabilizer that takes any off-line or on-line algorithm and "compiles" a self-stabilizing version of it is presented by Afek and Dolev [1]. The stabilizer has the advantage of being local, whereby local it is meant that as soon as the system enters a corrupt state, that fact is detected and second that the expected computation time lost in recovering from the corrupted state is proportional to the size of the corrupted part of the network. In a seminal paper by Arora and Gouda [3] a distributed reset protocol for shared memory is presented which tolerates fail-stop failures. Note that the fail-stop failure assumption (as opposed to the sudden crash faults) makes the protocol non-masking and thus doesn't truly tolerate permanent faults. Moreover it has a relatively costly convergence time.

Gopal and Perry [14] present a framework for unifying process faults and systemic failures, i.e. ongoing faults and self-stabilization. Their scheme works in a fully synchronous system and is a "compiler" that creates a self-stabilizing version of any fault-tolerant fully synchronous algorithm. They assume the non-stabilizing algorithm works in synchronous rounds. Assuming a fully synchronous system is a strong assumption as it obliterates the need to consider the loss of synchronization of the rounds following a transient failure. Their scheme only assumes the loss of agreement on the round number itself. To overcome this following a systemic (transient) failure, at each round some sort of "agreement" is done on the round number. They assume the register holding the round number is unbounded, which is not a realistic assumption. In a self-stabilizing scheme a transient failure can cause the register to reach its upper limit. Thus they do not handle the overflow and wrap-around of the round number which is a major flaw. The permanent faults that the framework tolerates are any corruption of process code. This may seem very similar to Byzantine faults but the difference hinges on a subtle but significant dissimilarity. It is assumed that corruption of process code cannot result in malicious or two-faced behavior whereas Byzantine failures allow for any adversary behavior. This difference results in the FLM result [13]

---

[1] Note that the pulse synchronization procedure used in [8] has a flaw, as pointed out by Mahyar Malekpour from NASA LaRC and Radu Siminiceanu from NIA. A correct version can be found in [9].

for Byzantine behavior, in which at least $3f + 1$ nodes are required to mask f failures. Conversely, corruption of process code imposes no such bound on the number of concurrent failures.

Note that being in an illegal global state is a stable predicate of the system state of a non-stabilizing program as otherwise it would either be self-stabilizing or not have the closure property that is required of any "rational" non-stabilizing algorithm (i.e. if in a legal state then stay in a legal state). A more general way of presenting our scheme is as a self-stabilizing Byzantine method for detection of stable predicates in semi-synchronous networks (see [21] for non fault-tolerant predicate detection in semi-synchronous networks). Distributed reset is just one particular action that can be done upon the detection of a certain predicate. Examples of other predicate detection uses are deadlock detection, threshold detection, progress detection, termination detection, state variance detection (e.g. clock synchronization), among others.

3   Model and Definitions

The environment is a semi-synchronous network model of n nodes that communicate by exchanging messages. We assume that the message passing allows for an authenticated identity of the senders. The communication network does not guarantee any order on messages among different nodes. Individual nodes have no access to a central clock and there is no external pulse system. The hardware clock rate (referred to as the *physical timers*) of correct nodes has a bounded drift, ρ, from real-time rate. When the system is not coherent then there can be an unbounded number of concurrent Byzantine faulty nodes, the turnover rate between faulty and non-faulty nodes can be arbitrarily large and the communication network may behave arbitrarily.

Definition 1. *A node is* **non-faulty** *at times that it complies with the following:*
1. *Obeys a global constant $0 < \rho << 1$ (typically $\rho \approx 10^{-6}$), such that for every real-time interval $[u, v]$:*

$$(1 - \rho)(v - u) \leq \text{ 'physical timer'}(v) - \text{ 'physical timer'}(u) \leq (1 + \rho)(v - u).$$

2. *Operates according to the instructed protocol.*
3. *Processes any message of the instructed protocol within π real-time units of arrival time.*

A node is considered **faulty** if it violates any of the above conditions. We allow for Byzantine behavior of the faulty nodes. A faulty node may recover from its faulty behavior once it resumes obeying the conditions of a non-faulty node. For consistency reasons, the "correction" is not immediate but rather takes a certain amount of time during which the non-faulty node is still not counted as a correct node, although it supposedly behaves "correctly"[2]. We later specify the time-length of continuous non-faulty behavior required of a recovering node to be considered **correct**.

---

[2] For example, a node may recover with arbitrary variables, which may violate the validity condition if considered correct immediately.

Definition 2. *The communication network is* **non-faulty** *at periods that it complies with the following:*

1. *Any message sent by any non-faulty node arrives at every non-faulty node within δ real-time units;*
2. *All messages sent by a non-faulty node and received by a non-faulty node obey FOFI order.*

Basic Notations:

- $d \equiv \delta + \pi$. Thus, when the communication network is non-faulty, d is the upper bound on the elapsed real-time from the sending of a message by a non-faulty node until it is received and processed by every correct node.
- A "*pulse*" is an internal event targeted to happen in tight synchrony at all correct nodes. A **Cycle** is the "ideal" time interval length between two successive pulses that a node invokes, as given by the user. The actual cycle length has upper and lower bounds and can be shortened to $cycle_{min}$ by faulty nodes. (see [9] for the details of the *pulse synchronization*).
- σ represents the upper bound on the real-time between the invocation of the pulses of different correct nodes (*tightness of pulse synchronization*)[3].
- *pulse_ conv* represents the convergence time of the underlying pulse synchronization module.
- *agreement_ duration* represents the maximum real-time required to complete the chosen Byzantine consensus/agreement procedure[4].

Note that n, f and *Cycle* are fixed constants and thus non-faulty nodes do not initialize with arbitrary values of these constants. It is required that *Cycle* is chosen s.t. $cycle_{min}$ is large enough to allow our protocol to terminate in between pulses.

A recovering node should be considered correct only once it has been continuously non-faulty for enough time to enable it to go through a complete "synchronization process". This is the time it takes, from any state, to complete two concomitant pulses that are in synchrony with all other correct nodes.

Definition 3. *A node is* **correct** *following pulse_ conv $+ 2 \cdot$ Cycle $+ \sigma$ real-time of continuous non-faulty behavior.*

Definition 4. *The system is said to be* **coherent** *at times that it complies with the following:*

1. *At least $n - f$ of the nodes are correct, where $n \geq 3f + 1$;*
2. *The communication network has been continuously non-faulty for at least pulse_ conv $+ 2 \cdot$ Cycle $+ \sigma$ real-time units.*

---

[3] The specific pulse synchronization used ([9]) achieves $\sigma \leq 3d$.

[4] We differentiate between *consensus* on an initial value held by all nodes and *agreement* on an initial value sent by a specific possibly faulty node.

The reference to correct instead of non-faulty nodes circumvents the ability of the turnover rate between faulty and non-faulty behavior of nodes to hinder the system from ever converging to a legal state. Hence, if the system is not coherent then there can be an unbounded number of concurrent faulty nodes; the turnover rate between faulty and non-faulty nodes can be arbitrarily large and the communication network may behave arbitrarily. When the system is coherent, then the network and a large enough fraction of the nodes $(n - f)$ have been non-faulty for a sufficiently long time period for the pre-conditions for convergence of the protocol to hold. The assumption in this paper, as underlies any other self-stabilizing algorithm, is that eventually the system becomes coherent. Note that being coherent does not imply that the system is in a legal state.

The self-stabilization paradigm assumes that all variables and program registers are volatile and thus prone to corruption or can initialize with arbitrary assignments. Conversely, it assumes that the code (the instructed protocol) is not dynamic and can thus be stored on non-volatile or non-corruptible storage. Furthermore, it is assumed in the paradigm that any access to an external module utilized by the system is eventually restored. E.g., any dependency on continuous time correlated to real-time without access to an external time source, can not be handled in the context of self-stabilization as no algorithm can restore the reference to external time without access to the external time source.

A *local state* of a node is comprised of the program counter and an assignment of values to the local variables. A node switches from one local state to another through a computation step. A *global state* of a system of nodes is the set of local states of its constituents nodes and the contents of the FIFO communication channels. A *local application state* is a subset of the variables of the local state that are relevant for the application. Two local states are said to be *distinct* if they represent local states on different nodes. A *global application state* is a collection of all the distinct constituent local application states at a certain moment. A *global application snapshot* is any collection of distinct local application states. An *execution* of a program P is a possibly infinite sequence of global states in which each element follows from its predecessor by the execution of a single computation step of P. We define E to be the set of all possible execution sequences of a program P.

Definition 5. *An initial state is said to be **normal** if the program counter of each correct node is 0 and the communication channels are empty.*

Definition 6. *A **normal execution** is an execution whose initial state is normal and has entirely occurred while the system is coherent.*

Definition 7. *A global application state is said to be **legal** if it could occur in a normal execution.*

Definition 8. *A **legal execution** is an execution that is a non-empty suffix of a normal execution.*

We define NE, $(NE \subset E)$, to be the set of normal executions of P (also denoted $NE(P)$). Equivalently, we define LE, $(LE \subset E)$, to be the set of legal executions of P (denoted $LE(P)$ respectively). The legal global states and the set of legal executions are determined by the particular task in the specific system and its respective normal executions. This cannot be characterized in general terms regardless of the actual problem definition that program P seeks to solve.

The self-stabilization of a system is informally defined by the requirement that every execution in E has a non-empty suffix in LE. We adopt the definitions of a self-stabilizing extension of a non-stabilizing program from [15]:

Definition 9. *A **projection** of a global state onto a subset of the variables and the messages on the channels is the value of the state for those variables and messages.*

Definition 10. *Program Q is an **extension** of program P if for each global state in $NE(Q)$ there is a projection onto all variables and messages of P such that the resulting set of sequences is identical to $NE(P)$, up to stuttering[5].*

Note that when one considers only those portions of Q's global state that correspond to P's variables and messages and if repetitions of states are ignored, then the legal executions of P and Q are identical. Thus, a state of Q is a legal state of Q iff the projection onto P is a legal state of P. The program P to be extended is called **the basic program**.

Definition 11. *Program Q is a **self-stabilizing extension** of a program P if Q is an extension of P and any execution in E(Q) has a non-empty suffix whose projection onto P is in LE(P).*

Thus, informally, if Q is a self-stabilizing extension of P then the projection of Q onto P is self-stabilizing. Therefore we refer to Q as a **stabilizer** of P.

4   A Byzantine Stabilizer

Intuitively, the task of stabilizing a program should supposedly be rather straightforward: Every period of time, make all nodes report their internal states, then sift through the collected states and search for a possibly global inconsistency in the algorithm as emerges from the global snapshot. Upon such an inconsistency make all nodes reset to a consistent state. Below we display a conceptual view of the scheme:

This greatly simplified scheme does not address the many subtle problems that surface when facing transient faults and permanent Byzantine faults: How do you synchronize the point in time for reporting the internal states? How do you ensure that the global snapshot is concurrent enough to be meaningful? How do you prevent Byzantine nodes from causing correct nodes to see differing global snapshots? How does the predicate detection mask Byzantine values?

We address the synchronization issue by employing an underlying Byzantine self-stabilizing pulse synchronization procedure. The pulse is essentially used as

---

[5] When comparing sequences, adjacent identical states are eliminated; this is called the elimination of stuttering in [15].

At *"time − to − exchange − states"* **do**
1. Send local state to all nodes and Byzantine Agree on every node's state;
2. All correct nodes now see the same global snapshot;
3. Check if global snapshot represents a legal state;
4. If not then reset the basic program;
5. If yes but your state is corrupt then repair state;

---

the event that helps to determine when to report the local state. The "meaningfulness" of the global snapshot is addressed by the observation that many algorithms have identifiable events in their executions. In a semi-synchronous protocol different nodes should execute the same events within a small bounded time of each other. If all correct nodes report their local states and clock time[6] at such an event (denoted *sampling point*) then the combination of clock time and the emergent global snapshot can be used for deducing whether the protocol is in a legal state. As an example, consider that the events are the beginning of a round, in case the basic program works in rounds. Thus all correct nodes should, whenever the system is in a legal state, reach the event of a specific round within bounded clock time of each other. By instructing the nodes to report their state (round number) and clock time at the specific round, it can be deduced whether this event indeed happened within the legal bounded time. If so, then that implies that the global snapshot taken carries meaningful information about the global state of the system. By evaluating this global predicate a decision can be made as of the legality of the global state and a reset can be done, if required. If the reported clock times are "too far" from each other then this is a sufficient indication that the system is not in a legal state and thus should be reset.

The issue of Byzantine nodes and values are tackled by initiating Byzantine agreement on the reported states. This ensures that all correct nodes have identical views of the global snapshot.

Our scheme stabilizes any Byzantine protocol that has such events (sampling points) during the execution, which can be identified by checking the program counter and local state. Otherwise, it is required that the basic program signals when to read and report the local state. We argue that this definition covers an extensive set of protocols. Programs that work in round structure is just a specific and easily identifiable example of such protocols. We assume for simplicity that the sampling points are taken at least 4σ apart on the same node in order to be able to differentiate between adjacent sampling points due to the synchronization uncertainties. It remains open whether this bound is really required. In Section 5 we give a detailed example of how to extend a specific clock synchronization algorithm that does not operate in a round structure.

Note that we do not aim at achieving a consistent global snapshot in the Chandy-Lamport sense (see [5]), which is not clearly defined in the Byzantine fault model. For our purposes a projection of the local state to the application

---

[6] Note that the clock time can be the elapsed time on a node's timer since the pulse. The synchronization of the pulses implies synchronization of these clocks.

state suffices in order to detect states that violate the assumptions of the basic program on its initial states, which rendered it non-stabilizing in the first place.

Generally, the extension of the basic program is established through a user-supplied wrapper function, so called because it "wraps" the basic program and functions as an interface between the basic program and the stabilizer. Note that the wrapper procedures must be supplied by the implementor. This is because it is a semantic matter to determine whether the global application state predicate indicates an illegal state that violates the assumptions of the basic program. For the sake of modularity and readability the wrapper is divided into two distinct modules according to its two main functions. The GETSTATE_WRAPPER() module interprets the local state of the basic program and returns the local state at the sampling points. The EVALSTATE_WRAPPER() module evaluates the agreed global application snapshot and determines whether it is legal with respect to the application. It also instructs a node how to repair its local application state as a function of the global application snapshot, should a node detect that its local application state is inconsistent with the legal global application snapshot.

Restrictions on the Basic Program:

R1: The basic program at all correct nodes can be initialize within at least σ real-time units apart. The procedure INIT_BASIC_PROGRAM initializes it.

R2: The basic program can tolerate that up to f of the nodes can choose to keep values from previous incarnations of the basic program (e.g. for replay of digital signatures).

R3: Has repeated *sampling points* during execution that can be identified through the local state. The sampling points are such that if all correct nodes report their state at the same corresponding sampling point then the global application snapshot is "meaningful" with respect to the application.

R4: During a legal execution all the correct nodes' sampling points are within Δ real-time units of each other. The background pulse algorithm implies that $\Delta \geq \sigma$, because the pulse skew may cause the nodes to reach the sampling points up to σ real-time units of each other.

R5: There exists a value Σ, such that in every time-window that is at least some Σ real-time units long every correct node has at least one sampling point. This value also covers the initialization period of the basic program.

R6: The set of legal application states of the basic program can be determined by evaluating a predicate on the application state variables. An additional requirement is that if up to f non-faulty nodes detect that their own local state is inconsistent with a legal global application snapshot then it can be repaired without needing a global reset[7].

R7: The basic program has a closure property with regards to the legal global states. I.e. if the system is in a legal state and the system is coherent then it stays in a legal state as long as the system stays coherent.

---

[7] A basic program that lacks this property might not converge to a legal state.

To formalize the intuition we give a more refined presentation of the algorithm:

At "*pulse*" event Do   /* *received the internal pulse event*   */
  1.   Revoke possible other instances of the algorithm and clear the data structures;
  2.   If (*reset*) then Do invoke INIT_BASIC_PROGRAM;/* *reset the Basic Program* */

/* *Lines 3,4 are executed by the* GETSTATE_WRAPPER() *procedure*   */
  3.   Upon a sampling point Do
  4.   Set $Timer$:= elapsed time since pulse;
  5.   Record app_state & invoke BYZ_AGREEMENT on (app_state, $Timer$);

/* *Line 6 is executed about agreement_ duration time after the $f{+}1^{st}$ agreement*   */
  6.   Sift through agreed values for a cluster of $\geq n - f$ values whose $Timer$s within
        2Δ of each other, thus comprising a meaningful global application snapshot;
  7.   If no such cluster exists then Do $reset$:= true;

/* *Lines 8,9,10 are executed by the* EVALSTATE_WRAPPER() *procedure*   */
  8.   Else Do predicate evaluation on the global application snapshot;
  9.   If global application snapshot is not legal Do $reset$:=true;
10.   Else If you are not part of the cluster Do Repair your application state;

The complete algorithm, denoted BYZSTABILIZER, is given below:

Algorithm 1. BYZSTABILIZER   /* *executed at node q* */

At "*pulse*" event Do   /* *received the internal pulse event* */
Begin
  1. Revoke possible other instances of BYZSTABILIZER and clear the data structures;
  2. $Timer$:= 0; T_{pivot} := 0;
  3. If (*reset*) then Do invoke INIT_BASIC_PROGRAM; /* *reset the Basic Program* */
  4. Wait until $Timer = \sigma \cdot (1 + \rho)$ time units;

/* *read&agree state at sampl. point; collect f+1 agreed states in window*   */
  5. Do
  6.   Invoke in the background $RecState$:= GETSTATE_WRAPPER();
  7.   If $RecState \neq \bot$ then Do invoke BYZ_AGREEMENT(q, $RecState$, $Timer$);
  8. AS := $\{(p, S, T) \mid$ BYZ_AGREEMENT returned $S \neq \bot\}$;   /* *add agreed state* */
  9. Agr_nodes := $\{p_i \mid (p_i, \_, T_i) \in AS, \sigma + \Delta \leq T_i \leq \Sigma + \Delta\}$;   /* *minimal T_i* */
10. Until ($\| Agr\_nodes \| \geq f + 1$ or $Timer > \Sigma + \Delta +$ agreement_ duration);

/* *collect agreed states, until no more possible states from correct nodes*   */
11. Do
12. AS := $\{(p, S, T) \mid$ BYZ_AGREEMENT returned $S \neq \bot\}$;   /* *add agreed state* */
13. Agr_nodes := $\{p_i \mid (p_i, \_, T_i) \in AS, \sigma + \Delta \leq T_i \leq \Sigma + \Delta\}$;   /* *minimal T_i* */
14.   Let $pivot$ be the $f{+}1^{st}$ node in Agr_nodes, in ascending order by their min. T_i;
15. Until $Timer \geq T_{pivot} + (\sigma + \Delta +$ agreement_ duration$) \cdot (1 + \rho)$ time units;

/* *seek cluster of $\geq n - f$ values whose Timers within 2Δ of each other*   */
16. $AS' := \{(p, S, T) \in AS \mid \sigma + \Delta \leq T \leq T_{pivot} + \Delta \cdot (1 + \rho)\};$
17. $Cluster\_rep := \{(p_c, S_c, T_c) \in AS' \mid$

$\qquad \| \{p' \mid (p', S', T') \in AS \ \& \ T_c \leq T' \leq T_c + 2\Delta \ \& \ S_c \sim S'\} \| \geq n - f\};$

/* *if no cluster do reset, otherwise evaluate snapshot of earliest cluster*   */
18. If $\| Cluster\_rep \| = 0$ then Do $reset := $ true;   /* *if no n-f sized cluster found* */
19. Else Do $(p_c, S_c, T_c) := \min_T \{(p, S, T) \in Cluster\_rep\};$ /* *else seek earliest cluster* */
20. $globAppSnapshot := \{(p', S', T') \in AS \mid T_c \leq T' \leq T_c + 2\Delta \ \& \ S_c \sim S'\};$
21. $reset := $ EVALSTATE_WRAPPER$(globAppSnapshot);$ /* *reset,repair or nothing* */
End

The internal pulse event is delivered by the pulse synchronization procedure (presented in [9]). The synchronization of the pulses ensures that the BYZSTABILIZER procedure is invoked within σ real-time units of its invocation at all other correct nodes. Note that we do not assume any correlation between the pulse cycle and any internal cycles or rounds of the basic program. Hence at the time of the pulse, the basic program may be in any of its states. The Byzantine agreement procedure used, BYZ_AGREEMENT, is essentially the consensus procedure of [6]. We present its agreement equivalent in Appendix.

Line 1: Following the pulse any possible on-going invocation of BYZSTABILIZER (and thus any on-going BYZ_AGREEMENT or instance of the wrappers, but not the execution of the basic program) is revoked and all data structures that are not used by the basic program are cleared. The exception is the "reset" variable that is not cleared. Note that the application state, as it belongs to the basic program, remains intact.

Line 2-3: Each node p initializes a $Timer$ that holds the elapsed clock time since the last pulse invocation, before possibly doing a reset of the basic program.

Lines 4-7: When the GETSTATE_WRAPPER() wrapper procedure encounters a sampling point subsequent to the pulse, at elapsed time $= Timer$, then it records the local application state into the $RecState$ variable. Agreement is then invoked on (p, $RecState$, $Timer$). The procedure GETSTATE_WRAPPER() sanity checks the state recorded at line 6, thus if it detects that the local application state is invalid or corrupt it will return $\perp$.

Lines 8-15: Target at identifying the $f + 1^{st}$ (time-wise) distinct node whose value has been agreed upon, denoted the $pivot$ node. Note that after a bounded time all correct nodes will identify the same pivot node. The time appearing in the agreed value of the pivot node is denoted T_{pivot}. The variable AS holds the set of agreed states. The variable Agr_nodes holds the set of nodes whose values have been agreed on.

Lines 16-17: A bounded period of time subsequent to T_{pivot}, all correct nodes must have terminated agreement on all nodes' values. It is then, that a cluster of at least $n - f$ agreed values is searched for, such that their $Timers$ are within 2Δ of each other.

Line 18: Such a cluster, if exists, comprises a meaningful global application snapshot. Otherwise, the global application state must be in an illegal state.

Lines 19-21: If a cluster is detected, then the EVALSTATE_WRAPPER procedure evaluates the global application snapshot. It determines whether the node must repair its local application state; whether a global reset should be scheduled at the next pulse invocation or whether the global application state is assumed to be legal and thus nothing is done. The $\sim$ notation denotes equality between cluster identifiers.

The following Lemma and Theorem apply as long as the system is coherent:

Lemma 1. *If the system is in an arbitrary global state then, within finite time, subsequent to line 17 of the* BYZSTABILIZER *algorithm there is agreement on the set Cluster_rep.*

Theorem 1. BYZSTABILIZER *is a self-stabilizing extension of any algorithm that complies with restrictions R1-R7.*

Proof. **Convergence:** Let the system be coherent but in an arbitrary global state, s, with the nodes holding arbitrary local application states. The pulse synchronization procedure is self-stabilizing, thus, independent of the system's initial state within a finite time the pulses are invoked regularly and synchronously with a tightness of σ real-time units. At the pulse invocation all remnants of previously invoked BYZSTABILIZER, inclusive of its sub-procedures such as the agreement and wrappers, are flushed by all the correct nodes. Following Lemma 1, subsequent to line 17 of BYZSTABILIZER there is consensus on the selected cluster (including of the empty cluster). At line 18 there may be one of two possibilities:

1. $\parallel$ *Cluster_rep* $\parallel = 0$: This necessarily implies the basic program is in an illegal state. In this case all correct nodes will do *reset* := *true*. At the next pulse all correct nodes will reset the basic program and thus converge to a legal state.

2. *A cluster was detected*: In this case subsequent to line 20 the variable globAppSnapshot, which holds the cluster whose states are the earliest agreed on since the pulse, will be generated at all correct nodes. Again, there are two cases to consider:

   (a) *The sampling points are within Δ real-time of each other*:
       Thus all correct nodes have initiated an agreement on their state within Δ real-time units of time T_{pivot} at the pivot node. Hence all correct nodes are represented in the cluster. The reset variable will be set at line 21 by the EVALSTATE_WRAPPER predicate detection procedure. If the procedure returns that the globAppSnapshot is legal then all correct nodes do nothing. Otherwise all correct nodes will reset the basic program at the next pulse and thus the system converges to a legal global state.

   (b) *The sampling points are not within Δ real-time of each other*: There are two cases to consider:

       i. *All correct nodes are represented in the cluster*:
          Thus the basic program is unsynchronized within the uncertainty window. If the EVALSTATE_WRAPPER procedure detects the illegality of the global state then all correct nodes will reset at next

pulse, otherwise the illegality will not be detected and all correct nodes will not reset the basic program at the next pulse.

ii. *At least one correct nodes is not represented in the cluster*: Again there are two cases:

A. *The* EVALSTATE_WRAPPER *procedure evaluates in line* 21 *the application snapshot as illegal*: Then all correct nodes reset at the next pulse and the system attains a legal global state.

B. *The* EVALSTATE_WRAPPER *procedure evaluates in line* 21 *the application snapshot as legal*: This is due to faulty nodes that "fill-in" for the lacking correct values, then these correct nodes that are not represented will detect so and must repair their local states. Thus no correct node does a reset at the next pulse. By restriction R6, a repair is done by the EVALSTATE_WRAPPER procedure as a function of the global application snapshot such that the new global state will be legal.   □

Closure: Following Lemma 1 the closure proof reduces to case (2.a.) in the proof of convergence, for the case in which the global state is legal. Thus, following restriction R4 the EVALSTATE_WRAPPER procedure evaluates correctly that the global snapshot is legal and thus all correct nodes do *reset* :=*false*.

This concludes the proof of the theorem.   □

5   Example of Stabilizing a Non-stabilizing Algorithm

To illustrate our method and to elucidate its generality we will provide a specific example of the conversion of a well known non-stabilizing algorithms to its stabilizing counterpart.

To stabilize the protocol using our scheme the following needs to be identified: the application state, the sampling points, the bound Δ on the real-time skew between correct nodes' sampling points in a legal state, the GETSTATE_WRAPPER procedure, the EVALSTATE_WRAPPER procedure and how it characterizes the legal states and how it does a repair, the initialization of the basic program following a global reset, the required minimal length of the cycle.

Consider the Byzantine clock synchronization algorithm in [10]. Informally that algorithm operates as follows: The processes resynchronize their clocks every *PER* time period. A process expects the time at the next resynchronization to equal *ET*. When a process's local time reaches *ET* it broadcasts a (signed) message stating "the time is *ET*". Alternatively, when a process receives such a message from $f + 1$ distinct nodes it knows that at least one correct node advanced its local time to *ET* and thus it resets its clock to *ET*. Note that this algorithm does not utilize a rounds structure.

It is interesting to note that the candidate protocol above uses signed messages in a way that does not comply with R2, because replay of signed messages from previous incarnations of the protocol can destroy the synchronization of the clocks of the correct nodes. One can transform the protocol to conform with R2, by using Byzantine Agreement instead of sending signed messages. The difficulty above is inherent in stabilizing protocols that use digital signatures.

- The application state will be comprised of the ET variable only.
- Practically any point throughout the inter-PER period avoiding the vicinity of the resynchronization events is safe for sampling. For illustrative purposes we will define a sampling point at every time that equals $ET + PER/2$. It is clear that the ET variable is quiescent around this point when the algorithm is in a legal global state.
- The algorithm can be initialized with the required bound of σ real-time units between the different nodes. This will not affect the precision of the algorithm which will stay d. That will yield a real-time skew between correct nodes' sampling points in a legal state of $\Delta = d + PER \cdot (1 + \rho)$.
- The sampling point is identified by the GETSTATE_WRAPPER procedure through the local state event of $clocktime = ET + PER/2$, at which the ET value is read into the localAppState variable.
- The EVALSTATE_WRAPPER procedure identifies the legal application states as those in which there are at least $n - f$ identical ET values. A repair is done by a node by setting its ET value to equal the other $n - f$ or more ET values in the application snapshot if it was evaluated as legal.
- Following a reset a node should initialize the algorithm by setting its ET variable to some pre-defined value, e.g. $ET = 0$. As mentioned before, the initial skew of σ will affect the accuracy but not the precision, as early and fast nodes will reach their subsequent ET before the others, but the others late and slow nodes will set their clock accordingly upon receiving $f + 1$ messages which is uncorrelated to the initialization skew.
- The required minimal cycle length equals $PER/2$ in case the pulse correlates with the reading of the sampling point and some correct nodes will have to wait until the next sampling point. The protocol then needs to allow for a full Byzantine agreement to terminate, in addition to a few round-trip rounds. Thus the required minimal cycle length equals $PER/2 + (2f + 3)$ rounds.

6   Analysis

We require $Cycle$ to be chosen s.t. $cycle_{min} > \sigma + \Sigma + agreement\_duration$.

From an arbitrary state in which the system is coherent it can take up to $pulse\_conv$ real-time until the pulses synchronize. Subsequent to the pulses it can take in the order of $\Sigma + agreement\_duratione$ real-time to reach a decision on a reset. The steady-state time complexity equals the time overhead from the pulse until the EVALSTATE_WRAPPER procedure terminates. Again this equals about $\Sigma + agreement\_duration$ time. With few faults and/or a fast network this becomes in the order of Σ, which is largely determined by the user and can be as low as $4d$ if the basic program allows for frequent sampling points. The message complexity is expressed in point-to-point messages. The message complexity of the steady state is roughly n^2 messages for the pulse synchronization procedure, and $f' \cdot n^2$ for the agreement algorithm.

Note that the agreement instances initiated by correct nodes will always terminate within 2 communication rounds, this is due to the early stopping property of the consensus algorithm which terminates within 2 rounds if all correct nodes hold the same initial agreement value. Thus the communication complexity is that of the actual number of faulty nodes.

The algorithm is *fault-containing*, in the sense that if faulty nodes behave "correctly" such that a correct node detects that it is not in synch with a legal global snapshot then the node can "repair" itself. Thus even though we present a reset-based protocol, repair is done up to a certain amount of concurrent faults. This is because our protocol is Byzantine resilient, thus a non-Byzantine fault or inconsistency will be masked by the protocol while the affected non-faulty node can perform a repair. Only if there should be more than f faults and inconsistencies would a system reset be performed.

The algorithm is also time-adaptive, the number of rounds executed in every cycle equals the number of actual faults, f'. This is due to the early-stopping feature of the agreement algorithm which terminates within $f' \leq f$ rounds.

Note that if solving a certain Byzantine problem can be reduced to consensus (or agreement) on the future value of the global state at the next pulse, (e.g. token circulation, see [6]), as opposed to reaching agreement on the current value of every node, then the agreement algorithm presented can be used to achieve 2-round early stopping subsequent to every pulse. Thus based on the global application snapshot at the last pulse, it can be calculated what the global state should be at this pulse. Thus if all correct nodes previously agreed on the state of every other node, which comprises the global snapshot, then they can enter agreement with consensus on the expected states for all nodes. The early stopping feature of the consensus algorithm in [6] ensures that if all correct nodes hold the same initial value to be agreed on then consensus is reached within two rounds. This makes the steady-state case extremely cost-efficient with a minimal overhead of 2 rounds. Only following a transient failure might full agreement be executed on the values of the faulty nodes, since different correct nodes may then hold different values for the same nodes.

Acknowledgements: We wish to thank Shlomi Dolev and Hanna Parnas for stimulating discussions with regards to the current result.

References

1. Y. Afek, S. Dolev, "*Local Stabilizer*", Proc. of the 5th Israeli Symposium on Theory of Computing Systems (ISTCS97), Bar-Ilan, Israel,74-84. June 1997.
2. A. Arora and S. Kulkarni, "*Component Based Design of Multitolerance*, IEEE Transactions on Software Engineering, Vol. 24, No.1, January 1998, pp. 63-78.
3. A. Arora and M. Gouda, "*Distributed Reset*, In Proceedings of the 10th Conference on Foundations of Software Technology and Theoretical Computer Science, number 472 in Lecture Notes in Computer Science, pages 316–333, 1990.

4. B. Awerbuch, B. Patt-Shamir and G. Varghese, *"Self-Stabilization by Local Checking and Correction*, In Proceedings of the 32nd IEEE Symp. on Foundation of Computer Science, 1991.

5. K. M. Chandy and L. Lamport, *"Distributed Snapshots: Determining Global States of Distributed Systems*, ACM Trans. on Computer Systems, Vol. 9(1):63–75, 1985.

6. A. Daliot, and D. Dolev, *"Self-Stabilizing Byzantine Token Circulation"*, Technical Report TR2005-77, Schools of Engineering and Computer Science, The Hebrew University of Jerusalem, June 2005. Url: http://leibniz.cs.huji.ac.il/tr/834.pdf

7. A. Daliot, D. Dolev and H. Parnas, *"Self-Stabilizing Pulse Synchronization Inspired by Biological Pacemaker Networks"*, In Proceedings of the Sixth Symposium on Self-Stabilizing Systems, DSN SSS '03, San Francisco, June 2003. See also LNCS 2704.

8. A. Daliot, D. Dolev and H. Parnas, *"Linear Time Byzantine Self-Stabilizing Clock Synchronization"*, In Proceedings of 7th International Conference on Principles of Distributed Systems (OPODIS-2003), La Martinique, France, December, 2003.

9. A. Daliot, D. Dolev and H. Parnas, *"Self-Stabilizing Byzantine Pulse Synchronization"*, Technical Report TR2005-84, Schools of Engineering and Computer Science, The Hebrew University of Jerusalem, Aug. 2005. Url: http://leibniz.cs.huji.ac.il/tr/841.pdf

10. D. Dolev, J. Y. Halpern, B. Simons, and R. Strong, *"Dynamic Fault-Tolerant Clock Synchronization"*, Journal of the ACM, Vol. 42, No.1, pp. 143-185, 1995.

11. S. Dolev, *"Self-Stabilization"*, The MIT Press, 2000.

12. S. Dolev, and J. L. Welch, *"Self-Stabilizing Clock Synchronization in the presence of Byzantine faults"*, Journal of the ACM, Vol. 51, Issue 5, pp. 780 - 799, 2004.

13. M. J. Fischer, N. A. Lynch and M. Merritt, *"Easy impossibility proofs for distributed consensus problems"*, Distributed Computing, Vol. 1, pp. 26-39, 1986.

14. A. S. Gopal and K. J. Perry, *"Unifying self-stabilization and fault-tolerance"*, IEEE Proceedings of the 12th annual ACM symposium on Principles of distributed computing, Ithaca, New York, 1993.

15. S. Katz, K. J. Perry, *"Self-Stabilizing Extensions for Message-Passing Systems"*, Distributed Computing 7(1): 17-26 (1993)

16. S. Kulkarni and A. Arora, *"Multitolerance in distributed reset*, Chicago Journal of Theoretical Computer Science, Special Issue on Self-Stabilization, 1998.

17. S. Kulkarni and A. Arora, *"Compositional Design of Multitolerant Repetitive Byzantine Agreement*, Proceedings of the 18th Int. Conference on the Foundations of Software Technology and Theoretical Computer Science, India, 1997.

18. S. Kutten and B. Patt-Shamir, *"Time-adaptive self stabilization*, In PODC97 Proceedings of the Sixteenth Annual ACM Symposium on Principles of Distributed Computing, pages 149-158, 1997.

19. J. Lundelius, and N. Lynch, *"An Upper and Lower Bound for Clock Synchronization,"* Information and Control, Vol. 62, pp. 190-205, Aug/Sep. 1984.

20. M. Nesterenko and A. Arora, *"Local Tolerance to Unbounded Byzantine Faults"*, IEEE SRDS, pages 22-31, 2002.

21. S. D. Stoller, *"Detecting Global Predicates in Distributed Systems with Clocks"*, Distributed Computing, 13(2):85-98, April 2000.

22. Sam Toueg, Kenneth J. Perry, T. K. Srikanth, *"Fast Distributed Agreement"*, SIAM Journal on Computing, 16(3):445-457, June 1987.

Appendix - The Byz_Agreement Procedure

The Byzantine Agreement module extends the approach taken in [6] in using explicit time bounds in order to address the variety of potential problems that may arise when the system is stabilizing.

We assume that timers of correct nodes are always within $\bar{\sigma}$ of each other. More specifically, we assume that nodes have timers that reset periodically, say at intervals $\leq$ *Cycle'*. Let $T_p(t)$ be the reading of the timer at node p at real-time t. We thus assume that there exists a bound such that for every real-time t, when the system is coherent,

$$\forall p, q \text{ if } \bar{\sigma} < T_p(t), T_q(t) < \text{Cycle}' - \bar{\sigma} \text{ then } |T_p(t) - T_q(t)| < \bar{\sigma} .$$

The bound $\bar{\sigma}$ includes all drift factors that may occur among the timers of correct nodes during that period. When the timers are reset to zero it might be, that for a short period of time, the timers may be further apart. The pulse synchronization algorithm [9] satisfies the above assumptions and implies that $\bar{\sigma} > d$.

We use the following notations in the description of the agreement procedure:

- Let $\bar{d}$ be the duration of time equal to $(\bar{\sigma} + d) \cdot (1 + \rho)$ time units on a correct node's timer. Intuitively, $\bar{d}$ can be assumed to be a duration of a "phase" on a correct node's timer.
- The *consensus-broadcast* and the *broadcast* primitives are defined in [6]. Note that an *accept* is issued within the broadcast primitive.

The BYZ_AGREEMENT algorithm is presented in a somewhat different style. Each step has a condition attached to it, if the condition holds and the timer value assumption holds, then the step is to be executed. Notice that only the step needs to take place at a specific timer value. It is assumed that the internal procedures invoked as a result of the BYZ_AGREEMENT procedure are implicitly associated with the agreement procedure.

The BYZ_AGREEMENT algorithm satisfies the following typical properties:

Termination: The protocol terminates in a finite time;
Agreement: The protocol returns the same value at all correct nodes;
Validity: If the initiator is correct, then the protocol returns the intiator's value;

Nodes stop participating in the BYZ_AGREEMENT protocol when they are instructed to do so. They stop participating in the broadcast primitive $2\bar{d}$ after they terminate BYZ_AGREEMENT.

Definition 12. *We say:*

*A node **returns** a value m if it has stopped and returned value $= m$.*
*A node p **decides** if it stops at that timer time and returns a value $\neq \perp$.*
*A node p **aborts** if it stops and returns $\perp$.*

```
Algorithm Byz_Agreement on (p, Val, T)          /* invoked at node q */

broadcasters := ∅;  value := ⊥;
if p = q then send (initialize, q, Val, T + d̄, 1) to all;     /* the General */
by time (T + d̄) :
    if received (initialize, p, Val, T + d̄, 1) then
        consensus-broadcast(p, Val, T + d̄, 1);
by time (T + 3d̄) :
    if accepted (p, v, T + d̄, 1) then
        value := v;
by time (T + (2f + 3)d̄) :
    if value ≠ ⊥ then
            broadcast (q, value, T + d̄, ⌊(T_q − T − d̄)/(2d)⌋ + 1);
            stop and return value.
at time (T + (2r + 1)d̄) :
    if (|broadcasters| < r − 1) then
            stop and return value.
by time (T + (2r + 1)d̄) :
    if accepted (p, v′, T + d̄, 1) and r − 1 distinct messages (p_i, v′, T + d̄, i)
            where ∀i, j  2 ≤ i ≤ r, and p_i ≠ p_j ≠ p then
        value := v′;
```

Fig. 1. The Byz_Agreement algorithm

Theorem 2. *The* Byz_Agreement *satisfies the Termination property. When $n > 3f$, it also satisfies the Agreement and Validity properties.*

Proof. The proof follows very closely to the proof of the Byz-Consensus algorithm in [6]. Notice, that there is a difference of one $\bar{d}$ resulting from the initiation of the protocol by a specific node, followed by a consensus. Another difference is that the General itself is one of the nodes, so if it is faulty there are only $f − 1$ potential faults left.

Lemma 2. *If a correct node aborts at time $T + (2r + 1)\bar{d}$ on its timer, then no correct node decides at a time $T + (2r + 1)'\bar{d} \geq T + (2r + 1)\bar{d}$ on its timer.*

Lemma 3. *If a correct node decides by time $T + (2r + 1)\bar{d}$ on its timer, then every correct node decides by time $T + (2r + 3)\bar{d}$ on its timer.*

Termination: Lemma 3 implies that if any correct node decides, all decide and stop. Assume that no correct node decides. In this case, no correct node ever invokes a broadcast $(p, v, T + \bar{d}, \_)$. By the consensus-broadcast properties in [6], no correct node will ever be considered as broadcaster. Therefore, by time $T + (2f + 3)\bar{d}$ on their timers, all correct nodes will have at most f broadcasters and will abort and stop.   □

Agreement: If no correct node decides, then all abort, and return to the same value. Otherwise, let q be the first correct node to decide. Therefore, no correct node aborts. The value returned by q is the value v of the accepted $(p, v, T + \bar{d}, 1)$ message. By the consensus-broadcast properties in [6], all correct nodes accept

$(p, v, T + \bar{d}, 1)$ and no correct node accepts $(p, v', T + \bar{d}, 1)$ for $v \neq v'$. Thus all correct nodes return the same value.   □

Validity: If the initiator q is correct, all the correct nodes invoke the consensus-broadcast with the same value v' and invoke the protocol with the same timer time $(T + \bar{d})$. By the consensus-broadcast properties in [6], all correct nodes will stop and return v'.   □

Thus the proof of the theorem is concluded.   □

Self-stabilization with r-Operators Revisited

Sylvie Delaët[1], Bertrand Ducourthial[2], and Sébastien Tixeuil[3]

[1] LRI – CNRS UMR 8623, Université Paris Sud, France
[2] Heudiasyc – UMR CNRS 6599, UTC, Compiègne, France
[3] LRI – CNRS & INRIA Grand Large, Université Paris Sud, France

Abstract. We present a generic distributed algorithm for solving silents tasks such as shortest path calculus, depth-first-search tree construction, best reliable transmitters, in directed networks where communication may be only unidirectional. Our solution is written for the asynchronous message passing communication model, and tolerates multiple kinds of failures (transient and intermittent).

First, our algorithm is self-stabilizing, so that it recovers correct behavior after finite time starting from an arbitrary global state caused by a transient fault. Second, it tolerates fair message loss, finite message duplication, and arbitrary message reordering, during both the stabilizing phase and the stabilized phase. This second property is most interesting since, in the context of unidirectional networks, there exists no self-stabilizing reliable data-link protocol. The correctness proof subsumes previous proofs for solutions in the simpler reliable shared memory communication model.

1 Introduction

Historically, research in self-stabilization over general networks has mostly covered undirected networks where bidirectional communication is feasible and carried out using shared registers (see [7]). This model permits algorithm designers to write elegant algorithms and proofs. To actually implement such self-stabilizing algorithms in real systems, where processors communicate by exchanging messages, transformers that preserve the self-stabilizing property of the original algorithm are needed. Such transformers are presented in [2,7], and are based on variants of the alternating bit protocol or the sliding window protocol. A common drawback to these transformers is that they require the receiver of a message to be able to send acknowledgments to the emitter periodically, so that the underlying message passing network must be bidirectional for the transformer to be correct. Also, those transformers still make the assumption that processors are aware of their neighboring processors (*i.e.* they know the identities of all of their neighbors).

Hence, in directed networks, acknowledgment-based transformers cannot be used to run self-stabilizing algorithms in message passing networks, since it is possible that there exist two neighbors in the network that are only connected through a unidirectional link. Moreover, in directed message passing networks, it is generally easy to maintain the set of input neighbors (by checking who has "recently"

T. Herman and S. Tixeuil (Eds.): SSS 2005, LNCS 3764, pp. 68–80, 2005.

sent a message), but it is very difficult (if not impossible) to maintain the set of output neighbors. For instance, in a satellite or a sensor network, a transmitter is generally not aware of who is listening to the information it communicates. Note also that wireless networks can be directed message passing networks, especially when power of emissions are not uniform: a node i can receive a message from j while the converse is not possible.

So, self-stabilizing algorithms that use implicit neighborhood knowledge to compare one node state with those of its neighbors and to check for consistency – a large subset of self-stabilizing algorithms – cannot be used in directed networks.

The particular system hypothesis and the lack of transformers has led authors to design specific self-stabilizing algorithms for directed networks [1,4,11,6,12,9]. The two solutions of [11,12] are generic (they can solve multiple problem instances with a single parameterized algorithm), but perform in the unidirectional shared memory model. In [12], the atomicity of communication is composite: in one atomic step, a processor is able to read the actual state of all of its neighbors and update its state, while in [11], the atomicity is read-write: in one atomic step, a processor is able to read the state of one neighbor, or update its state, but not both. Both approaches cannot be transformed to perform in unidirectional message passing networks using known self-stabilizing transformers (see above). The two solutions of [4,6,9] are specific (a single problem is addressed, the routing problem in [4], the census problem in [6], and the group communication problem in [9]), but perform in directed message passing networks. While [4,9] assume reliable communications (links do not lose, duplicate or reorder messages), [6] tolerates message loss, duplication, and reordering. [1] proposes a generic solution in the message passing model, but assumes that communications are reliable (with FIFO links), that nodes have unique identifiers, and that the network is strongly connected, three hypothesis that we do not make.

Our Contribution. In this paper, we concentrate on providing a generic algorithm (that can be instantiated to solve silent tasks, see [8]), that performs on general directed message passing networks. Our solution is not only self-stabilizing (it recovers in finite time from any initial global state), it also tolerates fair message loss, finite duplication, and arbitrary reordering both in the stabilizing and in the stabilized phase. Nice properties of our approach are that the network need not be strongly connected, and nodes need not know whether the network contains cycles, and no upper bound on the network size, diameter, or maximum degree. However, if such information is known, the stabilization time can be significantly reduced.

We provide, in more details, a parameterized algorithm that can be instantiated with a local function. Our parameterized algorithm enables a set of silent tasks to be solved self-stabilizingly, provided that these tasks can be expressed through local calculus operations called r-operators that operate over a set $\mathbb{S}$. The r-operators are general enough to permit applications such as shortest path calculus and depth-first-search tree construction on arbitrary graphs while remaining self-stabilizing.

The main differences between this paper and the most closely related work [11] are twofold. First, we consider an unreliable message passing communication network, instead of a reliable shared memory system. As noted above, unidirectional

Reference	Overhead	Atomicity	Reliability	Algorithm
[1]	yes	send/receive atomicity	reliable	generic (total order)
[4]	yes	send/receive atomicity	reliable	specific (routing)
[6]	yes	send/receive atomicity	unreliable	specific (census)
[9]	yes	send/receive atomicity	reliable	specific (group communication)
[12]	no	composite atomicity	reliable	generic (partial order on $\mathbb{S}$)
[11]	no	read/write atomicity	reliable	generic (total order on $\mathbb{S}$)
This paper	no	send/receive atomicity	unreliable	generic (total order on $\mathbb{S}$)

Fig. 1. A summary of related self-stabilizing algorithms in directed networks

read-write systems cannot be emulated in message passing networks by means of a known self-stabilizing transformer. The key difference is that shared registers may hold only the latest written value, while the communications links we consider may hold an unbounded number of (possibly erroneous) messages that can appear again once the network appears to have stabilized (due to the reordering assumption). Second, the proof technique that we use here is based on a completely different idea than that of [11]. In [11], it is first proved that a terminal configuration is eventually reached starting from any initial configuration, and then (using a complicated induction argument) that this terminal configuration is in fact legitimate. In contrast, in message passing networks, self-stabilizing systems cannot be terminating (otherwise deadlock situations could occur, see [13]), so the proof argument here is to prove the following two invariants: *(i)* the state of each processor is eventually lower than (or equal to) its legitimate state (in the sense of the order defined on $\mathbb{S}$), and *(ii)* the state of each processor is eventually greater than (or equal to) its legitimate state, so that the state of each processor is eventually legitimate. Not only is this new proof simpler and more elegant than that of [11], it also permits algorithm designers to abstract the communication media that is used, so that the same proof applies for shared memory and unreliable message passing systems.

In Figure 1, we capture the key differences between our protocol and the aforementioned related solutions ([1,4,11,6,12]) in general directed networks regarding the following criteria: communication, overhead, atomicity, reliability, and algorithm nature.

Outline. Section 2 presents a model for distributed systems we consider. Section 3 describes our self-stabilizing parameterized algorithm for general directed networks, along with our system hypothesis and the sketch of the proof of correctness (see [5] for complete proofs). Concluding remarks are proposed in Section 4.

2   Model

Processors and Links. Processors use *unidirectional communication links* to transmit messages from an origin processor o to a destination processor d. The link is interacting with one input port of d and one output port of o. A link may hold an arbitrary number of messages (although our algorithm also works for bounded capacity links). Depending upon the way messages are handled by a communication link, several properties can be defined on a link. A complete formalization of these properties is proposed in [14]. We only enumerate those that are related to our algorithm. There is a *fair loss* when, infinitely many messages being emitted by o, infinitely many messages are received by d. There is *finite duplication* when every message emitted by o may be received by d a finite (yet unbounded) number of times. There is *reordering* when messages emitted by o may be received by d in a different order than that they were emitted. There is *eventual delivery* if any message that is not lost is eventually received (*i.e.* no message remains forever in a communication link).

Distributed System. A *distributed system* is a 2-tuple $S = (P, L)$ where P is the set of processors and L is the set of communication links. Such a system is modeled by a *directed graph* (also called *digraph*) $G = (V, E)$, defined by a set of vertices V and a set E of edges (v_1, v_2), which are ordered pairs of vertices of V ($v_1, v_2 \in V$). Each vertex u in V represents a processor P_u of system S. Each edge (u, v) in E represents a communication link from P_u to P_v in S. In the remainder of the paper, we use interchangeably processors, nodes, and vertices to denote processors, and links and edges to denote communication links.

Graph Notations. The *in-degree* of a vertex v of G, denoted by δv is equal to the number of vertices u such that the edge (u, v) is in E. The incoming edges of each vertex v of G are indexed from 1 to δv. A *directed path* P_{v_0, v_k} in a digraph $G(V, E)$ is an ordered list of vertices $v_0, v_1, \ldots, v_k \in V$ such that, for any $i \in \{0, \ldots, k-1\}$, (v_i, v_{i+1}) is an edge of E (*i.e.*, $(v_i, v_{i+1}) \in E$). The *length* of this path is k. If each v_i is unique in the path, the path is *elementary*. The set of all elementary paths from a vertex u to another vertex v is denoted by $X_{u,v}$. A *cycle* is a directed path P_{v_0, v_k} where $v_0 = v_k$. The *distance* between two vertices u, v of a digraph G (denoted by $d_G(u, v)$, or by $d(u, v)$ when G is not ambiguous) is the minimum of the lengths of all directed paths from u to v (assuming there exists at least one such path). The *diameter* of a digraph G is the maximum of the distances between all couples of vertices in G between which a distance is defined. Finally, we denote as Γ_v^- (resp. Γ_v^+) the set of predecessors (resp. successors) of a vertex $v \in V$, that is the set of all vertices $u \in V$ such that there exists a path starting at u (resp. v) and ending at v (resp. u). The predecessors (resp. successors) u of v verifying $d_G(u, v) = 1$ (resp. $d_G(v, u) = 1$)) are called *direct-predecessors* (resp. *direct-successors*) and their set is denoted Γ_v^{-1} (resp. Γ_v^{+1}).

Configurations and Executions. The global system state, called a *system configuration* (or simply *configuration*) and generally denoted c, is the union of (i) the states of memories of processors of P and (ii) the contents of communication links of L. The set of configurations is denoted by C. The part of information in a configuration $c \in C$ related to the processors of P is denoted $c_{|P}$; the part related to a given processor $P \in P$ is denoted $c_{|P}$.

Starting from an *initial configuration* c_1, an *execution* $e_{c_1} = c_1, a_1, c_2, a_2, \ldots$ is a maximal alternating sequence of configurations and actions of such that, for any positive integer i, the transition from configuration c_i to configuration c_{i+1} is done through execution of action a_i. Maximal means that either the computation is infinite, or the computation is finite and no action is enabled in the final configuration. The notations $\mathcal{E}_c$, $\mathcal{E}_C$ and $\mathcal{E}$ denote respectively the set of all executions starting (i) from the initial configuration c, (ii) from any configuration $c \in C \subset \mathcal{C}$, or (iii) from any configuration of $\mathcal{C}$ ($\mathcal{E}_\mathcal{C} = \mathcal{E}$). The ordered list $c_1, c_2, \ldots \in \mathcal{C}$ of the configurations of an execution $e = c_1, a_1, c_2, a_2 \ldots$ is denoted by $e_{|\mathcal{C}}$. In the rest of this paper, we adopt the following convention: if $c_i \in e_{|\mathcal{C}}$ appears before $c_j \in e_{|\mathcal{C}}$, then $i < j$.

Distributed algorithms resolve either static tasks (*e.g.*, distance computation) or dynamic tasks (*e.g.*, token circulation). The aim of static tasks is to compute a global result, which means that after a running time, processors always produce the same output (*e.g.*, the distance from a source). A static task is characterized by a final processor output o_P for any processor $P \in \mathcal{P}$, called *legitimate output*. A *legitimate configuration* c for this task satisfies $c_{|P} = o_P$ for any processor $P \in \mathcal{P}$. A distributed protocol designed for solving a given static task is correct if the distributed system $\mathcal{S}$ running this protocol reaches in finite time a legitimate configuration for this task.

Self-stabilization. A set of configurations $C \subset \mathcal{C}$ is *closed* if, for any $c \in C$, any possible execution $e_c \in \mathcal{E}_c$ of system $\mathcal{S}$ whose c is initial configuration only contains configurations in C. A set of configurations $C_2 \subset \mathcal{C}$ is an *attractor* for a set of configurations $C_1 \subset \mathcal{C}$ if, any execution $e_c \in \mathcal{E}_{C_1}$ contains a configuration of C_2. Let $C \subset \mathcal{C}$ be a non-empty set of configurations. A distributed system $\mathcal{S}$ is *C-stabilizing* if and only if C is a closed attractor for $\mathcal{C}$: any execution e of $\mathcal{E}$ contains a configuration c of C, and any further configurations in e reached after c remains in C. Finally, consider a static task for the distributed system $\mathcal{S}$, and let $L \subset \mathcal{C}$ be the set of the legitimate configurations of $\mathcal{S}$. A distributed protocol designed for solving this static task is *self-stabilizing* if the distributed system $\mathcal{S}$ running this protocol is L-stabilizing.

3   Parametric Message Passing $\mathcal{P}\mathcal{A}$-MP Algorithm

In this section, we first describe the distributed system we consider before defining the $\mathcal{P}\mathcal{A}$-MP parametrized algorithm. We then introduce the r-operators, that are used as parameters. These operators are derived from the associative, commutative and idempotent operators (such as the minimum on the integers).

3.1   System

Let $\mathcal{S} = (\mathcal{P}, \mathcal{L})$ be the distributed system we consider in the following. The associated graph composed of processors of $\mathcal{P}$ and communications links of $\mathcal{L}$ is fixed, directed and unknown to the processors of $\mathcal{P}$. Communications between processors are performed by message passing (directed message passing network).

Each processor v of $\mathcal{P}$ owns an incoming memory denoted as IN_v, which is supposed to be unalterable; this can be implemented by a ROM memory

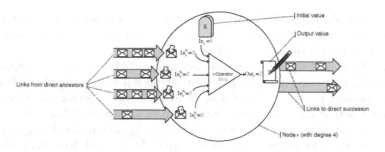

Fig. 2. Layout of a processor using the minc r-operator, defined by $minc(x, y) = min(x, y + 1)$

(*e.g.*, EPROM), or a memory that is regularly reloaded by any external process (human interface, captor, other independent algorithm, *etc.*). The value of this memory (that will never change) is called *initialization value*. For most provided applications (see [11]), this initialization value is equal to the identity element of the set $\mathbb{S}$ (except for a limited set of predecessors, see below). Moreover, for each link, starting at processor $u \in \mathcal{P}$ and ending at processor v, there exists a corresponding incoming memory IN_v^u in v, which is used by v to store incoming messages sent by u. Note that IN_v^u contains only one message. A processor v only stores the latest received message from u. In addition, processor v owns an output memory denoted by OUT_v. All these memories are private, and can only be read or written by v (note that v only reads IN_v, and only writes OUT_v). In the following, we identify the name of a memory with the value it contains. In the same way, a message is considered as equivalent to its value.

Processor v performs a calculation by applying an operator $\lhd$ (see § 3.3) on all of its incoming memories, and stores the result in its output memory OUT_v (see also Figure 2).

3.2 Algorithm

In [11] is defined a <u>P</u>arameterized distributed <u>A</u>lgorithm (denoted as $\mathcal{PA}$), and proved that it is self-stabilizing when $\lhd$ is a strictly idempotent r-operator (see § 3.3). That algorithm uses shared registers to permit communication between neighboring processors. In this paper, we design a similar parameterized distributed protocol for <u>M</u>essage <u>P</u>assing systems (denoted as $\mathcal{PA}$-MP). This protocol is composed of one local parameterized algorithm per processor v of $\mathcal{P}$, denoted by $\mathcal{PA}$-MP$|_{\lhd_v}$, where $\lhd_v$ is an operator used as a parameter (parameters could be slightly different on each processor, see Hypothesis 2).

This local algorithm calls three helper functions: $\text{Store}_v(m, u)$ stores in the local register IN_v^u the contents of the message m; $\text{Evaluate}_v(\lhd_v)$ stores in the local register OUT_v the result of the local computation $\lhd_v(\text{IN}_v, \text{IN}_v^{u_1}, \dots, \text{IN}_v^{u_k})$ where $u_1, \dots, u_k$ are direct predecessors of v ($\in \Gamma_v^{-1}$); Forward_v sends OUT_v to w for each processor $w \in \Gamma_v^{+1}$.

The local algorithm $\mathcal{PA}\text{-MP}|_\lhd$ on processor v is composed of two *guarded actions*, which are atomic sets of instructions (actions) executed when a precondition (guard) is fulfilled (see Figure 3).

Rule $\mathcal{R}_2$ makes use of a timeout mechanism. This timeout is required for stabilization purposes since [13] proved that no self-stabilizing algorithm could exist in message passing systems if no kind of timeout mechanism is available. The reason is that the system may start from an arbitrary global state where no messages are in transit, so if no node has a sending action that is triggered by a spontaneous timeout action, then the system is deadlocked. Rule $\mathcal{R}_2$ is also used in case of message loss. In a typical implementation of our algorithm in an actual system, the timeout mechanism should be tuned accordingly to the loss rate of the communication links, in order that not too many spontaneous messages are emitted, and that the stabilization time remains reasonable. Tuning this timeout is clearly beyond the scope of this paper.

Also, note that when the system is stabilized, only spontaneous messages are emitted (the condition of Rule $\mathcal{R}_1$ is never satisfied), so those spontaneous messages are never retransmitted. So, in the stabilized phase, the overall number of messages in the system is $O(m)$, where m is the number of links in the network.

3.3   r-Operators

An *infimum* (hereby called an *s-operator*) $\oplus$ over a set $\mathbb{S}$ is an associative, commutative and idempotent binary operator. Such an operator defines a partial order relation $\preceq_\oplus$ over the set $\mathbb{S}$ by $x \preceq_\oplus y$ if and only if $x \oplus y = x$ and then a strict order relation $\prec_\oplus$ by $x \prec_\oplus y$ if and only if $x \preceq_\oplus y$ and $x \neq y$.

It is generally assumed that there exists a greatest element on $\mathbb{S}$, denoted by $e_\oplus$, and verifying $x \preceq_\oplus e_\oplus$ for every $x \in \mathbb{S}$. Hence, the $(\mathbb{S}, \oplus)$ structure is an *Abelian idempotent semi-group* with $e_\oplus$ as identity element. The prefix *semi* means that the structure cannot be completed to obtain a group, because the law $\oplus$ is idempotent (see [3]).

When parameterized by such an *s-operator* $\oplus$, the $\mathcal{PA}\text{-MP}$ parametric local algorithm converges [10]. However, some counter examples show that it is not self-stabilizing [11].

$\mathcal{R}_1$ **Upon receipt of a message** m **sent by** u:
        `if` $m \neq IN_v^u$, `then`
              `Store`$_v (m, u)$
              `Evaluate`$_v (\lhd_v)$
              `Forward`$_v$
        `end if`
$\mathcal{R}_2$ **Upon timeout expiration:**
        `Evaluate`$_v (\lhd_v)$
        `Forward`$_v$
        `reset the timeout`

Fig. 3. Local algorithm $\mathcal{PA}\text{-MP}|_{\lhd_v}$ on processor v

In [10], a distorted algebra — the r-algebra — is proposed. This algebra generalizes the Abelian idempotent semi-group, and still allows convergence of wave-like algorithms: the three basic properties (associativity, commutativity, idempotency) defining the s-operators are generalized using a mapping (usually denoted r). For instance, the binary operator $\diamond$ defined on $\mathbb{N}$ by $x \diamond y = x + 2y$ is not associative. However we have $x \diamond (y \diamond z) = (x \diamond y) \diamond 2z = x \diamond y \diamond 2z = x + 2y + 4z$ and $\diamond$ is *r-associative* with the mapping $x \mapsto 2x$.

Definition 1. *The binary operator $\vartriangleleft$ on $\mathbb{S}$ is an r-operator if there exists a surjective mapping r called r-mapping, such that the following conditions are fulfilled: (i) r-associativity: $\forall x, y, z \in \mathbb{S}, x \vartriangleleft (y \vartriangleleft z) = (x \vartriangleleft y) \vartriangleleft r(z)$; (ii) r-commutativity: $\forall x, y \in \mathbb{S}, r(x) \vartriangleleft y = r(y) \vartriangleleft x$; (iii) r-idempotency: $\forall x \in \mathbb{S}, r(x) \vartriangleleft x = r(x)$ and (iv) right identity element: $\exists e_\vartriangleleft \in \mathbb{S}, x \vartriangleleft e_\vartriangleleft = x$.*

For example, the operator $\text{minc}(x, y) = \min(x, y + 1)$ is an r-operator on $\mathbb{N} \cup \{+\infty\}$, with $+\infty$ its right identity element.

Given an r-operator $\vartriangleleft$, one can show that the r-mapping r is unique, and is an homomorphism of $(\mathbb{S}, \vartriangleleft)$. Moreover, the r-operator defines an s-operator on $\mathbb{S}$ by $x \vartriangleleft y = x \oplus r(y)$, and $e_\oplus = e_\vartriangleleft$. We also have $r(e_\oplus) = e_\oplus$. For instance, the r-operator minc is based on the s-operator min and on the surjective r-mapping $r(x) = x + 1$.

If no fault appears in the distributed system $\mathcal{S}$, our $\mathcal{PA}$-MP algorithm stabilizes when it is parameterized by any idempotent r-operator $\vartriangleleft$. Idempotent r-operators verify $x \preceq_\oplus r(x)$ for any $x \in \mathbb{S}$. This last property leads to the definition of *strict idempotency*, verified for instance by the r-operator minc:

Definition 2. *An r-operator $\vartriangleleft$ is strictly idempotent if, for any $x \in \mathbb{S} \setminus \{e_\oplus\}$, we have $x \prec_\oplus r(x)$.*

The operator $\text{minc}(x, y) = \min(x, y + 1)$ (for minimum and increment) is a strictly idempotent r-operator on $\mathbb{N} \cup \{+\infty\}$, with $+\infty$ as its identity element. It is based on the s-operator min and on the surjective r-mapping $r(x) = x + 1$.

Finally, binary r-operators can be extended to accept any number of arguments. This is useful for our algorithm because a processor computes a result with one value per direct predecessor plus its own initialization value. An *n-ary r-operator* $\vartriangleleft$ consists in $n - 1$ binary r-operators based on the same s-operator, and we have, for any $x_0, \ldots, x_{n-1}$ in $\mathbb{S}$, $\vartriangleleft(x_0, \ldots, x_{n-1}) = x_0 \oplus r_1(x_1) \oplus \cdots \oplus r_{n-1}(x_{n-1})$. If all of these binary r-operators are (strictly) idempotent, the resulting n-ary r-operator is said (strictly) idempotent.

3.4   Hypotheses

In this section, we formalize some hypotheses, introduce some notations, and give basic lemmas that are used throughout the proofs.

Hypothesis 1. *In the distributed system $\mathcal{S}$, links may (fairly) lose, (finitely) duplicate, and (arbitrarily) reorder messages that are sent by neighboring processors. However, any message sent by u on the link (u, v) that is not lost is eventually received by v (i.e. no message may remain in a communication link forever).*

This is a weak hypothesis on link's reliability. However, the following lemma is immediate.

Lemma 1. *Let consider a communication link* $(u, v) \in \mathcal{L}$. *If the origin node* u *keeps sending the same message infinitely often, then this message is eventually received by the destination node* v.

Hypothesis 2. *In the distributed system* $\mathcal{S}$ *running the* $\mathcal{PA}$-*MP algorithm, any processor* v *runs the local algorithm defined in Figure 3 and parameterized by a strictly idempotent* $(\delta v + 1)$-*ary r-operator. Moreover, all these r-operators are defined on the same set* $\mathbb{S}$, *and are based on the same s-operator* $\oplus$, *with* $e_\oplus$ *their common identity element.*

In other words, this hypothesis ensures a form of homogeneity in the distributed system we consider. The following lemma is a direct application of Hypothesis 2, Definition 1, and `Evaluate` function:

Lemma 2. *Let* $\lhd_v$ *be the r-operator used by processor* v. *Then the computation of the* $\text{Evaluate}_v(\lhd_v)$ *function can be rewritten as:*
$$\lhd_v\left(\text{IN}_v, \text{IN}_v^{u_1}, \ldots, \text{IN}_v^{u_k}\right) = \text{IN}_v \oplus r_v^{u_1}\left(\text{IN}_v^{u_1}\right) \oplus \cdots \oplus r_v^{u_k}\left(\text{IN}_v^{u_k}\right).$$

Hence, there is one r-mapping per communication link. We now define the composition of these mappings along a path ($\mathcal{X}_{u,v}$ denotes the set of all elementary paths from u to v).

Definition 3. *Let* $P_{u_0,u_k} \in \mathcal{X}_{u_0,u_k}$ *be a path from processor* u_0 *to processor* u_k, *composed of the edges* (u_i, u_{i+1}) $(0 \le i < k)$. *Let* r_{i+1}^i, $0 \le i < k$, *be the r-mapping associated to the link* (u_i, u_{i+1}). *The r-path-mapping of* P_{u_0,u_k}, *denoted by* $r_{P_{u_0,u_k}}$, *is defined by the composition of the r-mappings* r_{i+1}^i, *for* $0 \le i < k$:
$$r_{P_{u_0,u_k}} = r_k^{k-1} \circ \cdots \circ r_1^0.$$

Our proofs of correctness assume that any result produced on a node with the `Evaluate`$_v(\lhd_v)$ function (see Lemma 2) is either the initial value of the node (IN_v) or one of its incoming value transformed by an r-mapping ($r_v^{u_i}(\text{IN}_v^{u_1})$). For this purpose, we admit that the order $\preceq_\oplus$ defines a total order. Note that with stronger nodes synchronization, such hypothesis is not necessary (see [12], where a proof for composite atomicity in a shared memory model is given).

Hypothesis 3. *The order relation* $\preceq_\oplus$ *is a total order relation:* $\forall x, y \in \mathbb{S}$, *either* $x \preceq_\oplus y$ *or* $y \preceq_\oplus x$.

Hypothesis 4. *The set* $\mathbb{S}$ *is either finite, or any strictly increasing infinite sequence of values of* $\mathbb{S}$ *is unbounded (except by* $e_\oplus$).

Assuming Hypothesis 3, Hypothesis 4 specifies that the values used in the distributed system $\mathcal{S}$ can be, for instance, integers but not reals. Note that truncated reals (as in any computer implementation) are also convenient. Hypotheses 2 and 4 give the following lemma:

Lemma 3. *The set $\mathbb{S}$ is either finite or any r-mapping r used in $\mathcal{S}$ verifies:* $\forall x \in \mathbb{S} \setminus \{e_\oplus\}, r(x) \prec_\oplus e_\oplus$.

Hypothesis 5. *Each processor v admits at least one predecessor $u \in \Gamma_v^-$ such that* $\text{IN}_u \neq e_\oplus$, u *is called a* non-null *processor.*

In the following, we denote by $\widehat{\text{OUT}}_v$ the legitimate output of processor v. Moreover, for any processor v, any predecessor u of v and any configuration c, we denote by $\text{OUT}_v(c)$ and $\text{IN}_v^u(c)$ the value of the memories OUT_v and IN_v^u in the configuration c.

3.5 Our Result

Our protocol is dedicated to static tasks. Such tasks (*e.g.*, the distance computation from a processor u) are defined by one output per processor v (*e.g.*, the distance from u to v), which is the legitimate output of v. With our $\mathcal{PA}$-MP algorithm, this means that, after finite time, each processor $v \in \mathcal{P}$ should contain this output (*e.g.*, $d(u,v)$) in its outgoing memory OUT_v. To solve static tasks with the $\mathcal{PA}$-MP distributed algorithm, one must use an operator as parameter (*e.g.*, minc for distance computation) such that the distributed system $\mathcal{S}$ reaches the legitimate configurations and do not leave them thereafter (*i.e.*, any processor reaches and then conserves its legitimate output). In this paper, we prove that if the operator is used to parameterize the $\mathcal{PA}$-MP distributed algorithm, then it is self-stabilizing, according to the hypotheses of § 3.4.

Let us define the legitimate outputs of the processor using the r-operators that parameterize the $\mathcal{PA}$-MP algorithm. For instance, to solve the distance computation problem, we state $\mathbb{S} = \mathbb{N} \cup \{+\infty\}$, and each local algorithm is parameterized by the minc r-operator (see § 3.3 and Figures 2). All processors v verify $\text{IN}_v = +\infty$ except a non null processor u verifying $\text{IN}_u = 0$ (0 is absorbing while $+\infty$ is the identity element for minc). Each r-path-mapping adds its length to its argument (*i.e.*, $r_P(x) = x + \text{length}(P)$), and we have:

$$d(u,v) = \min \left(\text{IN}_v, \min_{w \in \Gamma_v^-, P_{w,v} \in \mathcal{X}_{w,v}} \left\{ r_{P_{w,v}}(\text{IN}_w) \right\} \right)$$

We now define the legitimate output of a processor v in the general case.

Definition 4 (Legitimate output). *The* legitimate output *of processor v is:*

$$\widehat{\text{OUT}}_v = \text{IN}_v \oplus \bigoplus_{u \in \Gamma_v^-, P_{u,v} \in \mathcal{X}_{u,v}} r_{P_{u,v}}(\text{IN}_u)$$

The following lemma is given by Lemma 3, Hypothesis 5 and Definition 4; it is used for proving Theorem 1.

Lemma 4. *The set $\mathbb{S}$ is either finite or any processor $v \in \mathcal{P}$ verifies:* $\widehat{\text{OUT}}_v \prec_\oplus e_\oplus$.

Now we defined $\widehat{\mathtt{OUT}}_v$, we define the set of legitimate configurations $L \subset \mathcal{C}$ of the protocol $\mathcal{PA}$-MP (see Section 3 and Figure 3):

Definition 5 (Legitimate configuration). *For any configuration $c \in L$, for any processor $v \in \mathcal{P}$, $\mathtt{OUT}_v(c) = \widehat{\mathtt{OUT}}_v$.*

Finally, after defining the distributed system $\mathcal{S}$, the generic algorithm $\mathcal{PA}$-MP, the r-operators used as parameters and some Hypotheses, we can express the main result of this paper as follows, which is proved in the following section:

Theorem 1. *Algorithm $\mathcal{PA}$-MP parameterized by any strictly idempotent r-operator is self-stabilizing in directed message passing networks, despite fair loss, finite duplication and reordering of messages.*

Due to space constraints, only the sketch of the proof is given here; the detailed proof can be found in [5].

Proof. **(Sketch)** The message passing model that we consider leads to hard difficulties (compared for instance to shared memory model [11]). Indeed, with this model it is possible that an initially wrong message remains in a link for quite a long (finite) time (*e.g.* after several new messages have been exchanged) and then is delivered to cause havoc in the system. Despite weak hypotheses on the communication capabilities of every link (u, v), and possible transient failures that could corrupt data in links or nodes communication buffers $\mathtt{OUT}_u$ and $\mathtt{IN}_v^u$, we have to prove that eventually any input value read by v in $\mathtt{IN}_v^u$ has effectively been sent by u. Even though this is true, it does not imply that a value sent by u will be received by v. Hence, a legitimate value sent by u could be lost in (u, v), while the inputs of u that were used to produce it disappeared, either because of transient failures, or simply because they were overwritten by other incoming values. This means that legitimate values could completely be removed from $\mathcal{S}$.

We actually have to prove that a value received by v on (u, v) has been sent by u *after* a given configuration. This configuration is chosen such that the value of u fulfills some predicates. One of those predicates is that this value has been built using incoming values of u sent by its predecessors *after* a given configuration. This permits to use recursivity along paths of the network.

By weak fairness, any processor v calls **Evaluate** for updating its output $\mathtt{OUT}_v$ using its inputs. By properties of the r-operators, and using the total order Hypothesis (Hyp. 3), this output is either built with $\mathtt{IN}_v$ or with a received value, say $\mathtt{IN}_v^u$. After the last transient failure, and since duplications are finite on the link (u, v), any value received by v has been sent by u. Since every perturbation on the link is finite, there is a finite number of configurations between the sending of the value by u and its receipt by v. Thus, if we consider a configuration that is far enough in the execution, v must have updated its output using a value received by u after u has itself updated its output too. This way, we can prove that any output is smaller or equal than the legitimate value, which means that every large unlegitimate value eventually disappears from the network.

To complete the proof of correctness, we still have to prove that every processor v may not remain with a smaller value than its legitimate one. Suppose this is the case, then by reusing a recursive reasoning, we obtain an infinite path of processors, such that their outputs are strictly increasing along the path (by the strict idempotency property of the r-operators). Since such a path does not exists in the network (that is finite), it is a cycle. This means that, successive outputs of v increase without ever reaching its legitimate value. That contradicts Hypothesis 4.

4   Concluding Remarks

We presented a generic distributed algorithm for message passing networks applicable to any directed graph topology. This algorithm tolerates transient faults that corrupt the processors and communication links memory as well as intermittent faults (fair loss, reorder, finite duplication of messages) on communication media. Our contribution allows to envisage new applications for wireless networks (such as sensor networks), where nodes are not aware of their neighbors, and communications could be unidirectional (*e.g.*, non uniform power) and unreliable.

The algorithm can be instantiated to produce distributed algorithms for both fundamental and high level applications (see [11,12]). We quickly sketch two simple applications of the generic algorithm. First, to solve the shortest path problem with r-operators, it is sufficient to consider $\mathbb{N} \cup \{+\infty\}$ as $\mathbb{S}$, $+\infty$ as $e_\oplus$, min as $\oplus$, and $x \mapsto x + c_{u,v}$ as r_u^v (where $c_{u,v}$ is the cost of the link (u, v)). Second, in a telecommunication network where some terminals must chose their "best" transmitter, distance is not always the relevant criterium, and it can be interesting to know the transmitter from where there exists a least failure rate path, and to know the path itself. If we consider $[0, 1] \cap \mathbb{R}$ as $\mathbb{S}$, 0 as $e_\oplus$, max as $\oplus$, and $x \mapsto x \times \tau_u^v$ as r_u^v (where τ_u^v is the reliability rate of the edge between u and v, with $0 < \tau_u^v < 1$) our parameterized algorithm ensures that a best transmitter tree is maintained despite transient failures (in a self-stabilizing way). More complex applications can be solved with specific r-operators, though the completeness of r-operators is an open problem.

Acknowledgements. We are grateful to the anonymous reviewers that helped to improve the quality of our presentation. This work was supported in part by the FRAGILE and SR2I projects of the ACI "Sécurité et Informatique".

References

1. Y Afek and A Bremler. Self-stabilizing unidirectional network algorithms by power supply. *Chicago Journal of Theoretical Computer Science*, 4(3):1–48, 1998.
2. Y Afek and G M Brown. Self-stabilization over unreliable communication media. *Distributed Computing*, 7:27–34, 1993.

3. F Baccelli, G Cohen, G Olsder, and J-P Quadrat. *Synchronization and Linearity, an algebra for discrete event systems.* Wiley, Chichester, UK, 1992.
4. J A Cobb and M G Gouda. Stabilization of routing in directed networks. In *Proceedings of the Fifth Internationa Workshop on Self-stabilizing Systems (WSS'01), Lisbon, Portugal,* pages 51–66, 2001.
5. S Delaët, B Ducourthial, and S Tixeuil. Self-stabilization with r-operators in unreliable directed networks. Technical Report 1361, Laboratoire de Recherche en Informatique, April 2003.
6. S Delaët and S Tixeuil. Tolerating transient and intermittent failures. *Journal of Parallel and Distributed Computing,* 62(5):961–981, 2002.
7. S Dolev. *Self-stabilization.* The MIT Press, 2000.
8. S Dolev, MG Gouda, and M Schneider. Memory requirements for silent stabilization. *Acta Informatica,* 36(6):447–462, 1999.
9. Shlomi Dolev and Elad Schiller. Self-stabilizing group communication in directed networks. *Acta Inf.,* 40(9):609–636, 2004.
10. B Ducourthial. New operators for computing with associative nets. In *Proceedings of SIROCCO'98, Amalfi, Italia,* 1998.
11. B Ducourthial and S Tixeuil. Self-stabilization with r-operators. *Distributed Computing,* 14(3):147–162, 2001.
12. B Ducourthial and S Tixeuil. Self-stabilization with path algebra. *Theoretical Computer Science,* 293(1):219–236, 2003.
13. S Katz and K J Perry. Message passing extensions for self-stabilizing systems. *Distributed Computing,* 7(1):17–26, 1993.
14. N A Lynch. *Distributed Algorithms.* Morgan Kaufmann, 1996.

Self-stabilization Preserving Compiler*
(Extended Abstract)

Shlomi Dolev[1], Yinnon Haviv[1], and Mooly Sagiv[2]

[1] Department of Computer Science, Ben-Gurion University of the Negev,
Beer-Sheva, 84105, Israel
{dolev, haviv}@cs.bgu.ac.il
[2] School of Computer Science, Tel-Aviv University, Tel-Aviv 69978, Israel
msagiv@acm.org

Abstract. Self-Stabilization is an elegant approach for designing fault tolerant systems. A system is considered self-stabilizing if, starting in any state, it converges to the desired behavior. Self-stabilizing algorithms were designed for solving fundamental distributed tasks, such as leader election, token circulation and communication network protocols. The algorithms were expressed using guarded commands or pseudo-code. The realization of these algorithms requires the existence of (self-stabilizing) infrastructure for their execution such as a self-stabilizing microprocessor and a self-stabilizing operating system. Moreover, the high-level description of the algorithms needs to be converted into machine language of the microprocessor. In this work, we present a design for a self-stabilization preserving compiler designed for programs written in a language similar to the abstract state machine (ASM). The compiler preserves the stabilization property of the high level program.

1 Introduction

Self-stabilization is an important fault-tolerance paradigm [4,5]. A system that is designed to be self-stabilizing automatically recovers from an arbitrary state, which is a state reached due to unexpected failures. The self-stabilization property is not tied to replications as other well studied fault models are. In particular, to cope with Byzantine failures one needs to have redundancy in the number of processors. In fact, the self-stabilization property is orthogonal to replication techniques that are used to mask faults (e.g., [5,10,16]). Moreover, the traditional time/space redundancy techniques may be combined with self-stabilization to ensure automatic recovery, even in the cases in which the redundancy is not sufficient to mask the faults.

There are major investments for obtaining industrial systems with self-healing, self-controlled, automatic recovery, autonomic computing and similar

---

* Partially supported by Microsoft, IBM, NSF, Intel, Deutsche Telekom, Rita Altura Trust Chair in Computer Sciences, Intel, vaatat and Lynn and William Frankel Center for Computer Sciences.

T. Herman and S. Tixeuil (Eds.): SSS 2005, LNCS 3764, pp. 81–95, 2005.
© Springer-Verlag Berlin Heidelberg 2005

properties [12,14,3,9]. We believe that the self-stabilization property is fundamental for achieving the self management goals. Moreover, self-stabilization is a
property that is defined in terms of the states and the runs of the system and
therefore is rigorously verified.

Several existing algorithms for on-going tasks (as opposed to one shot tasks)
were designed to be self-stabilizing. For example, the routing tables of the Internet are based on a self-stabilizing algorithm (e.g., [22]). This is no coincidence,
since the operation of this algorithm should cope with unexpected situations,
which occur, for example, due to an undetected corrupted message arrival, transient errors or processor crashes.

Core components of computer and communication systems, such as micro-
processors and communication routers have to be self-stabilizing in order to
ensure recovery and continuous operation. In particular, a self-stabilizing microprocessor will ensure the execution of a program [6]. Then a self-stabilizing
operating system [11] should ensure that eventually the resources of the computer are well managed. In this work, we consider a very important building
block towards the vision of practical self-stabilizing systems. Namely, we examine high-level languages for writing self-stabilizing programs and the way to
compile them into machine code.

Languages that are based on state machines are natural candidates for writing and arguing about self-stabilizing programs. The reason for such a choice is
that the stabilization arguments consider any possible state, namely any content
of variables, and prove convergence to a subset of safe states from which the run
behaves as desired. Guarded commands [4], Input Output Automata [20], and
Abstract State Machine (ASM) [15] are three bold examples for state based programming languages. We note that a pseudo code description of self-stabilizing
algorithms stated in a different format, can be transferred to the above representation, integrating a mechanism that mimics a program counter into the
guards. We choose a variant of ASM as the high-level programming language,
that is inspired by the guarded commands language. We note that our results
are applicable to other choices of programming languages as well.

In order to enable the compilation of existing distributed self-stabilizing algorithms into machine code, we have also examined the Distributed Abstract State
Machine (DASM) language. Part of our contribution is a design that extends the
DASM primitives in a way that supports refined operations in the level of read
or write operations to safe, regular or atomic registers. The new primitives are
mapped directly to the underlined hardware (the exact communication register
used). The programmer is responsible for the correct operation (and proof) of
the program using the refined communication devices. We note that in [21] a
language and a compiler for protocols are described. Our work compliments the
work of [21] in the sense that we present a compiler that ensures convergence of
each processor (either in a stand-alone system or as a part of a distributed system) when started in an arbitrary state of the compiled program. We take into
account refined states produced by the compiler to implement the transitions
defined by the high level language.

We show that a usage of off-the-shelf (ASM) compiler with a consistency check, in which there is no given correspondence function between the original ASM state and the refined machine state, is a hard task. In fact we show, in Section 3, that given a refined machine state it is NP hard to find whether a corresponding state of the ASM program exists. We then turn to the positive side.

Given a self-stabilizing program written in ASM we would like to produce a machine code that eventually has the same input output relation as the original ASM program. Roughly speaking, we use the fact that ASM execution is composed of moves, each corresponding to the evaluation of a rule and the updating of the current state. The syntax of ASM allows only bounded loops within a rule, which causes each move to be executed in finite time. This enables our compiler to create a code that efficiently checks the validity of the state in between consecutive moves. We prove that the machine code portion produced by our compiler for an ASM rule can be executed from any point (program counter and arbitrary microprocessor state) and still terminate. The machine code produced is a sequence of portions, where each portion reflects a rule. Hence, no matter where we start the execution of the machine code the execution of a rule terminates and an additional portion of consistency check of the current state is executed. The consistency check verifies that the variables that correspond to the original ASM program are in their value range and the data structures used by the execution environment e.g., the scheduler of the ASM rules are also consistent.

Motivating Example: We now present a simple example for motivating the self-stabilization preserving compiler. Figure 1 consists of an example of IJVM code produced for the statement for i=0 to 9 do f(i). The commands used are analogous to the ones presented in [23]. Line 2 initiates the local variable i to zero. Lines $4 - 12$ contain the code for one iteration. Line $4 - 7$ call $f(i)$. Line 8 increases i by one. The end condition for the loop is checked in lines $9 - 11$. Line 9 makes a copy of i, line 10 pushes the value 10 to the stack and line 11 pops the two recently pushed values from the stack and branches out of the loop code if they are equal. Finally, if i is not equal to 10, then the loop execution is repeated due to the unconditional jump in line 12.

The programmer assumes that f(i) will be executed at most ten times (even when started

```
1: ...:
2:    PUSH 0 // i ← 0
3: LOOP:
4:    LDC_W objref
5:    LOAD 1 // i
6:    INVOKEVIRTUAL f //
      calling f(i)
7:    POP
8:    INC 0, 1 // i++
9:    LOAD 0
10:   PUSH 10
11:   IF_ICMPEQ END // if
      i = 10, exit
12:   GOTO LOOP
13: END:
14:   ...
```

Fig. 1. Example of code generated for a loop which does not preserve self-stabilization

at an arbitrary state). However, in case the value of i is equal to 11 (or -2^{30}) and the program counter is inside the loop (e.g., line 4) the loop, practically, becomes an infinite loop. The reason for the corruption of i may be a soft error in the memory or other transient fault, see e.g., [18].

Moreover, even when a range check of the loop variable is added to the code of the loop, an existing optimizer will consider the additional check as a redundant code and remove it. Thus, we have to examine and define the requirements for the compiler and the optimizer.

Our Contribution: (a) Examination of programming languages for writing self-stabilizing algorithms and a choice of automata like description, namely ASM. (b) The extension of ASM to *refined ASM* where each rule of the ASM includes at most one communication operation (e.g., read, write, send, receive) and a full correspondence of the communication operation to the given hardware; for example, a read that overlaps a write from/to a safe register returns an arbitrary value. (c) Definitions of the requirements for a self-stabilization preserving compiler. (d) Design of a self-stabilization preserving compiler.

The rest of the paper is organized as follows: The settings of the problem and technical description of ASM and DASM are described in Section 2, in particular we suggest special features and extensions in order to compose and compile self-stabilizing programs. In Section 3 we give an indication on the intricacy of the problem, proving that a usage of a black-box off-the-shelf compiler may be infeasible. The self-stabilization preserving compiler is described in Section 4.

2   Settings for Self-stabilization Preserving Compiler

We start with a brief description of a variant of the abstract state machine, that is inspired by Dijkstra's guarded commands. Then we describe the distributed and refined abstract state machines. We summarize by presenting the requirements for a self-stabilization preserving compiler.

2.1   Abstract State Machines and Guarded Commands

Abstract State Machines (*ASM*) [15,2] serve as an efficient tool for the design, description and provable refinement process of algorithms and systems. The algorithm designer may specify the algorithm in an abstract form that simplifies the correctness proof process. ASM is designed to support the refinements process in which the proof of the abstract description is preserved during the conversion of the algorithm into its implementation. Originally, ASM was defined by its *signature*, and its main *rule*. Roughly speaking, the *signature* is equivalent to the program variables definition and the set of function names, each associated with its arity. The program code is expressed in the form of a *rule*, which calculates the changes in the state. Inspired by Dijkstra's guarded commands notation, which is used intensively for describing self-stabilizing algorithms, we choose a more general syntax for ASM. Here a program consists of a set of rules, each of the form "upon ⟨condition⟩ do ⟨statement⟩".

Given an ASM program with a set of rules $\{rule_1, \ldots, rule_n\}$, a *move* of the ASM starts in a choice of a rule from the set of rules for which the condition of the rule is evaluated to true; then evaluating the statement that forms the body of the chosen rule. When evaluating the body of the chosen rule, we use the state prior to the activation of the rule. Updates to the state made by assignments are registered in the *update set* and delayed until the evaluation of the rule is finished. Finally, the obtained update set is used for changing the current state, resulting in the next state. A *run* $s_1, m_1, s_2, m_2, \cdots$ is alternating sequence of states and moves, such that, for every $i \geq 1$ s_{i+1} is obtained by the application of the move m_i to s_i. A run ru is a *fair* run iff every rule, $rule_i$, for which there are infinitely many states in ru in which the condition of $rule_i$ is true, is applied to the system state in infinitely many moves of ru.

The program *constructs* is partitioned into three sets, the first set of constructs is the *declaration constructs* used for declaring locations (the ASM equivalent to variables). For example the location x may be declared by: "location x as range(0,2)", which defines x to be an integer variable in the set $\{0, 1, 2\}$. The second set of constructs is the *term constructs* used for assembling arithmetic and boolean *terms*. The term constructs are evaluated to a value of one of the basic variable types (boolean, integer).

The third and last set of constructs is the *statement constructs* used for assembling statements, which evaluates to an update set. The most basic statement construct is the assignment i.e., $x(t_1, \ldots, t_n) := t$, where $t_1, \ldots, t_n$, and t are terms. Two more statement constructs are the *par* or *seq* which are used to create blocks of statements, both constructs are parameterized with a pair of statements, and evaluated as the *parallel* or *sequential* execution of the statements, respectively. Bounded loops are available using the *forall* statement construct which implies parallel evaluation of the statements in the loop for each item in the forall set, which is an integer range. The forall statement constructs allow the set that is iterated to be any continuous range of integers [1]. The *if* and the *let* statement constructs are also available.

For the sake of refining the DASM (discussed bellow) we added constructs for reading and writing shared registers, as well as constructs for serializing / deserializing data into/from a register variable.

2.2 Distributed and Refined Abstract State Machines

ASM assists also in the more complex settings of distributed systems. Distributed ASM (*DASM*) is used for describing distributed algorithms and is very helpful in specifying the behavior of protocols and proving their correctness [1]. A distributed system is modeled in DASM as a set of ASMs, also referred to as *agents*.

The asynchronous multi-agent ASM (asynchronous ASM) models a run as an interleaving sequence [19] of moves of the ASM agents in the system. This is a similar policy to the policy for activating guards in the guarded commands language under the central daemon. Each guard is composed of a boolean condition, and a body that is expressed using pseudo-code. The existence of a scheduler or central daemon in a multi-tasking single processor system may be justified. However, system hardware usually does not support a single global scheduler in distributed environments.

---

[1] ASM originally allows the expression of any set in the form of $\{x : \Psi(x)\}$, iterating such a set may not be computationally feasible.

It is important to refine the DASM and the guarded commands granularity execution to directly reflect the promise of the underlining hardware, leaving the responsibility for mimicking (the coarse) atomic execution of guards for the programmer (when such a mimic is desired) [8,5,13]. Note that such emulation restricts the set of schedules in which progress is made. One may like to be able to design the algorithm in a way that he/she is aware of and use the exact hardware promises in the most efficient way, thus avoiding the cost of mimicking the extra synchronization abstraction. In a way, the extreme of this tradeoff has some similarity to the tradeoff between wait-free algorithms and synchronous algorithms.

Our *refined DASM* (a) includes the register type as part of the DASM (where a register is associated with a location) (b) restricts the number of communication operations in the statement of every rule to be at most one, and (c) a *read* from a register and a *write* to a register are directly translated (by the compiler) to read and write communication operations supported by the given hardware.

The requirement of at most one communication operation in a rule allows us to keep the convention of rules interleaving, as if in every given time at most one move is executed (where a move is an execution of a rule). We note that in the case of *safe* or *regular* register the interleaving is in terms of the *beginning and the corresponding end of the communication operations*. A move in which a communication operation to such a register takes place, starts the communication operation that is then pending to be ended by the next move of that agent.

Note that the state of the system includes the registers states. The system state includes for every register *reg* the set of operations that are not finalized for *reg* and the values associated with them.

2.3   Self-stabilization Preserving Requirements

In this section we present the requirements from a stabilization preserving compiler. We restrict our attention to compilers which process the code of each of the ASM agents independently. Using such a compiler, the stabilization property of the entire system is preserved by the following arguments. Each processor (low level) program stabilizes into the behavior of the high level ASM program it was compiled from. Only then the system stabilizes due to the self-stabilization property of the original algorithm. We start with a few standard definitions needed for arguing concerning the compiled code. We define terms analogous to *move* and *run* of ASM for the (lower) processor level behavior description.

We view a processor as a state machine that changes state by executing *atomic steps* or simply steps. A state of a processor is defined by the contents of its memory including the program counter and other internal registers. We use $s \xrightarrow{a} s'$ to denote a state change of a processor from the state s to state s' due to the execution of a step a. We view the step a as an execution of a single machine command (of the compiled code). An *execution* is a sequence $s_1, a_1, s_2, a_2, \ldots$ such that $s_i \xrightarrow{a_i} s_{i+1}$ for every $i \geq 1$. In the scope of a distributed system we use the term *configuration* for a vector of processors states and communication entities states (either registers or communication channels).

Since the specification of legal system behavior is given by the required input output relation, and since our compiler wishes to preserve this behavior in some sense, we establish the term *trace* both for executions and for runs. Formally, each move and atomic step is associated with zero or one I/O operations. For example, if m is a move of a DASM that reads the value 42 from register r_{22} into internal variable v_{22} and changes the value of some more internal variables, then m is associated with the I/O operation $\langle read, r_{22}, 42 \rangle$. The trace of a run (or an execution) is obtained by first reducing the sequence only to moves (atomic steps, respectively) which are associated with an I/O operation, and then replacing those moves with their associated I/O operation. Given an ASM or a machine-code program A and a state s of A, we define $[\![A]\!](s)$ to be the set of traces of A, when started in s.

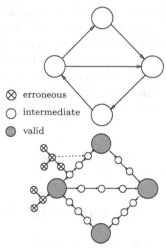

Existing compilers guarantee, when compiling a program PR_h into a program PR_l, that the set of traces exhibited by both programs, when started at their initial states will be the same. Formally, if s_h is the initial state of PR_h and s_l is the initial state of PR_l then traditional compilers guarantee that $[\![PR_h]\!](s_h) = [\![PR_l]\!](s_l)$. Our requirements are different. Since we would like our compiled program to be self stabilizing, we require that the trace of an execution of the compiled program, when started in *any* state, will eventually be a trace of a run of the original program started in *some* state. Formally, we require that for all state s_l of PR_l, and for each trace $tr \in [\![PR_l]\!](s_l)$, there exists a suffix tr' of tr, and a state s_h of PR_h, for which $tr' \in [\![PR_h]\!](s_h)$. When this condition holds, we say that PR_l *eventually behaves the same as* PR_h.

Fig. 2. Above, the state space of the original, high level, program. Below, the state space of the compiled, low level, program.

In particular, there may exist states of the compiled program that are not reachable from the initial state and do not correspond to states of the original program/programs. Nevertheless, we require that starting in these additional states the traces of the system will have a suffix that is the same as the traces of a run of the original ASM program.

Figure 2, illustrates the concept presented above. In the upper portion of Figure 2 an automaton of a given (refined) ASM is illustrated. States are represented by circles, and moves, defined by the possible ASM rule execution from each state, are represented by arrows between states. In the lower portion of Figure 2, the automaton of the compiled program is illustrated. Each move of the original program is refined into several steps in the compiled program. Since the state space of the compiled program includes erroneous states which are not reachable from any valid state, our compiled code must make sure that these erroneous states are transient and eventually the program reaches one of the valid states (i.e., the existence of the dotted arrows), and from which the input/output trace is the same as the input/output trace of the original program.

Caution Required While Optimizing: Most optimizations take advantage of the fact that there exist portions of code in the compiled program whose execution transforms the state from one valid state to another, traveling through intermediate states. These portions of code are replaced by the optimizer with more efficient portions, with respect to one or more efficiency measurements (time, space, instruction parallelism level, etc.). The replaced code is considered equivalent to the original code if it performs the same function on the state. Some of the optimizations use syntactic analysis of the target program, to obtain assertions on the state when certain program addresses are reached. Using such assertions allows the optimizer to relax the equivalence condition between the original and optimized code to states respecting the assertions.

Syntactic analysis is often used for omitting unnecessary code, usually checking conditions that will never (or always) be met. Notice that a code that implements a bounded loop such as "For i=0 to 9 do f(i)" in a self-stabilizing manner will check, in each iteration, that both the end condition is not reached and that $i \geq 0$, to ensure that the loop is executed at most ten times, even from a corrupted state. The code that checks that i is not negative will be considered redundant by the optimizer and will be removed, which will result in a non self-stabilizing code.

3   The Complexity of Using Off-the-Shelf Compiler

One possible way to create a self-stabilization preserving compiler might be to use an existing compiler and modify the code produced. Here we examine such an approach, in which one would like to add a procedure that repeatedly checks whether the state s_l of the a processor in the system (that executes the compiled code) corresponds to a state s_h of the original ASM.

More formally given an ASM program PR_h, a low level program PR_l, and two states s_h, s_l of the programs PR_h, PR_l, respectively, we say that s_h *directly corresponds* to s_l if the set of traces produced by PR_l when started in s_l is the same as the set of traces produced by PR_h when started in s_h. A state s_l of PR_l is called *valid* if there is a state s_h of PR_h such that s_l directly corresponds to s_h, and *invalid* otherwise. The STATE-CORRESPONDENCE-PROBLEM is defined as follows: Given PR_h, PR_l, s_h, and s_l as above, find whether s_l is a valid state. Using such a procedure, one can repeatedly check the validity of the current state and reset PR_l to a predefined state in case it is in invalid state.

First, we note that in the scope of self-stabilization the number of variables is bounded and so are their domains. A designer of a self-stabilizing program cannot assume that a counter of 64 bits that is repeatedly incremented by one may suffice (by claiming that reaching the upper bound will take longer than the time a system exists) since every initial value is possible, in particular equal to the maximal value [5]. This is in fact an observation on the computation power of processors in a self-stabilizing system. The computation power is the one of a bounded hardware systems, that may be well represented by a finite automata, as opposed to the infinite working tape of a Turing machine. Thus, the state spaces of both programs, PR_h and PR_l are finite.

The following theorem shows that when no knowledge on the compiler transformation exists, the use of a procedure that repeatedly checks, given s_l whether a given state s_l is valid is computationally intractable, (the proof can be found in [7]).

Theorem 1. *The* STATE-CORRESPONDENCE-PROBLEM *is NP-Hard.*

4 Self-stabilization Preserving Compiler

Figure 3(a) gives a bird's eye view on how the code generated from our compiler is structured. The code for evaluating the conditions of each of the transition rules is placed following the scheduling code (which is described in section 4.3). The code compiled from the body of each transition rule is placed just below the scheduling code. Executing the code compiled from a body of a transition results in an update set, which is applied in the *apply-update-set* section. The *enforce-invariants* section contains a code for ensuring that a state s_l of the produced code corresponding to a state s_h of the original ASM program is reached. Executing this code section from its first line ensures that s_l is a valid state, namely, that there is a state s_h such that the set of traces of the executions starting from s_l is equal to the set of traces of the runs that start in s_h. Thus, from this point on, the behavior is the same as the behavior of the original (refined) ASM. Details on the content of the *enforce-invariants* section are given in sub section 4.1.

The basic idea for designing the compiled code is to make sure that regardless of the current state, the program counter will reach the beginning of the *enforce-invariants* section, after which the execution corresponds to the ASM execution. Moreover, we design our compiler so that the *enforce-invariants* section is reached within $2 \cdot R_{max}$ steps, where R_{max} is the maximal number of steps used to implement a move of the original ASM.

We state two conditions on the transformation made by the compiler which together ensure that our compiler does preserve the self-stabilization property:

C1. Starting in an arbitrary state of PR_l the system reaches in $2 \cdot R_{max}$ steps a state in which the first line of PR_l is executed, namely the first line of the enforce-invariant section.
C2. Executing the *enforce-invariants* section from its first line results in a valid state. Moreover, if the state is already valid, executing the section will not change the state.

Satisfying condition $C1$ is carried out by ensuring that the execution of each of the sections described in Figure 3(a) terminates without any assumptions on the state, even when started within the section. When the execution of a section

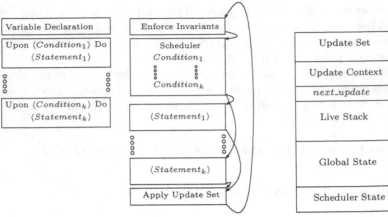

(a) On the right, the structure of the compiled code (with respect to the original refined ASM on the left). The arrows illustrate the program flow between the specified sections.

(b) The structure of the memory used by the target program

Fig. 3. The code and memory structure of the compiled program

terminates, the flow of the program continues by following one of the outgoing arrows from that section as described in Figure 3(a). Note that every cycle in the graph $G = (V, E)$, where V are the sections and E are the directed arrows in Figure 3(a), travels through the *enforce-invariants* node or section. Therefore, eventually the first instruction of the *enforce-invariants* section is reached, and condition $C1$ holds.

Satisfying condition $C2$ is explained in sub-section 4.1, which contains general definitions for the transformation. In particular, sub-section 4.1 explains how we map states of the original program to states of the compiled program and how the execution of the *enforce-invariant* section ensures that we are in the image of that mapping. sub-section 4.2 describe how terms and statements are transformed, and sub-section 4.3 describes our implementation for a fair scheduler. Each of the following sections shows that the execution of its corresponding code section terminates, without any assumptions on the validity of the state, and from any position within the code section.

4.1 General Definitions

Figure 3(b) describes the memory layout of the target program, PR_l. The state of the scheduler, which is described in sub-section 4.3 uses address $0 \ldots N + 1$, where N is the number of ASM rules in the source program PR_h. The next addresses are used for holding (a refinement of) the state of the original program.

Although IJVM, our target language, is stack machine oriented, we use only a portion of the memory, the "Live Stack", as a stack. Under normal operation, our stack pointer should always remain within the range of this section. Moreover, since we use the "Live Stack" only for temporal computations the *enforce-invariants* section may reset the stack pointer to the beginning of this memory section, denoted *live_stack_start*. Note that, due to the fact that ASM allows no recursion, we can bound the size of the stack a-priori.

In ASM, the update set is used for delaying updates, which in turn gives the programmer semantics which is similar to parallel execution. For example, the following statement swaps the value of locations x and y: "Par$\{x = y; y = x\}$". Therefore, as shown in sub-section 4.2, update statements do not immediately change the global state, instead they register the update which is later applied. The *next_update* variable, together with the "Update Set" section are used for representing the update set. The "Update Set" memory section is an array of word pairs, containing the *lvalue* (left value) and *rvalue* (right value) of an update. The *next_update* variable is used for pointing to the next free cell in the update set and advances upwards, starting from *us_start*, the first address of the "Update Set" memory section. ASM also supports the "Seq$\{\langle s_1 \rangle, \langle s_2 \rangle\}$" construct which implies sequential semantics; i.e., references made to locations in s_2 are evaluated in the presence of the updates induced by s_1. The "Update Context" section is used for supporting this feature, by representing the current partial update set. The update context is maintained as a stack of continuous updates, represented as pair of pointers to the "Update Set" section, marking the beginning and end of continuous update sections. The right portion of Figure 4 illustrates the update set and update context when the statement $r = x$ of the code presented on the left portion of Figure 4 is executed. sub-section 4.2 elaborates on the transformation of the Seq construct and explains how the update context is changed. The transformation of the assignment statement, which increases the update set can be found in [7].

Each variable v of PR_h (location, in ASM) is mapped to a specific memory address range m_v within the "Global State" section. Moreover, there exists a mapping from each value of v to a distinct value of m_v. The number of bits used for m_v suffices for representing every value of v. In some cases, as in the case of variables of type range, it is impossible (or inefficient) to represent the exact set of values associated with v by the values of m_v and there are a few extra unused values for m_v. One important task of the *enforce-invariants* section is to ensure that the current value of m_v does correspond to a value of v.

We say that the state of PR_l is *valid* if the following conditions hold: (a) All the m_v variables do correspond to the original range of their corresponding ASM variables (b) The update set is empty (c) The scheduler state is valid (see

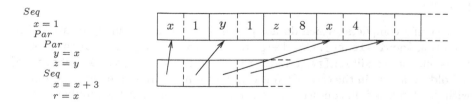

Fig. 4. The content of the update set and update context when executing statement $r = x$ of the code on the left. Here the initial value of y is 8.

Section 4.3) (d) The stack pointer is equal to *live_stack_start* (e) The program counter points to the beginning of the scheduling code. We say that a state is *intermediate* if it is not valid but can be reached from a valid state.

The *enforce-invariants* code section is responsible for achieving (a) to (e). It starts by setting the stack pointer to *live_stack_start*, which ensures (d). Then it performs, for each of the range variables, a range check and correction if necessary, and by that it achieves (a). The value of *next_update* is set to *us_start*, ensuring that (b) to holds. Next, the code for checking the validity of the scheduler state is executed (see section 4.3). In case of corruption in the scheduler state, the queue is set to the predefined $(\langle 1, \ldots, N \rangle)$ state. The (e) requirement is obtained by ending the enforce invariants code section and continuing sequentially to the scheduling code segment. We note that one may extend the model to allow the ASM programmer to define an initial state that should be enforced in case of a corruption.

Applying the Update Set: Applying the update set implies iterating over the updates and applying each of them. Since the upper bound for this loop is dynamic (*next_update*), and may be corrupted, care must be taken. We use a recursive computation on the parse tree to find an upper bound on the number of updates induced by a rule, denoted *max_updates*, and use it to calculate during compile time the *update_set_end* , which is a constant upper bound for the loop. Note that care must be taken also when applying an update since the *lvalue* of the update may be corrupted in a way that it points to the address of the loop variable, which may result in an infinite loop. The complete code for applying the update set can be found in [7].

4.2   Transforming Statements

We focus on the transformation of statements; details for the transformation of terms are similar and can be found in [7]. The code that is generated for a statement s, should fulfill the following conditions:

[**termination**] When started at any position, it should terminate with no latencies.
[**stack coherence**] When started in its initial position, it should terminate without changing any memory element below the initial stack position. Moreover, it should return with the stack pointer in its initial position.
[**equivalence**] When started in its initial position and in an intermediate state, it should terminate with the update set computed from s added to the initial update set.

Existing compilers (which do not preserve stabilization) may be satisfied by condition [equivalence]. Our design requires condition [termination], but it turns out that condition [termination] requires condition [stack coherence] to hold. Again, as in the case of transforming terms the requirement to terminate with "no latencies" in condition [termination] means that the number of steps until termination is not grater than the (worst case) number of steps under normal operation from of an intermediate state.

Implementing the Seq statement requires executing the second statement with the update context together with the updates induced by the first statement. The code generated for a Seq statement stores the value held in the *next_update* variable before and after executing s_1 in the next free pair of the update context. See [7] for the complete code generated for a Seq statement.

The code generated for a Forall statement appears in Figure 5. The code uses a local variable x for iterating the range, prepared in line 2. On each iteration, we check the variable x against the end of the loop (lines 5 − 8), but also ensure that x is not corrupted (lines 9 − 13). Note that increasing a loop variable and checking that it is in its range is not enough for ensuring that the [termination] condition holds for this code or even that the code terminates when started in a corrupted state. If the code generated for s, the body of the loop, does not satisfy condition [stack], it may repeatedly set our loop variable x to, say, the beginning of the loop range which will turn the loop into an infinite loop.

```
1:  ...:
2:      PUSH ⟨start⟩ // x ← start
3:      GOTO FIRST_LOOP_SHORTCUT
4:  LOOP:
5:      DUP
6:      PUSH ⟨end⟩
7:      SUB
8:      IFLT END_LOOP // if x > end
9:      DUP
10:     PUSH ⟨start⟩ + 1
11:     SWAP
12:     SUB
13:     IFLT ENFORCE_INVARIANTS //
            if x ≤ start
14: FIRST_LOOP_SHORTCUT:
15:     ⟨s⟩
16:     INC 0,1 // x + +
17:     GOTO LOOP
18: END_LOOP:
19:     POP // x
```

Fig. 5. Compiling a statement of the form "Forall $\langle x \rangle$ in $[\langle start \rangle, \langle end \rangle]$ do $\langle s \rangle$", where $\langle x \rangle$ is an identifier, $\langle start \rangle$ and $\langle end \rangle$ are integer literals and $\langle s \rangle$ is a statement

Lemma 1. *The code generated for a Forall statement satisfies condition* [termination].

Proof. Since the code for s satisfies the [termination] condition, eventually line 4 of Figure 5 is reached and the value of x is within its bounds. From that point on, the code for s is executed, in every iteration, from its first line and condition [stack coherence] on s ensures that x is not changed by s. The variable x is then advanced and checked against its bounds on each iteration, and the execution of the code terminates.

The FIRST_LOOP_SHORTCUT label is used not only to speed the execution of the generated code under normal operation, but also to ensure that the code of s is executed at most $end - start + 1$ times, as in a normal operation. Started in any state, once the first execution of the code generated for s terminates, lines 5 − 13 are iterated at most $end - start$ times. Therefore, there may be at most $end - start$ additional executions of the code generated for s before termination.

4.3   Implementing a Self-stabilizing Fair Scheduler

The scheduler, which is embedded in the compiled code, plays a crucial part in the execution of the program. It is supposed to examine the conditions of (some of) the transition rules, and *fairly* choose an *enabled* rule, that is, a rule for which the condition evaluates to *true*. As in ASM, we assume that in every state of the ASM, at least one of the rules is enabled. Notice that a simple round robin implementation will not achieve such fairness, simply because there may be a run in which a rule is enabled almost before every move, except before the move in which it is its turn to be examined. A common way to ensure fairness is to bound the number of times an enabled rule is not chosen until finally chosen. In case there exists such a bound, a rule which is enabled infinitely often is also chosen and executed infinitely often.

In order to achieve such a bound we choose to use a priority queue (see [17] for a similar, action driven converging, structure). Whenever the scheduler is required to choose a rule to execute, the rules conditions are examined according to their order in the priority queue. When an enabled rule is found, it is moved to the end of the queue and chosen as the next rule to be executed.

A straightforward implementation of the queue is using an array, containing rule numbers in the order the rules appear in the priority queue. When using this implementation, the queue will be considered consistent if the array contains a permutation of $\{1, \ldots, N\}$, where N is the number of rules. A code enforcing the existence of such a permutation can be added to the *enforce-invariants* section. Unfortunately, using this simple implementation takes $\Omega(N)$ steps to shift rules in order to move the chosen rule to the end of the queue. In order to avoid such latency, we use a more efficient implementation for the queue, which is equivalent to a linked list, and for which the consistency can be enforced. An array of size $N + 2$ denoted by Q is used for implementing the queue. The values in the first and last entries of Q ($Q[0]$ and $Q[N + 1]$) will be the index of the first rule and the last rule in the queue, respectively. The value in $Q[k]$ $1 \leq k \leq N$ is the index of the rule that follows the kst rule or 0 in case the kth rule is the last rule in the queue. For example, a queue with rules in the order $\langle 4, 2, 1, 3 \rangle$ will be represented using the following 6 entries array $[4, 3, 1, 0, 2, 3]$. Where $Q[0] = 4$ indicates rule number 4 is the first rule in the queue. Then $Q[4] = 2$ implies that rule number 2 follows. Continuing in the same manner we reach $Q[3] = 0$ indicating that rule number 3 is the last rule in the queue.

Using the above queue implementation allows one to move an element k in the queue to the end of the queue by four simple updates, provided that the element preceding k in the queue is also available. Moreover, queue consistency can be checked by simply iterating through the queue elements and checking that 0 is reached *exactly* after N hops.

Theorem 2. *The IJVM program, PR_l, generated by the compiler for an ASM program PR_h eventually behaves the same as PR_h.*

References

1. E. Borger, Y. Gurevich, and D. Rosenzweig, "The bakery algorithm: Yet another specification and verification. In E. Borger, editor, Specification and Validation Methods, pp. 231 – 243. Oxford University Press, 1995.
2. E. Borger and R. Stark, *Abstract State Machines: A Method for High-Level System Design and Analysis*, Springer-Verlag, 2003.

3. O. Brukman, S. Dolev, E. Kolodner, "Self-Stabilizing Autonomic Recoverer for Eventual Byzantine Software" *IEEE International Conference on Software-Science, Technology & Engineering*, (SwSTE03), pp. 20-29, Herzelia, 2003. Also in the *Workshop on Adaptive Distributed Systems* (WADiS03), Sorrento, Italy, 2003.

4. E. W. Dijkstra. Self-stabilizing systems in spite of distributed control. *Commun. ACM*, 17(11):643–644, 1974.

5. S. Dolev, *Self-Stabilization*, MIT Press, 2000.

6. S. Dolev, Y. Haviv, "Self-Stabilizing Soft Error Resilient Microprocessor" *17th International Conference on Architecture of Computing Systems*, LNCS:2981, (ARCS04), 2004. Also to appear in *IEEE Transaction on computers*.

7. S. Dolev, Y. Haviv, M. Sagiv "Self-Stabilization Preserving Compiler" *Technical Report #2005-06*, http://www.cs.bgu.ac.il/~haviv/PHD/sspc-techreport.ps 2005.

8. S. Dolev, A. Israeli, and S. Moran. Self-stabilization of dynamic systems assuming only read/write atomicity. *Distributed Computing*, 7(1):3–16, 1993.

9. S. Dolev, R. Kat. "Self-Stabilizing Distributed File Systems", *International Workshop on Self-Repairing and Self-Configurable Distributed Systems*, (RCDS 2002), pp. 384-389, To appear in *Journal of High Speed Networks*, special issue on self-stabilizing systems.

10. S. Dolev, and J. L. Welch, "Self-Stabilizing Clock Synchronization in the Presence of Byzantine Faults,", *Journal of the ACM*, Vol. 51, No. 5, pp. 780-799, September 2004.

11. S. Dolev, R. Yagel, "Toward Self-Stabilizing Operating Systems" *2nd International Workshop on Self-Adaptive and Autonomic Computing Systems* (SAACS04), pp. 684-688, 2004.

12. A. Fox and D. Patterson. "Self-Repairing Computers", *Scientific American*, June, 2003.

13. M. G. Gouda and F. F. Haddix, "The alternator," *WSS*, pp. 48-53, 1999.

14. J. O. Kephart, D. M. Chess. "The Vision of Autonomic Computing", *IEEE Computer*, 41-50, January, 2003.

15. Y. Gurevich. Evolving Algebras 1993: Lipari Guide. In E. Boerger, editor, *Specification and Validation Methods*, pages 9–36. Oxford University Press, 1995.

16. C. N. Hadjicostis, *Coding Approaches to Fault Tolerance in Combinational and Dynamic Systems*, Kluwer Academic Publishers, 2002.

17. T. Herman, I. Pirwani, "A Composite Stabilizing Data Structure" *5th Workshop on Self-Stabilizing Systems*, LNCS:2194, 167-182 (WSS2001), 2001.

18. M. Kistler, P. Shivakumar, L. Alvisi, D. Burger, and S. Keckler. "Modeling the effect of technology trends on the soft error rate of combinational logic". In *ICDSN*, volume 72 of *LNCS*, pages 216–226, 2002.

19. L. Lamport, *Time, Clocks, and the Ordering of Events in a Distributed System*, Communications of the ACM, 21(7):558-565, July 1978.

20. N. A. Lynch. *Distributed Algorithms*. Morgan Kaufman, 1996.

21. T. M. McGuire, M. G. Gouda, *The Austin Protocol Compiler*, Springer, 2005.

22. R. Perlman, *Interconnections: Bridges, Routers, Switches, and Internetworking Protocols*, Addison Wesley, 1999.

23. A. Tanenbaum, *Structured Computer Organization; (2nd ed.)*, Prentice-Hall, Inc., 1984.

Self-stabilizing Mobile Node
Location Management and Message Routing*

Shlomi Dolev[1],[**], Limor Lahiani[1],[**], Nancy Lynch[2],[***], and Tina Nolte[2],[***]

[1] Department of Computer Science, Ben-Gurion University of the Negev,
Beer-Sheva, 84105, Israel
{dolev, lahiani}@cs.bgu.ac.il
[2] MIT CSAIL, Cambridge, MA 02139, USA
{lynch, tnolte}@theory.csail.mit.edu

Abstract. We present simple algorithms for achieving self-stabilizing location management and routing in mobile ad-hoc networks. While mobile clients may be susceptible to corruption and stopping failures, mobile networks are often deployed with a reliable *GPS oracle*, supplying frequent updates of accurate real time and location information to mobile nodes. Information from a GPS oracle provides an external, shared source of consistency for mobile nodes, allowing them to label and timestamp messages, and hence aiding in identification of, and eventual recovery from, corruption and failures. Our algorithms use a GPS oracle.

Our algorithms also take advantage of the *Virtual Stationary Automata* programming abstraction, consisting of mobile clients, virtual timed machines called virtual stationary automata (VSAs), and a local broadcast service connecting VSAs and mobile clients. VSAs are distributed at known locations over the plane, and emulated in a self-stabilizing manner by the mobile nodes in the system. They serve as fault-tolerant building blocks that can interact with mobile clients and each other, and can simplify implementations of services in mobile networks.

We implement three self-stabilizing, fault-tolerant services, each built on the prior services: (1) VSA-to-VSA geographic routing, (2) mobile client location management, and (3) mobile client end-to-end routing. We use a greedy version of the classical depth-first search algorithm to route messages between VSAs in different regions. The mobile client location management service is based on *home locations*: Each client identifier hashes to a set of home locations, regions whose VSAs are periodically updated with the client's location. VSAs maintain this information and answer queries for client locations. Finally, the VSA-to-VSA routing and location management services are used to implement mobile client end-to-end routing.

Keywords: Virtual infrastructure, location management, home locations, end-to-end routing, hash functions, self-stabilization, GPS oracle.

* Longer version available as MIT LCS Technical Report MIT-LCS-TR-999.
** Partially supported by IBM, NSF, Rita Altura Trust Chair in Computer Sciences and Lynn and William Frankel Center for Computer Sciences.
*** Supported by DARPA contract F33615-01-C-1896, NSF ITR contract CCR-0121277, and USAF, AFRL contract FA9550-04-1-0121.

T. Herman and S. Tixeuil (Eds.): SSS 2005, LNCS 3764, pp. 96–112, 2005.
© Springer-Verlag Berlin Heidelberg 2005

1   Introduction

A system with no fixed infrastructure in which mobile clients may wander in the plane and assist each other in forwarding messages is called an ad-hoc network. The task of designing algorithms for constantly changing networks is difficult. Highly dynamic networks, however, are becoming increasingly prevalent, and it is therefore important to develop and use techniques that simplify this task. In addition, mobile nodes in these networks may suffer from crash failures or corruption faults, which cause arbitrary changes to their program states. Self-stabilization [4,5] is the ability to recover from an arbitrarily corrupt state. This property is important in long-lived, chaotic systems where certain events can result in unpredictable faults. For example, transient interference may disrupt wireless communication, violating our assumptions about the broadcast medium.

Mobile networks are often deployed with "reliable" GPS services, supplying frequent updates of real time and region information to mobile nodes. While the mobile clients may be susceptible to corruption and stopping failures, the GPS service may not be. Each of our algorithms utilizes such a reliable *GPS oracle*. Information from this oracle provides an external, shared source of consistency for nodes, and aids in identification of, and recovery from, failures.

In this paper we describe self-stabilizing algorithms that use a reliable GPS oracle to provide geographic routing, a mobile client location management service, and a mobile client end-to-end routing service. Each service is built on the prior services such that the composition of the services remains self-stabilizing [11]. To simplify the service implementations, we mask the unpredictability of mobile nodes by using a self-stabilizing *virtual* infrastructure, consisting of mobile clients, timing-aware and location-aware machines at fixed locations, called *Virtual Stationary Automata* (VSAs) [6,7], that mobile clients can interact with, and a local broadcast service connecting VSAs and mobile clients.

Self-stabilization and *GPS Oracles*. Traditionally, self-stabilizing systems are those systems that can be started from arbitrary configurations and eventually regain consistency *without external help*. However, mobile clients often have access to some reliable external information from a service such as GPS. Each algorithm in this paper uses an external GPS service (or an equivalent) as a reliable *GPS oracle*, providing periodic time and location updates, to base stabilization upon; our algorithms use timestamps and location information to tag events. In an arbitrary state, recorded events may have corrupted timestamps. Corrupted timestamps indicating future times can be identified and reset to predefined values; new events receive newer timestamps than any in the arbitrary initial state. This eventually allows nodes in the system to totally order events. We use the eventual total order to provide consistency of information and distinguish between incarnations of activity (such as retransmissions of messages).

Virtual Stationary Automata Programming Layer. In prior work [6,9,8], we developed a notion of "virtual nodes" for mobile ad hoc networks. A virtual node is an abstract, relatively well-behaved active node that is implemented using less well-behaved real physical nodes. The GeoQuorums algorithm [9] proposes storing data at fixed locations; however it only supports atomic objects, rather than general automata. A more general virtual mobile automaton is suggested in [8]. Finally, the virtual automata presented in [6,7] (and used here) are more powerful than those of [8], providing timing capabilities.

The static infrastructure we use in this paper includes virtual machines with an explicit notion of real time, called *Virtual Stationary Automata* (VSAs), distributed at known locations [6,7]. Each VSA represents a predetermined geographic area and has broadcast capabilities similar to those of the mobile nodes, allowing nearby VSAs and mobile nodes to communicate with one another. Many algorithms depend significantly on timing, and many mobile nodes have access to reasonably synchronized clocks. In the VSA layer, VSAs also have access to *virtual* clocks, guaranteed to not drift too far from real time. The layer provides mobile nodes with a fixed virtual infrastructure, reminiscent of better understood wired networks, with which to coordinate. An important property of the VSA layer implementation described in [6,7] is that it is self-stabilizing. Corruptions at physical nodes can result in inconsistency in the emulation of a VSA. However, emulations recover after corruptions to correctly emulate a VSA.

Geographic/VSA-to-VSA Routing. A basic service running on the VSA layer that we describe and use repeatedly is that of VSA-to-VSA (or region-to-region) routing (VtoVComm), providing a form of geocast. GeoCast algorithms [24,3], GOAFR [19], and algorithms for "routing on a curve" [23] route messages based on the location of the source and destination, using geography to delivery messages efficiently. GPSR [17], AFR [20], GOAFR+ [19], polygonal broadcast [10], and the asymptotically optimal algorithm [20] are algorithms based on greedy geographic routing algorithms, forwarding messages to the neighbor that is geographically closest to the destination. The algorithms also address "local minimum situations", where the greedy decision cannot be made. GPSR, GOAFR+, and AFR achieve, under reasonable network behavior, a linear order expected cost in the distance between the sender and the receiver. We implement VSA-to-VSA routing using a persistent greedy depth-first search (DFS) routing algorithm that runs on top of the VSA layer's fixed infrastructure. Our scheme is an application of the classical DFS algorithm in a new setting.

Location Management. Finding the location of a moving client in an ad-hoc network is difficult, much more so than in cellular networks where a fixed infrastructure of wired support stations exist (as in [16]), or sensor networks where some approximation of fixed infrastructure may exist [2]. A *location service* is a service that allows any client to discover the location of any other client using only its identifier. The paradigm for location services that we use here is that of a home location service: Hosts called *home location servers* are responsible for storing and maintaining the location of other hosts in the network [1,14,21]. Several ways to determine home location servers have been suggested.

The locality aware location service in [1] for ad-hoc networks is based on a hierarchy of lattice points for destination nodes, published with locations of associated nodes. Lattice points can be queried for the desired location, with a query traversing a spiral path of lattice nodes increasingly distant from the source until it reaches the destination. Another way of choosing location servers is based on quorums. A set of hosts is chosen to be a *write* quorum for a mobile client and is updated with the client's location. Another set is chosen to be a *read* quorum and queried for the desired client location. Each *write* and *read* quorum has a nonempty intersection, guaranteeing that if a *read* quorum is queried, the results will include the latest location written to a *write* quorum. In [14], a uniform quorum system is suggested, based on a virtual backbone of quorum representatives. Geographic quorums based on focal points are suggested in [9].

Location servers can also be chosen using a hash table. Some papers [21,15,25] use geographic locations as a repository for data. These use a hash to associate each piece of data with a region of the network and store the data at nodes in the region. This data can be used for routing or other applications. The Grid location service (GLS) [21] maps client ids to geographic coordinates. A client C_p's location is saved by clients closest to the coordinates p hashes to.

The scheme we present is based on hash tables and built on top of the VSA layer and VSA-to-VSA routing service. VSAs and mobile clients are programmed to form a self-stabilizing distributed data structure, where VSAs serve as home locations for clients. Each client's id hashes to a VSA region, the client's home location, whose VSA is responsible for maintaining the location of the client. To tolerate crashes of a limited number of VSAs, each mobile client id actually maps to a set of VSA home locations; the hash function returns a sequence of region ids as the home locations. We can use any hash function that provides a sequence of regions; one possibility is a *permutation hash function*, where permutations of region ids are lexicographically ordered and indexed by client id.

End-to-end Routing. Another important service in mobile networks is end-to-end routing. Our self-stabilizing implementation of a mobile client end-to-end communication service is simple, given VSA-to-VSA routing and the home location service. A client sends a message to another client by using the home location service to discover the destination client's region and then has a local VSA forward the message to the region using the VSA-to-VSA service.

2 Datatypes and System Model

We assume the *Virtual Stationary Automata* programming abstraction [6], which includes mobile client nodes and the virtual stationary automata (VSAs) the mobile nodes emulate, as well as a local broadcast service, V-bcast, between them (see Figure 1). The network is a fixed, closed, and bounded connected region R of the 2-D plane. R is partitioned into known connected subregions called *regions*, with unique ids from the set of region ids U. We define a neighbor relation *nbrs* on ids from U. This relation holds for any two regions u and v where the supremum distance between points in u and v is bounded by a constant r_{virt}.

2.1   Client Nodes

For each physical node identifier p from P, we assume a mobile timed I/O automaton client C_p, whose location in R at any time is referred to as $loc(p)$. Mobile client speed is bounded by a constant v_{max}. Clients receive region and time information from the GPS oracle. A $\mathsf{GPSupdate}(u, now)_p$ happens every ϵ_{sample} time at each client, indicating to the client the region u where it is located and the current time now. Clients accept now as the value of their own local clock. For simplicity, this local variable progresses at the rate of real time.

Each client C_p is equipped with a local broadcast service V-bcast (see Section 2.3), allowing it to communicate with nearby VSAs and clients with $\mathsf{bcast}(m)_p$ and $\mathsf{brcv}(m)_p$. Clients are susceptible to stopping and corruption failures. After a stopping failure, a client performs no additional local steps until restarted. If restarted, it starts again from an initial state. If a node suffers a corruption, it experiences a nondeterministic change to its program state. Additional interface actions and local state at the client are allowed. Local steps take no time.

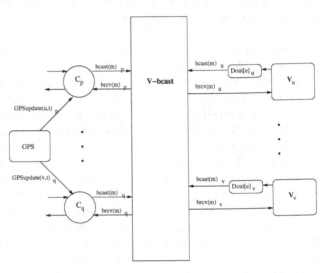

Fig. 1. VSA layer. VSAs and clients communicate with V-bcast. VSA outputs may be delayed in Dout.

2.2   Virtual Stationary Automata (VSAs)

A self-stabilizing implementation of VSAs using a GPS oracle and physical mobile nodes can be found in [6,7]. An abstract VSA is a timing-enabled virtual machine that may be emulated by the mobile nodes in its region in the network. A VSA for region u, V_u, is a TIOA whose program is a tuple of its action signature, sig_u, valid states, $states_u$, a start state function mapping clock values to start states, $start_u$, a discrete transition function, δ_u, and a set of valid trajectories [18], τ_u. The state of V_u is referred to collectively as $vstate$ and is assumed to include a variable corresponding to real time, $vstate.now$. To guarantee we can emulate a VSA using mobile nodes, its interface must be emulatable by the nodes; a VSA V_u's external interface is restricted, including only stopping, corruption, and restart inputs, and the ability to broadcast and receive messages.

Since a VSA is emulated by physical nodes in its region, its failures are defined in terms of client failures: (1) If no clients are in the region, the VSA is crashed, (2) If no client failure occurs in an alive VSA's region over some interval, the VSA does not suffer a failure during that interval, and (3) A VSA may suffer a corruption only if a mobile client in its region suffers a corruption; the self-stabilizing implementation of a VSA in [6,7] guarantees that starting from an arbitrary configuration, the emulation's external trace will eventually look like that of the abstract VSA, starting from a corrupted abstract state.

Due to message delays or node failure, emulations might be behind real time by up to some time e. It is then a *delay-augmented TIOA*, an augmentation of V_u with timing perturbations, represented with buffers Dout$[e]_u$. The buffer delays messages by a nondeterministic time $[0, e]$, where e is more than V-bcast's broadcast delay, d (see Section 2.3).

2.3   Local Broadcast Service (V-bcast)

Communication is in the form of local broadcast V-bcast, with broadcast radius r_{virt} and message delay d. It allows communication between VSAs and clients in the same or neighboring regions. The service allows the broadcasting and receiving of message m at each port $i \in P \cup U$ through bcast$(m)_i$ and brcv$(m)_i$.

We assume V-bcast guarantees two properties: integrity and reliable local delivery. *Integrity* guarantees for any brcv$(m)_i$ that occurs, a bcast$(m)_j, j \in P \cup U$ previously occurred. *Reliable local delivery* roughly guarantees a transmission will be received by nearby ports: If port i in region u transmits a message, then every port j in region u or neighboring regions during the entire time interval starting at transmission and ending d later receives the message by the end of the interval. (Here, due to GPSupdate lag, a client is said to be "in" region u if it has just left u but has not yet received a GPSupdate with the change.)

We assume broadcast buffers are large enough that overflows do not occur in normal operation. In the event of overflow, overflow messages are lost.

3   Problem Specifications

We describe the services we will build over the VSA layer: VSA-to-VSA routing, a location service, and client-to-client routing, and describe our requirement that implementations be self-stabilizing.

The following constants (explained/used shortly) are globally known: (1) $f < |U|$, a limit on "home location" VSA failures for a client, (2) h, a function mapping each client id to a sequence of $f + 1$ distinct region ids, (3) $ttl_{VtoV} > d$, delivery time for the VtoVComm service, (4) $ttl_{HLS} \geq \epsilon_{sample} + 2d + 3e + 2ttl_{VtoV}$, response time of the location management service, and (5) ttl_{hb}, a refresh period. We assume the following client mobility and VSA crash failure conditions:

(1) Each client spends at least ϵ_{sample} time in a region before moving to another,
(2) At any time, each alive client's current region or a neighboring region has a non-crashed VSA that remains alive for an additional ttl_{HLS} time,
(3) For any interval of length $ttl_{VtoV} + e$, VSAs alive over the interval are connected via at least one path of non-crashed VSAs over the whole interval, and

(4) For any interval of length $ttl_{hb} + 2ttl_{VtoV} + 2e + d$, and any alive client q, at least one VSA from $h(q)$ does not crash during the interval.

3.1   VSA-to-VSA Communication Service (VtoVComm) Specification

The first service is an inter-VSA routing service, where a VSA from some region u can send a message m through $VtoVsend(v, m)_u$ to a VSA in another (potentially non-neighboring) region v. Region v's VSA later receives m through $VtoVrcv(m)_v$. The service guarantees two properties:

(1) If a VSA at region u performs a $VtoVsend(v, m)$, and region u and v VSAs are alive over the interval beginning with the send and ending ttl_{VtoV} later, then the VSA at region v performs a $VtoVrcv(m)$ before the end of the interval, and
(2) If a message is received at some VSA, it was previously sent to that VSA.

3.2   Location Service Specification

A location service answers queries from clients for the locations of other clients. A client node p can submit a query for a recent region of client node q via a $HLquery(q)_p$ action. If q has been in the system for a sufficient amount of time, the service responds within bounded time with a recent region location of q, $qreg$, through a $HLreply(q, qreg)_i$ action. More precisely, the service guarantees that if a client p performs a $HLquery$ to find an alive client q that has been in the system longer than $\epsilon_{sample} + d + ttl_{VtoV} + e + ttl_{HLS}$ time, and p does not crash or change regions for ttl_{HLS} time, then:

(1) Within ttl_{HLS} time, client p will perform a $HLreply$ with a region for q, and
(2) If p performs a $HLreply(q, qreg)$, then p had requested q's location and q was either: (a) alive in region $qreg$ within the last ttl_{HLS} time, or (b) failed for at most $ttl_{hb} + ttl_{HLS} - \epsilon_{sample}$ time.

3.3   Client End-to-End Routing (EtoEComm) Specification

End-to-end routing is an important application for ad-hoc networks. The V-bcast service provides a local broadcast service where VSAs and clients can communicate with VSAs and clients in neighboring regions. VtoVComm allows arbitrary VSAs to communicate. End-to-end routing (EtoEComm) allows arbitrary clients to communicate: a client p sends message m to client q using $send(q, m)_p$, which is received by q in bounded time via $receive(m)_q$.

If clients p and q do not crash for ttl_{HLS} time, clients do not change regions for ttl_{HLS} time after a send, and q has been in the system at least $ttl_{HLS} + \epsilon_{sample} + d + ttl_{VtoV} + e$ time, then:

(1) If p sends m to q, q receives m within $ttl_{HLS} + 2d + 2e + ttl_{VtoV}$ time, and
(2) Any message received by a client was previously sent to the client.

3.4   Self-stabilizing Implementations

We require implementations of the services to be self-stabilizing. A system configuration is *safe* with respect to a specification and implementation if any admissible execution fragment of the implementation starting from the configuration is an admissible execution fragment of the specification. An implementation is *self-stabilizing* if starting from any configuration, an admissible execution of the implementation eventually reaches a safe configuration. Notice if an implementation is self-stabilizing, then any long enough execution fragment of the implementation will eventually have a suffix that looks like the suffix of some correct execution of the specification, until a corruption occurs.

Each of the above services' self-stabilizing implementations will be built on top of self-stabilizing implementations of other services: VtoVComm over the VSA layer, the location service over the VSA layer and VtoVComm service, and EtoEComm over the VSA layer, VtoVComm, and location services. Each self-stabilizing implementation uses lower level services without feedback, so lower level service executions are not influenced by the upper level services. This allows us to guarantee that higher level service implementations are still self-stabilizing through *fair composition* [11].

Our service implementations, starting from an arbitrary system configuration, stabilize within the following times: VtoVComm: $ttl_{VtoV} + d$ time after the VSA layer stabilizes, the location service: $max(ttl_{HLS}, 2e + 3ttl_{VtoV} + ttl_{hb} + 2d)$ time after VtoVComm stabilizes, and EtoEComm: $ttl_{pb} + 2d + 2e + ttl_{VtoV}$ time after the location service has stabilized.

4   VSA-to-VSA Communication Implementation

The VSA-to-VSA communication (VtoVComm) service allows communication of messages between any two VSAs through VtoVsend and VtoVrcv actions, as long as there is a path of non-failed VSAs between them. The VtoVComm service is built on top of the V-bcast service [6], which supports communication between two neighboring VSAs.

VSA-to-VSA communication is based on greedy DFS. When a VSA receives a message for which it is not the destination, it chooses a neighboring VSA that is on a shortest path to the destination VSA and forwards the message in a forward message to that neighbor. If the VSA does not receive an indication through a found message that the message has been delivered to the destination within some bounded amount of time, it then forwards the message to the neighboring VSA on the next shortest path to the destination VSA, and so on. This choice of neighbors is greedy in the sense that the next neighbor chosen to receive the forwarded message is the one on a shortest path to the destination VSA, excluding the neighbors associated with previous tries. The greedy DFS can turn into a flood in pathological situations in which the destination is that last VSA reached. Self-stabilization of the algorithm is ensured by the use of a real time timestamp to identify the version of the DFS. Too old versions are eliminated from the system and new versions are handled as completely new attempts to complete a greedy DFS towards the destination.

We present a simple greedy DFS that gradually expands the search until all paths are checked. This algorithm will find a path to the destination if such a path exists throughout the DFS execution. We also have a modification of the algorithm to produce a persistent version in which each VSA repeatedly tries to forward messages along previously unsuccessful paths to take advantage of recoveries of VSAs that may result in a viable path [13].

4.1 Detailed Code Description

The following code description refers to the code for VSA V_u^{VtoV} in Figure 2. The main state variable $DFStable$ keeps track of information for messages that are still waiting to be delivered. For each such unique message, the table stores

---

```
     Signature:
 2    Input VtoVsend(d, m)_u, d ∈ U, m arbitrary
      Input brcv(m)_u, m ∈ ({found}× Msg)
 4       ∪ ({forward} × Msg × U × {u})
      Output bcast(m)_u, m arbitrary
 6    Output VtoVrcv(m)_u, m arbitrary
      Internal DFStimeout(msg)_u, msg ∈ Msg
 8    Internal DFSclean(msg)_u, msg ∈ Msg
      Msg = M× U× U× ℝ,
10    of the form ⟨m, v2vs, v2vd, ts⟩

12  State:
      analog now ∈ ℝ, the current real time
14    bcastq, VtoVrcvq, message queues, initially ∅
      DFStable, a table indexed on Msg tuples,
16      with entries in (nbrs(u) × 2^{nbrs(u)} × ℝ),
        initially ∅
18    curNbr ∈ U, initially ⊥

20  Trajectories:
      satisfies
22      d(now) = 1
        constant bcastq, VtoVrcvq, DFStable,
24                curNbr
      stops when
26      Any precondition is satisfied.

28  Actions:
      Output bcast(m)_u
30    Precondition:
        m ∈ bcastq
32    Effect:
        bcastq ← bcastq \ {m}
34
      Input VtoVsend(d, m)_u
36    Effect:
        if u = d then
38         VtoVrcvq ← VtoVrcvq ∪ {m}
           else DFStable(⟨m, u, d, now⟩)
40             ← ⟨u, nbrs(u), now⟩
```

```
  Internal DFStimeout(msg)_u                    42
  Precondition:
      DFStable(msg) = ⟨*, *, to⟩                 44
      to ∉ (now, now + δ(u, msg.v2vd))]
  Effect:                                        46
      if (DFStable(msg)= ⟨i,NS,to⟩∧ NS≠ ∅) then
         curNbr ← NxtNbr(NS, i, u, msg.v2vd)     48
         DFStable(msg)
             ← ⟨i,NS\{curNbr},now+δ(u,msg.v2vd)⟩  50
         bcastq← bcastq ∪ {⟨forward,msg,u,curNbr⟩}
         else DFStable(msg) ← null               52

  Input brcv(⟨forward, msg, isrc, u⟩)_u          54
  Effect:
      if msg.ts ∈ [now -ttl_{VtoV}, now] then     56
         if u = msg.v2vd then
            bcastq ← bcastq ∪ {⟨found, msg⟩}      58
            VtoVrcvq ← VtoVrcvq ∪ {msg.m}
         else if DFStable(msg) = null then        60
            DFStable(msg)
                ← ⟨isrc, nbrs(u)\{isrc}, now⟩      62

  Input brcv(⟨found, msg⟩)_u                      64
  Effect:
      if DFStable(msg) ≠ null then                66
         DFStable(msg) ← null
         if u ≠ msg.v2vs then                     68
            bcastq ← bcastq ∪ {⟨found, msg⟩}
                                                  70

  Output VtoVrcv(m)_u
  Precondition:                                   72
      m ∈ VtoVrcvq
  Effect:                                         74
      VtoVrcvq ← VtoVRcvq \ {m}
                                                  76
  Internal DFSclean(msg)_u
  Precondition:                                   78
      DFStable(msg) ≠ null
      msg.ts ∉ [now -ttl_{VtoV}, now]              80
  Effect:
      DFStable(msg) ← null                        82
```

Fig. 2. Greedy DFS algorithm at V_u^{VtoV} for region u

the intermediate source of the message, the set of VSA neighbors that have yet to have the message forwarded to them, and a timeout for the neighbor currently being tried for forwarding the message.

A source VSA V_u^{VtoV} for region u sends a message m to a destination VSA in region d using VtoVsend$(d, m)_u$ (line 35). If $u = d$ then V_u^{VtoV} receives m through VtoVrcv$(m)_u$ (lines 37-38). Otherwise the destination VSA is another VSA and VSA V_u^{VtoV} sets the $DFStable$ mapping of an augmented version of the message, $\langle m, u, d, now \rangle$, to $\langle u, nbrs(u), now \rangle$. This enables the start of a new DFS execution to forward the message to its destination (line 39-40).

Whenever the forwarding of a message to a neighbor in $DFStable$ times out, it triggers forwarding to the next neighbor in the DFS, if possible. If the message hasn't yet been forwarded to all of the relevant neighbors, then the next neighbor closest to the destination VSA that has not yet had a message forwarded to it, $curNbr$, is selected and the message tuple msg is then forwarded in a forward message to it using the V-bcast service (lines 42-52). The timeout for this attempt at forwarding is set to $\delta(curNbr, msg.v2vd)$ later, where $\delta : \{U\} \times \{U\} \to \mathcal{N}$ is a bound on the time required for a message to arrive from x to y. If the message has already been forwarded to all the relevant neighbors, then $DFStable(msg)$ is set to null, indicating that nothing more can be done.

If a tuple msg whose destination is u is received in a forward message from $isrc$, then V_u^{VtoV} broadcasts a $\langle found, msg \rangle$ message via the V-bcast service and VtoVrcv's the message $msg.m$. The found message notifies neighbors still participating in the DFS for msg that it has reached its destination. No forwarding is required (lines 56-59). Otherwise, if msg is not destined for V_u^{VtoV} and V_u^{VtoV} does not already have an entry in $DFStable$ for msg, then the message must be forwarded to its destination. $DFStable(msg)$ is set to $\langle isrc, nbrs(u) \backslash \{isrc\}, now \rangle$ (lines 61-62), storing the intermediate source, initializing the set of neighbors that have yet to have the message forwarded to them, and setting a timeout to now. Setting the timeout to now immediately enables the DFStimeout action for msg, triggering the forwarding of msg to one of V_u^{VtoV}'s neighbors.

When a found message is received for a message tuple msg that is mapped by $DFStable$, the entry in $DFStable$ is erased, preventing additional forwarding (line 67). If $u \neq msg.v2vs$ then VSA V_u^{VtoV} broadcasts a found message via the V-bcast service (lines 68-69), notifying neighbors that are still participating for msg that it has been delivered. Clearly, if $u = msg.v2vs$, then no found message is required and no further action needs to be taken.

4.2   Correctness

Let the source VSA be V_s^{VtoV}, the destination VSA be V_d^{VtoV}, the message sent be m, and a DFS execution exe from V_s^{VtoV} to V_d^{VtoV} be as defined above. Any non-negative wait time is sufficient for correctness. However, a wait time dependent on hop count between regions will be the most message-efficient. If no corruptions occur and the status (failed or non-failed) of every VSA doesn't change during exe, then the following holds:

Lemma 1. *If V_s^{VtoV} performs a $\mathsf{VtoVsend}(d,m)$ at time t, and there exists a path of non-failed VSAs between V_s^{VtoV} and V_d^{VtoV} from t to time $t + ttl_{VtoV}$, then V_d^{VtoV} performs a $\mathsf{VtoVrcv}(m)$ in the interval $[t, t + ttl_{VtoV}]$, for $ttl_{VtoV} \geq [e + d + (max_{u,v \in U} \delta(u, v) \cdot max_{u \in U} |nbrs(u)| - 1)] \cdot (|U| - 1)$.*

Lemma 2. *The number of times a message tuple is re-broadcast is bounded.*

Lemma 3. *Once corruptions stop and the VSA layer has stabilized, it takes up to $d + ttl_{VtoV}$ time for VtoVComm to stabilize.*

5   Home Location Service (HLS) Implementation

The location service allows a client to determine a recent region of another alive client. In our implementation, called the *Home Location Service (HLS)*, we accomplish this using *home locations*. Recall that the home locations of a client node p are $f + 1$ regions whose VSAs are occasionally updated with p's region. The home locations are calculated with a hash function h, mapping a client's id to a list of VSA regions, and is known to all VSAs. These home location VSAs can then be queried by other VSAs to determine a recent region of p.

The HLS implementation consists of two parts: a client-side portion and a VSA-side portion. C_p^{HL} is a subautomaton of client p that interacts with VSAs to provide HLS. It notifies local VSAs of its region. It also handles $\mathsf{HLquery}(q)_p$ requests, by broadcasting the query to local VSAs. It translates responses from the VSAs into $\mathsf{HLreply}$ outputs. For the VSA-side, V_u^{HL} and V_v^{HL} are home location VSAs corresponding to regions u and v of the network; they are sub-automata of VSAs V_u and V_v. V_u^{HL} takes a request from a local client for client node q's region, calculates q's home locations using the hash function, and then sends location queries to the home locations using VtoVComm. Home locations respond with region information they have for q, which is then provided by V_u^{HL} to the requesting client. V_u^{HL} also is responsible both for informing the home locations of each client p located in its region or neighboring regions of p's region, and answering queries for the regions of clients for which it is a home location.

Time and region information from the GPS oracle is used throughout the HLS algorithm, by clients and VSAs, to timestamp and label information and messages. This information is used to guarantee timeliness of replies from the HLS service, and to stabilize the service after faults. Timestamps are used to determine if information is too old or too new, while region information allows clients and VSAs to know which other clients and VSAs to interact with.

5.1   HLS Client Actions

Clients receive $\mathsf{GPSupdates}$ every ϵ_{sample} time from the GPS automaton, making them aware of their current region and the time. If a client's region has changed, the client immediately sends a $\mathsf{heartbeat}$ message with its id, current time and region information. The client periodically reminds its current and neighboring region VSAs of its region by broadcasting additional $\mathsf{heartbeat}$ messages every ttl_{hb} time, where ttl_{hb} is a known constant.

C_p^{HL} also handles the HLquery(q) inputs it receives. This request for q's location is stored in a $queryq$ table and, once the client knows its own region, translated into a $\langle$clocQuery, $q\rangle$ message that is broadcast, together with the VSA region, to local regions' VSAs. If C_p^{HL} eventually receives a $\langle$clocReply, $q, qreg\rangle$ message from its current or neighboring region's VSA for a client q in $queryq$, indicating that node q was in region $qreg$, it clears the entry for q in $queryq$, and outputs a HLreply($q, qreg$) of the information. If the request goes unanswered for more than $ttl_{HLS} - \epsilon_{sample}$ time, then the request has failed and is removed.

5.2 HLS VSA Actions

The code for automaton V_u^{HL} appears in Figure 3. The VSA knows of local clients through heartbeat messages. If a VSA hears a heartbeat from a client p claiming to be in its region or a neighboring region, the VSA sends a locUpdate message for p, with p's heartbeat timestamp and region, through VtoVComm to the VSAs at home locations of client p (lines 40-44); home locations are computed using a known hash function h from $P \times \{1, \cdots, f + 1\}$ to U.

When a VSA receives one of these locUpdate messages for a client p, it stores both the region indicated in the message as p's current region and the attached heartbeat timestamp in its loc table (lines 46-49). This location information for p is refreshed each time the VSA receives a locUpdate for client p with a newer heartbeat timestamp. Since a client sends a heartbeat message every ttl_{hb} time, which can take up to $d + e$ time to arrive at and trigger a VSA to send a locUpdate message through VtoVComm, which can take ttl_{VtoV} time to be delivered at a home location, an entry for client p is erased if its timestamp is older than $ttl_{hb} + d + e + ttl_{VtoV}$ (lines 51-55).

The other responsibility of the VSA is to receive and respond to local client requests for location information on other clients. A client p in a VSA's region or a neighboring region v can send a query for q's current location to the VSA. This is done via a mobile node's broadcast of a $\langle\langle$clocQuery, $q\rangle, v\rangle$ message. When the VSA at region u receives this query, if no outstanding query for q exists, it notes the request for q in $lquery(q)$, and sends a vlocQuery message to q's $f + 1$ home locations, querying about q's location (lines 57-64). Any home location that receives such a message and has an entry for q's region responds with a vlocReply to the querying VSA with the region (lines 66-70).

If the querying VSA at u receives a vlocReply in response to an outstanding location request for a client q, it stores the attached region information in $lquery(q)$ (lines 72-75), broadcasts a clocReply message with q and its region to local clients, and erases the entry for $lquery(q)$ (lines 77-81). If, however, $2ttl_{VtoV} + 2e$ time passes since a request for q's region was received by a local client and there is no entry for q's region, $lquery(q)$ is just erased (lines 83-87).

5.3 Correctness

We make the system assumptions described in Section 3. For the following two lemmas and theorem, assume the system starts in a safe configuration, and no corruptions occur.

```
   Constants:                                    Input VtoVrcv(⟨v, ⟨locUpdate, q, t⟩⟩)ᵤ      46
2  h, a hash function from P × {1, · · · , f + 1} to   Effect:
   U such that for p ∈ P, x, y ∈ {1, · · · , f + 1}    if loc(q).ts < t ≤ now then              48
4  if x ≠ y, then h(p, x) ≠ h(p, y)                   loc(q) ← ⟨v, t⟩
                                                                                              50
6 Signature:                                      Internal cleanLoc(q)ᵤ
   Input brcv(⟨m, v⟩)ᵤ, m ∈ ({heartbeat}× ℝ× P)   Precondition:                             52
8            ∪ ({clocQuery} × P), v ∈ U             loc(q).ts ∉ [now-ttlₕ_b-d-e-ttl_{VtoV}, now]
   Input VtoVrcv(⟨v, m⟩)ᵤ, v ∈ U,                  Effect:                                   54
10   m ∈ ({locUpdate} × P × ℝ)∪                      loc(q) ← null
     ({vlocQuery}× P)∪ ({vlocReply}× P× U)                                                   56
12   Output bcast(⟨⟨clocReply, q, qreg⟩, u⟩)ᵤ,     Input brcv(⟨⟨clocQuery, q⟩, v⟩)ᵤ
     q ∈ P, qreg ∈ U                               Effect:                                   58
14   Output VtoVsend(v, m)ᵤ, v ∈ U                   if ([lquery(q) = null ∨ lquery(q).ts< now]
     Internal updateHL(q)ᵤ, q ∈ P                        ∧ v ∈ nbrs(u)∪ {u}) then             60
16   Internal cleanLoc(q)ᵤ, q ∈ P                     lquery(q) ← ⟨⊥, now + 2ttl_{VtoV} + 2e⟩
     Internal cleanLquery(q)ᵤ, q ∈ P                  for i = 1 to f+1                        62
18                                                      vtovq ← vtovq ∪
   State:                                                 {⟨h(q,i), ⟨u, ⟨vlocQuery, q⟩⟩⟩}    64
20  loc, lquery, tables indexed on process ids with
     entries from U × ℝ^{≥0}, of the form ⟨reg, ts⟩  Input VtoVrcv(⟨v, ⟨vlocQuery, q⟩⟩)ᵤ     66
22  vtovq, a queue of tuples from U × msg          Effect:
     (Above all initially empty)                     if loc(q) ≠ null then                   68
24  analog now ∈ ℝ^{≥0}, the current real time        vtovq ← vtovq ∪
                                                       {⟨v, ⟨u, ⟨vlocReply, q, loc(q).reg⟩⟩⟩} 70
26 Trajectories:
   satisfies                                       Input VtoVrcv(⟨v, ⟨vlocReply, q, qreg⟩⟩)ᵤ 72
28   d(now) = 1                                     Effect:
     constant loc, lquery, vtovq                      if lquery(q) ≠ null then               74
30   stops when                                        lquery(q).reg ← qreg
     Any precondition is satisfied.                                                          76
32                                                 Output bcast(⟨⟨clocReply, q, qreg⟩, u⟩)ᵤ
   Actions:                                         Precondition:                            78
34   Output VtoVsend(v, m)ᵤ                           qreg = lquery(q).reg ≠ ⊥
     Precondition:                                  Effect:                                  80
36     ⟨v, m⟩ ∈ vtovq                                 lquery(q) ← null
     Effect:                                                                                 82
38     vtovq ← vtovq \ {⟨v, m⟩}                      Internal cleanLquery(q)ᵤ
                                                    Precondition:                            84
40   Input brcv(⟨⟨heartbeat, t, p⟩, v⟩)ᵤ              lquery(q).ts∉ [now, now + 2ttl_{VtoV} + 2e]
     Effect:                                        Effect:                                  86
42     if (v∈ nbrs(u)∪ {u}∧ now-d≤ t≤ now) then       lquery(q) ← null
         for i = 1 to f+1
44         vtovq← vtovq∪ {⟨h(q,i),⟨v,⟨locUpdate,q,t⟩⟩⟩}
```

Fig. 3. HLS's V_u^{HL} automaton with parameters ttl_{VtoV} and ttl_{hb}

Lemma 4. *For any VSA u, if there is a request for q's region in lquery, it was submitted through a HLquery(q) within the last $\epsilon_{sample} + d + 2ttl_{VtoV} + 2e$ time.*

Lemma 5. *Starting $\epsilon_{sample}+d+e+ttl_{VtoV}$ time after client p enters the system and until p fails, for each interval of length $ttl_{VtoV} + e$, all but f of p's home locations will have a non-null loc(p) entry for the entire interval. If client p is alive and there is some VSA u such that loc(p) is not null, p was alive and located in loc(p).reg within the last $\epsilon_{sample} + d + e + ttl_{VtoV}$ time.*

Theorem 1. *Every client p searching for a non-failed client q that has been in the system longer than $ttl_{HLS} + \epsilon_{sample} + d + ttl_{VtoV} + e$ time will perform a HLreply(q, qreg) within time ttl_{HLS}, such that q was located in region qreg no* more than ttl_{HLS} time ago. No reply will occur if q has been failed for more than $ttl_{hb} + ttl_{HLS} - \epsilon_{sample}$ time. Any reply is in response to a query.

Proof sketch: By the prior lemma, once client q has been in the system for $\epsilon_{sample} + d + e + ttl_{VtoV}$ time, any queries of its home locations will succeed in producing a result. However, a new HLquery request "piggybacks" on any prior unexpired HLquery requests. Since one of these requests could have been initiated just before the client q's home locations are updated, we can only guarantee a response will be received for a new request if any outstanding requests will be answered. If the client has been in the system for this total $ttl_{HLS}+d+e+ttl_{VtoV}$ time after receiving its first GPSupdate, then any response to a query can take as much as ttl_{HLS} time: ϵ_{sample} time for the querying client to receive its first GPSupdate, d time for the query to be transmitted and received by a local VSA, $e+ttl_{VtoV}$ for the local VSA to query a home location, $e+ttl_{VtoV}$ for the response to arrive at a local VSA, e time for the local VSA to transmit the response to its requesting clients, and d time for the transmission to be received and translated into HLreplys at clients. By the prior lemma, we know that information can only be out of date by $\epsilon_{sample} + ttl_{VtoV} + e + d$ time when a home location responds to a query by another VSA. The response can take $e + ttl_{VtoV}$ time to arrive at the querying VSA, followed by $e + d$ time for the querying VSA to get the information to the clients that prompted the query. The oldest the information could be is the total.

For the second statement, note that a failed client will not send a heartbeat message. Since $loc(p)$ entries are cleared once $ttl_{hb} + d + e + ttl_{VtoV}$ time has passed since the heartbeat message upon which it was based was broadcast, and the information from the entry can only take as much as $e + ttl_{VtoV}$ time to reach a querying VSA and $e + d$ time to reach any querying clients, the total is the maximum time a HLreply can occur after the client fails.

For the third statement, a query expires after ttl_{HLS} time. Hence, any response generated must be for a query that is not older. □

Theorem 2. *Starting from an arbitrary configuration, after VtoVComm has stabilized, it takes $max(ttl_{HLS}, 2e+3ttl_{VtoV}+ttl_{hb}+2d)$ time for HLS to stabilize.*

Proof sketch: Once lower levels have stabilized, most client state is made locally consistent within ϵ_{sample} time, the time for a GPSupdate. This action resets most variables if the region is updated. The remaining state is made consistent instantaneously with local correction, except for the heartbeat timer and $query_q$ variables. The heartbeat timer can affect operations for at most ttl_{hb} time. The $query_q$ variable can affect operations for ttl_{HLS} time, when it would be deleted.

For VSAs, there are two variables that are not instantaneously corrected: loc and $lquery$. The loc variable will be consistent within time $e+2ttl_{VtoV}+ttl_{hb}+d$. At worst, there could be a corrupted message that arrives at a VSA after ttl_{VtoV} time, adding a bad entry that takes $e + ttl_{VtoV} + ttl_{hb} + d$ time to expire. If the client referred to is in the system, it might not be until the next update after the timestamp of the corrupted message (which could have been delivered as late as

ttl_{VtoV} after corruptions stopped) arrives for the information to be cleaned up. This time is exactly what the offset term for loc timeouts describes. Hence, the variable might not be cleaned until ttl_{VtoV} plus that offset term.

However, there may be responses based on this bad loc table information that were sent right at $e + 2ttl_{VtoV} + ttl_{hb} + d$, and that take $e + ttl_{VtoV}$ to arrive at the VSA. The resulting transmission (taking d time to complete) to local clients is then incorrect. However, those incorrect transmissions cease after the total time $2e + 3ttl_{VtoV} + ttl_{hb} + 2d$ elapses.

The $lquery$ variable is cleaned up within ttl_{HLS} time. An entry in $lquery$ only has a total of $2ttl_{VtoV} + 2e$ time in the data structure. It could be the case that a spurious request was transmitted in the beginning, which adds d time. If a region response is received it results in immediate correction of the state through erasure. Hence, the time required to be consistent is the time that it takes for a query to be accounted for. The maximum of ttl_{HLS} and $2e + 3ttl_{VtoV} + ttl_{hb} + 2d$ is the maximum stabilization time.   □

6   Client End-to-End Routing (EtoEComm) Implementation

Our implementation of the end-to-end routing service, EtoEComm, uses the location service to discover a recent region location of a destination client node and then uses this location in conjunction with VtoVComm to deliver messages. As in the implementation of the Home Location Service, there are two parts to the implementation: the client-side portion and the VSA-side portion.

A message m is sent to another client q via $\mathsf{send}(q, m)_p$. This input to client-side C_p^{E2E} results in the forwarding of the message to p's current region u's and neighboring VSAs through a local broadcast of the message with the the the destination q and q's location, if q's location is known. If a recent region for q is not known, C_p^{E2E} queries HLS to determine one. A timeout for response to the location request is set for ttl_{HLS} later. Once a response is received from HLS in the form of $\mathsf{HLreply}(q, qreg)_p$, indicating q was in region $qreg$, the location of q is stored and kept for ttl_{pb} time. For each message waiting to be sent to q, the message, labeled with q and $qreg$, is forwarded to p's current and neighboring regions' VSAs through a local broadcast, as before.

Messages for client p from other clients are received from p's current region or a neighboring region v's VSA through a local broadcast from a local VSA. The message is subsequently delivered through the output $\mathsf{receive}(m)_p$.

The VSA V_u^{E2E} portion is very simple. A client may send it information to be transmitted to other VSAs, which it forwards through VtoVComm, or another VSA may send it information to be delivered at a client in its own or a neighboring region, which it forwards through V-bcast.

The receipt of a locally broadcast message m from a client p in region u or a neighboring region to q at region $qreg$ results in the subsequent forwarding of the message to the virtual automata at regions $\mathsf{calcregs}(qreg)$ and their neighboring regions, via the virtual automata VtoVComm service. The set of VSA regions calcregs($qreg$) describes the regions that q may occupy by the time the message is delivered to it. The receipt, via VtoVComm of message m intended for client p in region u or a neighboring region results in the forwarding of the message to p through a local broadcast.

7 Concluding Remarks

We described how both the GPS oracle and the VSA layer could help implement self-stabilizing geocast routing, location management, and end-to-end routing services. The self-stabilizing VSA layer provides a virtual fixed infrastructure useful for solving a variety of problems. It acts as a fault-tolerant, self-stabilizing building block for services, allowing applications to be built for mobile networks as though base stations existed for mobile clients to interact with.

The GPS oracle's frequently refreshed and reliable timing and location information made providing self-stabilization easier. The paradigm of an external service providing reliable information that can be used in a self-stabilizing service implementation is an especially important and relevant one in mobile networks. Mobile networks demonstrate many properties that naturally require self-stabilizing implementations, such as a need for self-configuration, or the possibility of unpredictable kinds of failures, but also often have access to reliable external knowledge that can act as a source of shared consistency in the network; here, accurate region knowledge allowed nodes to determine who they should be communicating with (current region and neighboring region nodes), and time information allowed them to order messages and assess timeliness of information.

References

1. Abraham, I., Dolev, D., and Malkhi, D., "LLS: A Locality Aware Location Service for Mobile Ad Hoc Networks", *Proceedings of the DIALM-POMC Joint Workshop on Foundations of Mobile Computing (DIALM-POMC)*, pp. 75-84, 2004.
2. Arora, A., Demirbas, M., Lynch, N., and Nolte, T., "A Hierarchy-based Fault-local Stabilizing Algorithm for Tracking in Sensor Networks", *8th International Conference on Principles of Distributed Systems (OPODIS)*, pp. 207-217, 2004.
3. Camp, T., Liu, Y., "An adaptive mesh-based protocol for geocast routing", *Journal of Parallel and Distributed Computing: Special Issue on Mobile Ad-hoc Networking and Computing*, pp. 196–213, 2002.
4. Dijkstra, E.W., "Self stabilizing systems in spite of distributed control", *Communications of the ACM*, pp. 643-644, 1974.
5. Dolev, S., *Self-Stabilization*, MIT Press, 2000.
6. Dolev, S., Gilbert, S., Lahiani, L., Lynch, N., and Nolte, T., "Timed Virtual Stationary Automata for Mobile Networks", Technical Report MIT-LCS-TR-979a, MIT CSAIL, Cambridge, MA 02139, 2005.
7. Dolev, S., Gilbert, S., Lahiani, L., Lynch, N., and Nolte, T., "Brief Announcement: Virtual Stationary Automata for Mobile Networks", *Proceedings of the 24th Annual ACM Symposium on Principles of Distributed Computing (PODC)*, pp. 323, 2005.

8. Dolev, S., Gilbert, S., Lynch, N., Schiller, E., Shvartsman, A., and Welch, J., "Virtual Mobile Nodes for Mobile Ad Hoc Networks", *International Conference on Principles of Distributed Computing (DISC)*, pp. 230-244, 2004.

9. Dolev, S., Gilbert, S., Lynch, N., Shvartsman, A., Welch, J., "GeoQuorums: Implementing Atomic Memory in Ad Hoc Networks", *17th International Conference on Principles of Distributed Computing (DISC)*, Springer-Verlag LNCS:2848, pp. 306-320, 2003. Also to appear in *Distributed Computing*.

10. Dolev, S., Herman, T., and Lahiani, L., "Polygonal Broadcast, Secret Maturity and the Firing Sensors", *Third International Conference on Fun with Algorithms (FUN)*, pp. 41-52, May 2004. Also to appear in *Ad Hoc Networks Journal*, Elseiver.

11. Dolev, S., Israeli, A., and Moran, S., "Self-Stabilization of Dynamic Systems Assuming only Read/Write Atomicity", *Proceeding of the ACM Symposium on the Principles of Distributed Computing (PODC 90)*, pp. 103-117. Also in *Distributed Computing* 7(1): 3-16 (1993).

12. Dolev, S., Pradhan, D.K., and Welch, J.L., "Modified Tree Structure for Location Management in Mobile Environments", *Computer Communications*, Special issue on mobile computing, Vol. 19, No. 4, pp. 335-345, April 1996. Also INFOCOM 1995, Vol. 2, pp. 530-537, 1995.

13. Dolev, S. and Welch, J.L.,"Crash Resilient Communication in Dynamic Networks", *IEEE Transactions on Computers*, Vol. 46, No. 1, pp.14-26, January 1997.

14. Haas, Z.J. and Liang, B., "Ad Hoc Mobility Management With Uniform Quorum Systems", *IEEE/ACM Trans. on Networking*, Vol. 7, No. 2, pp. 228-240, April 1999.

15. Hubaux, J.P., LeBoudec, J.Y., Giordano, S., and Hamdi, M., "The Terminodes Project: Towards Mobile Ad-Hoc WAN", *Proceedings of MOMUC*, pp. 124-128, 1999.

16. Imielinski, T., and Badrinath, B.R., "Mobile wireless computing: challenges in data management", *Communications of the ACM*, Vol. 37, Issue 10, pp. 18-28, 1994.

17. Karp, B. and Kung, H. T., "GPSR: Greedy Perimeter Stateless Routing for Wireless Networks", *Proceedings of the 6th Annual International Conference on Mobile Computing and Networking*, pp. 243-254, SCM Press, 2000.

18. Kaynar, D., Lynch, N., Segala, R., and Vaandrager, F., "The Theory of Timed I/O Automata", Technical Report MIT-LCS-TR-917a, MIT LCS, 2004.

19. Kuhn, F., Wattenhofer, R., Zhang, Y., Zollinger, A., "Geometric Ad-Hoc Routing: Of Theory and Practice", *Proceedings of the 22nd Annual ACM Symposium on Principles of Distributed Computing (PODC)*, pp. 63-72, 2003.

20. Kuhn, F., Wattenhofer, R., and Zollinger, A., "Asymptotically Optimal Geometric Mobile Ad-Hoc routing", *Proceedings of the 6th International Workshop on Discrete Algorithms and Methods for Mobile Computing and Communications (Dial-M)*, pp. 24-33, ACM Press, 2002.

21. Li, J., Jannotti, J., De Couto, D.S.J., Karger, D.R., and Morris, R., "A Scalable Location Service for Geographic Ad Hoc Routing", *Proceedings of Mobicom*, pp. 120-130, 2000.

22. Malkhi, D., Reiter, M., and Wright, R., "Probabilistic Quorum Systems", *Proceeding of the 16th Annual ACM Symposium on the Principles of Distributed Computing (PODC 97)*, pp. 267-273, Santa Barbara, CA, August 1997.

23. Nath, B., Niculescu, D., "Routing on a curve", *ACM SIGCOMM Computer Communication Review*, pp. 155-160, 2003.

24. Navas, J.C., Imielinski, T., "Geocast- geographic addressing and routing", *Proceedings of the 3rd MobiCom*, pp. 66-76, 1997.

25. Ratnasamy, S., Karp, B., Yin, L., Yu, F., Estrin, D., Govindan, R., and Shenker, S., "GHT: A Geographic Hash Table for Data-Centric Storage", *First ACM International Workshop on Wireless Sensor Networks and Applications*, pp. 78-87, 2002.

Memory Management for Self-stabilizing Operating Systems[*]
(Extended Abstract)

Shlomi Dolev[1] and Reuven Yagel[1,2]

[1] Department of Computer Science,
Ben-Gurion University of the Negev, Beer-Sheva, 84105, Israel
{dolev, yagel}@cs.bgu.ac.il
[2] Rafael 3M, POB 2205, Haifa, Israel

Abstract. This work presents several approaches for designing the memory management component of self-stabilizing operating systems. We state the requirements which a memory manager should satisfy. One requirement is *eventual memory hierarchy consistency* among different copies of data residing in different (level of) memory devices e.g., RAM and disk. Another requirement is *stabilization preserving* where the memory manager ensures that every process that is proven to stabilize independently, also stabilizes under the (self-stabilizing scheduler and the) memory manager operation. Three memory managers that satisfy the above requirements are presented. The first allocates the entire physical memory to a single process in every given point of time, the second uses fixed partition of the memory among processes, and the last uses memory leases for dynamic memory allocations.

1 Introduction

This work presents new directions for building self-stabilizing memory management as a component of a self-stabilizing operating system kernel. A system is *self-stabilizing* [7,8] if it can be started in any possible state and converge to a desired behavior. A *state* of a system is an assignment of arbitrary values to the systems variables. The usefulness of such a system in critical and remote systems cannot be over estimated. Entire years of work maybe lost when the operating system of an expensive complicated device e.g., a spaceship, may reach an arbitrary state due to say, soft errors (e.g., [14]), and be lost forever.

An operating system kernel usually contains the basic mechanisms for managing the hardware resources. The classical Von-Neumann machine includes a processor, a memory device and external *i/o* devices. In this architecture memory management is an important task of the kernel of the operating system. Our memory management uses the primitive building blocks from [10] where simple self-stabilizing process schedulers are presented.

[*] Partially supported by Rafael, Microsoft, IBM, NSF, Intel, Deutsche Telekom, Rita Altura Trust Chair in Computer Sciences and Lynn and William Frankel Center for Computer Sciences.

T. Herman and S. Tixeuil (Eds.): SSS 2005, LNCS 3764, pp. 113–127, 2005.
© Springer-Verlag Berlin Heidelberg 2005

Management of memory influenced the development of computer architecture and operating systems [2]. Various memory organization schemes and appropriate requirements have been suggested during the years. Here we add two important requirements called the *eventual memory hierarchy consistency* requirement and the *stabilization preserving* requirement. Since memory hierarchies and caching are key ideas in memory management, the memory manger must eventually provide consistency of the various memory levels. Secondly, once stabilization is proven for a process, the fact that process and scope switching occurs and memory is actually shared with other processes, will not damage the stabilization property of the process. These requirements are an addition to the usual efficiency concerns which operating systems must address.

We present three basic design solutions that, roughly speaking, follow the evolution of memory management techniques. The first approach allocates the whole available memory to the running process, thus ensuring exclusion of memory access. This method is simple but not efficient, since each process switch requires expensive disk operations. The second solution partitions the memory among several running processes, exclusive access is achieved through segmentation and stabilization of the segment partitioning algorithm. Both solutions constrain program referencing to addresses in the physical memory only (or even in the partition size) and allow only static use of memory. Then we present lease based dynamic schemes, where the application must renew memory leases in order to ensure the correct operation of a self-stabilizing garbage collector.

Demonstration implementations (which appear in [11]) using the Intel Pentium processor architecture [13] were composed. The implementations are written in assembly language, and are directly assembled into the processor's opcode (in our experiments we have used the NASM open-source assembler [16]). The methodology we used for building such critical systems is to examine, with extra care, every instruction. This is achieved by writing the code directly according to the machine semantics (not relying on current compilers to preserve our requirements), together with line by line examination. This style is sometimes tedious, but is essential to demonstrate the way one should ensure the correctness of a program from any arbitrary initial state. Such a method is specially important when dealing with such a basic component as an operating system kernel. Higher level components and applications can then be composed in ways discussed in [4]. The Intel Pentium processor contains various mechanisms which support robust design of memory management like segmentation, paging and ring protection. However, the complexity of the processor (partially due to previous processors compatibility requirements) carries a risk of the entering into undesirable states, thereby causing undesirable execution. Our proof and prototype show that it is possible to design a self-stabilizing memory manager that preserves the stabilization of the running processes which is an important building block of an infrastructure for industrial self-stabilizing systems.

Previous Work: Extensive theoretical research has been done toward self-stabilizing systems [7,8,21] and recovery-oriented/autonomic-computing/self-repair, e.g., [12,17,22]. Fault tolerance properties of operating systems (e.g., [19]), including the memory management layer were extensively studied as well. For example in [1] important operating system memory regions are copied into a special area for fast recovery. The design of the Multics operating system pioneered issues of data protection and sharing, see [6] and [18]. However, none of the above suggest a design for an operating system, and particularly memory management that can automatically recover from an arbitrary state (that may be reached after a combination of unexpected faults).

Paper Organization: In the next section we define the system settings and requirements. The three solutions: total swapping, fixed partition and dynamic memory allocation, are presented in Section 3, Section 4 and Section 5, respectively. Concluding remarks appear in Section 6.

2   System Settings, Assumptions and Requirements

We start with a brief set of definitions related to states and state transitions (see [9,10] for more details). The *system* is modeled by a tuple ⟨*processor, memory, i/o connectors*⟩. The *processor* (or microprocessor) is defined by an operation manual, e.g., Pentium [13]. The processor *state* is defined by the contents of its internal memory (registers).

The *registers* includes a *program counter* (*pc*) register and a *processor status word* (*psw*) register, which determines the current mode of operation. In particular, the psw contains a bit indicating whether interrupts are enabled. A *clock tick* triggers the microprocessor to *execute a processor step* $ps_j = (s, i, s', o)$, where the inputs i and the current state of the processor s are used to define the next processor state s' and the outputs o. The *inputs and outputs* of the processor are the values of its *i/o connectors* whenever a clock tick occurs. The processor uses the i/o connectors values to communicate with other devices, mainly with the memory via its data lines. In fact the processor can be viewed as a transition function defined by, e.g., [13]. A *processor execution* $PE = ps_1, ps_2, \cdots$ is a sequence of processor steps such that for every two successive steps in PE, $ps_j = (s, i, s', o)$ and $ps_{j+1} = (\bar{s}, \bar{i}, \bar{s}', \bar{o})$ it holds that $s' = \bar{s}$.

The *interrupt connector* which is connected to external i/o devices, is used to signal the processor for (urgent) service requests. The NMI (Non-Maskable Interrupt) *connector* role is similar to the interrupt connector, except that the NMI request is not masked by the interrupt flag. In the Pentium, whenever one NMI is handled, other NMI's are ignored until an `iret` operation is executed.

The *memory* is composed of various devices (Figure 1 presents some common *memory hierarchy*). Here we consider *main memory* and *secondary storage*. The main memory is composed of ROM and RAM components. Read-only parts are assumed non-volatile. The secondary storage is also organized as a combination of read-only parts, such as CD-ROM and other disks. The read-only requirement is a must for ensuring correctness of the code. Otherwise, the Byzantine fault model [15] must be assumed. Processor caches, at least in the current Pentium design can not be controlled directly by the operating system, and therefore are not considered here.

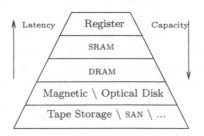

Fig. 1. A Common Memory Hierarchy

The *i/o state* is the value of the *connectors* connecting to peripheral devices. We assume that any information stored in the interface cards for these devices, is also part of the memory.

A *system configuration* is a processor state and the content of the system memory. A *system execution* $E = (c_1, a_1, c_2, a_2, ...)$ is a sequence of alternating system configurations and system steps. A system step consists of a processor step together with the effect of the step on the memory (and other non stateless devices, if they exist). Note that the entire execution can be defined by the first configuration (for achieving self-stabilization usually assumed arbitrary) and the external inputs at the clock ticks.

Additional Necessary and Sufficient Hardware Support: We assume that in every infinite processor execution, PE, the processor executes fetch-decode-execute infinitely often. Moreover, the processor executes a fetched command according to its specification where the state of the processor, when the first fetch starts is arbitrary. (Means for achieving such a behavior are presented in [9]).

We assume there is a *watchdog* device connected to the NMI connector which is guaranteed to periodically generate a signal every predefined time. Watchdog devices are standard devices used in fault-tolerant systems e.g., [5,10]. We have to design the watchdog to be self-stabilizing as well. The watchdog state is in fact a countdown register with a maximal value equal to the desired interval time. Starting from any state of the watchdog, a signal will be triggered within the desired interval time and no premature signal will be triggered thereafter. The watchdog guarantee execution of critical operating system code such as code refresh and consistency checks [10] as well as the memory management operations addressed in this work.

In order to guarantee that the processor will react to an NMI *trigger*, we suggest the addition of an internal countdown register or NMI *counter* as part of the processor architecture. This NMI counter will be decremented in every clock tick until it reaches zero. Whenever an NMI handler is executed (the processor can detect this according to a predefined program counter value), the NMI counter is raised to its maximal value (chosen to be a fixed value greater than the expected execution length of the NMI handler). The processor does not react to NMIs when the NMI counter does not contain zero. In addition, the `iret` operation assigns

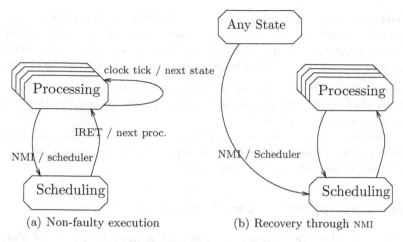

Fig. 2. System Transitions

zero to the NMI counter. Thus, we guarantee that NMIs will eventually be handled from any processor state. In addition, while one NMI is handled, all other NMI's will be masked. We say that a processor is in an NMI *state* whenever the NMI connector is set and the NMI counter contains 0, which means that the next operation to be executed is the first operation of the NMI handler procedure[1].

A read only memory should be used for storing fixed values. Specifically, the ROM will contain at least the interrupt table entry for the NMI and the NMI handler routine. This is needed in order to guarantee the execution of the NMI interrupt handler which in turn will regain consistency.

Figure 2(a) illustrates the legal execution of the system. The system is composed of various processes which are executing each in turn. Additionally, there is a scheduler which is part of the NMI handler. The scheduler established its own consistency and carries the process switch operation. It then validates the next process' state and sets the program counter so that the next chosen process will be executed. Due to a fault, the system may reach any possible state, as seen in Figure 2(b), but due to the NMI trigger design, eventually the scheduler code will be called and will establish the required behavior.

The Error Model: we assume that every bit of the system's variables might change following some transient fault (e.g. soft-error). We also assume that code portions are kept in read-only nonvolatile memories which can not be corrupted (say by means of hardwired ROM cheaps) and thus are not part of the system's state. We remark that a corruption of the code may lead to an arbitrary (Byzantine) behavior!

The memory manager requirements includes both the **consistency** and the **stabilization preserving** requirements:

---

[1] Note that the Pentium design has a similar mechanism that ensures that no NMI is executed immediately after an `sti` instruction.

Consistency: as the system executes, the memory manager keeps the memory hierarchy consistent (Analogously to the consistency requirement for non-stabilizing operating systems). Namely we have to show that the contents of say, the main memory and the disk are kept mutually consistent. **Stabilization**

Preserving: the fact that process and scope switching occurs, and the memory is actually shared with other processes, will not falsify the stabilization property of each process in the system.

A *self-stabilizing memory manager* is one that ensures that every infinite execution of the system has a suffix in which both the consistency and the stabilization preserving requirements hold.

3   Total Swapping — One Process at a Time

In the first solution the memory management is done by means of allocating (almost) all the available memory (RAM) to every process.

The settings for this solution are: N code portions, one for each process in the system, reside in a persistent read only secondary storage. The soft state of each process is repeatedly saved in the disk. The operating system includes a self-stabilizing scheduler which activates processes in a round robin fashion. Whenever a process is activated the process has all the memory for its operation (except the portion used by the scheduler). The scheduler actions include saving the state of the stopped process in the disk and loading the state of the new process whenever a process switch occurs.

The scheduler executes process switch whenever a fixed time elapses since the last process switch[2]. The processor state (register values) is saved in the stack. Note that we ensure that for every processor state, stack operations will not prevent the execution of the NMI handler, and the scheduler code will be started.

The implementation uses the Pentium processor in its real (16 bit) operation mode, thus paging and protection mechanisms are not used. This configuration may not be acceptable for modern desktop operating system but is more common in embedded systems and also serves as a simplified model to investigate the application of the self-stabilization paradigm to operating systems. The protected mode mechanisms might be used in satisfying the stabilization requirement, but once the processor exits this mode, there is no guarantee anymore. Thus, we assume the processor's mode is hardwired during the system execution so the mode flag is not part of the system's (soft) state. For now, the disk driver operations are assumed to be atomic and stateless (achieving this abstraction is left for future research).

The main drawback of this solution is of course the need to switch the whole process state in every context switch. This might not be acceptable for all systems.

---

[2] Note that a counter of clock interrupts may form a self-stabilizing mechanism for triggering process switch, the counter upper bound is achieved no matter what is the counter value when counting begins.

```
SWAP-PROCESS(PT, i)
 1   MEMORY-SAVE-PROCESSOR-STATE(PT, i)
 2   DISK-SAVE-PROCESS-STATE(i)
 3   i ← (i + 1) modulo N
 4   CD-ROM-LOAD-PROCESS-CODE(i)
 5   DISK-LOAD-PROCESS-STATE(i)
 6   MEMORY-LOAD-PROCESSOR-STATE(PT, i)
```

Fig. 3. Total Swapping Algorithm

The scheduler algorithm which appears in Figure 3 carries the memory management task. The algorithm uses an array in memory that is used for the process table denoted by PT. PT keeps the entire processor state (the register values of the processor) for each running process p_i and i acts as a process pointer. Recall that N is the (fixed) number of processes in the system. The scheduler saves the state of the running process to the process table (line 1), and disk (line 2), then increments the process counter (line 3), and loads the next process to be activated. The loading is carried by reloading the process code from the read-only storage (line 4), process state from disk (line 5) and processor state from PT in memory (line 6). The correctness of the algorithm is based on the fact that the various procedures that save and load data depend only on the value of i (that represents p_i) which by itself is bounded by the number of processes in the system.

4   Fixed Partition — Multiple Residing Processes

In this section we follow a better memory utilization which allows the partitioning of the memory among several processes. This reduces the number of accesses to disk, thereby improving system performance. Still, when one partition is free the processes in other partitions can not use this free memory. So although the second design does not require the system to repeatedly transfer the entire data between memory levels, the second design still constrains the size of the applications.

The decision concerning the set of processes that should be activated depends on outside environmental inputs. This is needed since the main advantage of this solution is rescheduling processes without costly disk operations. However, since a priority mechanism is not used, all memory frames are occupied if N > M (M is the number of partitions) so every context switch causes costly disk operations, and the main advantage is lost. The process table is a natural candidate to hold the additional activity status for each process. The entity which generates this information as input to the memory manager is responsible for the correctness and stability of this value.

The settings for this solution are: the code of N programs reside in a persistent read only secondary storage. The operating system consists of (memory hardwired) resident NMI handler and a scheduler process. The memory for the

Process Table:

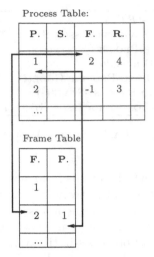

Fig. 4. Fixed Partition Consistency Check

applications is partitioned into M fixed equal length memory segments which are called frames. Thus, programs are constrained to use the size of a frame. The operating system uses a frame table FT which describes the currently residing process in each memory frame. In addition there is a process table PT. The i'th entry of PT consists of: (a) the last processor state of p_i, for uploading in case the process should be scheduled, (b) the frame number (address in RAM) used by p_i (NIL if not present), (c) refresh down counter, when the value of the counter is zero, and p_i is rescheduled, the code of p_i is reloaded from CD-ROM to make sure it is not corrupted. The remaining state of the processes is kept on a disk. The locations on disk, and CD-ROM, are calculated from the process identifier i.

Upon the periodic NMI trigger, the processor execution context (register values) is saved to the stack and execution of the scheduler code is started. The scheduler saves the processor state of the interrupted process to PT, selects the next ready process, and then carries out the memory management actions necessary for executing this process. The pseudo code for the algorithm appears in Figure 5. In case the next process is not present in memory or there is an inconsistency between the process and frame tables (line 1), a new frame is chosen (line 2) and the currently residing process is saved to disk (line 3). The refresh counter is decreased for every activation of a process (line 4). In case this value equals zero (line 5), the new process' code is loaded from CD-ROM (line 6).

The algorithm **Find-Frame** searches the frame table for a free frame. In case all frames are used, some frame is chosen for replacement. First the frame currently pointed to by this process' entry is validated to be in range (line 1). Next a search over FT starts from the pointed frame's successor (line 2-4) until an empty frame is found or the whole table is searched. Even if due to a fault, say an error in the program counter which causes bypassing of lines 1 and 2 which calculate the loop limit value, the execution will eventually bypass this loop. First, the size of the field used for storing the frame number in PT can be

```
SELECT-NEXT-PROCESS-AND-FRAME(PT, FT, i)
1   if frame[PT[i]] = NIL or FT[frame[PT[i]]] ≠ i
2     then nf ← FIND-FRAME(PT, FT, i)
3         SWAP-PROCESS(PT, FT, i, nf)
4   decrease refresh[PT[i]]
5   if refresh[PT[i]] = 0
6     then CD-ROM-LOAD-PROCESS-CODE(i, PT)


FIND-FRAME(PT, FT, i)
1   frame[PT[i]] ← frame[PT[i]] modulo M
2   nf ← (frame[PT[i]] + 1) modulo M
3   while nf ≠ frame[PT[i]] and FT[nf] ≠ NIL
4   do nf ← (nf + 1) modulo M
5   return nf


SWAP-PROCESS(PT, FT, i, nf)
1   if FT[nf] ≠ NIL
2     then DISK-SAVE-PROCESS-STATE(FT[nf], nf)
3         frame[PT[FT[nf]]] ← NIL
4   FT[nf] ← i
5   frame[PT[i]] ← nf
6   DISK-LOAD-PROCESS-STATE(i, nf)
7   refresh[PT[i]] ← 1  ▷ Causes code to be loaded.
```

Fig. 5. Fixed Partition Algorithm

bounded by M thus, increments of nf (line 4), must reach the loop limit value. Secondly, the system is designed as that eventually an NMI will be triggered, and the code will be re-executed from the first line.

The Swap-Process algorithm checks if there is a swapped out process due to loading the new one (line 1), it saves to disk the state of this process (line 2), and marks its frame entry in PT as NIL (line 3). The entries of FT and PT are updated with the new assignment (lines 4-5) and the state of the new process is loaded to main memory (line 6). Finally, the code refresh bit is set to one (line 7), which will cause the main procedure to decrement it further to zero, and thereafter load the new process' code.

After the execution of the above algorithm the scheduler continues with the swap, by loading the processor state of the new process from PT.

The correctness of the algorithm is based on the ongoing consistency checks of FT and PT. Figure 4 demonstrates the consistency check made when assigning a frame to a process. Frame 1 is assigned to p_2, thus 1 is entered in the 2nd entry of FT. Additionally, the frame field in the entry of p_2 in PT (column marked with F) is marked with the new frame number. The arrow lines demonstrate the exclusive ownership to the selected frame, for every scheduled process. Additionally the refresh field (column marked with R) shows the refresh counter which ensures periodically refreshing of the code for the processes. (The S column represent the processor state for each process).

We remark that the fixed partition restriction of the above solution can be relaxed. Applications can be of variable size. The partition of main memory is not fixed and a record of occupied space is maintained. Whenever a process is about to be scheduled, the record is searched for a big enough space and the application is loaded there. To ensure fulfillment of our requirements this record must be kept consistent with the process table. Additional care, using standard techniques, must be taken to address fragmentation of main memory and avoid process starvation. The next section addresses variable memory sizes by means of dynamic allocations.

5   Dynamic Allocation

Further enhancement of memory usage would be to remove the static allocation nature of the programs and allow them to allocate memory in a malloc/free style. Of course the operating system must keep track of memory usage according to some policy. To ensure that there is no memory that is marked as used, due to some fault, when it is in fact unused, a leasing mechanism is suggested where applications must extend their lease from time to time. This way, memory that is not in use will eventually become free (assuming no malicious Byzantine behavior of processes). To be more precise, we would like to support a dynamic memory allocation scheme where additional memory beyond the fixed memory required for the code and the static variables may be on-demand allocated. To support the management of the additional memory allocations in a self-stabilizing fashion, a *lease* mechanism which limits the allocation of a new memory portion for the use of a process either by time, or the number of steps the process performed since the allocation, is used.

A memory manager process is responsible for allocating, and for memory garbage collection. The dynamic memory manager uses bookkeeping to manage the dynamic memory allocations. Allocations are tracked using a table that holds for each allocation unit, the number of the owner process and the remaining lease period. The dynamic memory manager repeatedly checks for memory portions allocated to a process for which the lease expired, and returns every such memory portion to the available memory pool for reallocation. The lease policy leaves the responsibility for refreshing the leases to the programmer of the processes, and at the same time allows simple and stabilizing dynamic memory management. We can argue that starting in an arbitrary configuration, where the dynamic memory is allocated randomly to processes, eventually no memory will be allocated to a process which did not (recently) requested memory. Also, assuming no malicious process behavior, in every infinite execution, repeated allocation requests will be infinitely often respected. Up until this solution, programs were totally ignorant of operating system services. Here the operating system exposes an application programming interface for memory requests. Thus programs now should also deal with temporary rejections of requests while the operating system satisfies that eventually all legal requests will be respected.

Figure 6 presents the algorithms which implement the interface which programs can call in order to use dynamic memory. The MM-Alloc procedure is used for requesting memory allocation. With MM-ExtendLease a lease extension is possible. The applications are restricted to use the allocated memory through a special segment selector register, the procedure MM-NextSegment is the only way of accessing the different segments allocated to an application. At last, applications can release their allocations with MM-Free. The operating system contains a specialized process called _MM-Validator (the leading underscore marks a procedure internally called by the operating system) that validates the system's state concerning dynamic allocation. The algorithm is presented in Figure 7. Additionally, we use several simple service procedures which are presented in Figure 8.

Next we describe how the algorithms work. The MM-Alloc algorithm inputs are the number of allocations units (segments) required by the process and expi-

---

MM-ALLOC($quantity, expiration$)
1 **if** $seg(PT[currentProcess]) \neq$ NIL
2   **then return**
3 **if** $quantity <= freeSegments$
4   **then** _MM-ASSIGN($currentProcess, quantity, expiration$)
5   _MM-ENQUE($currentProcess, quantity, expiration$)

MM-EXTENDLEASE($newExpiration$)
1 $s \leftarrow seg(PT[currentProcess])$
2 **if** $owner(ST[s]) = currentProcess$
3   **then** $lease(ST[s]) \leftarrow newExpiration$

MM-NEXTSEGMENT()
1 $currentSegment \leftarrow seg(PT[currentProcess])$
2 **if** $currentSegment \neq$ NIL
3   **then for** **each** s **in** $\{(currentSegment + 1)$ modulo $NUM\_SEG..$
4      $(currentSegment - 1)$ modulo $NUM\_SEG\}$
5   **do if** $owner(ST[s]) = currentProcess$
6   **then** $seg(PT[currentProcess]) \leftarrow s$
7   **break**

MM-FREE()
1 $currentSegment \leftarrow seg(PT[currentProcess])$
2 MM-NEXTSEGEMNT($currentProcess$)
3 **if** $currentSegment \neq$ NIL
4   **then if** $currentSegment = seg(PT[currentProcess])$
5   **then** $seg(PT[currentProcess]) \leftarrow$ NIL
6   **if** $owner(ST[currentSegment]) = currentProcess$
7   **then** $owner(ST[currentSegment]) \leftarrow NIL$
8          $freeSegments \leftarrow freeSegments + 1$

Fig. 6. Dynamic Allocation Services

```
_MM-VALIDATION()
 1    for  each p in {0..NUM_PROC − 1}
 2    do usingDynamic[p] ← false
 3    freeSegments ← 0
 4    for  each s in {0..NUM_SEG − 1}
 5    do p ← owner(ST[s])
 6        if p ≠ NIL
 7          then lease(ST[s]) :← lease(ST[s]) − 1
 8              if lease(ST[s]) = 0
 9                then owner(ST[s]) ← NIL
10                else  usingDynamic[p] ← true
11        if owner(ST[s]) = NIL
12          then freeSegments ← freeSegments + 1
13    for  each p in {0..NUM_PROC − 1}
14    do if usingDynamic[p] = false
15          then seg(PT[p]) ← NIL
16    q ← top(Q)
17    if q ≠ NIL and quantity(q) <= freeSegments
18      then _MM-DEQUEUE()
19          _MM-ASSIGN(process(q), quantity(q), expiration(q))
```

Fig. 7. Dynamic Allocation Validation

ration period needed. The expiration is the number of activations of the process
for which the allocation will be valid, and this number is of course bounded(at
least) by the parameter length. After this period the validator will reclaim those
segments and mark them as free. In line 1 of the algorithm, the *dynamic selector*
(which in the implementation is realized in a specific processor segment register)
is checked to hold an empty address. If this is not the case it means that this
process is already using dynamic memory and the request is rejected in line 2
(for simplicity reasons we allow only one allocation at a time). In line 3 we check
whether there's enough allocation units for this request through a global variable that holds this count. We assign the requested quantity to the requesting
process with the _MM-Assign procedure which simply go over all the segments
in the segment table ST and mark the needed quantity as occupied. This procedure also updates the free segment variable (line 5), and sets the dynamic
selector value with the address of one of the allocated segments (line 9). In case
not enough segments are available the request is queued through the procedure
_MM-Enqueue which first checks that there isn't already a queue entry for this
process, and then finds an empty slot to enqueue the request. The queue size is
equal to the process number, thus exactly one slot for each process is reserved.

The MM-ExtendLease procedure carries it's task by validating that the requested segment is own by the requesting process and enlarge the lease counter
value. Again, this operation is allowed assuming there isn't a malicious behavior
of processes. A different approach might be enabling the extension just in cases
where the queue is empty, thus preventing a repeated extension of a lease by
a particular process. As mentioned before, a process can access the allocated

```
_MM-Assign(process, quantity, expiration)
1   for  each s in {0..NUM_SEGMENTS − 1}
2   do if owner(ST[s]) = NIL
3         then owner(ST[s]) ← process
4              lease(ST[s]) ← expiration
5              freeSegments ← freeSegments − 1
6              quantity ← quantity − 1
7              if quantity = 0
8                 then break
9   seg(PT[process]) ← s


_MM-Enqueu(process, quantity, expiration)
1   for  each p in {0..NUM_PROC − 1}
2   do if process(Q[p]) = process
3         then return
4   for  each p in {0..NUM_PROC − 1}
5   do if process(Q[p]) = NIL
6         then process(Q[p]) ← process
7              quantity(Q[p]) ← quantity
8              expiration(Q[p]) ← expiration
9              break


_MM-Dequeue()
1   for  each p in {0..NUM_PROC − 2}
2   do Q[p] ← Q[p + 1]
3   q[NUM_PROC − 1] ← NIL
```

Fig. 8. Dynamic Allocation Service Procedures

segment through a selector which it can not change. In order to move between allocated segments, the process calls MM-NextSegment which looks in the segment table for all other segments and if another one is also occupied by the calling process, it's number is returned in the selector (line 6). The MM-Free procedure carries it's task by first updating the selector with another segment address (lines 1-2) then it checks if this selector is the only one owned by this process, which means that the selector should be cleared too (line 5). In lines 6-8 the released segment is checked to be owned by the process and then marked as free. The global counter of free segments is updated respectively.

The garbage collector algorithm (_MM-Validation) works as follow. In lines 1-2 it marks all processes as not using dynamic memory, this will allow initialization of the dynamic selector for processes that are incorrectly marked as already using dynamic memory. Thus subsequently such a process will be able to request (and get!) allocations. In line 3 the global counter for free segments is reset, thus only really used segments will be counted (in lines 11-12). The loop of lines 4-12 iterates over all segments and decreases the lease for each of them. In case a lease reaches zero, the segment is marked free (line 9). Otherwise we mark the process as using dynamic memory (line 10). Lines 13-15 reset the dynamic selector for processes that do not currently use dynamic memory. Then we check the queue top and in case the first waiting process can be satisfied with the current free segments, it is deleted from the queue (line 18) and assigned with the free segments (line 19). The _MM-Dequeue procedure just moves all the entries in the array implementing the queue one cell towards the queue top, and marks the last entry as free.

Note that the memory manager can protect itself from a greedy process by designing the MM-ExtendLease procedure such that extensions are allowed only when the queue is empty. This way when there is a pending request, a process that holds memory will eventually loose it. Thus, from any system state eventually, enough segments will be freed for the top queue process and thereafter it will be granted with it's request. So eventually every request will be respected.

6   Concluding Remarks

We have presented three classes of self-stabilizing memory management schemes, total swapping, fixed partition and dynamic memory allocation.

In order to also support virtual addressing, the page tables have to be kept consistent, which will allow correct address translation made by the MMU (memory management unit). The page tables are usually also cached in a special memory (TLB) so consistency must also be examined for this structure. (To date, the Pentium's TLB is not accessible by the operating system).

We have run the presented system using the BOCHS [3] simulator. During some executions we totally changed the contents of the RAM, and observed that stabilization is achieved. Namely, the processor eventually continues to execute the correct code of the operating system. At last we believe that self-stabilization operating systems will be part of every critical computing system in the near future. Proof sketches and prototype implementations, including machine code, can be found in [11] and [20].

References

1. M. Baker, M. Sullivan. "The Recovery Box: Using Fast Recovery to Provide High Availability in the UNIX Environment", *Proceedings of the Summer 1992 USENIX Conference*, Texas, June 1992
2. L. A. Belady, R. P. Parmelee, C. A. Scalzi. "The IBM History of Memory Management Technology", *IBM Journal of Research and Development 25(5)*, pp. 491-504, 1981.
3. Bochs IA-32 Emulator Project. http://bochs.sourceforge.net/
4. O. Brukman, S. Dolev, H. Kolodner. "Self-Stabilizing Autonomic Recoverer for Eventual Byzantine Software", *Proceedings of IEEE International Conference on Software-Science Technology & Engineering*, (SwSTE03), Israel, 2003.
5. M. Castro, B. Liskov. "Proactive Recovery in a Byzantine-Fault-Tolerant System", *Proceedings of the Fourth Symposium on Operating Systems Design and Implementation*, pp. 273-288, San Diego, CA, October 2000.

6. R. C. Daley , J. B. Dennis. "Virtual memory, processes, and sharing in Multics", *Proceedings of the first ACM symposium on Operating System Principles*, p.12.1-12.8, January 1967, Gatlinburg, TN.
7. E. W. Dijkstra. "Self-Stabilizing Systems in Spite of Distributed Control," *Communications of the ACM,* Vol. 17, No. 11, pp. 643-644, 1974.
8. S. Dolev. *Self-Stabilization*, The MIT Press, Cambridge, 2000.
9. S. Dolev, Y. Haviv, "Self-Stabilizing Soft Error Resilient Microprocessor" *17th International Conference on Architecture of Computing Systems*, LNCS:2981, (ARCS04), 2004. Also to appear in *IEEE Transaction on computers.*
10. S. Dolev, R. Yagel. "Toward Self-Stabilizing Operating Systems", *Proceedings of the 15th International Conference on Database and Expert Systems Applications, 2nd International Workshop on Self-Adaptive and Autonomic Computing Systems* (SAACS04,DEXA), pp. 684-688, Zaragoza, Spain, August 2004.
11. S. Dolev and R. Yagel. "Memory Management for Self-Stabilizing Operating Systems". Technical report, #05-05, Computer Science, Ben-Gurion University, Beer-Sheva, Israel, June 2005.
12. IBM. Autonomic computing initiative, http://www.research.ibm.com/autonomic, 2001.
13. Intel Corporation. "The IA-32 Intel Architecture Software Developer's Manual", http://developer.intel.com/design/pentium4 /documentation.htm, 2005.
14. M. Kistler, P. Shivakumar, L. Alvisi, D. Burger, and S. Keckler. "Modeling the effect of technology trends on the soft error rate of combinational logic". In *ICDSN*, volume 72 of *LNCS*, pages 216–226, 2002.
15. L. Lamport, R. Shostak, and M. Pease. "The Byzantine Generals Problem", *ACM Trans. on Programming Languages and Systems*, Vol. 4, No. 3, pp. 382-401, 1982.
16. The Netwide Assembler. http://nasm.sourceforge.net.
17. D. Patterson, A. Brown, P. Broadwell, G. Candea, M. Chen, J. Cutler, P. Enriquez, A. Fox, E. Kiciman, M. Merzbacher, D. Oppenheimer, N. Sastry, W. Tetzlaff, J. Traupman, N. Treuhaft. "Recovery Oriented Computing(ROC): Motivation, definition, techniques and case studies", UC Berkeley Computer Science Technical Report UCB/CSD-02-1175, Berkeley, CA, March 2002.
18. Jerome H. Saltzer. "Protection and the control of information sharing in multics", *Communications of the ACM*, v.17 n.7, p.388-402, July 1974.
19. M. M. Swift, B. N. Bershad, H. M. Levy. "Improving the reliability of commodity operating systems", *Proceedings of the 19th ACM Symposium on Operating Systems Principles - SOSP'03*, Bolton Landing, NY, October 2003.
20. http://www.cs.bgu.ac.il/~yagel/sos
21. http://www.selfstabilization.org
22. Sun Microsystems, Inc., "Predictive Self-Healing in the Solaris™10 Operating System", White paper http://www.sun.com/software/whitepapers /solaris10/self_healing.pdf, September 2004.

Code Stabilization

Felix C. Freiling[1] and Sukumar Ghosh[2,*]

[1] Laboratory for Dependable Distributed Systems,
RWTH Aachen University, Germany
[2] The University of Iowa, Iowa City, USA

Abstract. Dijkstra's concept of self-stabilization assumes that faults can only affect the variables of a program. We study the notion of self-stabilization if faults can also affect (i.e., augment) the program code of a system. A *code stabilizing* system automatically recovers from (almost) arbitrary perturbations of its program code. We prove some lower bounds for code stabilizing systems and argue that code stabilization has many resemblances to the area of integrity management in the domain of security.

1 Introduction

The concept of self-stabilization by Dijkstra [4] describes the fact that a system will eventually return to good behavior when starting from an arbitrary state. The arbitrary state was used as a tool to model the effects of transient faults that changed the values of variables stored in volatile memory. The program code however was always assumed to remain unchanged.

Interestingly, the assumption that the program code is not affected by faults has remained unchallenged for a long time. Usually it is argued that the program code resides in non-volatile read-only memory and can therefore be assumed to remain constant. This is however only true for small and specialized systems (like embedded systems) today. Most software which runs on PCs is stored on hard disks which—while being non-volatile—still can be subject to changes through faults. Moreover, the threats from unauthorized code alterations through malicious software (like worms or viruses) are steadily increasing. Hence we feel that it is time to investigate the notion of self-stabilization where faults can also affect the code of the program.

In this paper we ask the question: How and when can self-stabilizing systems recover not only from perturbations of the data but also from perturbations of the program code? To answer this question we first give a formal definition of what we call *code stabilization*. In analogy to self-stabilization (which we in contrast call *data stabilization*) we define code stabilization to mean eventual recovery of the program code to a "legal state". Our definition is a clean extension of Dijkstra's definition: If the legal state of the code is a self-stabilizing algorithm, then code stabilization implies also data stabilization.

---

* Work by Sukumar Ghosh was supported in part by a fellowship from Alexander von Humboldt Foundation while visiting RWTH Aachen University.

T. Herman and S. Tixeuil (Eds.): SSS 2005, LNCS 3764, pp. 128–139, 2005.

We further investigate the amount of perturbation tolerable in code stabilization and prove that code stabilization is impossible if the entire code space can be perturbed. Hence, a minimal nucleus of unaltered code space must always remain. This is in clear contrast to self-stabilization where faults could affect all the variables. We show that this minimal nucleus must have a size in the order of the entire program. This result implies that code stabilization is a very costly concept. However, in a distributed system it is possible to reduce the space requirement of this nucleus to about the size of the code which is stored in only *one* process.

Finally, we relate our findings to observations made in the area of security. We discuss the area of software integrity management and argue that the concept of code stabilization underlies many practical methods used in this area.

In summary, we provide the following contributions in this paper:

- We extend the definition of self-stabilization to code perturbations.
- We prove some lower bounds for this type of stabilization.
- We relate the new type of stabilization to practical methods from the area of security.

To the best of our knowledge, the investigation of code perturbations in the context of self-stabilization is novel. In can be seen as standing in a line of research which considers stabilization as a useful abstraction in the area of security (see for example work by Gouda [8]).

The paper is structured as follows: In Section 2 we present the system model and the definition of code stabilization. In Section 3 we consider code stabilization in the context of local (non-distributed) computations and subsequently extend our findings to distributed computations in Section 4. In Section 5 we relate code stabilization to concepts from the area of security. We conclude in Section 6.

2   Code Stabilization: Definition

In this section we present a definition of code stabilization and relate it to the concept of self-stabilization.

2.1   Systems, Programs, Code, and Data

A *system* is a general purpose computing machine that consists of an execution unit and memory. Intuitively the execution unit is a microprocessor and the memory is some form of data storage like RAM, ROM or external memory (e.g. hard disk). The memory of a system is separated into two parts: a *code part* and a *data part*. The code part stores the *program* which the system should execute. We are not concerned here with the way in which the program is encoded in memory except that we assume that it be executable. To execute the program, the system chooses the next instruction from the code part, loads it into the execution unit and executes the instruction, thereby possibly changing the data or code part of memory. Choice of the next program instruction can be done deterministically (e.g. by using an explicit program counter stored in the data part) or non-deterministically (like in the language of guarded commands [5]). Note that we allow a program to update also the code part of memory, i.e., we allow programs to be *self-modifying*.

The data part of memory can hold many different values. A particular assignment of values to the variables in the data part is called a *state* of the program. Let $\mathcal{D}$ denote the set of all possible states, i.e., all possible combinations of values which may be stored in the data part.

A representation of the program in memory is called the *code of the program* (or simply *code*). The code part of memory may hold many different codes (i.e., many different programs). Let $\mathcal{C}$ denote the set of all different codes that may be stored in the code part of memory.

2.2 Distributed Systems and Executions

The definitions above can be easily extended to cover aspects of (geographical) distribution. In a *distributed system*, the concept which we called a system above is called a *process*. Each process has its individual execution unit and memory. The code part of the memory of the distributed system is the union of all the code parts of the processes. Similarly, the data part of the memory of the distributed system is the union of the data part of the memories of all processes.

In a distributed system, processes need a method to communicate. Here we assume that processes communicate through shared memory, i.e., we assume that portions of the processes' memory can be accessed by other processes. The *topology* of the distributed system defines which process has access to the memory of which other process. The type of access can be distinguished by its type (read and/or write access) and the portion of the memory which it affects (code and/or data part of the memory). We will differentiate special types of access later in Section 4 where we consider distributed systems.

In general, for any system (be it distributed or not), the state of the entire memory can be expressed as an element $(c, d) \in \mathcal{C} \times \mathcal{D}$ where c identifies the code and d identifies the data state. An *execution* of a system is a sequence $\sigma = ((c_1, d_1), (c_2, d_2), \ldots)$ of such code/data state pairs for which holds that for all i, (c_{i+1}, d_{i+1}) results from executing the fetch-execute cycle described above on state (c_i, d_i).

2.3 Memory Perturbations

We adopt here the standard fault-assumption of self-stabilization, i.e., the type of faults we assume here are transient faults that can alter the state stored in memory. This is a very general fault assumption encompassing things like transient memory faults (e.g., bit flips), faults during data transmission, brown-outs due to transiently weak power supply, and effects of cosmic rays on memories. We rule out faults that permanently affect the execution unit. We model the effect of a fault by assuming that memory can spontaneously change into a certain "bad" state. Recovery of faults is achieved if the system by itself manages to return into a "good" state, as we explain shortly. Given some type of fault, the *fault span* [2] of that fault is the largest set of memory values which can be reached by faulty behavior.

2.4   Data Stabilization

We now recall the definition of self-stabilization [1,4]. To distinguish it from other forms of stabilization, we use the term *data stabilization* instead of self-stabilization.

Intuitively, data stabilization means that, given some set A of states, starting from a state in A, a system always eventually reaches a set of *legal* states. If it enters a legal state, then, as long as no faults occur, the next state of the system is also legal. In the following, let $D \subseteq \mathcal{D}$ denote the set of legal states.

Definition 1 (data stabilization). *Let $A \subseteq \mathcal{D}$ be a set of (data) states that includes D (i.e., $D \subseteq A$). A system* data stabilizes *from A to D if the following conditions hold for every execution $\sigma = ((c_1, d_1), (c_2, d_2), \ldots)$ of the system:*

- *(closure) for any (c_i, d_i), if $d_i \in D$ then $d_{i+1} \in D$.*
- *(convergence) for any (c_i, d_i) such that $d_i \in A$ there exists a $j \geq i$ such that $d_j \in D$.*

If $A = \mathcal{D} = \text{true}$ we omit mentioning the set A in the definition and simply say that a system data stabilizes. Data stabilization from $\mathcal{D} = A$ is equivalent to the notion of self-stabilization as introduced by Dijkstra [4].

2.5   Code Stabilization

We assume that the set of all codes $\mathcal{C}$ contains some programs that are *illegal* (they do not solve the problem for which the system was built by, e.g., going into an infinite loop). Conversely, we assume that there exists a set $C \subset \mathcal{C}$ of *legal* codes.[1]

We now define *code stabilization* in analogy to data stabilization.

Definition 2 (code stabilization). *Let $B \subseteq \mathcal{C}$ be a set of codes that includes C (i.e., $C \subseteq B$). A system* code stabilizes *from B to C if the following conditions hold for every execution $\sigma = ((c_1, d_1), (c_2, d_2), \ldots)$ of the system:*

- *(closure) for any (c_i, d_i), if $c_i \in C$ then $c_{i+1} \in C$.*
- *(convergence) for any (c_i, d_i) such that $c_i \in B$ there exists a $j \geq i$ such that $c_j \in C$.*

---

[1] Note that our definition allows the case where more than one code is legal, e.g., if there are different syntactic representations which are semantically equivalent.

We define *probabilistic code stabilization* (with probability p) as code stabilization where the convergence property holds only probabilistically (i.e., with probability p). Clearly, any system that is code stabilizing is also probabilistically code stabilizing, therefore probabilistic code stabilization is a weaker concept that code stabilization.

2.6   Relations Between Code and Data Stabilization

Code and data stabilization are defined independently, but they are not orthogonal since data stabilization relies on execution of correct code.

If faults are only allowed to perturb the data, then the code can be initialized to some chosen value. If the code happens to be data stabilizing algorithm, then we get the usual setting of self-stabilization. However, in the following assume that faults may happen in data *and* code. In this case, data stabilization depends on code stabilization.

Lemma 1. *For any system, if the set of legal codes C contains only data stabilizing algorithms, then the system data stabilizes only if it code stabilizes.*

Proof. For a contradiction, assume that the code does not stabilize to a legal code in C. This means that the code remains in a state which is not data stabilizing. Hence, the system does not data stabilize.   □

Note that Lemma 1 cannot be strengthened to an equivalence. To see this consider the case where a system does not code stabilize. In this case it may be stuck in an arbitrary program, e.g. one that executes an infinite loop. Clearly, such a system will not data stabilize. So data stabilization of some system is by no means sufficient for code stabilization of that system.

We define a system to be *completely stabilizing* if and only if it is code stabilizing and data stabilizing. A completely stabilizing system can tolerate a larger fault-span than a data stabilizing system because an additional level of perturbation is possible: corruptions of code space (see Figure 1). Code stabilization can therefore be explained as driving the fault-span past the border of the variable state space.

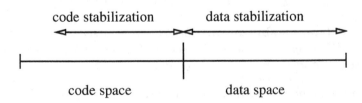

Fig. 1. Code stabilization: Moving the fault-span past to the left of the border between code and data

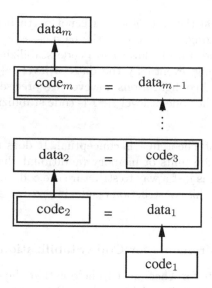

Fig. 2. Hierarchical construction of code stabilization. The code at level i is regarded as the data at level $i - 1$.

3   Code Stabilization for Local Computations

In this section we consider code stabilization in a non-distributed setting, i.e., where the system consists of only one execution unit (one process).

3.1   A Technique to Establish Code Stabilization

How can code stabilizing systems be constructed? One simple way to do this is to apply a layered approach and regard the code of one layer as the data of the next layer (see Fig. 2). This approach builds upon the ideas of *fair composition* of stabilizing protocols by Dolev, Israeli, and Moran [6]. If the system at one level i is not code stabilizing, we enlarge the system by adding another code part at level $i - 1$ which can modify the code at level i (the code of level i is the data of level $i - 1$). Now define the correct codes of level i as the set of legal states for code at level $i - 1$, then if the code of level $i - 1$ is data stabilizing, the code at level i is code stabilizing.

If the code at the lowest layer (layer 1) is not affected by faults, then we can show that the entire system is code stabilizing.

Theorem 1. *Given the system as constructed in Fig. 2 in which the code of every layer is a data stabilizing algorithm. If the code of level 1 is not perturbed by faults, then the system is code stabilizing.*

Proof. The proof is similar to the proof of self-stabilizing algorithms using the idea of a *convergence stair* as introduced by Gouda and Multari [9]. The proof is by induction over the levels.

Since we assume that the code of level 1 is not perturbed by faults, this code is trivially code stabilizing, which proves the base case.

Assume that all codes up to level i are code stabilizing. Since the code at level i is data stabilizing, eventually the data of level $i + 1$ will reach a legal configuration. The legal configurations however are precisely the set of codes of level $i + 1$. Therefore, the code at level $i + 1$ is code stabilizing, which proves the induction step.   □

The construction of Theorem 1 is conceptual. It does not necessarily mean that additional execution units or memory (additional "hardware") need to be added to the system. It is just a way to structure the code and memory space of a system. Note here that this construction results in programs which are inherently self-modifying.

3.2   Minimal Requirements for Code Stabilization

One central prerequisite for Theorem 1 to hold is that the code of level m is not perturbed by faults. This raises the question whether this assumption is really necessary, i.e., is there a way to construct code stabilizing systems such that the entire code part of the memory may be perturbed by faults? Unfortunately, this is not the case, as we now explain.

The code of a program holds some form of information about this program. We define the *size* of a code as the amount of information which it encodes. Taking into consideration all possible programs that generate the same output as the given program and choosing the shortest one, we get the minimal description of it. (If there exist more than one program of the same minimal length, select the lexicographically first among them.) The Kolmogorov complexity is the length of the minimal description, and this defines the size k of the program [12]. We now show that some minimal part of the code space must be safe from perturbations in order to achieve code stabilization.

Theorem 2. *In general, a code stabilizing system of size k requires an area of non-perturbation of size at least $O(k)$.*

Proof. The most unfavorable case is one where faults perturb the entire code and data space. Assuming that a code stabilizing system could recover from this case would mean that the information contained in the original program must be reconstructed from some source. However, if faults have perturbed the entire state space, it is impossible to recover the data from anywhere. In general, the amount of unperturbed storage corresponds directly to the size of the program (the amount of information which is expressed by the code). Hence, for a code of size k at least $O(k)$ storage needs to be maintained and this storage must be always unperturbed.   □

Note that Theorem 2 is rather general. It holds for any type of system (even ones with self-modifying code) and also for probabilistic code stabilization. In a sense, it prescribes for any program of size k a "safe nucleus" of size $O(k)$

from which it can be reconstructed. This makes code stabilization fundamentally different from data stabilization because in data stabilization *all* data can be perturbed without losing the ability to stabilize.

4   Code Stabilization for Distributed Computations

We now investigate how code stabilization can be achieved in distributed systems and what the minimal requirements are to achieve code stabilization.

4.1   Uniformity Issues and Types of Remote Access

Let p and q be two processes. In the context of distributed systems with shared memory, we need to distinguish among different types of access from p to q. Process p has *remote read access* to q if p can read the entire code part of the memory of q. Process p has *remote write access* to q if p can write to the entire code part of q. If p has neither remote read nor remote write access to any other process, we say that p has *local access*. Note that local access does not prohibit processes to communicate since communication can still be done through some shared data part of memory.

Many distributed algorithms assume the fact that individual processes can be named using unique identifiers. Usually, these identifiers are assumed to be hard coded into the algorithm. In the terminology of this paper, unique identifiers are a part of the code. If faults can perturb the entire memory of a process, then also these identifiers can change. This is not a problem if the algorithm is *uniform*, i.e., it does not rely on the existence of unique identifiers and all processes in the system execute an identical copy of the same code. However, due to issues of symmetry breaking, uniform algorithms are faced with many problems. Nevertheless, in the following we focus on uniform algorithms. We discuss the impact of unique identifiers on our results later.

4.2   Techniques to Achieve Code Stabilization

Theorem 2 states that any program of size k needs an unperturbed memory portion of size $O(k)$ to code stabilize. In distributed systems with uniform algorithms, the code is stored redundantly at all processes. Therefore, it is possible to exploit this redundancy to achieve lower bounds for code stabilization than were possible in the non-distributed setting.

In the following, let k be the size of the code of an individual process. A simple and sufficient bound for code stabilization follows directly from Theorem 2. Since every process can be regarded as a non-distributed system, if all processes have only local access, then it is sufficient that all processes contain unperturbed code space of size $O(k)$. If processes have remote read and write access, this bound can be improved.

Theorem 3. *If some processes p has remote write access to all other processes and all other processes do not have remote write access to p, then it is sufficient that p contains unperturbed code space of size $O(k)$.*

Proof. We prove the theorem by sketching a solution that achieves code stabilization using unperturbed code space at a single process. The idea is as follows: The code of every process is augmented with a program part that regularly tries to write a copy of its own code to the code space of all other processes at once. Even if all processes have been perturbed, eventually process p will overwrite the perturbed code with an unperturbed copy of the code. Since p itself will not be perturbed, eventually all processes contain a version of the unperturbed code, yielding code stabilization.   □

Note that Theorem 3 needs special read/write restrictions on the topology of the system. These are necessary in order to prevent a perturbed process from writing a perturbed version of the code into p. This cannot be prevented even if we assume that processes contain unique identifiers which cannot be perturbed by faults.

The atomic update of the entire code state of the system is also necessary since otherwise two perturbed processes could "re-perturb" each other infinitely often if one of them is overwritten by p. For example, consider a setting with three processes p, q and r and let p be the process containing the write-protected and unperturbed code. If q and r have been perturbed, then the following sequence of write operations can happen and—if repeated infinitely—do not ensure stabilization:

- p updates q to correct code.
- r perturbs q again to incorrect code.
- p updates r to correct code.
- q perturbs r again to incorrect code.

The assumption about the atomic update can be relaxed if we place restrictions on the scheduling of processes. For example, if the scheduler ensures that a sequence like the one sketched above never happens (or happens only with low probability), then we also achieve (probabilistic) code stabilization.

Alternatively, we can weaken all of the above assumptions by assuming a local checking mechanism and reverting to probabilistic code stabilization, at the expense of requiring at least a constant size of unperturbed code space at *every* process.

Theorem 4. *If all processes have only remote read access to each other (and no remote write access), then it is sufficient that some process contains unperturbed code space of size $O(k)$ and all other processes contain unperturbed code space of size $O(1)$ to achieve probabilistic code stabilization.*

Proof. The central idea to construct a solution with the above characteristics is to use cryptographic hash functions [13]. A cryptographic hash function maps any finite string of bits to a fixed-size bit string, the *fingerprint*. Hash functions have the property that it is very hard to find *collisions*, i.e., two input strings that have the same fingerprint. In other words, it is very improbable that an arbitrary (random or intentional) perturbation of some bit string results in a bit string with the same fingerprint.

We augment every process with the following integrity checker program: Periodically, the process applies a cryptographic hash function to its own code and compares the resulting fingerprint with the value stored in its unperturbed code space. In case there is a mismatch, the process reads the code space of the totally unperturbed process and overwrites its own code with that copy. By doing this, any local code perturbations are erased. The only case that this does not happen is when code is perturbed to a state which has the same fingerprint as the legal code. The properties of cryptographic hash functions make this sufficiently improbable. The integrity checker together with the fingerprint can be implemented in constant space. Hence, probabilistic code stabilization with the claimed space requirements is achieved.   □

In the proof of Theorem 4, it is necessary that all processes know from where to copy the unperturbed code. This information must be encoded in the constant size unperturbed part of their own code. Note also that the fingerprint must not be stored locally, it can be stored remotely at the same location where the unperturbed code resides or even can be computed on-the-fly. The method to implement the integrity check (a cryptographic hash function) can also be replaced by some form of error detecting code (like a CRC checksum) as long as faults can be assumed to be random.

5 Related Work and Concepts

The techniques described in Section 4 to achieve code stabilization in distributed systems have some similarities to other work in the area self-stabilization, namely the principle of local checking and correction [3] and work by Katz and Perry [11]. The idea is to regularly aquire a (local or global) snapshot of the state of the system and in case of discovered inconsistencies to locally correct or globally reset the system into a legal state. The problem in this area is to construct snapshot and reset procedures that are themselves self-stabilizing. In practice these methods can be found in the form of automatically generated or handcrafted runtime assertions within program code and exception handler mechanisms that perform corrective measures. However note, that all of these methods rely on the fact that the program code itself is unchanged.

Interestingly, there are close resemblances between our methods and the approaches from the area of security, more specifically from the area of (operating system) integrity management. There, *integrity* is defined as protection against unauthorized modification of the data and/or the code of a program. Integrity violations usually occur due to malicious actions by attackers. A common threat is a Trojan horse, a software which pretends to do something useful (like a screensaver or a computer game) but in fact alters your operating system in unforseen and unpleasant ways. Popular alterations are the installation of sniffers and keyloggers that capture sensitive data processed by the system, and post it on the Internet. Another typical alteration is the installation of a back door for a hacker, which enables unauthorized access to the system to outsiders. Modern operating systems have become so complex that these alterations usually are not noticed by the user or system administrator. Integrity management assumes that code is stored on writable media (like a hard disk) and aims at detecting even subtle modifications and wherever possible also to correct them.

Concepts to prevent the effect of these types of modifications are read-only files or filesystems that are supported by many of today's Unix-like operating systems (for example BSD 4.4 Unix offers read-only and append-only files, for a more involved discussion see Garfinkel, Spafford and Schwartz [7]). However, the most general approach in integrity management requires "clean" original copies of all the data and code which is part of the operating system. On a regular basis, the files of the running operating system are compared with the originals. If unauthorized alterations are found, the compromised version is replaced by the original version. The problems in integrity management correspond to the minimal requirements of code stabilization: Care must be taken that the original versions are unaltered and that the comparison and replacement software is also not compromised.

Maintaining a full clean copy of the original files and comparing it with the current ones on a computer is cumbersome in practice. This gave rise to a tool called *Tripwire* that exists in a commercial [16] and a freely available open source variant [15]. Tripwire maintains a database of cryptographic checksums of important files. This database has to be initialized by creating checksums of a known and unaltered baseline. At regular intervals, Tripwire takes snapshots of the system by comparing the checksums of the current version with the clean stored checksums. By reporting on mismatches, integrity violations can be detected or accepted changes merged into the database. Again it is vital that Tripwire itself is unaltered when it is run. Ideally, the filesystem is checked after booting a clean and original version of the operating system from CD including the Tripwire program itself. If Tripwire is executed off a compromised operating system, it may not operate in a trustworthy way [10]. The paradigm of Tripwire closely resembles the observations made in Theorem 4. Note that Tripwire needs to use cryptographic hash functions and not CRC checksums for example.

6   Conclusion

As noted by Ken Thompson in his 1984 Turing Award lecture [14], it is (almost) impossible to trust a system which you have not checked down to the transistor level. Today, integrity management software allows you to place trust on the integrity of your operating system. Integrity means prevention of unauthorized code or data modifications. Integrity is an increasingly important concern in today's computer systems, but requires a minimal amount of trustworthy code to be manageable.

In this paper we have revisited the notion of self-stabilization in a new context. Instead of allowing only data to be corrupted, we asked the question: To what extent can code corruptions be tolerated? We extended the notion of self-stabilization to also cover code corruptions. Our results on minimal unperturbed storage space and on techniques to achieve code stabilization directly reflect structures in the area of integrity management, and therefore can be used as a theoretical foundation for this important area of security.

Acknowledgments

We wish to thank the anonymous reviewers for their constructive comments regarding Theorems 2 and 3.

References

1. A. Arora and M. Gouda. Closure and convergence: A foundation of fault-tolerant computing. *IEEE Transactions on Software Engineering*, 19(11):1015–1027, 1993.
2. A. Arora and S. S. Kulkarni. Component based design of multitolerant systems. *IEEE Transactions on Software Engineering*, 24(1):63–78, Jan. 1998.
3. B. Awerbuch, B. Patt-Shamir, and G. Varghese. Self-stabilization by local checking and correction. In *FOCS91 Proceedings of the 31st Annual IEEE Symposium on Foundations of Computer Science*, pages 268–277, 1991.
4. E. W. Dijkstra. Self stabilizing systems in spite of distributed control. *Communications of the ACM*, 17(11):643–644, 1974.
5. E. W. Dijkstra. Guarded commands, nondeterminacy, and formal derivation of programs. *Communications of the ACM*, 18(8):453–457, Aug. 1975.
6. S. Dolev, A. Israeli, and S. Moran. Self-stabilization of dynamic systems assuming only read/write atomicity. *Distributed Computing*, 7:3–16, 1993.
7. S. Garfinkel, G. Spafford, and A. Schwartz. *Practical UNIX & Internet Security*. O'Reilly & Associates, 2003.
8. M. G. Gouda. Elements of security: Closure, convergence, and protection. *Information Processing Letters*, 77(2–4):109–114, 2001.
9. M. G. Gouda and N. J. Multari. Stabilizing communication protocols. *IEEE Transactions on Computers*, 40(4):448–458, Apr. 1991.
10. Halflife. Bypassing integrity checkers. *Phrack Magazine*, 7(51), Sept. 1997.
11. S. Katz and K. J. Perry. Self-stabilizing extensions for message-passing systems. *Distributed Computing*, 7:17–26, 1993.
12. M. Li and P. Vitányi. *An introduction to Kolmogorov complexity and its applications*. Springer, 2nd edition, 1997.
13. A. J. Menezes, P. C. V. Oorschot, and S. A. Vanstone. *Handbook of Applied Cryptography*. CRC Press, Boca Raton, FL, 1997.
14. K. L. Thompson. Reflections on trusting trust. *Communications of the ACM*, 27(8):761–763, Aug. 1984.
15. Open Source Tripwire. Internet: `http://www.sourceforge.net/projects/tripwire/`.
16. Tripwire change auditing solutions. Internet: `http://www.tripwire.com`.

Stabilizing Certificate Dispersal

Mohamed G. Gouda and Eunjin (EJ) Jung

Department of Computer Sciences,
The University of Texas at Austin,
Austin, TX U.S.A.
{gouda,ejung}@cs.utexas.edu

Abstract. A certificate issued by a user u for another user v enables any user that knows the public key of u to obtain the public key of v. A *certificate dispersal* D assigns a set of certificates $D.u$ to each user u in the system so that user u can find a public key of any other user v without consulting a third party. In this paper, we present a stabilizing certificate dispersal protocol that tolerates transient faults and changes in the certificate system. For example, when a certificate is issued or revoked, this change may lead the system into a state where the set of certificates assigned to each user no longer constitutes a certificate dispersal. Our "dynamic dispersal" protocol eventually brings the system back to a legitimate state where the set of certificates assigned to each user constitutes a certificate dispersal.

1 Introduction

In a distributed system, public key cryptography is often used to provide security features such as authentication and authorization. For example, when a client wants to have assurance that he is communicating with the correct server, then the client can use the public key of the server for authentication. The client may pick up a random number and encrypt it with the public key of the server. When the server receives the encrypted message, the server decrypts the message with the matching private key and sends the number back to the client. When the client receives the correct number, the client can authenticate the server. In fact, this is how customers authenticate the web servers using Secure Socket Layer (SSL) [1] in the Internet. This use of public key cryptography necessitates that the users know the public keys of other users in the system.

The public keys can be advertised through *certificates*. A certificate (u, v) issued by a user u for another user v contains the public key of user v and is signed with the private key of user u. Any user who knows the public key of user u can verify this certificate and obtain the public key of user v. A *certificate dispersal* D assigns a set of certificates $D.u$ to each user u in the system so that user u can find a public key of any other user v without consulting a third party. In this paper, we show a stabilizing certificate dispersal protocol that tolerates transient faults and changes in the certificate system.

The concept of stabilization [2,3] was first introduced by Dijkstra [4]. His definition of a stabilizing system was "regardless of its initial state, it is guaranteed

T. Herman and S. Tixeuil (Eds.): SSS 2005, LNCS 3764, pp. 140–152, 2005.

to arrive at a legitimate states in a finite number of steps." This concept is very useful in building a fault-tolerant system under a model of transient failures. For example, when a certificate is issued or revoked, this change may lead the system into a state where the set of certificates assigned to each user no longer constitutes a certificate dispersal. Our "dynamic dispersal" protocol eventually brings the system back to a legitimate state where the set of certificates assigned to each user constitutes a certificate dispersal. In Section 5, we prove that our dynamic dispersal protocol is stabilizing.

In the following sections, we give formal definitions of certificate systems and present our dynamic dispersal protocol. We prove that this protocol is stabilizing and discuss some events that may lead the system out of the legitimate states and show that the dynamic dispersal protocol eventually brings the system back to a legitimate state.

2   Certificate Systems

We consider a system where each user u has a private key $R.u$ and a public key $B.u$. In this system, in order for a user u to securely send a message m to another user v, user u needs to encrypt the message m using the public key $B.v$, before sending the encrypted message, denoted $B.v\{m\}$, to user v. This necessitates that user u know the public key $B.v$ of user v.

If a user u knows the public key $B.v$ of another user v in this system, then user u can issue a certificate, called a certificate from u to v, that identifies the public key $B.v$ of user v. This certificate can be used by any user in the system that knows the public key of user u to further acquire the public key of user v. An example of such system is Pretty Good Privacy (PGP) [5].

A certificate from user u to user v is of the following form:

$$\langle u, v, B.v, \texttt{expr}, \texttt{sig} \rangle$$

This certificate is signed using the private key $R.u$ of user u, and it includes five items:

u is the identity of the issuer,
v is the identity of the subject,
$B.v$ is the public key of the subject v,
$\texttt{expr}$ is the expiration date, and
$\texttt{sig}$ is an encrypted message digest of
       this certificate.

$\texttt{sig}$ is constructed by computing a message digest of all other four items in this certificate and encrypting the message digest with the private key $R.u$ of issuer u.

For simplicity, a certificate $\langle u, v, B.v, \texttt{expr}, \texttt{sig} \rangle$ is denoted (u, v). Any user x that knows the public key $B.u$ of user u can use $B.u$ to decrypt $\texttt{sig}$ in (u, v). If the decrypted message matches the message digest of all other four items in

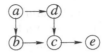

Fig. 1. A certificate graph example

the certificate, then user x can accept the key $B.v$ in certificate (u, v) as the public key of user v. A *valid* certificate (u, v) is an unexpired certificate with the correct signature.

Even though public key cryptography has strong guarantees, a public key can be used only for a finite amount of time. (A dictionary attack will eventually succeed.) Therefore, each certificate has an expiration date and every certificate system requires some degree of clock synchronization. In practice, the expiration of certificates happens daily, and the lifetime of a certificate is often quite long, say a year, so the clock may be skewed by hours and this certificate system would still run correctly. As an alternative, we can also assume the clock rates of all users are the same. (In this case, we need to use version numbers instead of expiration dates.) All users will agree on the number of clock ticks as the lifetime of a certificate and use version numbers to verify the freshness of certificates. For simplicity, we assume that we have perfect clock synchronization in this paper. However, the protocol works as long as the clock skew is small enough that users will be able to detect expired certificates not too late.

The certificates issued by different users in a system can be represented by a directed graph, called the *certificate graph* of the system. Each node u in the certificate graph represents a user u and its corresponding public and private key pair $B.u$ and $R.u$. Each directed edge (u, v) from node u to node v in the certificate graph represents a certificate $\langle u, v, B.v, \texttt{expr}, \texttt{sig} \rangle$.

Fig. 1 shows a certificate graph for a system with five users: a, b, c, d, and e. According to this graph,

> user a issued two certificates (a, b) and (a, d)
> user b issued one certificate (b, c)
> user c issued one certificate (c, e)
> user d issued one certificate (d, c)
> user e issued no certificates.

A simple path $(v_0, v_1), (v_1, v_2), \cdots, (v_{k-1}, v_k)$ in a certificate graph G, where the nodes $v_0, v_1, \cdots, v_k$ are all distinct, is called a *certificate chain* from v_0 to v_k in G of *length* k. Node v_0 in this chain can accept all the keys $B.v_1 \cdots B.v_k$ in the certificates in this chain as the public keys of the users $v_1 \cdots v_k$, respectively. For example, user a in Fig. 1 may use the certificate chain $(a, b)(b, c)$ to accept the public keys $B.b$ and $B.c$ of user b and user c.

3   Certificate Dispersal

In a certificate system, when a user u wants to securely communicate with another user v, u needs to find a certificate chain from u to v to obtain the public key of user v. Therefore, each user can store a subset of certificates in the certificate system to securely communicate with each other.

A *certificate dispersal* of a certificate graph G is a function that assigns a set of certificates $CERT.u$ to each user u in G such that the following condition holds. If there is a certificate chain from a user u to a user v in G, then u and v can find a chain from u to v using the certificates in the set $CERT.u \cup CERT.v$.

A certificate dispersal is *optimal* if and only if the average number of certificates stored in each user due to this dispersal is minimum.

For the certificate graph in Fig. 1, an optimal certificate dispersal is as follows:

$CERT.a := \{(a, d), (a, b), (b, c)\}$
$CERT.b := \{(b, c)\}$
$CERT.c := \{\}$
$CERT.d := \{(d, c)\}$
$CERT.e := \{(c, e)\}$

Based on this dispersal, when user a wishes to securely communicate with user c, user a can use the two certificates (a, b) and (b, c) in $CERT.a$ to obtain the public key of user c. Also, when user b wishes to securely communicate with user e, user b can use the two certificates (b, c) in $CERT.b$ and (c, e) in $CERT.e$ to obtain the public key of user e.

In general, an optimal dispersal is hard to compute [6]. A certificate dispersal, that is not necessarily optimal, can be obtained by storing a "maximal reach tree" of certificates in each users. A *maximal reach* tree of a graph is a tree that contains all the reachable nodes from the root. Lemma 4 in [7] proves the following theorem.

Theorem 1. *A certificate dispersal of a certificate graph G is obtained by storing in each $CERT.u$ the certificates in a maximal reach tree rooted at u for each user u in G.*

For the certificate graph in Fig. 1, the certificate dispersal using reach trees is as follows:

$CERT.a := \{(a, d), (a, b), (b, c), (c, e)\}$
$CERT.b := \{(b, c), (c, e)\}$
$CERT.c := \{(c, e)\}$
$CERT.d := \{(d, c), (c, e)\}$
$CERT.e := \{\}$

Note that a maximal reach tree rooted at user u does not necessarily include all the users in the certificate graph. Each reach tree rooted at user u includes only the reachable users from u in the certificate graph. For example, the maximal reach tree rooted at user d includes only users d, c, and e. Also, there can be multiple reach trees in the certificate graph for the same root. For example, there are two possible maximal reach trees rooted at user a as shown in Fig. 2. CERT.a needs to contain the certificates of only one of the two reach trees. The example dispersal above contains the certificates from the reach tree in Fig. 2(b).

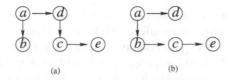

(a)   (b)

Fig. 2. Two possible reach trees

4   Dynamic Dispersal

In the previous section, we discussed the concept of certificate dispersal. Algorithms in [7] show how to compute a certificate dispersal for a "static" certificate graph, i.e. the topology of the certificate graph does not change over time. However, in many certificate systems, certificate graphs do change due to issuing new certificates, adding new users, revoking old certificates, and removing old users. To maintain the certificate dispersal of a dynamic certificate graph, the changes in the graph need to be propagated to the appropriate users.

Fig. 3 shows the inputs and output of our dynamic dispersal protocol. The dynamic dispersal protocol running at each user has two inputs FORE and BACK. FORE in user u is the set of the certificates that have been issued by user u, and BACK in user u is the set of users that have issued certificates for u. Note that the two inputs FORE and BACK in all users define the certificate graph of the system. We assume that FORE and BACK are maintained by an outside protocol that issues new certificates and revokes old ones. We also assume that FORE and BACK are always *correct* and so they are always *consistent*. For example, if at any time a certificate (u, v) is in FORE.u of user u, then u is in BACK.v of user v at the same time.

The dynamic dispersal protocol maintains a variable CERT.u at each user u. At stabilization, the value of CERT.u is a maximal reach tree rooted at user u. Thus, by Theorem 1, the values of CERTs at stabilization constitute a certificate dispersal of the system.

The dynamic dispersal protocol in user u is shown in Protocol 1 below. Protocol 1 consists of three actions.

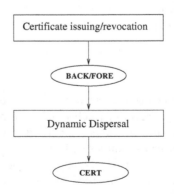

Fig. 3. Inputs and Output of Dynamic Dispersal Protocol

In the first action, when the timer of user u expires, user u uses its input FORE.u to update the variable CERT.u and sends a copy of CERT.u to each user v in BACK.u. Then u updates its timer to expire after ltime time units, and the cycle repeats. For convenience, we refer to CERT.u messages that user u has sent in this action as a round of gossip. If user u does not change its CERT.u and does not observe any change in its inputs FORE.u and BACK.u, then the time period between two consecutive rounds of gossip by u is ltime time units. The value ltime is expected to be in the range of days or months.

In the second action, user u receives a certificate tree sent by a user v (where u is in BACK.v). In this case, u updates its CERT.u using its input FORE.u, and then merges its CERT.u with the received certificate tree. If the update or merge operations change CERT.u then u reduces the value of its timer to at most stime time units. Note that the value stime is in the range of minutes or hours so it is much less than the value ltime. In other words, any change in the variable CERT.u causes u to initiate its next round of gossip after no more than stime time units.

In the third action, when user u observes that its inputs BACK.u or FORE.u has changed, then user u sets its timer to be at most stime time units. This change causes u to initiate its next round of gossip after no more than stime time units.

4.1 Issuing certificates

When a user u issues a certificate (u, v), there are two events that need to occur. (Note that these two events happen outside the dynamic dispersal protocol.) The first event is to add (u, v) to FORE.u, and the second action is to add u to BACK.v. These events cause users u and v to execute the third action in the protocol and to reduce their timers to be at most stime time units. In stime time units, the timers in both users u and v will expire and then users u and v will execute the first action and update their CERTs accordingly and send a copy to the users in their BACKs.

4.2 Revoking Certificates

When a user u wants to revoke a certificate (u, v) it has issued before, two events need to occur in users u and v. (Note that these two events happen outside the dynamic dispersal protocol.) The first event is to remove (u, v) from FORE.u, and the second action is to remove u from BACK.v.

When user u observes the change in FORE.u, u executes the third action and set its timer to be at most stime. When the timer expires, u will update CERT.u and send it to users in BACK.u. When user x in BACK.u receives the newly updated CERT.u from user u, x will merge it with its own CERT.x. During this merge, the revoked certificate (u, v) and any path using that certificate will be removed from CERT.x.

4.3 Expired Certificates

We assume that when a certificate (u, v) expires, it is removed from FORE.u and u is removed from BACK.v in user v. This triggers user u to set its timer to be at most

---

PROTOCOL 1. dynamic dispersal

```
user u

const   stime, ltime              //stime is a short time period
                                  //ltime is a long time period
                                  //ltime is greater than stime

input   BACK      : {x| x has issued a certificate (x,u)}
        FORE      : {(u,x) | u has issued a certificate (u,x)}

var     CERT      : a certificate tree rooted at u
        tree      : a certificate tree
        timer     : 0..ltime
        v         : any user other than u

begin
        timer=0 ->          update(CERT, FORE);
                            for each user v in BACK, send CERT to v;
                            timer:=ltime

    [] rcv tree from v -> update(CERT, FORE);
                            merge(CERT, tree);
                            if CERT has changed, timer:=min(timer, stime)

    [] BACK or FORE has changed -> timer:=min(timer,stime)

end
```

---

stime and user u will update its CERT.u accordingly and send a copy of CERT.u to users in BACK.u. Similarly to the case of certificate revocation, when a node x in BACK.u receives CERT.u, then x will update CERT.x and remove (u, v) from it.

4.4 update Procedure

Procedure update(CERT,FORE) is defined as follows.

It is convenient to explain this procedure by an example. Consider user a where FORE.a in user a contains one certificate (a, b) and CERT.a contains two certificates $(a, b), (b, c)$ as shown in Fig. 4(a). When user a issues a new certificate

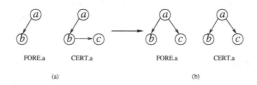

FORE.a   CERT.a   FORE.a   CERT.a

(a)   (b)

Fig. 4. update of CERT.a due to change in FORE.a

PROCEDURE 1. update(CERT, FORE)

```
INPUT: a certificate tree CERT rooted at u and
       a set of certificates FORE issued by u
OUTPUT: a certificate tree CERT rooted at u

var tmp: a certificate tree rooted at u

begin

    add all the valid certificates in FORE to tmp;
    while there is a valid certificate (x,y) in CERT where
        x != u,
        x is in tmp, and
        v is not in tmp
    do add (u,v) to tmp;
    CERT:=tmp;

end
```

(a, c), FORE.a changes into $\{(a, b), (a, c)\}$. This change causes user a to execute its third action and then after stime time units to execute its first action. In the first action, procedure update(CERT.a,FORE.a) is executed. First, all the certificates in FORE.a are added to a certificate tree tmp and tmp becomes $\{(a, b), (a, c)\}$. Certificate (b, c) cannot be added to tmp because user c is already in tmp. In the last step, tmp is copied to CERT.a, and CERT.a becomes $\{(a, b), (a, c)\}$ as shown in Fig. 4(b).

4.5   merge Procedure

Procedure merge(CERT,tree) is defined as follows.

It is convenient to explain this procedure by an example. Consider user a where FORE.a contains two certificate $(a, b), (a, c)$ and CERT.a contains three certificates $(a, b), (a, c), (b, d)$ as shown in Fig. 5(a). When user b revokes certificate (b, d), FORE.b changes into $\{(b, c)\}$. This change causes user b to execute its third action and after stime time units to execute its first action. In the first action, user b updates its CERT.b to be $\{(b, c)\}$. User a still does not know about

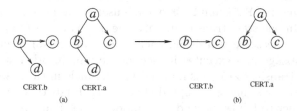

CERT.b   CERT.a   CERT.b   CERT.a

(a)   (b)

Fig. 5. merge of CERT.a due to change in CERT.b

PROCEDURE 2. merge(CERT, tree)

INPUT: a certificate tree CERT rooted at u and
       a certificate tree ''tree'' rooted at t, where
       t != u
OUTPUT: a certificate tree CERT

```
begin

    if CERT has a certificate (u,t) ->
        remove all the certificates in the subtree rooted at t from CERT;
        while tree has a valid certificate (x,y) where
                x is in CERT and
                y is not in CERT
        do add y and certificate (x,y) to CERT;
    [] CERT has no certificate (u,t) ->
        skip
    fi

end
```

---

this revocation, so CERT.a remains the same as shown in Fig. 5(a). After stime time units, user b sends a copy of its CERT.b to user a. When user a receives the certificate tree $\{(b,c)\}$, user a executes its second action, and procedure merge(CERT.a,tree) is executed with CERT.a and the received tree $\{(b,c)\}$. Procedure merge(CERT.a,tree) first checks if there is certificate (a,b) in CERT.a. There is certificate (a,b), so the subtree rooted at user b, (b,d) in CERT.a is removed from CERT.a. Then, certificate (b,c) is considered, but is not added to CERT.a because c is already in CERT.a. In result, CERT.a becomes $\{(a,b),(a,c)\}$ as shown in Fig. 5(b).

5   Stabilization of Dynamic Dispersal

The dynamic dispersal algorithm in Section 4 is based on a message passing model. In [8], it is shown to be hard to design stabilizing protocols in the traditional message passing model where there are channels between users. In this paper, we use a non-conventional model of communication. A state consists of the values of timer and CERT of all the users in the system. As mentioned in Section 4, we assume that FORE and BACK of each user remain correct and consistent in every state. In one state transition, only one user can execute its first action. Furthermore, in the same transition, each user v in BACK.u receives the same copy of this message and executes its second action. In other words, we have no messages in transit, so there is no need for channels in the state description. There are two reasons that we adopted this model. First, this model allows the proofs to be easier to follow. Second, this model is sensible, given that the time it takes for the timer in each user to expire is very large compared to the time each state transition takes. stime is in the range of minutes and hours, and each state transition takes only milliseconds, so we can assume that no two timers expire at the same time.

For the proofs of convergence and closure, we define a *computation* to be a sequence of states of the system where along with this computation FORE and BACK of all the users remain unchanged. In the following theorems, we show that the dynamic dispersal protocol eventually stabilizes into a legitimate state, where the values of CERTs of all users constitute a certificate dispersal of the certificate graph of the system. Following the proof technique in [9], we show the convergence and the closure of this protocol to prove its stabilization.

Theorem 2. *(Convergence) Each computation of the dynamic dispersal protocol has a state where the value of each CERT.u in the protocol is a maximal reach tree rooted at u in the certificate graph of the protocol (as defined by the two inputs FORE and BACK of all users in the protocol).*

Proof Sketch. To prove that CERT.u eventually becomes a maximal reach tree rooted at node u of the certificate graph G, we first prove that CERT.u eventually becomes a tree rooted at u, and then prove that every node that is reachable from u in G is reachable in CERT.u.

There are two procedures, update(CERT.u,FORE.u) and merge(CERT.u,tree), that can change CERT.u. The procedure update(CERT.u,FORE.u) constructs a tree by starting from the certificates in FORE.u. All the certificates in FORE.u are issued by user u, so the resulting tree from update(CERT.u,FORE.u) is rooted at u. Similarly, the procedure merge(CERT.u,tree) adds certificates in the received tree to CERT.u, a certificate tree rooted at u. Therefore, the resulting tree from merge(CERT.u,tree) is also rooted at u. Based on these observations, after a state transition in this computation, CERT.u in user u becomes a tree rooted at u.

Now we prove that CERT.u is a maximal reach tree, i.e. any node that is reachable from node u in G is also CERT.u. Assume that there is a path from u to another node v in G, $(u, u_1)(u_1, u_2) \cdots (u_k, v)$. Node u_k has the certificate (u_k, v) in its FORE, so the certificate (u_k, v) is in its CERT. Node u_k sends its CERT periodically to node u_{k-1}, so node u_{k-1} will have a path from itself to node v in its CERT. Repeatedly, each node on the path will send its CERT to the previous node in the path and node u will have a path from itself to node v in its CERT. Therefore, every node v that is reachable from node u in G is also reachable in CERT.u. ∎

Note that our dynamic dispersal protocol is different from stabilizing spanning tree algorithms. The spanning tree algorithms in [10,11,12] build a single spanning tree for the whole system that covers every process in the system, and build one tree rooted at a special process (usually referred as a leader). Each process in these algorithms stores the parent node identifier, the distance from the root, and possibly the root identifier. On the other hand, our dynamic dispersal protocol stores a maximal reach tree in each user, which does not necessarily cover every user in the system. Also, in our dynamic dispersal protocol, there is no leader, and each user u maintains a maximal reach tree rooted at u.

Theorem 3. *(Closure) Executing any step of the dynamic dispersal protocol starting from a state, where the value of each variable CERT.u in the protocol is a maximal reach tree rooted at u, leaves the values of all CERT variables unchanged.*

Proof Sketch. In a computation, the inputs BACK and FORE remain unchanged. Therefore, only two types of steps can be executed: time propagation and the first action. Time propagation cannot change the value of CERT. When the time propagation causes the timer in user u to expire, the first action in the dynamic dispersal protocol will be executed. When the timer expires, user u updates its CERT.u with FORE.u, but CERT.u remains the same since FORE.u remains unchanged. Now user u sends a copy of its CERT.u to each user v in BACK.u. User v receives a tree and merge it with its own CERT.v. Since CERT.u is the same, merge(CERT,tree) will not change CERT.v. Therefore, when the certificate graph of the system does not change, CERT.u in each user u, a maximal reach tree rooted at u, remains unchanged.   ∎

6   Time Complexity

In this section, we compute the time in terms of the two timers stime and ltime that takes to bring the system to stabilization. Note that each state transition is triggered by a timer expiration in a user, so the time between any two state transitions may be between 0 to ltime. Every state transition but the first one towards stabilization is triggered by a timer whose value is at most stime, which is shown below.

Theorem 4. *In each computation of the dynamic dispersal protocol, the protocol reaches a legitimate state in at most T time units, where*

$$T = ltime \times \text{ the length of the longest path in the certificate graph -1}$$

Proof Sketch. A legitimate state of the dynamic dispersal protocol is one where the value of CERT.u of every user u in the system is a maximal reach tree rooted at u.

After the first ltime time units in the computation, each CERT.u is a tree rooted at u, and the first two levels of this tree are correct. After the second ltime time units, each user sends a copy of its CERT to the users in the BACK, so the top three levels of each CERT are correct. The cycle repeats, and after ltime $\times$ (the length of the longest path in the certificate graph-1) time units, all the levels of each tree CERT are correct, so CERT.u becomes a maximal reach tree rooted at u.   ∎

We believe that the upper bound on the convergence span described in Theorem 4 is quite loose. It is an interesting problem to compute a tight upper bound of the convergence span.

7 Dispersal in Client/Server Systems

This dynamic dispersal protocol is useful in any dynamic certificate systems. Consider a client/server system, where there are much fewer servers than clients in the system. We can run the dynamic dispersal protocol among the servers and let any server issue a certificate for a client. Each server will have an maximal reach certificate tree in its CERT, so each server will be able to find a certificate chain from itself to any client that has a certificate issued by an authenticated server.

For example, many coffee shops offer free Internet connection for their customers. To prevent free-riders that are not customers, coffee shops may require the customers to register. For convenience, a customer needs to register only once at any coffee shop (the coffee shop issues a certificate for the customer), and the customer can use the free connection at all coffee shops that are participating in this membership without logging in or getting temporary authorization each time he or she goes to a coffee shop, since any coffee shop has a certificate chain from itself to the customer. The authentication using the certificate chain does not require any interaction with the customer, so once the customer registers to get a certificate from one coffee shop, the customer does not need to know how he or she gets authenticated and authorized for the Internet connection.

Also, this client/server system can help two clients authenticate each other. A client $c1$ has issued a certificate for a server $s1$ and $s1$ issued a certificate for $c1$. A client $c2$ has issued a certificate for a server $s2$ and $s2$ issued a certificate for $c2$. When client $c1$ wants to securely communicate with client $c2$, client $c1$ can ask server $s1$ for a certificate chain from $s1$ to $s2$ and use the chain and the certificates $(c1, s1)$ and $(s2, c2)$ to find the public key of client $c2$.

A hierarchical certificate authorities used in Lotus Notes [13] is a special case of such client/server system. In a system with a hierarchical certificate authorities, the certificate graph between certificate authorities constitutes a star graph, where the root certificate authority has issued a certificate for each non-root certificate authority and each non-root certificate authority has issued a certificate for the root certificate authority. In such a system, when a client $c1$ who has issued a certificate for a certificate authority $ca1$ wants to securely communicate with another client $c2$ who has issued a certificate for a certificate authority $ca2$, $c1$ can contact $ca1$ for certificates $(ca1, root)(root, ca2)$. In Lotus Notes, $ca1$ also finds the certificate $(ca2, c2)$ from $ca2$ so that $c1$ can use the public key of $c2$ safely without communicating with $c2$.

8 Concluding Remarks

Public key cryptography is often used to provide security features in a distributed system. For users to use public key cryptography, they need to know the public keys of other users. Certificates are useful to advertise public keys to other users. In particular, when a user u wishes to securely communicate with another user v, user u needs to find a certificate chain from u to v. A certificate dispersal D assigns a set of certificates $CERT.u$ to each user u so that user u can find such a chain in $CERT.u \cup CERT.v$.

We present the dynamic dispersal protocol, which eventually stabilizes a certificate system into the legitimate states where the set of certificates assigned to each user constitutes a certificate dispersal when a certificate graph of the certificate system is dynamic. We prove the convergence and the closure of the protocol, and show the time complexity of the convergence.

References

1. Dierks, T., Rescorla, E.: The TLS protocol version 1.1. Internet Draft (draft-ietf-tls-rfc2246-bis-08.txt) (2004)
2. Dolev, S.: Self-Stabilization. MIT Press (2000)
3. Herman, T.: A comprehensive bibliography on self-stabilization. Chicago Journal of Theoretical Computer Science (1996)
4. Dijkstra, E.W.: Self-stabilization in spite of distributed control. ACM Communications **17** (1974) 643–644
5. Zimmerman, P.: The Official PGP User's Guide. MIT Press (1995)
6. Jung, E., Elmallah, E.S., Gouda, M.G.: Optimal dispersal of certificate chains. In: Proceedings of the 18th International Symposium on Distributed Computing (DISC '04), Springer-Verlag (2004)
7. Gouda, M.G., Jung, E.: Certificate dispersal in ad-hoc networks. In: Proceedings of the 24th International Conference on Distributed Computing Systems (ICDCS '04), IEEE (2004)
8. Gouda, M.G., Multari, N.: Stabilizing communication protocols. EEE Transactions on Computers, Special Issue on Protocol Engineering **40** (1991) 448–458
9. Arora, A., Gouda, M.G.: Closure and convergence: A foundation of fault-tolerant computing. IEEE Transactions on Software Engineering **19** (1993) 1015–1027
10. Dolev, S., Israeli, A., Moran, S.: Self-stabilization of dynamic systems. In: Proceedings of the 9th Annual ACM Symposium on Principles of Distributed Computing, ACM (1990)
11. Arora, A., Gouda, M.G.: Distributed reset. In: Proceedings of the 22nd International Conference on Fault-Tolerant Computing Systems. (1990)
12. Chen, N.S., Yu, H.P., Huang, S.T.: A self-stabilizing algorithm for constructing spanning trees. Inf. Process. Lett. **39** (1991) 147–151
13. Nielsen, S.P., Dahm, F., Lüscher, M., Yamamoto, H., Collins, F., Denholm, B., Kumar, S., Softley, J.: Lotus notes and domino r5.0 security infrastructure revealed (1999)

On the Possibility and the Impossibility of Message-Driven Self-stabilizing Failure Detection[*]

Martin Hutle and Josef Widder[**]

Technische Universität Wien, Embedded Computing Systems Group 182/2,
Treitlstraße 3/2, A-1040 Vienna (Austria)
{hutle, widder}@ecs.tuwien.ac.at

Abstract. This paper considers message-driven self-stabilizing implementations of unreliable failure detectors. We show that it is impossible to give a deterministic implementation using just bounded memory if there is no known upper bound on the number of messages that may be in transit simultaneously. With relaxed assumptions we then introduce two algorithms that solve the problem.

We use self-stabilization to show that message-driven and time-driven semantics are different regarding expressiveness: Comparison with work by Beauquier and Kekkonen-Moneta (1997) reveals that the discussed problem has a time-driven solution but cannot have a message-driven one.

1 Introduction

Generally, the discipline of distributed computing considers sets of distributed processes that execute algorithms where each execution consists of a sequence of events. In the context of reliable agreement problems, much work [5,8,10] focuses on timing constraints of these events; e.g. upper bounds between send and receive events of messages between processes. Another issue is event generation. We distinguish here two kinds of models, i.e., time-driven and message-driven. In time-driven models, events occur due to passage of time and are triggered by clocks or timers. In contrast, after a message-driven algorithm was started, all events happen as immediate reaction to a received message while clocks are either not part of the model or are just not employed by the algorithms.

Note, however, that the issues of timing constraints and event generation are orthogonal. Consider, e.g., the well known failure detector (FD) based consensus algorithms of [5] which work in an asynchronous model of computation (often referred to as "time-free" model, reflecting the absence of timing bounds). These algorithms must be attributed as time-driven as steps can be taken — independently of the presence or absence of messages in input buffers — just by

---

[*] The results were presented as brief announcement at ACM PODC 2005.
[**] Supported by the Austrian bmvit FIT-IT project *DCBA* (proj. no. 808198), and by the FWF project *Theta* (proj. no. P17757-N04).

T. Herman and S. Tixeuil (Eds.): SSS 2005, LNCS 3764, pp. 153–170, 2005.

the passage of time respectively the progress of the program counter. It seems obvious that solutions to the same problem can be achieved with message-driven algorithms if (1) messages are immediately processed upon reception, (2) the FD module triggers the consensus algorithm if new suspicions have been added and (3) the FD implementation itself is message-driven. Most existing FD implementation in the literature [5,1,3] are not message-driven as they periodically send messages (e.g. heartbeats). Exceptions are the message-driven FD implementations by Le Lann and Schmid [17,20].

We investigate whether time-driven and message-driven semantics are equivalent regarding expressiveness; in other words whether the same set of problems have solutions in both models. We answer the question in the negative. To this end, the problem of self-stabilizing [7,9] implementation of FDs is investigated. FDs [5] provide processes with information about process crashes. The first self-stabilizing (SS) FD implementations were introduced by Beauquier and Kekkonen-Moneta [3]. Their implementations send messages with every clock tick, in other words, they are time-driven. These algorithms satisfy the FD semantics and stabilize within finite time in systems that obey a fair ordering property which is in fact an abstract synchrony assumption: If a process p receives m messages from a process q, then p must receive at least one message by any other correct process. In this paper we reconcile the work by Beauquier and Kekkonen-Moneta [3] and the work by Le Lann and Schmid [17,20] and investigate SS message-driven FD implementations.

SS FD implementations cannot be purely message-driven as inaccurate FD information can never be corrected after a state was reached where no messages are in transit such that no process will ever make a step afterwards. To overcome such situations, several approaches can be taken. We could augment the system model with the requirement that at least one message must always be in transit. Since for the states where no messages are in transit convergence cannot be ensured we could not argue that recovery from *all* states is guaranteed. Moreover, when considering practical solutions this does not seem reasonable (e.g. this does not cover system booting [19,20] where no messages are in transit initially). Therefore we add a local deadlock prevention event, which however has no timing constraints except that in every infinite run it happens an infinite number of times, where the duration between two events is finite. In other words this event cannot be used as a (even weak [11]) clock. Strictly speaking, using this approach, our algorithms are not message-driven anymore. Our proofs, however, reveal that they do not rely on the deadlock prevention event if messages are in transit. In this paper we show that under certain circumstances it is impossible to implement FDs in message-driven models even with such a deadlock prevention event. Trivially, this result also holds for purely message driven systems. Therefore, having this deadlock prevention event in the system model makes the impossibility result even stronger as it holds not only for message-driven systems but also for message-driven systems with deadlock prevention.

Apart from self-stabilization, FDs were explored with regard to weak synchrony assumptions [4,1,11]. In [1], e.g., eventually some link in the system must have some unknown upper bound on communication delays. From a theoretical viewpoint, such algorithms require unbounded memory as the timeout value has to be stored (and increased on false suspicions). Assuming an unbounded timeout variable for SS algorithms is problematic as an overly pessimistic timeout might emanate from the unstable period and render the performance of such an algorithm unusable, while decreasing timeout values may violate FD properties. Therefore we focus on bounded memory FD algorithms under quite conservative synchrony assumptions, i.e., there exists some upper bound on message end-to-end delays that is different from the lower bound. For our implementations — but not for the impossibility result — we require the lower bound to be greater than 0.

Under these assumptions it turns out that the number of messages that can be in transit at any given time becomes an important factor. Messages from the unstable period could produce message patterns which look identical to correct ones but which are much denser in the sense that the elapsed time of such a faulty pattern is just a fraction of the duration of a corresponding correct pattern. We show in Sect. 3 that this behavior leads to the impossibility of implementing even the weakest FD [4] that allows solving consensus, i.e., the eventually strong FD $\diamond \mathcal{S}$ (as defined in [5]) in fully connected networks if the number of messages that are simultaneously in transit is unknown. According to the reduction in [4], this result also holds for the leader oracle Ω which gained some attention in literature recently [1,15]. In fact our impossibility proof (of Theorem 1) can be applied literally to show the impossibility of implementing Ω in our setting.

By devising two FD implementations that also work in sparse networks [15] we show how to circumvent this impossibility result. The first algorithm in Sect. 4 copes with an unbounded number of messages but requires unbounded space. Since we also want to give a practical solution, we devise a second algorithm in Sect. 5 which requires just bounded space. This algorithm, however, requires knowledge of M, an a priori known upper bound on the number of messages that may be in transit simultaneously. Since real networks are finite, we consider this upper bound as not very restrictive. For many networks, M can be analytically derived as the capacity of links (determined by memory allocated to queues at the network layers) is bounded as well. However, this bound has no influence on the detection time of our algorithm and the space requirements are just logarithmic in M. So even in networks where it is difficult to find a tight upper bound, one can still use an extremely conservative one.

2   System Model

We consider a set $\Pi = \{1 \ldots n\}$ of processes, where each process is modeled as a state machine. Processes communicate by *message passing* over links. An edge $\lambda = (p, q)$ of the communication graph G stands for a bidirectional link between p and q. For our impossibility result, we assume a fully-connected graph and FIFO links in order to strengthen the result. For our algorithms, this can be dropped as they work on non-FIFO sparse graphs. Let $\mathrm{nb}(p)$ be the set of neighbors of process p $(p \notin \mathrm{nb}(p))$, and $\deg(p) = |\mathrm{nb}(p)|$ be the number of neighbors.

Execution Model. Processes operate by performing *steps*. A step can be either a message reception step or a deadlock prevention step. A message reception step includes reception of one or more messages, the computational step of the state machine and (optional) sending of messages. Formally, a message reception step is defined by $a = (p, s_p, R, S, s'_p)$, where $R = \{(msg_1^r, \lambda_1^r), \ldots, (msg_k^r, \lambda_k^r)\}$ and $S = \{(msg_1^s, \lambda_1^s), \ldots, (msg_\ell^s, \lambda_\ell^s)\}$, meaning p is in state s_p, p receives messages msg_i^r from links λ_i^r and sends messages msg_j^s over links λ_j^s, and s'_p is the state of p after execution of this step. We assume that processes are able to receive several numbers of messages from incoming links concurrently, thus the λ_i^r are not necessarily disjoint. The λ_j^s must be disjoint, however. A deadlock prevention step is defined as $a = (p, s_p, S, s'_p)$, meaning p is in state s_p, sends messages S and is in state s'_p after the spontaneous deadlock prevention event.

Let m be the number of links in the system. For $p \in \Pi$, S_p denotes the set of states of p. A *configuration* of the system is a vector of states of all processes together with m lists, one list for every link, of messages on that link. A configuration is denoted by $C = (s_1, s_2, \ldots, s_n, L_{\lambda_1}, L_{\lambda_2}, \ldots, L_{\lambda_m})$ where $s_i \in S_i$ and L_{λ_j} is a list of messages on λ_j. Let C be a configuration as above, and $a = (p, s_p, R, S, s'_p)$ be a message reception step. Then a is *applicable* to C, if p is in state s_p, and for every $(msg_j^r, \lambda_j) \in R$ it holds that $msg_j^r \in L_{\lambda_j}$. A deadlock prevention step $a = (p, s_p, S, s'_p)$ is applicable if p is in s_p. For every $s_p \in S_p$ such a step exists, thus for every configuration there is a deadlock prevention step that is applicable. Application of a step a to C yields the resulting configuration C'.

An *execution*, $\sigma = C_0 a_1 C_1 a_2 \ldots$ is a (finite or infinite) sequence, which starts with some configuration C_0 and where, for every $i > 0$, a_i is applicable to C_{i-1} and results in C_i. An execution σ_1 is applicable to a finite execution σ_0, if the last configuration of σ_0 is equal to the first of σ_1. A *timed execution* is a sequence $\sigma = C_0 a_1 t_1 C_1 a_2 t_2 \ldots$, where $C_0 a_1 C_1 a_2 \ldots$ is an execution and $t_i \in \mathbb{R}$ is the real-time the step a_i occurs, with $t_i \le t_{i+1}$ holding for all i.

Let $\sigma = C_0 a_1 t_1 C_1 a_2 t_2 \ldots$ be a timed execution. Then we say a message msg is *in transit* from p to q at time t, if msg is in $L_{(p,q)}$ in the last configuration before t (note that this does not include messages sent at t). In other words, msg is in transit in the interval $(t_s, t_r]$, if it is sent in a step at t_s and received in a step at t_r. Further, we denote with $Q(p, q, t)$ the set of messages which are in transit from p to q or vice versa at time t, and with $Q(p, t) = \bigcup_{q \in \Pi} Q(p, q, t)$ all messages in transit from or to p. Further, $Q'(p, q, t)$ denotes the set of all messages from p to q or vice versa after a step at time t.

Additionally we define $v_p(t)$ to be the value of variable v at process p at time t before the step at time t, and $v'_p(t)$ to be the value of variable v at p and time t after the step at time t, if there is a step at t.

Timing Model. Let t_{GST} denote the time where our timing becomes correct in the following way: A timed execution is *timely*, if for every message msg that is sent by a_i there is some a_j where msg is received, and $\tau^- \leq t_j - t_i \leq \tau^+$ if $t_i \geq t_{GST}$ and $t_j < t_{GST} + \tau^+$ else. Moreover, every message that is in transit at time t_{GST} is received before $t_{GST} + \tau^+$. The impossibility result holds for any system with $\tau^- < \tau^+$. (This covers timing constraints as in (partially) synchronous models or the Θ-Model.) Our algorithms assume that there is a known bound $\Xi > \Theta$ on the ratio $\Theta = \tau^+/\tau^-$ while τ^+ and τ^- are not known in advance. We further define $\varepsilon = \tau^+ - \tau^-$ as the timing uncertainty.

To overcome the problem of deadlocks [13] in SS message passing systems, we introduce the deadlock prevention event which fulfills the following fairness property: for every time t and process p, there is a $t' > t$ where a deadlock prevention step is taken at p; $t' - t$ is finite. For timing analysis we assume that the deadlock prevention event is triggered at process p by time $t_{GST} + \eta$, where η is not known to processes. Note that the actual value of η has no influence on the correctness of our algorithms.

Failure Model. Processes behave correctly until they crash. Crashes need not be clean, i.e. may occur during a step. After a process has crashed it does not take any step, messages sent to such a process are lost. A process is called *correct* if it never crashes. At some unknown time t_{GST} the timing stabilizes and the system is in an arbitrary configuration. We call the time before t_{GST} the *unstable period*. Process crashes may occur at any time and processes do not recover after t_{GST}, i.e., crashes are permanent. We assume $f < \deg(p)$ for all p, where f is the upper bound on the number of faulty processes after t_{GST}.

Failure Detectors. An FD is a module at each processor that provides for some applications information about other processes. We assume the FD outputs a list of processes that are suspected to have crashed. If a process q is in the suspect list of a process p at some time t, we say p suspects q. For our impossibility result we consider the *eventually strong FD* $\diamond\mathcal{S}$ as defined in [5]. It satisfies:

Strong Completeness. Eventually every process that crashes is permanently suspected by all correct processes.

Eventual Weak Accuracy. There is a time after which some correct process is never suspected by any correct process.

We now define an *eventually perfect local* FD. Such an FD has to satisfy the same properties as an eventually perfect FD $\diamond\mathcal{P}$ [5], but just for neighbors:

Local Completeness. Eventually every process that crashes is permanently suspected by all correct neighbors.

Eventual Local Accuracy. There is a time after which correct processes are never suspected by any correct neighbor.

The class of eventually perfect local FDs is denoted by $\diamond\mathcal{P}_\ell$. We give implementations for this class in Sect. 4 and Sect. 5. Note that a $\diamond\mathcal{P}_\ell$ FD can be easily transformed to a $\diamond\mathcal{P}$ FD by an asynchronous SS algorithm: Every process just has to broadcast the local lists of suspects. Every process then obtains the global list of suspects by intersecting the most recent versions of the local lists.

In concordance with the self-stabilization requirements [9], an SS algorithm needs a set of legal executions which must be reached from any system state. We define all executions that guarantee the properties of completeness and accuracy as legal executions of an SS FD implementation.

3   Impossibility Result

In this section we show the impossibility of implementing message-driven SS failure detectors with bounded memory. The intuitive argument is as follows: Due to the bounded memory assumption, every algorithm has to reuse messages and there are executions of this algorithm that run in cycles. Since processes have no notion of real-time, they are not able to distinguish messages from a previous cycle from new ones. Initiated by a sufficiently large number of messages from the unstable period, it is hence possible that processes perceive a compressed notion of time. Since the FD is message-driven, this will trigger the generation of new messages according to this compressed time, which may go on perpetually. Since the FDs run much faster than they should, incorrect suspicions will occur. Due the self-stabilization and the bounded memory assumption they are not able to recover from this and thus no process stops being suspected forever.

The formal argumentation assumes by ways of contradiction, that such an FD algorithm exists and constructs a non-timely cyclic execution of this algorithm. Such an execution must exist because of the bounded memory assumption. By excessively delaying messages, the FD can be forced to suspect every process at least once. By showing indistinguishableness from a timely execution with messages from the unstable period we get the required contradiction.

Theorem 1. *There is no deterministic message-driven self-stabilizing bounded memory implementation of the eventually strong FD $\diamond S$ in system with $\varepsilon > 0$ and unknown channel capacity.*

Proof. Assume by contradiction that such an algorithm $\mathcal{A}$ exists. We first construct the following timed (but not timely; cf. Sect. 2) execution σ_0 of $\mathcal{A}$. Note that the adversary can control the receive times of messages and the times of the deadlock prevention events in such a run.

1. No process ever crashes. We start in a configuration $C_1^{(1)}$. Our run proceeds in lock-step, i.e., the algorithm receives and sends messages only at times $t_k = k\tau_0$, with $\tau^- \leq \tau_0 \leq \tau^+$. All timely messages are sent at times t_k and received at times t_{k+1}. Note that at all times t_k no messages are in transit (except those received at time t_k) such that the configuration following t_k is solely determined by the local states. The time between t_k and t_{k+1} is a round.

2. For every $p \in \{1, \ldots, n\}$: Starting from a configuration $C_{2p-1}^{(1)}$, the adversary fires the deadlock prevention event at p, and all messages from and to process p are delayed (at least for one round), until some process suspects p. Such a configuration is reached eventually, since such a behavior is indistinguishable

from a situation where p has crashed, and thus by strong completeness, p must eventually be suspected by some process. After that, the adversary delivers all delayed messages and we end up in a configuration $C_{2p}^{(1)}$. Between $C_{2p-1}^{(1)}$ and $C_{2p}^{(1)}$, p is suspected at least once. After $C_{2p}^{(1)}$, timing becomes correct for one round, resulting in configuration $C_{2p+1}^{(1)} = C_{2(p+1)-1}^{(1)}$. Finally, every process was suspected at least once by another process, and we end up in a configuration $C_1^{(2)} \triangleq C_{2n+1}^{(1)}$.

3. Starting repeatedly again from (2), we get chains of configurations $C_1^{(1)}$ ... $C_{2n}^{(1)}$ ... $C_1^{(i)}$ ... $C_{2n}^{(i)}$. We call the run from $C_i^{(j)}$ to $C_{i+1}^{(j)}$ a phase and the run from $C_1^{(i)}$ to $C_{2n+1}^{(i)}$ an epoch.

4. Since every configuration $C_1^{(j)}$ depends only on the (finite) local states and the messages sent in $C_{2n}^{(j-1)}$ (which depend on the finite local states of $C_{2n}^{(j-1)}$), there are only a finite number of configurations $C_1^{(j)}$. Thus, there are numbers u and v ($u < v$), such that $C_1^{(u)} = C_1^{(v)}$. Let $E = u - v$ be the number of epochs. Every epoch has obviously $2n$ phases, where the number of rounds in phase ϕ of epoch e is $R(e, \phi)$, with $0 \leq \phi < 2n$, $0 \leq e < E$. The execution from $C_1^{(u)}$ to $C_1^{(v)}$ we refer to as cycle.

5. Since $C_1^{(u)}$ and $C_1^{(v)}$ are identical, the execution from $C_1^{(u)}$ to $C_1^{(v)}$ is applicable to itself. σ_0 is the execution that comprises Z cycles of the execution from $C_1^{(u)}$ to $C_1^{(v)}$, where Z has to be determined yet. The times t_k which have not been assigned yet are assumed such that σ_0 starts at time $t_0 = t_{GST} = 0$. $\sigma_{0,\infty} = \sigma_0 \sigma_0 \dots$ is the infinite run composed by infinitely many iterations of σ_0. Note that in $\sigma_{0,\infty}$, for every process and every time t there is a time $t' > t$, where it is suspected by some other process.

We define k to be a unique round number in σ_0 by the function $k(z, e, \phi, r) = z \sum_{e'=0}^{E-1} \sum_{\phi'=0}^{2n-1} R(e', \phi') + \sum_{e'=0}^{e} \sum_{\phi'=0}^{2n-1} R(e', \phi') + \sum_{\phi'=0}^{\phi-1} R(e, \phi') + r$.

It can easily be seen that $k(z, e, \phi, r)$ maps every tuple (z, e, ϕ, r) one-to-one to a value k, thus we can define the inverse functions $z(k)$, $e(k)$, $\phi(k)$ and $r(k)$. The times the algorithms start round r in phase ϕ of epoch e and cycle z is given by $t(z, e, \phi, r) = t_{k(z,e,\phi,r)} = k(z, e, \phi, r)\tau_0$. The total number of rounds in σ_0 is $R_{total} = Z \sum_{e=0}^{E-1} \sum_{\phi=0}^{2n-1} R(e, \phi)$.

Now we introduce a compressed run σ_1 that is indistinguishable from σ_0 for all processes. To that end, we define a function that maps all times t_k to times t'_k, such that $t'_{R_{total}} - t'_0 = \tau^-$, whereas the temporal order of the steps is preserved. Since the processes perceive only the message pattern and have no other time information, processes in the compressed execution σ_1 behave in the same way as in σ_0. The time transformation function is given by:

$$t'_k \triangleq f(t_{k(z,e,\phi,r)}) = \left(2nEz + 2ne + \phi + \frac{r}{R(e, \phi)}\right)\gamma, \tag{1}$$

where $\gamma \triangleq \frac{\tau^-}{2nEZ}$ gives the compressed length of a phase. Additionally, we choose $Z \geq \frac{\tau^-}{2nE\varepsilon}$, which implies $\gamma \leq \varepsilon$. The temporal order of the message delivery times is preserved, if $f(t_k)$ is a monotonically increasing function in t_k:

Lemma 1. *The function* $f(t_k) = (2nEz + 2ne + \phi + \frac{r}{R(e,\phi)})\gamma$ *is monotonically increasing in* t_k.

Proof. Obvious from (1) and the fact that $\frac{r}{R(e,\phi)} < 1$, $\phi < 2n$, and $e < E$.   □

We now show that $\sigma_{1,\infty} = \sigma_1\sigma_1\dots$ is indistinguishable from an infinite and timely execution $\sigma_{2,\infty} = \sigma_{2,0}\sigma_{2,1}\dots$, if sufficiently many messages are in the links at $t_{GST} = 0$. The argument is as follows. During a single execution σ_1 all messages sent in σ_1 are received in σ_1. The following lemma constructs identical executions $\sigma_{2,i}$ where messages from $\sigma_{2,i-1}$ are received in $\sigma_{2,i}$ while the new messages are received in $\sigma_{2,i+1}$. Locally, temporal order of message receptions is maintained; thus σ_1 and $\sigma_{2,i}$ are indistinguishable.

Lemma 2. *For all processes, σ_1 is indistinguishable from an execution $\sigma_{2,i}$ that runs from $i\tau^-$ to $(i+1)\tau^-$, for any $i \geq 0$. At the end of $\sigma_{2,i+2}$ no messages from $\sigma_{2,i}$ are in transit. For $i > 0$, every message that is received in $\sigma_{2,i}$ satisfies $\tau^- \leq t_r - t_s \leq \tau^+$.*

Proof. By induction on i. For $i = 0$, recall that σ_0 has $2nEZ$ phases, and the duration of each phase is γ; thus $t'_{R_{total}} = \tau^-$. Hence, for every time t'_k a process receives a message in σ_1, the adversary delivers an identical message from the instable period in $\sigma_{2,0}$ at t'_k. Since all messages sent in $\sigma_{2,0}$ are delivered after τ^- and thus not within $\sigma_{2,0}$, $\sigma_{2,0}$ is indistinguishable from σ_1.

For the induction step $i > 0$, we assume that the lemma holds for $i - 1$. For every message that is sent at t'_k in σ_1 and received at t'_ℓ in σ_1, by the induction hypothesis there is a send event at time $t_s = (i-1)\tau^- + t'_k$. The adversary delivers this message at time $t_r = i\tau^- + t'_\ell$. To see that this message is indeed timely, recall that — by the construction of σ_0 — every message is delivered in the same phase in which it was sent, and by our compression function, the length of each phase in σ_1 is of length $\gamma \leq \varepsilon$. Thus, $t'_\ell - t'_k \leq \varepsilon$, and therefore $t_r - t_s = (i\tau^- + t'_\ell) - ((i-1)\tau^- + t'_k) \leq \tau^+$. Since both, t'_k and t'_ℓ are nonnegative, $t_r - t_s = (i\tau^- + t'_\ell) - ((i-1)\tau^- + t'_k) \geq \tau^-$ follows trivially.

As there are no messages in transit from $\sigma_{2,i-2}$, and all messages from $\sigma_{2,i-1}$ are delivered in $\sigma_{2,i}$ on times $i\tau^- + t'_k$, the algorithm indeed behaves as in σ_1.   □

Note that in $\sigma_{2,0}$ only messages from the unstable period are received, and all other messages fulfill $\tau^- \leq t_r - t_s \leq \tau^+$. Thus, the execution $\sigma_{2,\infty}$ is timely and indistinguishable from $\sigma_{1,\infty}$, which is indistinguishable from $\sigma_{0,\infty}$. In the latter, however, no correct process ever stops from being suspected. The maximum number of messages (per process) from the unstable period is $M = n \cdot R_{total}$ and thus only depends on the algorithm, i.e., for any algorithm there is a channel capacity where no correct process may stop from being suspected forever, although all processes are correct, which contradicts eventual weak accuracy.   □

```
1    state variables
2        ∀q ∈ nb(p) :  lastmsg_p[q] ∈ ℕ
3
4    if received (p, k) from q
5        if k > lastmsg_p[q]
6            lastmsg_p[q] ← k
7            if k = max_{r∈nb(p)}{lastmsg_p[r]} and ∄s, s ≠ q : lastmsg_p[s] = lastmsg_p[q]
8                suspect {r ∈ Π | k − lastmsg_p[r] ≥ Ξ}
9                send (p, k + 1) to all neighbors
10
11   if received (q, k) from q
12       send (q, k) to q
13
14   on deadlock-prevention-event do
15       send (p, max_{q∈nb(p)}{lastmsg_p[q]} + 1) to all neighbors
```

Fig. 1. Algorithm for process p with no bounds on number of messages on a link

4   Unbounded Link Capacity

In this section we describe an implementation of $\diamond\mathcal{P}_\ell$ which handles an unbounded number of messages on the links but requires unbounded memory.

The algorithm is given in Fig. 1. Process p exchanges (p, k) messages with its neighbors, where k is an integer. When a neighbor q receives such a message, q just returns it to p (lines 11–12). For every neighbor q, p holds a variable $lastmsg_p[q]$, where it stores the highest integer k received in a (p, k) reply from q. We also use $lastmsg_{p,q}$ for $lastmsg_p[q]$. The highest value among all $lastmsg_{p,q}$ determines the *round* for process p. Thus we define $round_p(t) \triangleq \max_{q \in \Pi}\{lastmsg_{p,q}(t)\}$ and $round'_p(t)$ respectively. Every time a new round is reached (by receiving a message (p, k) such that $k > round_p$), p sends a $(p, round_p + 1)$ message to all neighbors.

The "fastest neighbor" determines the progress, i.e., $round_p + 1$ is started when the first neighbor returns the $(p, round_p)$ message to p. By our timing model, this requires at least $2\tau^-$. The reply of the slowest neighbor requires at most $2\tau^+$. At this time, $round_p$ has reached at most $2\tau^+/2\tau^- < \Xi$ additional rounds. Thus, for every correct neighbor $round_p - lastmsg_{p,q}$ is less than Ξ, whereas for every faulty neighbor p eventually stops updating $lastmsg_{p,q}$. So, the processes q with $round_p - lastmsg_{p,q} \geq \Xi$ (line 8) are suspected.

From time to time the last message is resent to every neighbor by line 14 in order to prevent a deadlock when messages are lost during the unstable period. Note that this has no influence on the operation of the algorithm, since all messages with $k \leq lastmsg_{p,q}$ are dropped, therefore only the first message that is received has an influence on the behavior of p.

The proof follows the following observation: All messages from the unstable period are received by time τ^+ and responses to these message by $2\tau^+$. After this there cannot be messages in transit greater than $round_p$ for all processes p. That is, from then on the increase from $round_p = i$ to $i + 1$ takes at least $2\tau^-$ which suffices to detect faults. We start with some preliminary lemmas.

Lemma 3 (Monotonicity). *After* t_{GST}, $round_p(t)$ *is monotonically increasing with time* t, *i.e.,* $t_{\mathrm{GST}} \leq t_1 \leq t \Rightarrow round_p(t_1) \leq round_p(t) \leq round'_p(t)$.

Proof. Obvious, since $round_p$ is the maximum of all $lastmsg_{p,q}$, and by lines 5 and 6 $lastmsg_{p,q}$ is monotonically increasing. □

Lemma 4 (Progress). *There is a time* t, $t_{\mathrm{GST}} \leq t < t_{\mathrm{GST}} + \max\{2\tau^+, \eta\}$, *such that at time* t, p *broadcasts* $(p, round'_p(t) + 1)$.

Proof. At time t_{GST} we have to distinguish two cases:
(1) There is at least one neighbor q of p, such that at least one message (p, ℓ), with $round_p(t_{\mathrm{GST}}) < \ell$ is in $Q(p, q, t)$. Let (p, k) be the first of them to be received by p at some time $t \geq t_{\mathrm{GST}}$. Obviously, $t < t_{\mathrm{GST}} + 2\tau^+$. Since by assumption this is the first message after t_{GST} that changes $round_p$, we have $round_p(t) = round_p(t_{\mathrm{GST}})$. Thus, $lastmsg_{p,q}(t) \leq round_p(t) < k$, p executes lines 6 and 9 and hence broadcasts $(p, round'_p(t) + 1)$, with $round'_p(t) = k$.
(2) No such message exists. Then by time $t = t_{\mathrm{GST}} + \eta$, line 15 is executed, and also $(p, round_p(t) + 1)$ is broadcast.
    Thus, by time $t_{\mathrm{GST}} + \max(2\tau^+, \eta)$ the required message is broadcast. □

Lemma 5 (Stabilization). *For every message* (p, k), *which is received by* p *at some time* $t \geq t_{\mathrm{GST}} + 2\tau^+$, *it holds that* $k \leq round_p(t) + 1$.

Proof. Since sending a message to a neighbor and receiving the answer takes at most $2\tau^+$, there is a time $t_1 \geq t_{\mathrm{GST}}$ when p has broadcast (p, k). However, since we are after t_{GST}, k must be equal to $round'_p(t_1) + 1$, since p can broadcast only $(p, round'_p(t_1) + 1)$ messages (lines 9,15). By Lemma 3, $round_p$ is monotonically increasing with time. Therefore from $t \geq t_1$ follows $round'_p(t) + 1 \geq round_p(t) + 1 \geq round_p(t_1) + 1 = k$. □

    Let $t_{stable} \overset{\Delta}{=} t_{\mathrm{GST}} + \max(2\tau^+, \eta)$, which is the time by which we have progress (Lemma 4) and correct message pattern (Lemma 5).

Lemma 6 (Fastest Progress). *Let process* p *broadcast* (p, k) *at some time* $t \geq t_{stable}$ *for the first time. Then* p *does not broadcast* $(p, k + \ell)$ *before* $t + 2\ell\tau^-$.

Proof. By induction on ℓ. For $\ell = 1$ assume by contradiction that p broadcasts $(p, k+1)$ before time $t + 2\tau^-$. If $(p, k+1)$ is sent by line 15 it was sent also by line 9 before (since after t_{stable} by Lemma 4 at least one message was sent by line 9), which would not be the first time. Since $(p, k + 1)$ is sent by line 9, p received a (p, k) message which was sent before time $t + \tau^-$ by some q (as response – line 11) and before time t by p. Contradiction.
    Now assume p broadcasts $(p, k+\ell-1)$ not before $t + 2(\ell-1)\tau^-$ the first time. By the same argument, p does not broadcast $(p, k + \ell)$ before time $t + 2\ell\tau^-$. □

Lemma 7 (Slowest Progress). *Let correct process p broadcast (p, k) at some time $t > t_{stable}$ for the first time. p broadcasts $(p, k + \ell)$ by $t + 2\ell\tau^+$.*

Proof. By induction on ℓ. Since p broadcasts (p, k) at time t, all neighbors of p receive this message by time $t + \tau^+$ and every correct neighbor (since $\deg(p) > f$ there exists at least one) returns it. These messages are received by p by time $t + 2\tau^+$. Consider the time of the reception of the first of these messages. Because of Lemma 5 (note that $k = round'_p(t) + 1$), p receives no message (p, k') with $k' > k$ by $t + 2\tau^+$, thus p broadcasts $(p, k + 1)$.

For $\ell > 1$, assume p broadcasts (p, k) by time $t + 2(\ell - 1)\tau^+$. By the same argument, p broadcasts $(p, k + \ell)$ by time $t + 2\ell\tau^+$.   □

Lemma 8. *For every time $t > t_{stable} + 2\tau^+ \Xi$ and every correct neighbor q of correct process p, it holds that $round'_p(t) - lastmsg'_{p,q}(t) < \Xi$.*

Proof. Since all variables are non-decreasing, the condition could be only violated by increasing $round_p$. So we consider only times t, where $round'_p(t) > round_p(t)$. By Lemma 5 we have $round'_p(t) = round_p(t) + 1$. By Lemmas 4, 5 and 6, a message $(p, round'_p(t) - \Xi + 1)$ was broadcast by p at time $t_s \le t - 2\tau^- \Xi$, by Lemma 7, $t_s > t_{stable}$, so this message really exists. The reply to this message is received from every correct neighbor q by time $t_r \le t_s + 2\tau^+$, thus $lastmsg'_{p,q}(t_r) \ge round'_p(t) - \Xi + 1 > round'_p(t) - \Xi$. Because of $\Xi > \Theta$ we have $t_r \le t_s + 2\tau^+ \le t - 2\tau^- \Xi + 2\tau^+ \le t$. Since $lastmsg'_{p,q}$ is monotonically increasing it follows that $lastmsg'_{p,q}(t) \ge lastmsg'_{p,q}(t_r)$. Hence we derive our desired condition $round'_p(t) - lastmsg'_{p,q}(t) < \Xi$.   □

Theorem 2 (Local Completeness). *Eventually every non-correct neighbor of p is suspected by p.*

Proof. Let t_{crash} be the time q crashes, and $t = \max\{t_{crash}, t_{GST}\}$. Then no message from q to p is received after $t + \tau^+$. After this, $lastmsg_{p,q} \le round_p$ remains unchanged. By Lemma 7, $round_p$ reaches $round_p(t) + \Xi$ by time $\max\{t_{crash} + \tau^+, t_{stable}\} + 2\Xi\tau^+$. Since $round_p$ is nondecreasing, q remains suspected.   □

Theorem 3 (Eventual Local Accuracy). *Eventually p stops suspecting every correct neighbor of p.*

Proof. Follows directly from Lemma 8 and line 8 of the algorithm.   □

Corollary 1. *The algorithm in Fig. 1 is an SS implementation of $\diamond\mathcal{P}_\ell$.*

After stabilization, a crashed process is suspected Ξ rounds after it crashed, i.e., the worst case failure detection time is $2\Xi\tau^+$.

5   Bounded Link Capacity

We now provide an FD implementation that requires an a priori known bound on the number of messages which can be in transit at the same time from or to a single process. In contrast to the previous algorithm, this one requires just bounded memory size. Hence, this result is of practical interest: Real computers have bounded memory, which is not only used to store variables of our algorithms, but also to store messages in various queues. Since queues — which are the significant parts of links — essentially determine the link capacity, the assumption that the number of messages is bounded is reasonable.

The algorithm given in Fig. 2 works similar to the one in Sect. 4. However, since the integers are bounded, we need to wrap-around the round number. We call such a cycle a *phase*. To avoid that messages from previous phases interfere with the current one, we use phase numbers. Since the range of the phase numbers has to be bounded as well, we have to ensure that there are sufficiently many distinct phase numbers such that no interference is possible. We show that if there are at most M messages in all links of a process, $M + 2$ phases are sufficient to ensure stabilization. The idea behind this is that there exists at least one phase which cannot be shortened by faulty messages from the unstable period. In contrast to the algorithm in Sect. 4 this algorithm broadcasts only on a phase switch, whereas the previous one broadcasts every round.

```
1    state variables
2        phase_p ∈ {0, ..., M + 1}
3        ∀q ∈ nb(p) :  lastmsg_p[q] ∈ {0, ..., Ξ}
4
5    if received (p, ph, k) from q
6        if ph = phase_p and k > lastmsg_p[q]
7            if k < Ξ
8                lastmsg_p[q] ← k
9                send (p, phase_p, k + 1) to q
10           else
11               suspect {r ∈ Π | lastmsg_p[r] = 0}
12               phase_p ← (phase_p + 1) mod (M + 2)
13               ∀r ∈ nb(p) :  lastmsg_p[r] ← 0
14               send (p, phase_p, 1) to all neighbors
15
16   if received (q, ph, k) from q
17           send (q, ph, k) to q
18
19   on deadlock-prevention-event do
20       ∀q ∈ nb(p) :  send (p, phase_p, lastmsg_p[q] + 1) to q
```

Fig. 2. Algorithm for process p with known upper bound on number of messages

By our assumption, $|Q(p, t_{\text{GST}})| \leq M < \infty$ for all processes p. For any phase number ph we further define $next(ph) \triangleq (ph + 1) \bmod (M + 2)$ and $prev(ph) \triangleq (ph + M + 1) \bmod (M + 2)$.

Lemma 9. *For every process p, in any execution of our algorithm, there exists at least one phase number ph_0, such that no message (p, ph_0, k) is in $Q(p, t_{GST})$ and $ph_0 \neq phase_p(t_{GST})$.*

Proof. Obviously, $|Q(p, t_{GST})| = x \leq M$. At time t_{GST}, process p can be in one phase only. The number of phase numbers is $M + 2 > x + 1$ such that at least one phase number remains.   □

We now give two properties that define the legitimate states for process p. The stability property ensures that there are no faulty messages in transit. The progress property guarantees that the system is not deadlocked, i.e., that there are sufficiently many messages in transit to keep the FD working.

Definition 1 (Stability). $\mathcal{PS}(p, t)$ *holds for process p at time t iff there is no $next(phase_p(t))$ message in transit. Formally,*
$$\mathcal{PS}(p, t) \equiv \nexists k : (p, next(phase'_p(t)), k) \in Q(p, t)$$

Definition 2 (Progress). $\mathcal{PP}(p, t)$ *holds for process p at time t iff there is at least one correct neighbor q of p, from or to which a message for the current phase with $k > lastmsg_{p,q}(p, t)$ is in transit. Formally,*
$$\mathcal{PP}(p, t) \equiv \exists q \in (\mathcal{C} \cap \mathrm{nb}(p)) \; \exists k > lastmsg_{p,q}(p, t) : (p, phase_p(t), k) \in Q(p, q, t)$$

We start by showing closure of progress $\mathcal{PP}$.

Lemma 10. *If there is a time $t_0 \geq t_{GST}$, where $\mathcal{PP}(p, t_0)$ holds, then $\mathcal{PP}(p, t)$ holds also for all times $t > t_0$. Formally,*
$$\exists t_0 \geq t_{GST} : \mathcal{PP}(p, t_0) \Rightarrow \forall t > t_0 \; \mathcal{PP}(p, t)$$

Proof. Assume by contradiction that there is a time $t > t_0$, where $\mathcal{PP}(p, t)$ does not hold for the first time. Since by assumption the predicate held before that, for some non-faulty q, either $lastmsg_{p,q}(t) \neq lastmsg'_{p,q}(t)$ or $(p, phase_p(t), k) \notin Q'(p, q, t)$. In both cases, p has received a $(p, phase_p(t), k')$ message with $k' > lastmsg_{p,q}(t)$ and thus sends either a $(p, phase'_p(t), lastmsg'_{p,q}(t) + 1)$ or a $(p, phase'_p(t), round''_p(t)+1)$ message and sets $lastmsg_{p,q} = 0$. In both cases $\mathcal{PP}(p, t)$ holds. Contradiction.   □

Lemma 11. *For all times $t \geq t_{GST} + \eta$, $\mathcal{PP}(p, t)$ holds.*

Proof. By time $t_{GST} + \eta$, p sends a $(p, phase_p, lastmsg_{p,q} + 1)$ to every neighbor q. Since $f < \deg(p)$, at least one of them is non-faulty and thus $\mathcal{PP}$ holds for p at this time. By Lemma 10 after that $\mathcal{PP}$ holds forever.   □

We have seen that our algorithm stabilizes such that $\mathcal{PP}$ always holds after bounded time after t_{GST}. We now turn our attention to the $\mathcal{PS}$ property and start with some preliminary lemmas.

Lemma 12 (Fastest Progress). *Assume p starts phase $ph = phase_p(t)$ by broadcasting $(p, ph, 1)$ at time $t > t_{GST}$, and $\mathcal{PS}(p, t)$ holds. Then p does not broadcast $(p, next(ph), 1)$ by time $t + 2\tau^- \Xi > t + 2\tau^+$.*

Proof. Since $\mathcal{PS}(p,t)$ holds, no messages (p, ph, ℓ) are in transit at t. Therefore, if p receives a (p, ph, ℓ) message for $1 \leq \ell \leq \Xi$ after time t, it is a correct response to one of p's (p, ph, ℓ) messages. The minimum time of such a round trip is $2\tau^-$. By line 9 and line 7, the next phase is started after Ξ round trips. Thus, not before $t + 2\tau^-\Xi$. Since $\Xi > \Theta$ (cf. Sect. 2) $t + 2\tau^-\Xi > t + 2\tau^+$.   □

Lemma 13 (Slowest Progress). *Assume p starts phase ph by broadcasting $(p, ph, 1)$ at time t. Then p broadcasts $(p, next(ph), 1)$ by $t + 2\tau^+\Xi$.*

Proof. Note that p broadcasts $(p, next(ph), 1)$ if it receives a (p, ph, Ξ) message from one of its neighbors and is still in phase ph. If p is no more in phase ph we are done, so it remains to show that p receives a (p, ph, Ξ) message by time $t + 2\tau^+\Xi$. Sending a message to a neighbor and back requires at most time $2\tau^+$. By line 9 and line 7, the next phase is started after Ξ round trips. Thus p receives (p, ph, Ξ) by time $t + 2\tau^+\Xi$.   □

Lemma 14. *Assume $phase_p(t) = ph$. Then $phase_p(t_1) = prev(ph)$ for some times $t_1 > t > t_{\mathrm{GST}}$ only if p was in all phases in the time interval $[t, t_1]$.*

Proof. By line 12 of the algorithm, p changes its phase only to $next(phase_p(t))$ and thus has to adopt all other values before reaching $prev(phase_p(t))$.   □

Lemma 15. *$\mathcal{PS}(p,t)$ holds at time $t = t_{\mathrm{GST}} + 2\tau^+$.*

Proof. We have to show that no messages (p, ℓ, k) for $\ell = next(phase_p(t))$ and some k are in transit at time $t = t_{\mathrm{GST}} + 2\tau^+$. Obviously, no message which is in transit at time t was already in transit at time t_{GST}. Moreover, no message which is in transit at time t is a reply from one of p's neighbors to a faulty message which was in $Q(p, t_{\mathrm{GST}})$ since all these responses must be received by p before t. Thus, message (p, ℓ, k) can only be in transit at time t if p was in phase ℓ at some time t_1, $t_{\mathrm{GST}} \leq t_1 \leq t$. It remains to show that this is not possible.

As p is in phase $prev(\ell)$ at time t it must, by Lemma 14, have been in all phases $(0..M+1)$ between t_1 and t, thus there must be some time t_2, $t_1 \leq t_2 \leq t$ such that $phase_p(t_2) = prev(ph_0)$, i.e., phase ph_0 from Lemma 9 was started then. Thus $\mathcal{PS}(p, t_2)$. By Lemma 12 this phase can only be terminated after $t_2 + 2\tau^+ \geq t$ which is a contradiction to p being in phase $prev(\ell)$ at time t.   □

It remains to show closure, i.e., if $\mathcal{PS}$ is reached once, it holds forever.

Definition 3. *We define $t_{ph}(p, t, ph)$ as the first time after t, where p reaches phase ph. Formally, $t_{ph}(p, t, ph) \triangleq \min\{t' > t \mid phase_p(t') = ph \wedge \nexists t''(t < t'' < t' \wedge phase_p(t'') = ph)\}$.*

Lemma 16. *From $\mathcal{PS}(p,t)$ where $t \geq t_{\mathrm{GST}}$ follows that $\mathcal{PS}(p, t')$ holds for all times t', $t \leq t' < t_{ph}(p, t, next(phase_p(t)))$.*

Proof. Since $phase_p$ remains unchanged, no spontaneous messages are generated after t_{GST} and p sends $phase_p(t)$ messages only.   □

Lemma 17. *Let $\mathcal{PS}$ hold at p and time $t_{ph}(p, t, ph)$ where $t \geq t_{\text{GST}}$. Then $\mathcal{PS}(p, t')$ holds at time $t' = t_{ph}(p, t, next(ph))$.*

Proof. By Lemma 12 p terminates phase ph after $t_{ph}(p, t, ph) + 2\tau^+$. All messages which are in transit to p at time $t_{ph}(p, t, ph)$ are received by time $t_{ph}(p, t, ph) + \tau^+$. All messages for other phases than ph are ignored by p (and hence no messages are sent). All messages for phases other than ph which are in transit from p to its neighbors are answered by them by line 17. The answers are received by p by $t_{ph}(p, t, ph) + 2\tau^+$ and ignored as well since p is still in phase ph. Thus, no messages for other phases than ph are in transit at time t'. Since $next(next(ph)) \neq ph$ the lemma holds.   □

Lemma 18. *After time $t_{stable} = t_{\text{GST}} + 2\tau^+$, $\mathcal{PS}$ holds at all phase switches.*

Proof. By Lemma 15, $\mathcal{PS}(p, t)$ holds at time $t = t_{\text{GST}} + 2\tau^+$. By Lemma 16, $\mathcal{PS}(p, t')$ holds for all times t', $t \leq t' < t_{ph}(p, t, next(phase_p(t)))$. From an inductive application of Lemma 17 it follows that $\mathcal{PS}$ holds at all phase switch times after that.   □

From these lemmas it follows that after some time, all phases are sufficiently long to timeout processes. Thus we can show the FD properties.

Theorem 4 (Local Completeness). *Eventually every non-correct neighbor of p is suspected by p.*

Proof. Assume neighbor q of p has crashed. By Lemma 11, $\mathcal{PP}$ holds by time $t_{\text{GST}} + \eta$. Note that every message (p, ph, k) from q, with $k > lastmsg_{p,q}$ and $ph = phase_p$ causes either a message $(p, ph, k+1)$ (for $k < \Xi$) or a $(p, ph+1, 1)$ message. Consequently, eventually p reaches $k = \Xi$ and switches to the next phase (lines 11–14). When p reaches $k = \Xi$ in the next phase, $lastmsg_{p,q} = 0$, since there was no message from q. According to line 11, p suspects q.   □

Theorem 5 (Eventual Local Accuracy). *Eventually p stops suspecting every correct neighbor of p.*

Proof. By Lemma 18 and Lemma 12 all phases that are started after $t_{\text{GST}} + 2\tau^+$ are longer than $2\tau^+$. This is long enough for all answers of correct process p's correct neighbors q to p's $(p, ph, 1)$ message to be received by p before it executes line 11 at some time t. Thus, $lastmsg_{p,q}(t) > 0$ for every correct neighbor q when p executes line 11 such that no correct processes will ever be suspected by p.   □

Corollary 2. *The algorithm in Fig. 2 is an SS implementation of $\diamond\mathcal{P}_\ell$.*

When a process crashes in a phase (after replying to at least one message) it is suspected at the end of the next phase. Thus, the worst case failure detection time is $(4\Xi - 1)\tau^+$ once the FD has stabilized.

6 Discussions

This paper is in the context of distributed fault-tolerant SS algorithms [12,2,18,6] and considers the implementation of message-driven SS failure detectors. In contrast to time-driven algorithms [3,10], where local clocks can be employed to periodically send messages independently of the rate of received messages, message-driven algorithms can only react to received messages. The time between send events thus depends solely on the incoming message pattern. Due to arbitrary system states perceived time can be compressed arbitrarily such that the message pattern provides unreliable time information. This leads to our impossibility result in Sect. 3.

However, there are ways to circumvent the impossibility: We presented a simple solution, which requires unbounded memory, an assumption that is not reasonable when considering SS algorithms for implementations in real systems. We therefore presented a practical solution in Sect. 5 which requires only bounded memory but assumes a known bound on the channel capacity. This solution can be used in real systems, as the memory requirement of the algorithm is just $\log(M)$, M being a bound on the number of messages simultaneously in transit.

In [16] we devised two other algorithms which—in conjunction with the timed algorithms in [3]—contribute to the exploration of alternatives for circumventing our impossibility result: We show that the problem can be solved (1) by randomization and (2) in systems without timing uncertainty (where $\tau^+ = \tau^-$). The randomized algorithm is a variant of the algorithm in Sect. 5 with only 3 different phases where upon phase switch the next phase number is determined via a coin toss. The algorithm stabilizes with high probability.

Howell, Nesterenko, and Mizuno [14] discussed finite state SS protocols. The states include the messages that are in the buffer, and they consider a model where a message is lost if a process tries to write into a full buffer (belonging to a link between two processes). In the executions we construct in the impossibility proof of Sect. 3, the adversary delivers the messages in such a way that this does not happen—and we give the size of the buffer such that the adversary can do so. The algorithm in Sect. 4 has infinite buffers, and in concordance with the result in [13], it requires infinite legitimate states as some round number is ever increasing. Regarding our algorithm in Sect. 5 we consider a weaker adversary as in [14]. We assume that the adversary is fair in that it never forces an algorithm to put a message into a full outgoing buffer. Finding an algorithm that handles the adversary of [14] is an open topic.

Our results relate time-driven and message-driven solutions of agreement problems. We have shown that for the one very specific problem of SS failure detector implementations there is a difference regarding solvability. Hence, system models that allow just message-driven algorithms are weaker than models that allow time-driven algorithms. These results just show how much clocks or timers help when invalid message patterns have to be tolerated.

Acknowledgments. We are grateful to Felix Freiling for valuable discussions on the subject and to an anonymous reviewer for pointing out the relation of our work to [14]. Bettina Weiss helped us improving the presentation of the results by patiently reading and commenting earlier drafts of this paper.

References

1. Marcos K. Aguilera, Carole Delporte-Gallet, Hugues Fauconnier, and Sam Toueg. On implementing Omega with weak reliability and synchrony assumptions. In *Proceeding of the 22nd Annual ACM Symposium on Principles of Distributed Computing (PODC'03)*, 2003.
2. Efthymios Anagnostou and Vassos Hadzilacos. Tolerating transient and permanent failures (extended abstract). In *Proceedings of the 7th International Workshop on Distributed Algorithms (WDAG'93)*, volume 725 of *LNCS*, pages 174–188, Lausanne,Switzerland, Sept 1993.
3. Joffroy Beauquier and Synnöve Kekkonen-Moneta. Fault-tolerance and self-stabilization: Impossibility results and solutions using self-stabilizing failure detectors. *International Journal of Systems Science*, 28(11):1177–1187, 1997.
4. Tushar Deepak Chandra, Vassos Hadzilacos, and Sam Toueg. The weakest failure detector for solving consensus. *Journal of the ACM*, 43(4):685–722, June 1996.
5. Tushar Deepak Chandra and Sam Toueg. Unreliable failure detectors for reliable distributed systems. *Journal of the ACM*, 43(2):225–267, March 1996.
6. Ariel Daliot, Danny Dolev, and Hanna Parnas. Linear time byzantine self-stabilizing clock synchronization. In *Proceedings of the 7th International Conference on Principles of Distributed Systems*, Dec 2003.
7. Edsger W. Dijkstra. Self-stabilizing systems in spite of distributed control. *Communications of the ACM*, 17(11):643–644, 1974.
8. Danny Dolev, Cynthia Dwork, and Larry Stockmeyer. On the minimal synchronism needed for distributed consensus. *Journal of the ACM*, 34(1):77–97, January 1987.
9. Shlomi Dolev. *Self-Stabilization*. MIT Press, 2000.
10. Cynthia Dwork, Nancy Lynch, and Larry Stockmeyer. Consensus in the presence of partial synchrony. *Journal of the ACM*, 35(2):288–323, April 1988.
11. Christof Fetzer, Ulrich Schmid, and Martin Süßkraut. On the possibility of consensus in asynchronous systems with finite average response times. In *Proceedings of the 25th International Conderence on Distributed Computing Systems (ICDCS'05)*, Columbus, Ohio, USA, 2005.
12. Felix Gärtner. On crash failures and self-stabilization. Presentation at Journées Internationales sur l'auto-stabilisation, CIRM, Luminy, France, October 2002.
13. Mohamed G. Gouda and Nicholas J. Multari. Stabilizing communication protocols. *IEEE Transactions on Computers*, 40(4):448–458, April 1991.
14. Rodney R. Howell, Mikhail Nesterenko, and Masaaki Mizuno. Finite-state self-stabilizing protocols in message-passing systems. *Journal of Parallel and Distributed Computing*, 62:792–817, May 2002.
15. Martin Hutle. On omega in sparse networks. In *Proc. 10th International Symposium Pacific Rim Dependable Computing (PRDC'04)*, Papeete, Tahiti, March 2004.
16. Martin Hutle and Josef Widder. Self-stabilizing failure detector algorithms. In *Proc. IASTED International Conference on Parallel and Distributed Computing and Networks (PDCN'05)*, Innsbruck, Austria, February 2005.
17. Gérard Le Lann and Ulrich Schmid. How to implement a timer-free perfect failure detector in partially synchronous systems. Technical Report 183/1-127, Department of Automation, Technische Universität Wien, January 2003.

18. Mikhail Nesterenko and Anish Arora. Tolerance to unbounded byzantine faults. In *Proceedings of the 21st IEEE Symposium on Reliable Distributed Systems (SRDS'02)*, pages 22–29, Suita, Japan, 2002. IEEE Computer Society.
19. Josef Widder. Booting clock synchronization in partially synchronous systems. In *Proceedings of the 17th International Symposium on Distributed Computing (DISC'03)*, volume 2848 of *LNCS*, pages 121–135, Sorrento, Italy, October 2003. Springer Verlag.
20. Josef Widder, Gérard Le Lann, and Ulrich Schmid. Failure detection with booting in partially synchronous systems. In *Proceedings of the 5th European Dependable Computing Conference (EDCC-5)*, volume 3463 of *LNCS*, pages 20–37, Budapest, Hungary, April 2005. Springer Verlag.

Approximation of Self-stabilizing Vertex Cover Less Than 2

Jun Kiniwa

Department of Applied Economics, University of Hyogo,
8-2-1 Gakuen nishi-machi, Nishi-ku, Kobe-shi 651-2197, Japan
Phone: +81-78-794-5844, Fax: +81-78-794-6166
kiniwa@econ.u-hyogo.ac.jp

Abstract. A vertex cover of a graph is a subset of vertices such that each edge has at least one endpoint in the subset. Determining the minimum vertex cover is a well-known NP-complete problem in a sequential setting. Several techniques, e.g., depth-first search, a local ratio theorem, and semidefinite relaxation, have given good approximation algorithms. However, some of them cannot be applied to a distributed setting, in particular self-stabilizing algorithms. Thus only a 2-approximation solution based on a self-stabilizing maximal matching has been obviously known until now. In this paper we propose a new self-stabilizing vertex cover algorithm that achieves $(2 - 1/\Delta)$-approximation ratio, where Δ is the maximum degree of a given network. We first introduce a sequential $(2 - 1/\Delta)$-approximation algorithm that uses a maximal matching with the high-degree-first order of vertices. Then we present a self-stabilizing algorithm based on the same idea, and show that the output of the algorithm is the same as that of the sequential one.

1   Introduction

Self-stabilization is the most fundamental concept of automatic recovery in distributed systems. A lot of researchers have paid attention to its fault tolerance. A transient fault is the fault that only perturbs the system state, but not the program code. Self-stabilizing algorithms tolerate the transient fault in such a way that the system eventually converges to a legitimate state without any aid of external actions. Thus the algorithms must be designed to run for any initial system state. The execution of self-stabilizing algorithms is guaranteed to repair faulty states and to keep legitimacy thereafter.

Given an undirected graph $G = (V, E)$, a vertex cover is a subset $C \subseteq V$ such that each edge $e \in E$ has at least one endpoint in C. It is often required to find the minimum C, while it is known to be NP-complete[4]. Instead of finding an exact solution, many approximation algorithms have been developed[7,13,15,17]. Though the problem has been primary considered in sequential algorithms, it also has a wide application to distributed systems, e.g., monitoring link failures[1], placement of agents[11], and managing vector clocks[5]. The placement of such agents or processes cannot be designed in a centralized fashion for large-scale

T. Herman and S. Tixeuil (Eds.): SSS 2005, LNCS 3764, pp. 171–182, 2005.

networks. So it is significant to obtain a good approximation distributed algorithm. Furthermore, we would like to add the property of fault-tolerance. Hence our chief concern is to construct a self-stabilizing and as small vertex cover as possible.

Some approximation techniques used in sequential algorithms cannot be applied to distributed algorithms because only local computation is allowed. There, however, seem to be at least two applicable methods — a maximal matching and covering a high-degree vertex first. A maximal matching M is a maximal set of edges with no two of them share the same vertex. It is known that a set of both endpoints of every edge in M form a vertex cover with at most twice the optimum. On the other hand, it is also well-known that the worst example of the greedy method, i.e., covering a high-degree vertex first, is $O(\log n)$ times as large as the optimum. We, however, do not often experience such worst cases when using the greedy method. Instead, it sometimes works better than the maximal matching approximation that always covers both endpoints of the matched edges even if it is not necessary. Hence we combine the greedy method with the maximal matching to ensure the approximation ratio, that is, a maximal matching with the high-degree-first order of vertices.

From the sequential point of view, there have been many approximation approaches, depth-first search[15], a local-ratio theorem[17], semidefinite relaxation [7], and a graph theoretical algorithm[13]. However, Håstad[9] recently showed that there is no $(7/6 - \epsilon)$-approximation algorithm for the problem for any $\epsilon > 0$ unless $P = NP$. From the distributed point of view, there does not exist so much work for the vertex cover problem. The significance of this approach, however, has been continuing to grow since large-scale networks, e.g., Internet, mobile ad hoc and sensor networks emerged. Recently, a 2-approximation (weighted) vertex cover algorithm has been proposed[6]. The approximation ratio can be achieved by including matched vertices when a maximal matching is determined. As a part of the vertex cover, algorithms for finding a maximal matching were well-studied. The algorithm presented by Hanckowiack et al.[8] computes a maximal matching in $O(\log^4 n)$ rounds, while the one by Panconesi and Rizzi[14] in $O(\Delta + \log^* n)$ rounds, where n is the number of vertices and Δ is the maximum degree. A stabilizing maximal matching algorithm was also proposed by Hsu and Huang[12] and its performance was re-evaluated[10,16], furthermore, the computation model was recently sophisticated[2]. As far as we know, no self-stabilizing vertex cover algorithm with less than 2-approximation ratio is known.

In this paper we develop a self-stabilizing vertex cover algorithm with $(2 - 1/\Delta)$-approximation ratio, where Δ is the maximum degree of a network. To introduce our idea, we first describe a sequential version of our algorithm and derive its approximation ratio. Next we state our self-stabilizing algorithm and its correctness proofs. Then we claim that our main algorithm converges to the same solution as the one the sequential algorithm outputs. The features of our method are:

- the approximation ratio is better than that of an obvious solution based on the self-stabilizing maximal matching, and
- finding an adjacent vertex with the minimum degree locally (i.e., local optimization) is equivalent to those operations in the high-degree-first order (i.e., global optimization).

The rest of this paper is organized as follows. Section 2 states our self-stabilization model. Section 3 describes a sequential approximation algorithm to prepare for our main algorithm. Section 4 presents our method that finds as small a vertex cover as possible. Section 5 proves the correctness and the properties of our algorithm. Finally, Section 6 concludes the paper.

2   Model

Here we describe a model used in our discussion. There are n processes $P = \{1, 2, \ldots, n\}$, where each process is identified by the hardwired unique name. A network consists of n processes of finite state machines connected arbitrarily with bidirectional communication links, where each process $i \in P$ has shared state variables with a finite set of states Σ_i. We assume that transient faults sometimes occur at the variables and the interval between faults is sufficiently long compared to a stabilization time. The global state of all processes is called a *configuration*. The set of all configurations is denoted by $\Gamma = \Sigma_1 \times \Sigma_2 \times \cdots \times \Sigma_n$.

A network is represented by a graph $G = (V, E)$, where $V (= P)$ is a set of vertices (processes) and E is a set of edges (communication links). For convenience, we use the corresponding terms process–link and vertex–edge interchangeably. A vertex $i \in V$ is *adjacent* to another vertex j and an edge $e \in E$ is *incident* to i or j if there is an edge $e = (i, j)$. Each process i is assumed to maintain a set of adjacent processes $N(i)$ correctly. Let $N^+(i) = \{i\} \cup N(i)$ denote process i with its adjacent processes. The number of edges incident to vertex i is called a *degree* (or particularly called a *pure degree*), denoted by $\delta_i \leq \Delta$, where Δ is the maximum (pure) degree of a graph G. We define an *identified degree* d_i as (δ_i, i) to make the degree of a vertex unique. Then we say that $d_k < d_i$, called d_k is *lower* than d_i (or d_i is *higher* than d_k), if $\delta_k < \delta_i$ or $(\delta_k = \delta_i) \wedge (k < i)$. A vertex i with the *highest* (*maximum*) degree means that there is no vertex with higher degree in $N(i)$ for distributed algorithms, or in $V \backslash i$ for sequential algorithms. The *lowest* (*minimum*) degree is similarly defined. When we just refer to a degree without notice, e.g., high-degree-first, it means the identified degree[1].

We assume a *state-reading model* for simplicity, that is, each process directly reads the shared variables of adjacent processes and updates only the variables of its own. Each process has a program of internal computations, "**if** *Guard* **then** *Action*", or denoted by *Guard* $\Rightarrow$ *Action*. If *Guard* is true in a process i, the process is said to be *enabled*. A transient fault may perturb states of processes, where the number of enabled processes may be more than one. From the set of enabled processes $EP \subseteq P$, a scheduler D-*daemon* (distributed

---

[1] We explicitly use the pure degree only in Lemma 1.

daemon) selects, or called *activates*, a non-empty set of processes $A \subseteq EP$ at a configuration $c_j \in \Gamma$. An *atomic step* consists of reading the states of adjacent processes, an internal computation, and writing its own state. We say that c_{j+1} is reached from c_j for such a transition of configurations. An *execution E* is a sequence of configurations $E = c_0, c_1, \ldots, c_j, c_{j+1}, \ldots$ such that $c_{j+1} \in \Gamma$ is reached from $c_j \in \Gamma$. The definition of *round* complexity[3] is as follows. The first round e is the minimal prefix of an execution E in which every process executes at least one action. Let e' be the suffix of E such that $E = ee'$. The second round e'' of E is the first round of e', and so forth. The daemon is assumed to be *fair*, that is, every process is activated infinitely often.

The state variables of each process contain a pointer. The pointer *points to* one of adjacent processes to make a matching. We say that process i makes a *proposal* to $k \in N(i)$ if i points to k, denoted by $i \rightarrow k$, when k does not point to i. Conversely, we say that process i *accepts* a proposal of $k \in N(i)$ if i points to k against the k's proposal to i. That is, $i \rightarrow k$ and $k \rightarrow i$ hold and are abbreviated to $i \leftrightarrow k$. In that case, we say that process i is *matched* (with process k) and it is denoted by $i \in Matched$ or $(i, k) \in Matched$. If $i \notin Matched$, it is called *unmatched*. A set of matched processes are partitioned into two subsets, *Proposer* and *Acceptor*, where processes in *Proposer* have made proposals and those in *Acceptor* have accepted them. A vertex is said to be *covered* when it is contained in the vertex cover $C \subseteq V$, or otherwise *uncovered*. Additionally, an edge is also said to be covered when it is incident to some vertex in C.

3   Preliminaries

To introduce our self-stabilizing algorithm, here we state an underlying sequential algorithm. Our basic idea is partly based on a simple greedy approach : (1) take a vertex v with the maximum degree and delete v with its all incident edges, and (2) iterate this until there are no edges left. Though the greedy method seems to be usually good, its approximation ratio is known to be $O(\log n)$ times the optimal vertex cover in the worst case. To achieve a better approximation ratio, we need other techniques.

On the other hand, our idea is also partly based on a 2-approximation algorithm that makes use of a maximal matching. This approximation ratio is derived by the fact that a vertex cover is always included in any maximal matching. Since the algorithm always outputs both the matched vertices, the approximation is not good if the matching is close to the maximum matching. The bounded approximation ratio, however, is attractive to researchers.

Hence our method is to combine these algorithms so that it usually works well with the guarantee of the bounded worst case. Furthermore, we would like to achieve a better approximation ratio than 2, which is known to be the best one in a distributed setting[6]. First, we construct a high-degree-first maximal matching, where the vertex with the maximum degree is matched first, and then cover the vertex (one endpoint of the matched edge), and so forth. Finally, we

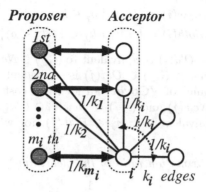

Fig. 1. Each edge cost incident to i

cover some vertices in order to complete a vertex cover by using the information of degrees.

Now we outline a sequential algorithm **VCover**, in which we use some expressions similar to the self-stabilizing algorithm. Let L be a sorted list whose top is the vertex with the maximum degree. A vertex v, the top element of L, is iteratively selected. Since the selected vertex v corresponds to the process making a proposal, we call v a *proposal vertex* and express $v \in Proposer$. Likewise, the minimum degree vertex u matched with the proposal vertex v is called an *acceptance vertex*. We call the i-th selected vertex in *Proposer* the i-*th proposal vertex*.

1. Sort vertices into the high-degree-first order and construct a list L according to the order.
2. For each vertex v at the top of L, iterate (a)–(c) (until no vertex can be selected):
   (a) Select its adjacent vertex u with the minimum degree and join (u, v) to a matching.
   (b) Cover the vertex v (not u).
   (c) Remove u and v from the list L.
3. If there is some uncovered vertex $v \notin Proposer$ which is adjacent to some uncovered vertex u with a lower degree, cover the vertex v.

Notice that the vertex v is matched with the vertex u having the minimum degree because the matching in **VCover** must be exactly the same as the one in our self-stabilizing algorithm. Since the degree is defined as the identified degree, it is uniquely determined.

The following lemma shows the performance of **VCover**. Let $Inc(i)$ be a set of incident edges to vertex i. The set $Inc(i)$ is partitioned into three disjoint subsets, i.e., $Inc(i) = Old(i) \cup New(i) \cup Both(i)$, where $|Old(i)| = m_i$ and $|New(i) \cup Both(i)| = k_i$. Hence $\delta_i = m_i + k_i$. For simplicity, we denote $New(i) \cup Both(i)$ by $E(i)$. The subsets are defined as

$$Old(i) = \{(i, j) \mid \delta_i \le k_j\},$$

$$New(i) = \{(i,j) \mid \delta_j \leq k_i\} \text{ and}$$
$$Both(i) = \{(i,j) \mid k_j < \delta_i, \ k_i < \delta_j\}.$$

In other words, $(i,j) \in Old(i)$ is equivalent to $(i,j) \in New(j)$ because $k_i < \delta_i \leq k_j \leq \delta_j$ holds. Conversely, $(i,j) \in Old(j)$ is equivalent to $(i,j) \in New(i)$. To estimate the performance of **VCover**, an identical cost defined below is given for $(i,j) \in Old(i) \cap New(j)$ and $(i,j) \in New(i) \cap Old(j)$. On the other hand, $(i,j) \in Both(i)$ is equivalent to $(i,j) \in Both(j)$, for which separate costs are given.

Lemma 1. *The approximation ratio of the algorithm* **VCover** *is*

$$2 - \frac{1}{\Delta}.$$

Proof. The proof proceeds by assigning costs c_{ij} and c_{ji} to each edge $(i,j) \in E(i) = New(i) \cup Both(i)$, and then using the costs to derive the relationship between the size of the optimal vertex cover $|C^*|$ and the size of the output $|C|$ of **VCover**. The cost c_{ij} is defined as evenly distributing the cost of 1 over every edge $(i,j) \in E(i)$. Notice that any edge $(i,j) \in Both(i) \cap Both(j)$ has two separate costs $c_{ij} = 1/k_i$ and $c_{ji} = 1/k_j$, while the other edge $(i,j) \in New(i) \cap Old(j)$ has the identical cost $c_{ij} = c_{ji} = 1/k_i$.

We can construct the three subsets of edges in the process of **VCover**. In most cases, the edges covered for the first time by i belong to $E(i)$ because the high-degree-first ordered list L is used. The only exception is that the edge (i,j) firstly covered by i may belong to $New(j)$. Since this case requires both i and j to be covered due to $\delta_i \leq k_j$, shifting the "firstly covered vertex" to j unlike **VCover**, does not change the number of covered vertices. Hence the sum of the entire edge costs $\sum_{(i,j) \in E(i)} c_{ij}$ for all vertex $i \in V$ is equivalent to $|C|$.

The sum of costs for k_i edges in $E(i)$ is $k_i \cdot 1/k_i = 1$ (see Fig. 1). On the other hand, the edge cost $c_{ji} = 1/k_j$ for an edge $(i,j) \in Old(i)$ is bounded by $1/\delta_i$. Since there are m_i edges in $Old(i)$, the entire cost for $Inc(i)$ is

$$\sum_{(i,j) \in Inc(i)} c_{ij} \leq 1 + \frac{m_i}{\delta_i} = 2 - \frac{k_i}{\delta_i}.$$

Thus we obtain

$$|C| \leq \sum_{i \in C^*} \sum_{(i,j) \in Inc(i)} c_{ij}$$
$$\leq |C^*|(2 - \frac{1}{\Delta}).$$

$\square$

4   Self-stabilizing Algorithm

Now we present our self-stabilizing algorithm **SSVC**. The **SSVC** is a distributed version of the **VCover** stated above. To execute operations locally, some techniques are contained in the algorithm.

First, each process has a variable *color* in order to construct the high-degree-first matching. The color is defined as the identified degree of a process if not matched, and as the same color as that of the proposal process if matched. If an unmatched process can detect some adjacent, lower colored processes, it makes a proposal to the minimum degree one. Thus the color determines whether or not it can make a proposal. Even if more than one processes concurrently make proposals to the same process i, the process i accepts the proposal of the maximum degree process j. Then process i's color is boosted up to process j's one. Thus lower colored processes cannot make proposals to i thereafter. After i has been matched with j, the unmatched, proposal processes must give up their proposals to i. To make it possible, we use a totally ordered degree, i.e., an identified degree, for each process.

Second, every process that can make a proposal is covered with respect to the vertex covering. Then the remaining covered processes are determined as follows. Let i be a non-proposal process. If every adjacent process $k \in N(i)$ has been matched with $j \neq i$ and has higher degree than i, process i is not covered. Otherwise, i is covered.

In Summary, we use a shared variable $\mathtt{col}_i \in \{(\delta_j, j) \mid 1 \leq \delta_j \leq \Delta,\ j \in P\}$ representing process i's color, and $\mathtt{col}_i = (\delta_i, i)$ when i is unmatched. Each process i has a variable $\mathtt{cover}_i \in \{true, false\}$, representing a covered process when $\mathtt{cover}_i = true$, which may not be shared.

The **SSVC** is formally described as follows.

Definition of Sets

$$Low_i = \{k \in N(i) \mid \mathtt{col}_k < \mathtt{col}_i\}$$
$$High_i = \{k \in N(i) \mid \mathtt{col}_i < \mathtt{col}_k\}$$
$$Other_i = \{k \in N(i) \mid k \to j \neq i\}$$
$$dmin(i) = \{k \mid \min_{k \in Low_i} d_k\}$$
$$dmax(i) = \{k \mid \max_{k \in High_i} d_k,\ k \to i\}$$

Notice that $dmin(i)$ is the minimum degree vertex among the lower colored vertices adjacent to i, and that $dmax(i)$ is the maximum degree vertex among the higher colored adjacent vertices that point to i.

High-Degree-First Matching

$$(\forall k \in N(i) : i \not\leftrightarrow k) \wedge (\mathtt{col}_i \neq d_i) \Rightarrow \mathtt{col}_i := d_i \qquad \text{(a)}$$

$$(\exists k \in N(i) : i \leftrightarrow k) \wedge (\mathtt{col}_i \neq \max(d_i, d_k)) \Rightarrow \mathtt{col}_i := \max(d_i, d_k) \qquad \text{(b)}$$

$$\exists dmax(i) : (dmax(i) \to i) \wedge (i \not\to dmax(i)) \Rightarrow i \to dmax(i) \ ;\ \mathtt{col}_i := d_{dmax(i)} \ ;$$
$$\mathtt{cover}_i := false \qquad \text{(c)}$$

$$\exists k \in High_i : (i \to k) \wedge (k \not\to i) \Rightarrow i \to null \ ;\ \mathtt{col}_i := d_i \ ;$$
$$\mathtt{cover}_i := false \qquad \text{(d)}$$

$$(\exists dmax(i) : (dmax(i) \not\to i))$$
$$\wedge(\exists dmin(i) : (i \not\to dmin(i))) \Rightarrow i \to dmin(i) \ ;\ \mathtt{cover}_i := true \qquad \text{(e)}$$

Non-proposal Covered Vertices

$$(\forall k \in Other_i : (d_i < d_k) \land cover_i)$$
$$\lor(\exists k \in Other_i : (d_k < d_i) \land (\neg cover_i)) \Rightarrow cover_i := \neg cover_i \quad (f)$$

Each statement above is informally explained in what follows.

(a) Every wrong color of unmatched processes is corrected.
(b) Every wrong color of matched processes is corrected.
(c) The proposal of a process with the (locally) maximum degree is accepted if at least one proposal is made.
(d) A proposal to a higher colored process is discarded.
(e) If a process is not pointed by any higher degree process and is adjacent to some lower colored processes, it makes a proposal to the minimum degree process among them.
(f) If a process i is adjacent to only processes with pointing others and i has the minimum degree among them, it is not covered. Conversely, if such a process does not have the minimum degree, it is covered.

Figure 2 intuitively illustrates how our **SSVC** stabilizes. First, given an arbitrary configuration, each vertex determines its color which is totally ordered. The leftmost figure shows that each vertex has a color of its own degree because no matched edge has been generated. For example, the label $(4, 8)$ means that the vertex has a col of $i = 8$ and degree $\delta_i = 4$. Furthermore, it shows that covered vertices, indicated by shaded vertices, are arbitrarily scattered. Next, the high-degree-first matching is executed in the second figure. After a maximal set of proposals to distinct vertices have been stabilized, covered vertices in *Proposer* are determined. Finally, the covered vertices not in *Proposer* are determined in such a way that every adjacent matched vertex has a higher degree as in the rightmost figure.

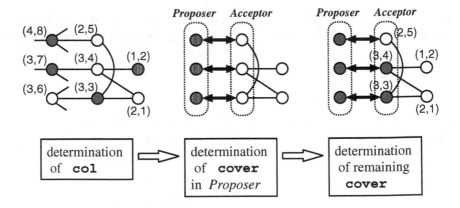

Fig. 2. Progress of stabilization

5   Correctness and Properties

To show that **SSVC** is deadlock-free, we introduce the following predicate. When $\mathcal{VC}$ is true, it means the system reaches a legitimate configuration.

$$\mathcal{VC} \equiv (\forall e = (i,j) \in E : (\text{cover}_i = true) \vee (\text{cover}_j = true))$$

Lemma 2. *If $\mathcal{VC}$ is false, there exists at least one process which can apply some rule in* **SSVC**.

Proof. (**by contradiction**) Suppose that there is some edge $e = (i,j)$ whose both ends are not covered. Then neither of them has executed (e). There are two cases.

(1) Neither i nor j is in *Matched* :
    Since $d_i < d_j$ or $d_j < d_i$ holds, the higher degree process between i and j can execute (e).
(2) Either i or j is in *Matched* :
    Suppose that i is matched and j is not. If $d_i < d_j$, then ($\exists i \in Other_j : (d_i < d_j) \wedge (\neg\text{cover}_j)$) in (f) is true for process j. Otherwise, the same rule is applied to process i.

Therefore, every edge is eventually covered.   □

To show that **SSVC** converges to a legitimate configuration, we define the following pseudo-legitimate states and use the proof method of *convergence stairs*.

$$Eligible = \{i \mid Low_i \neq \phi\},$$
$$Lowest = \{i \mid \forall k \in Other_i : d_i < d_k\}$$

$P1 \equiv (\forall i \notin Matched : (\text{col}_i = d_i)) \wedge (\forall(i,k) \in Matched : (\text{col}_i = \max(d_i, d_k)))$
$P2 \equiv P1 \wedge (\forall i \in Eligible : (i \leftrightarrow dmin(i)) \wedge (\text{cover}_i = true))$
$P3 \equiv P2 \wedge (\forall i \in \neg Proposer \wedge \neg Lowest : (\text{cover}_i = true))$
$\qquad \wedge (\forall i \in \neg Proposer \wedge Lowest : (\text{cover}_i = false))$

Lemma 3. *P1 eventually holds.*

Proof. Let i be a process in $\neg Matched$. If i has a wrong col_i, that is, $\text{col}_i \neq d_i$, then it is corrected by (a). Suppose that i moves from $\neg Matched$ to $Matched$. If several processes in $High_i$ point to i, then i selects the process $dmax(i)$ with the maximum degree among them and sets col_i to the same degree as $dmax(i)$ by (c). Conversely, if i is pointed by a process $k \in Low_i$, i just points to k but col_i remains unchanged. Thus $\forall(i,k) \in Matched : (\text{col}_i = \max(d_i, d_k))$ holds.

On the other hand, let i be a matched process with k. If i has a wrong col_i, that is, $\text{col}_i \neq \max(d_k, d_i)$, then it is corrected by (b). Suppose that (i,k) has changed from $Matched$ to $\neg Matched$. If k changes its pointer to another process, then col_i is reset to d_i (if necessary) by (d). Thus $\forall i \notin Matched : (\text{col}_i = d_i)$ holds.

After every process has been activated, P1 is satisfied.   □

Lemma 4. *P2 eventually holds.*

Proof. (**by induction**) Suppose that $P1 \wedge \neg P2$ holds. Hence every information about `col` is true. Let $K = \{i_1, i_2, \ldots, i_k\}$, where $d_{i_1} > d_{i_2} > \cdots > d_{i_k}$, be a set of processes such that $i \in K$ belongs to *Eligible* and $k \in N^+(i) : k \not\rightarrow dmin(k)$. Let j represent $dmin(i_1)$ for simplicity. Without loss of generality, we assume that $i_2 \leftrightarrow j \, (= dmin(i_1))$ and $d_{i_2} > d_j$. Since $i_1 \not\rightarrow dmin(i_1)$, i_1 eventually points to j, that is, $i_1 \rightarrow j$, and $\text{cover}_{i_1} := true$ by rule (e). Since $\text{col}_j = \text{col}_{i_2} < \text{col}_{i_1}$, rule (c) can be applied to j. Thus $i_1 \leftrightarrow j$ holds and i_1 is removed from K. At this time, $\text{col}_j := d_{i_1}$ and thus $\text{col}_j > \text{col}_{i_2}$ holds. Then by rule (d), $i_2 \rightarrow null$ holds. If Low_{i_2} is not empty, i_2 can select $dmin(i_2)$ from Low_{i_2}.

Notice that if Low_i becomes empty for some $i \in K$, such i is automatically removed from K. Since the same argument holds for any $i_j, i_{j+1} \in K$ as long as they belong to *Eligible*, the lemma follows by induction. □

Lemma 5. *P3 eventually holds.*

Proof. Suppose that $P2 \wedge \neg P3$ holds and that some process i in $\neg Proposer \wedge \neg Lowest$ has $\text{cover}_i = false$. Then the portion $(\exists k \in Other_i : (d_k < d_i) \wedge (\neg \text{cover}_i))$ in rule (f) will correct such process i. Next suppose that some process i in $\neg Proposer \wedge Lowest$ has $\text{cover}_i = true$. Then the portion $(\forall k \in Other_i : (d_i < d_k) \wedge \text{cover}_i)$ in rule (f) corrects such an error. □

Let M_s be a matching eventually determined by **SSVC**. The following theorem shows the efficiency of our method.

Theorem 1. **SSVC** *is a self-stabilizing distributed vertex cover algorithm whose stabilization time is $|M_s| + 2$ rounds.*

Proof. For the j-th round, the j-th highest-degree vertex makes a correct proposal and the $(j-1)$-st proposal is accepted. Hence, a maximal matching is completed in the $(|M_s| + 1)$-st round. Since non-proposal vertices, which have some adjacent lower degree vertices, locally know the necessity of being covered, they are covered in the $(|M_s| + 2)$-nd round. □

We show Lemmas 6 and 7 which claim the output of our self-stabilizing algorithm is equivalent to that of the sequential one.

Lemma 6. *Let M_v be a matching determined by **VCover**. We claim*

$$M_s = M_v.$$

Proof. (**by induction**) Let i_k be the k-th proposal vertex, and $i_s^k \in N(i_k)$ the matched vertex with i_k in **VCover**. Since i_s^1 is the vertex with the minimum degree in $N(i_1)$, the edge (i_1, i_s^1) belongs to M_v. On the other hand, i_1 makes a proposal to i_s^1 by rule (e) in **SSVC**. Then the proposal is eventually accepted irrespective of whether i_s^1 has already matched or not. Hence the edge (i_1, i_s^1) also belongs to M_s.

Suppose that every vertex $\{i_1, \ldots, i_k\}$ in **SSVC** has the same edge $\{i_s^1, \ldots, i_s^k\}$ as in **VCover**. Further suppose that (i_{k+1}, i_s^{k+1}) belongs to M_v. Then i_s^{k+1} is the vertex with the minimum degree in $N(i_{k+1})$. In **SSVC**, if i_{k+1} has made a proposal to $i_s^t \in \{i_s^1, \ldots, i_s^k\}$, i_s^t will reject the proposal and then i_{k+1} will eventually select the vertex with the minimum degree by rules (d) and (e). Since the vertex with the minimum degree in $N(i_{k+1})$ is uniquely determined, the edge (i_{k+1}, i_s^{k+1}) will also be contained in M_s. ☐

Lemma 7. *Let C_s and C_v be sets of vertex cover determined by **SSVC** and **VCover**, respectively. We claim*

$$C_s = C_v.$$

Proof. By Lemma 6, $C_s = C_v$ holds with respect to *Proposer* in M_s and M_v. The remaining covered vertices are uniquely determined by only degree information, which is equivalent in two algorithms. Thus $C_s = C_v$ also holds in the remaining portion. ☐

By Lemmas 1 and 7, we obtain the following theorem.

Theorem 2. *The approximation ratio of **SSVC** is $2 - 1/\Delta$.* ☐

6 Conclusion

We proposed a self-stabilizing algorithm for finding as small a vertex cover as possible in distributed systems. It has a wide application to the placement of agents or facilities in networks. The obtained approximation ratio is at most $2 - 1/\Delta$. It is interesting that the priority of vertices generates the same output as a sequential algorithm.

Our future work will include developing self-stabilizing approximation algorithms for other distributed combinatorial problems, improving their approximation ratios, and investigating their practical applications.

References

1. Y.Bejerano and R.Rastogi, Robust monitoring of link delays and faults in IP networks, In *Proceedings of the IEEE INFOCOM*, March (2003).
2. S.Chattopadhyay, L.Higham and K.Seyffarth, Dynamic and self-stabilizing distributed matching, In *Proceedings of the 21st Annual ACM Symposium on Principles of Distributed Computing*, July (2002) 290–297.
3. S.Dolev, A.Israeli and S.Moran, Uniform dynamic self-stabilizing leader election, *IEEE Transactions on Parallel and Distributed Systems*, **8**(4) (1997) 424–440.
4. M.R.Garey and D.S.Johnson, Computers and intractability. a guide to the theory of NP-completeness, *Freemann* (1979).
5. V.K.Garg and C.Skawratananond, On timestamping synchronous computations, In *Proceedings of the IEEE International Conference on Distributed Computing Systems (ICDCS'02)* , July (2002).

6. F.Grandoni, J.Könemann, and A.Panconesi, Distributed weighted vertex cover via maximal matchings, In *Proceedings of the 11th International Computing and Combinatorics Conference (COCOON'05)*, August (2005).
7. E.Halperin, Improved approximation algorithms for the vertex cover problem in graphs and hypergraphs, *SIAM Journal on Computing* **31**(5) (2002) 1608–1625.
8. M.Hańćkowiak, M.Karoński, and A.Panconesi, On the distributed complexity of computing maximal matchings, *SIAM Journal on Discrete Mathematics* **15**(1) (2001) 41–57.
9. J.Håstad, Some optimal inapproximability results, *Journal of the ACM*, **48**(4), (2001) 798–859.
10. S.T.Hedetniemi, D.P.Jacobs, and P.K.Srimani, Maximal matching stabilizes in time $O(m)$, *Information Processing Letters* **80** (2001) 221–223.
11. T.A.Hegazy, A distributed approach to dynamic autonomous agent placement for tracking moving targets with application to monitoring urban environments, Ph.D. Thesis, *School of Electrical and Computer Engineering, Georgia Institute of Technology* (2004).
12. S.-C.Hsu and S.-T.Huang, A self-stabilizing algorithm for maximal matching, *Information Processing Letters* **43** (1992) 77–81.
13. H.Nagamochi and T.Ibaraki, An approximation of the minimum vertex cover in a graph, *Japan Journal of Industrial and Applied Mathematics* **16** (1999) 369–375.
14. A.Panconesi and R.Rizzi, Some simple distributed algorithms for sparse networks, *Distributed Computing*, **14**, (2001) 97–100.
15. C.Savage, Depth-first search and the vertex cover problem, *Information Processing Letters* **14**(5) (1982) 233–235.
16. G.Tel, Maximal matching stabilizes in quadratic time, *Information Processing Letters* **49** (1994) 271–272.
17. R.Bar-Yehuda and S.Even, A local-ratio theorem for approximating the weighted vertex cover problem, *Annals of Discrete Mathematics*, **25** (1985) 27–46.

Self-stabilization in Spite of Frequent Changes of Networks: Case Study of Mutual Exclusion on Dynamic Rings

Toshimitsu Masuzawa* and Hirotsugu Kakugawa**

Osaka University, Toyonaka 560-8531, Japan
{masuzawa, kakugawa}@ist.osaka-u.ac.jp

Abstract. It is generally said that a self-stabilizing protocol is inefficient in distributed systems with frequent faults or topological changes and, what is worse, it might never converge to its intended behavior forever. Its main reason is that a new fault or topological change brings the system into an unexpected configuration, and thus, the system restarts convergence to its intended behavior *from scratch*. But the reasoning seems too pessimistic.

This paper provides a novel observation about self-stabilization on frequently changing networks: by quantifying influence of steps of a self-stabilizing protocol and that of a topological change, efficiency of the convergence can be estimated with considering topological changes that occur during the convergence. To show the feasibility and effectiveness of the approach, this paper presents a simple self-stabilizing mutual exclusion protocol on a dynamic ring where processes can join and leave the ring at any time. This paper clarifies what restrictions on frequency of joins and leaves are sufficient to guarantee the convergence and to guarantee the intended behavior after the convergence. The restrictions are not strict and thus the protocol can complete convergence and can continue its intended behavior on a frequently changing ring.

1 Introduction

A *self-stabilizing protocol* is a protocol that achieves its intended behavior regardless of the initial network configuration (i.e., global state) [4]. Thus, a self-stabilizing protocol is resilient to *any number* and *any type* of *transient* faults and is adaptive to *any number* and *any type* of *topological changes* of networks: after the last fault or the last topological change occurs, the protocol starts to converge to its intended behavior. These advantages make self-stabilizing protocols extremely attractive for designing highly dependable distributed systems.

---

* This work is supported in part by JSPS, Grant-in-Aid for Scientific Research ((B)15300017), MIC, Strategic Information and Communications R&D Promotion Programme, and MEXT, "The 21st Century Center of Excellence Program."
** This work is supported in part by JSPS, Grant-in-Aid for Encouragement of Young Scientist (15700017).

T. Herman and S. Tixeuil (Eds.): SSS 2005, LNCS 3764, pp. 183–197, 2005.
© Springer-Verlag Berlin Heidelberg 2005

The self-stabilization has attracted a great deal of attention of researchers and practitioners working in the field of distributed systems.

A self-stabilizing protocol can converge to its intended behavior, but *the convergence is guaranteed only when the distributed system experiences no new fault or topological change during the convergence.* When the system experiences a new fault or topological change before completing the convergence, the configuration immediately after the disturbance is regarded as an arbitrary one, which is regarded as a new initial configuration. Thus, in distributed systems where faults or topological changes frequently occur, a self-stabilizing protocol is quite inefficient and, what is worse, it might never converge to its intended behavior forever.

On the other hand, because of a rapid increase in the size of distributed systems and development of dynamic distributed systems such as P2P systems and mobile systems, self-stabilizing protocols that can tolerate frequent faults and frequent topological changes are highly desired. However, to the best of our knowledge, the problem has been tackled by few works and waits further investigation.

1.1   Contribution of This Paper

It is generally said that self-stabilizing protocols are inefficient in distributed systems with frequent faults or topological changes. Its main reason is that a new fault or topological change brings the system into an unexpected configuration, and thus, the system restarts convergence to its intended behavior *from scratch*. But the reasoning seems too pessimistic. Should a single new fault or topological change spoil all the efforts a self-stabilizing protocol made before the disturbance? This is the question that motivated us to start this research.

Our insight into the question is as follows. Each action of a self-stabilizing protocol can be regarded as a forward step to the convergence, but a fault or topological change can be regarded as a backward step. If we can quantify influence of the forward step and the backward step, we can estimate efficiency of the convergence with considering faults or topological changes that occur during the convergence. In other words, by evaluating the degree of regression a fault or topological change can bring about, we can evaluate the total number of the protocol's steps required to complete the convergence despite the disturbance.

The most important contribution of this paper is to provide such a novel observation about self-stabilization on frequently changing networks. To show the feasibility and effectiveness of our approach, we present a simple self-stabilizing protocol that can converge to its intended behavior from an arbitrary configuration and can continue its intended behavior on a frequently changing network.

We propose a self-stabilizing mutual exclusion protocol on a dynamic ring where processes can join and leave the ring at any time. The protocol is based on Dijkstra's self-stabilizing mutual exclusion protocol [3]. We clarify what restrictions on frequency of joins are sufficient to guarantee the convergence and to guarantee the intended behavior after the convergence. The restrictions are not strict and thus the protocol can complete convergence and can continue its intended behavior on a ring whose size frequently varies with time.

1.2   Related Works

Because of high adaptability of self-stabilizing protocols to topological changes, many works study self-stabilizing protocols on dynamic networks [1,2,5,6,7,8]. Most of the proposed protocols can converge to their intended behavior under the assumption that networks remain static during the convergence [1,6,7], and can continue its intended behavior until a new topological change occurs. Thus, these protocols cannot be applied to networks with frequent topological changes. The self-stabilizing mutual exclusion protocol proposed in [2] also requires that networks remain static during its convergence. The distinct advantage of this protocol is that it can guarantee its intended behavior in spite of (loosely restricted) topological changes after the convergence.

Instead of prohibiting topological changes, the self-stabilizing group communication protocol proposed in [5] requires the assumption that an agent can traverse a network by random walk despite topological changes. The assumption hides the affect of topological changes from the protocol. The paper also proves impossibility of the group communication under (malicious) frequent topological changes.

The concept of reconfiguration tolerance introduced in [8] is most related to this paper. The concept is introduced with some restriction on topological changes and guarantees the convergence and the intended behavior of a self-stabilizing protocol as long as topological changes do not violate the restriction. The self-stabilizing token circulation protocol proposed in [8] can complete the convergence and can continue its intended behavior if the interval of consecutive topological changes is longer than the time required for a token to traverse a spanning tree twice. However, the admissible interval of topological changes is longer than the convergence time of the protocol, and thus, the protocol actually requires that the network remains static during the convergence.

1.3   Organization of This Paper

The rest of this paper is organized as follows. Section 2 introduces the computation model of dynamic rings and defines stabilization in the dynamic rings. Section 3 shows a self-stabilizing mutual exclusion protocol on dynamic rings and analyzes its efficiency. Finally, Section 4 contains some concluding remarks.

2   Model

2.1   Dynamic Ring Networks

A *dynamic directed ring network* (simply called a ring) is a ring network where the number of processes forming the ring varies from time to time. The number of processes in the ring is called the *size* of the ring. Processes can join and leave the ring at any time. Each process p in the ring can identify its predecessor $pred(p)$ in the ring at any instance: while the process specified by $pred(p)$ varies from time to time because of joins and leaves of processes, $(V, \{(pred(p), p) \mid p \in V\})$

forms a directed ring at any instance where V denotes the set of processes in the ring. In other words, we assume that the adequate update of $pred(p)$ is atomically executed when a process joins or leaves the ring. The details of the update mechanism is not presented in this paper. Since a ring network is the basis of several structures, maintenance of a dynamic ring is investigated in some works [9,10]. When $pred(p) = q$ holds for two processes p and q, q is called a *predecessor* of p and p is called a *successor* of q. We also assume that there exists a single designated process called a *head process* at any instance. The head process p remains the head process until it leaves the ring. When the head process p leaves the ring, its successor becomes the new head process. The details of the mechanism for maintaining the single head process is not presented in this paper.

Each process p is a (possibly infinite) state machine. Each process can directly read its predecessor's state and can change its own state depending on its current state and its predecessor's state. The *normal action* of each process p is defined by *guarded actions* in the following form:

$$\langle guard_p \rangle \rightarrow \langle statement_p \rangle.$$

The guard $\langle guard_p \rangle$ of process p is a boolean expression on the states of p and its predecessor. When the guard is evaluated to be true, $\langle statement_p \rangle$ is executed to change the state of p. We assume that the guarded action can be atomically executed: evaluation of the guard and execution of the statement are executed in one atomic action.

A *configuration* (or a global state) of the ring is represented by a vector of process states. The length of the vector is equal to the current size of the ring. Let $\sigma = (s_0, s_1, s_2, \ldots, s_{n-1})$ be the configuration. Its entry s_i $(0 \le i \le n - 1)$ denotes the state of process p_i, where p_0 is the head process and p_j $(1 \le j \le n-1)$ is the successor of p_{j-1}. Since the size of the ring varies with time, the process denoted by p_i $(0 \le i \le n - 1)$ may also vary with time. To avoid the confusion, we use the following notations: $n[\sigma]$ denotes the size of the ring at configuration σ, $p_0[\sigma]$ denotes the head process at σ, and $p_j[\sigma]$ $(1 \le j \le n[\sigma] - 1)$ denotes the successor of $p_{j-1}[\sigma]$ at σ.

Now we consider transition of the configuration from σ to σ'. The configuration transitions are classified into the following three cases.

1. Transition by a *normal action* of a process: A process p is said to be *enabled* at a configuration σ when p has a guarded action whose guard is true at σ. A process p is said to be *disabled* at σ when it is not enabled at σ. Let p be an enabled process at $\sigma = (s_0, s_1, \ldots, s_{n[\sigma]-1})$, and $\sigma' = (s'_0, s'_1, \ldots, s'_{n[\sigma]-1})$ be the configuration resulting from σ by p's normal action. It is clear that $n[\sigma'] = n[\sigma]$ holds. When $p = p_i[\sigma]$ $(0 \le i \le n[\sigma]-1)$, s'_i is the state of p after executing the guarded action. Notice that $s_j = s'_j$ holds for each j $(\ne i)$.
2. Transition by a *join* of a process: Processes can join the ring at any time. When a process newly joins the ring, the size of the ring increases by one. Let p be a process that joins the ring at $\sigma = (s_0, s_1, \ldots, s_{n[\sigma]-1})$, and $\sigma' = (s'_0, s'_1, \ldots, s'_{n[\sigma']-1})$ be the configuration resulting from σ by p's join action.

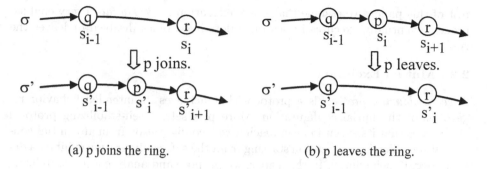

(a) p joins the ring.   (b) p leaves the ring.

Fig. 1. Dynamic changes in the ring

It is clear that $n[\sigma'] = n[\sigma] + 1$ holds. When $p = p_i[\sigma']$ $(1 \leq i \leq n[\sigma'] - 1)^1$ (or p joins between $p_{i-1}[\sigma]$ and $p_i[\sigma]$), $s'_j = s_j$ holds for each j $(0 \leq j \leq i-1)$ and $s'_{k+1} = s_k$ holds for each k $(i \leq k \leq n[\sigma] - 1)$ (Fig. 1(a)). We assume that the state s'_i of p is determined from the state s_{i-1} of its predecessor.

3. Transition by a *leave* of a process: Processes can leave the ring at any time. When a process leaves the ring, the size of the ring decreases by one. Let p be a process that leaves the ring at $\sigma = (s_0, s_1, \ldots, s_{n[\sigma]-1})$, and $\sigma' = (s'_0, s'_1, \ldots, s'_{n[\sigma']-1})$ be the configuration resulting from σ by p's leave. It is clear that $n[\sigma'] = n[\sigma] - 1$ holds. When $p = p_i[\sigma]$ $(0 \leq i \leq n[\sigma] - 1)$, $s'_j = s_j$ holds for each j $(0 \leq j \leq i - 1)$, and $s'_k = s_{k+1}$ holds for each k $(i < k \leq n[\sigma'] - 1)$ (Fig. 1(b)). We assume that the state s'_i (or the state of p's successor) is determined from its state and the state s_i of p.

When configuration changes from σ to σ' by a normal action, a join or a leave, the transition is denoted by $\sigma \mapsto \sigma'$.

As the execution model, we adopt the *sequential execution* model (sometimes called the *central daemon*) where no two processes execute actions at the same time. This assumption is made only for simplicity, and the protocol presented in the next section works correctly even when two or more enabled processes execute actions at the same time (i.e., *distributed daemon*). Complexity analysis in the next section can be easily modified for the distributed daemon.

An *execution* of a protocol is represented by an infinite sequence of configurations in the order they appear in the execution: an infinite sequence of configurations $E = \sigma_0, \sigma_1 \ldots$ is an execution if and only if $\sigma_i \mapsto \sigma_{i+1}$ holds for every i $(i \geq 0)$. The configuration σ_0 is called the *initial configuration* of E. A *partial execution* is denoted by $E[\sigma_i, \sigma_j] = \sigma_i, \sigma_{i+1} \ldots, \sigma_j$ $(i \leq j)$.

The execution is not uniquely determined only from the initial configuration, since there may exist several actions that can be executed at each configuration: normal actions of enabled processes, a join into every place of the ring and a leave of every process. One of them is arbitrary chosen to be executed. In the

---

[1] Since p does not become the head process when it newly joins, we don't consider the case of $p = p_0[\sigma']$.

rest of this paper, we assume that every execution is *weakly fair*: every enabled process eventually executes its action unless it becomes disabled or leaves the ring.

2.2 Mutual Exclusion

A *self-stabilizing protocol* is a protocol that achieves its intended behavior regardless of the initial configuration. More precisely, a self-stabilizing protocol guarantees that its execution can reach a *safe* configuration from any initial configuration, where any execution starting from the safe configuration exhibits a desired "legal" behavior[4]. In this paper, we propose and analyze a self-stabilizing protocol for *the mutual exclusion problem*. A self-stabilizing mutual exclusion protocol on the dynamic ring networks is defined as follows.

Definition 1. (safe configuration of mutual exclusion) *Configuration σ_0 is a* safe configuration *of the mutual exclusion problem iff every execution $E = \sigma_0, \sigma_1 \ldots$ starting from σ_0 satisfies the following two conditions.*

1. **(safety)** *For every configuration σ_i $(i \geq 0)$, there exists at most one process that has a privilege.*
2. **(liveness)** *Every process p has a privilege infinitely often in E unless p leaves the ring.*   □

Definition 2. (self-stabilizing mutual exclusion protocol) *A protocol is a* self-stabilizing mutual exclusion protocol *if any execution starting from an arbitrary configuration eventually reaches a safe configuration* (**convergence**).   □

2.3 Complexity Measures

We evaluate efficiency of the convergence of a self-stabilizing protocol. We use two complexity measures.

The *step complexity* is defined to be the maximum number of *normal actions* executed until executions reach safe configurations. The maximum function is taken over all executions starting from all possible configurations.

The step complexity of a self-stabilizing protocol on "static" rings is usually represented as a function of the ring size. In "dynamic" rings, however, the step complexity cannot be simply represented as a function of the ring size since the ring size varies with time. Thus, the step complexity is represented as a function of the initial ring size and the numbers of joins and leaves executed in executions.

Definition 3. (step complexity) *The* step complexity *of a self-stabilizing mutual exclusion protocol is (at most) $f(n_0, \#J, \#L)$ if any execution E from any initial configuration σ_0 with size n_0 satisfies the following:*

Let σ be any configuration appearing in E. Let $\#N$, $\#J$ and $\#L$ be respectively the numbers of normal actions, joins and leaves that are executed in $E[\sigma_0, \sigma]$. If $\#N \geq f(n_0, \#J, \#L)$, then σ is a safe configuration.   □

Intuitively the inequality $\#N \geq f(n_0, \#J, \#L)$ implies that sufficiently larger number of normal actions are executed than joins and leaves in a prefix $E[\sigma_0, \sigma]$ of E. In other words, the step complexity guarantees that the execution E reaches a safe configuration if it has a *relatively static* prefix of the execution. This can throw a new light on advantages of self-stabilizing protocols.

From the above explanation, readers may think of the deferred penalty of joins and leaves: when huge number of joins and leaves are executed in the beginning part of E, the huge number of normal actions must be executed until $\#N \geq f(n_0, \#J, \#L)$ becomes true. However, in the context of self-stabilization, we can escape the deferred penalty of joins and leaves by considering some configuration after the period of great dynamic changes as an initial configuration. Consequently, the execution E reaches a safe configuration if it has a *relatively static* period in any part of E.

By adopting *asynchronous rounds* (simply called a *round*) instead of the steps, the *round complexity* is similarly defined. Let $E = \sigma_0, \sigma_1, \ldots$ be any execution. The first round is defined to be the minimal prefix $E_1 = \sigma_0, \sigma_1, \ldots, \sigma_k$ such that all enabled processes at σ_0 make (normal or leave) actions or become disabled in E_1. The second round is the first round of $E^1 = \sigma_k, \sigma_{k+1}, \ldots$, and so on.

The round complexity of a self-stabilizing protocol is defined as follows.

Definition 4. (round complexity) *The round complexity of a self-stabilizing protocol is (at most) $f(n_0, \#J, \#L)$ if any execution E from any initial configuration σ_0 with size n_0 satisfies the following:*

Let σ be the last configuration of the R-th round of E for any R. Let $\#J$ and $\#L$ be respectively the numbers of joins and leaves that are executed in $E[\sigma_0, \sigma]$. If $R \geq f(n_0, \#J, \#L)$, then σ is a safe configuration.   □

3 Self-stabilizing Mutual Exclusion on Dynamic Rings

Dijkstra[3] proposed a self-stabilizing mutual exclusion protocol on *static* directed rings. We apply Dijkstra's protocol to *dynamic* rings as it is. We simply add join and leave actions that are executed when processes join and leave the ring respectively.

Each process p has a state variable st_p that takes a nonnegative integer in $\{0, 1, \ldots, K - 1\}$ where K is a constant that is greater than the ring size at any instance. Each process has a single guarded action as a normal action and is considered to be *privileged* when the guard of the action is true. A self-stabilizing mutual exclusion protocol on *dynamic* rings is presented as follows.

1. **Normal action of the head process p:**
   $st_p = st_{pred(p)} \rightarrow st_p := (st_p + 1) \bmod K$.
2. **Normal action of process p other than the head process:**
   $st_p \neq st_{pred(p)} \rightarrow st_p := st_{pred(p)}$.
3. **Join action:**
   A newly joining process p executes the following action.
   $st_p := st_{pred(p)}$.
   The process p recognizes that it is not the head process.

4. **Leave action**:
   When the head process q leaves the ring, its successor p executes the following action.
   $st_p := st_q$.
   The process p recognizes that it newly becomes the head process.
   (When the leaving process is not the head process, no action is executed.)

In Dijkstra's protocol for *static* rings of size n, it is known that any configuration $\sigma = (st_0, st_1, \ldots, st_{n-1})$ satisfying the following condition $\mathcal{SC}$ is safe: there exists i $(0 \leq i \leq n-1)$ such that

- $st_j = st_0$ for each j $(0 \leq j \leq i)$, and
- $st_j = (st_0 - 1) \bmod K$ for each j $(i < j \leq n - 1)$.

We can easily see that only the process $p_{(i+1)\bmod n}$ is privileged in the safe configuration. The configurations satisfying the condition $\mathcal{SC}$ are called $\mathcal{SC}$-configurations in what follows.

First, we show that any $\mathcal{SC}$-configuration is also a safe configuration for *dynamic* rings. To show this property, we need some constraint on frequency of joins from the following reason. At a configuration where process p is privileged, the privilege moves to p's successor when p executes the normal action. By consecutive executions of normal actions of privileged processes, the privilege circulates along the ring. However, on a *dynamic* ring, the privilege cannot complete the circulation if joins have higher frequency than normal actions.

Definition 5. (nice execution)   *An execution $E = \sigma_0, \sigma_1, \ldots$ is said to be nice if E satisfies the following condition:*
For any configuration σ_i, there exists σ_j $(j > i)$ such that the number of normal actions executed in $E[\sigma_i, \sigma_j]$ is larger than that of joins executed in $E[\sigma_i, \sigma_j]$.   □

Lemma 1. *Any $\mathcal{SC}$-configuration of the (dynamic) ring is a safe configuration for nice executions.*

(Proof)   Consider any nice execution E starting from any $\mathcal{SC}$-configuration. We have to show E satisfies the safety and the liveness properties in Definition 1.

Safety: Let $\sigma = (s_0, s_1, \ldots, s_{n[\sigma]-1})$ be any $\mathcal{SC}$-configuration and $\sigma' = (s'_0, s'_1, \ldots, s'_{n[\sigma']-1})$ be any configuration resulting from σ by execution of a single action act. It is sufficient to show that σ' is also a $\mathcal{SC}$-configuration since only a single process is privileged in any $\mathcal{SC}$-configuration.

From the correctness of Dijkstra's protocol on static rings, it is obvious that σ' is a $\mathcal{SC}$-configuration if the action act is a normal action. From the statements of the join and leave actions, it is clear that σ' is a $\mathcal{SC}$-configuration if the action act is a join or a leave.

Liveness: For contradiction, assume that a process p remains in the ring forever but never becomes privileged after some configuration σ in E. It follows from the proof of the safety that any configuration appearing in E is a $\mathcal{SC}$-configuration and has a single privileged process.

Let d (≥ 1) be the minimum distance from the privilege to p throughout the execution after σ. Let σ' be the configuration after σ in E where the distance from the privilege to p is exactly d. Consider the execution starting from σ'. The followings hold.

- From the statements of the normal and the leave actions, we can see that the privilege moves to the successor of the privileged process when the privileged process executes the normal or the leave action. Thus, the distance from the privilege to p decreases by one.
- Execution of the join action by a new process has no influence on the privilege. Thus, when a new process joins into the part of the ring from the privilege to p, the distance from the privilege to p increases by one.

Since E is a nice execution, there appears a configuration σ'' after σ' in E such that the number of the normal actions executed in $E[\sigma', \sigma'']$ is larger than that of the joins executed in $E[\sigma', \sigma'']$. From the above observations, the distance from the privilege to p at σ'' is smaller than d; this contradicts the definition of d. □

Notice that the proof of the safety in Lemma 1 does not require the assumption that the execution is nice. Thus, any execution starting from any safe configuration satisfies the safety: there appears no configuration where two or more processes have privileges at the same time. This is the advantage that the protocol in [2] also has. The assumption of the nice executions is required to guarantee only the liveness property.

In what follows, we prove the convergence of the protocol. It is sufficient to prove that any execution starting from an arbitrary configuration eventually reaches a SC-configuration. In the proof of the convergence, we focus on the privileges at the initial configuration[2] and trace their movement in E. To trace the privileges, we first clarify movement of privileges.

Let σ be any configuration and σ' be a configuration resulting from σ by an action act.

- Case that act is a normal action of process p: It is clear that p is privileged at σ and is not privileged at σ'. When p's successor (say q) is privileged at σ', we say that the privilege p has at σ moves to q (or q receives a privilege from p). When q is not privileged at σ', we say that the privilege p has at σ is discarded. In both cases, we say that the privilege q has at σ (if it has) is discarded.
- Case that act is a join of p (p joins the ring): Since p simply copies the state from its predecessor, it is clear that σ and σ' have the same privileged processes. Thus, join actions bring no movement of privileges.
- Case that act is a leave of p (p leaves the ring): When the successor (say q) of p is privileged at σ', we can see that either p or q is privileged at σ.

---

[2] From the definition of privileged processes, every configuration has at least one privileged process.

- When p is privileged at σ, we say that the privilege p has at σ *moves* to q and that the privilege q has at σ (if it has) is *discarded*.
- When p is not privileged and q is privileged at σ, we consider that the leave brings no movement of privileges.

When the successor (say q) is not privileged at σ', we say that the privileges p and q have at σ (if they have) are *discarded*.

From the movement of privileges clarified in the above, we can trace privileges and regard execution of the protocol as circulation of privileges. Since no action can create a new privilege, it is sufficient to trace privileges that exist in the initial configuration. Notice that there exist at most $n[\sigma_0]$ privileges at any configuration in any execution starting from σ_0, since there exist at most $n[\sigma_0]$ privileges at the initial configuration σ_0.

Let E be any execution starting from an arbitrary configuration σ_0. To prove that E reaches a $\mathcal{SC}$-configuration, we assign a *lap number* to each privilege. Notice that the lap number is introduced only for the proof and cannot be used in the protocol. The lap number of each privilege at the initial configuration σ_0 is defined to be *zero*. The lap number of each privilege is incremented by one at each time the privilege goes past the head process. That is, the lap number of each privilege is incremented by one, when the privilege moves from the head process to its successor by the normal action of the head process.

The following lemma clearly holds since no privilege passes others.

Lemma 2. *The lap numbers of privileges that the head process receives are monotonically non-decreasing.*   □

The next lemma is a key lemma for analysis of the convergence.

Lemma 3. *At most one privilege can get the lap number of two. (All other privileges are discarded before their lap numbers become two.)*

(Proof) Let $E = \sigma_0, \sigma_1, \ldots$ be any execution starting from an arbitrary configuration σ_0. For contradiction, assume that the lap numbers of two privileges x and y become *two*. Let $\sigma_{x(1)}$ and $\sigma_{y(1)}$ be the configurations immediately after the lap numbers of x and y become *one* respectively[3]. Without loss of generality, we can assume $x(1) < y(1)$. Let $\sigma_{x(2)}$ be the configuration immediately after the lap number of x becomes *two*. Then, from Lemma 2, $x(1) < y(1) < x(2)$ holds.

Let $st = v$ ($0 \le v \le K - 1$) hold at the head process at $\sigma_{x(1)}$. The state of the head process at $\sigma_{x(2)-1}$ (i.e., at the configuration immediately before x gets the lap number of *two*) also satisfies $st = v$ since the head process executes the normal action at $\sigma_{x(2)-1}$ to move x to its successor. The head process increments its state by one when and only when a privilege passes the head process. Since the state of the head process increases by one at $\sigma_{y(1)}$, the state is incremented K times in $E[\sigma_{x(1)}, \sigma_{x(2)-1}]$. However, since the number of privileges in the ring is $n[\sigma_0]$ or less, at most $n[\sigma_0]$ privileges can pass the head process in $E[\sigma_{x(1)}, \sigma_{x(2)-1}]$. This is contradiction since $K > n[\sigma_0]$ holds.   □

---

[3] At $\sigma_{x(1)}$ (resp. $\sigma_{y(1)}$) the successor of the head process has x (resp. y).

Lemma 4. *Assume the lap number of a privilege (say x) becomes* two. *The configuration immediately before x gets the lap number of* two *(i.e., the configuration at which the head process executes the normal action to move x to its successor) is a safe configuration for nice executions.*

(Proof). From the proof of Lemma 3, we can see that the privilege x is the last privilege that gets the lap number of *one*, and that x with the lap number of *one* completes circulation of the ring and gets the lap number of *two*. It is clear that all processes have the same state when x completes the circulation (i.e., at the configuration where the head process has x). The configuration is a SC-configuration and thus is safe for nice executions from Lemma1.   □

Lemma 4 implies that we can prove the convergence if we can show that a privilege eventually gets the lap number of *two*. Also Lemma 4 implies that we can estimate the numbers of steps and rounds required for the convergence by estimating the numbers of steps and rounds required until a privilege gets the lap number of *two*. Unfortunately, the constraint defining the nice executions is insufficient to guarantee the convergence. In what follows, we consider the numbers of steps and rounds required until a privilege gets the lap number of *two*, which are sufficient conditions on executions to guarantee the convergence.

3.1   Step Complexity of Convergence

In this subsection, we evaluate the number of steps required until a privilege gets the lap number of *two*. Let E be any execution starting from an arbitrary configuration σ_0. To evaluate the number of steps, we associate a *lifetime*, a non-negative integer, with each privilege at any configuration σ. The lifetime $life(x)[\sigma]$ of a privilege x at σ is defined by

$$life(x)[\sigma] = \begin{cases} dist(x)[\sigma] + n[\sigma] & \text{if } x \text{ has the lap number of } zero, \text{ and} \\ dist(x)[\sigma] & \text{if } x \text{ has the lap number of } one, \end{cases}$$

where $dist(x)[\sigma]$ denotes the distance from the privilege x to the head process at σ. Intuitively $life(x)[\sigma]$ gives an upper bound of the steps (movements) that x can experience during its lap number *zero* or *one*, provided that the ring size remains unchanged.

Our aim is to evaluate the number of steps required until a privilege gets the lap number of *two*. From Lemma 4, the configuration immediately before a privilege (say x) gets the lap number of *two* is a safe configuration and has no privilege other than x. This implies that the lifetime of x at the configuration is *zero*. Thus, the total of the lifetime over all privileges at σ (denoted by $TLIFE[\sigma]$) gives an upper bound of the steps required to reach a safe configuration provided that the ring size remains unchanged.

Now we consider the influence of actions to the value of $TLIFE$. Let σ be any configuration and σ' be a configuration resulting from σ by an action act.

- Case that *act* is a normal action of process p: The privilege (say y) that p has at σ moves to p's successor or is discarded[4]. This implies $life(y)[\sigma'] \leq life(y)[\sigma] - 1$, and thus, $TLIFE(\sigma') \leq TLIFE(\sigma) - 1$ holds.
- Case that *act* is a join of p (p joins the ring): Let y be any privilege at σ. When p joins into the part of the ring from y to the head process, then $dist(y)$ increases by one. The size of the ring also increases by one. This implies $life(y)[\sigma'] \leq life(y)[\sigma] + 2$. In the case that y is located at the head process, $dist(y)$ does not increase and $life(y)[\sigma'] \leq life(y)[\sigma] + 1$ holds. Also in the case that y has the lap number of *one*, $life(y)[\sigma'] \leq life(y)[\sigma] + 1$ holds.
  Since the initial configuration σ_0 has at most $n[\sigma_0]$ privileges, the number of privileges at any configuration cannot exceed $n[\sigma_0]$. When $n[\sigma_0]$ privileges exist in the initial configuration, one is located at the head process at σ_0. Thus, in any configuration after the initial configuration with $n[\sigma_0]$ privileges, at least one privilege is located at the head process or has the lap number of *one*. Consequently, $TLIFE(\sigma') \leq TLIFE(\sigma) + 2n[\sigma_0] - 1$ holds.
- Case that *act* is a leave of p (p leaves the ring): Let y be any privilege at σ. It is clear that the leave cannot increase the value of $TLIFE$. While the difference between $life(y)[\sigma]$ and $life(y)[\sigma']$ depends on the location of the leaving process and the lap number of y, $life(y)[\sigma] - 2 \leq life(y)[\sigma'] \leq life(y)[\sigma]$ clearly holds. Thus, we ignore the influence of leaves on the value of $TLIFE$.

From the above observation about influence of actions to the value of $TLIFE$, we can prove the following theorem. Intuitively, the theorem implies that a single join can spoil the efforts of at most $2n[\sigma_0] - 1$ normal actions. It cannot spoil all the efforts that the protocol has made.

Theorem 1. *Let E be any execution starting from an arbitrary configuration σ_0. Let σ be any configuration in E, and $\#N[\sigma]$ (resp. $\#J[\sigma]$) be the number of normal actions (resp. joins) executed in $E[\sigma_0, \sigma]$. Then, the configuration σ is safe for nice executions if the following holds:*

$$\#N[\sigma] \geq \frac{3n[\sigma_0]^2 - n[\sigma_0]}{2} + 2n[\sigma_0] \cdot \#J[\sigma] - \#J[\sigma]$$

(Proof)   The initial configuration σ_0 has at most $n[\sigma_0]$ privileges. Since each process has at most one privilege at any configuration,

$$TLIFE[\sigma_0] \leq \frac{n[\sigma_0](n[\sigma_0] - 1)}{2} + n[\sigma_0]^2 = \frac{3n[\sigma_0]^2 - n[\sigma_0]}{2}$$

holds. Since each normal action decreases $TLIFE$ by at least one and each join increases $TLIFE$ by at most $2n[\sigma_0] - 1$,

$$TLIFE[\sigma] \leq TLIFE[\sigma_0] - \#N[\sigma] + (2n[\sigma_0] - 1) \cdot \#J[\sigma]$$

holds. From this inequality,

---

[4] The privilege that p's successor has at σ is also discarded if exists.

$$TLIFE[\sigma_0] - \#N[\sigma] + (2n[\sigma_0] - 1) \cdot \#J[\sigma] \leq 0$$

implies $TLIFE[\sigma] = 0$, which guarantees that σ has exactly one privilege x: x is located at the head process and has the lap number of *one*. This implies that σ is a $\mathcal{SC}$-configuration, and thus, σ is a safe configuration.

From the above inequalities, we can see that $TLIFE[\sigma] = 0$ holds, if the inequality of the theorem holds. □

Theorem 1 does not overestimate the step complexity so much. Consider the initial configuration $\sigma_0 = (0, n - 2, n - 3, \ldots, 1, 0)$ where $n = n[\sigma_0]$ (Fig. 2). When $\#J$ processes consecutively join the ring as the predecessors of the head process, the configuration changes to $\sigma_{\#J} = (0, n - 2, n - 3, \ldots, 1, 0, 0, \ldots, 0)$. Figure 2 shows an execution starting from $\sigma_{\#J}$ that requires

$$\frac{3n[\sigma_0]^2 - 3n[\sigma_0]}{2} + 2n[\sigma_0] \cdot \#J - 2\#J - 1$$

steps until it reaches a safe configuration. In Fig. 2, the small numbers in parentheses show the order processes execute the normal actions between the configurations. While the execution does not include leaves, it is easy to add leaves (in the last part of the execution) without reducing the step complexity.

Remarks About Transient Faults During Convergence: From Theorem 1, we can claim that the protocol is robust against joins of processes: (at most) only the $2n[\sigma_0] - 1$ normal actions can be spoiled by a single join. However, the protocol is vulnerable to transient faults during convergence. Consider configuration $\sigma_{\#J+n(\#J+n-1)}$ in Fig. 2 and assume, for simplicity, that $\#J = 0$ holds. When a transient fault changes the state of p_0 from $n - 1$ into 0, the resultant configuration is $\sigma = (0, n - 2, n - 3, \ldots, 1, 1)$ and is the same as $\sigma_{\#J+1}$ resulting from $\sigma_{\#J}$ by an action of p_{n-1}. This implies that the single transient fault spoils all the $n^2 - n - 1$ normal actions executed between $\sigma_{\#J+1}$ and $\sigma_{\#J+n(\#J+n-1)}$.

3.2 Round Complexity of Convergence

In this subsection, we evaluate the number of rounds required until the protocol reaches a safe configuration. Since every privilege makes at least one movement in each round unless it is discarded, we use the maximum of the lifetime over all privileges at σ (denoted by $MLIFE[\sigma]$) instead of $TLIFE[\sigma]$.

It is clear that $MLIFE[\sigma] \leq 2n[\sigma_0] - 1$ at the initial configuration σ_0 and that configuration σ is safe if $MLIFE[\sigma] = 0$ holds. Since normal actions executed in a round decreases $MLIFE$ at least one and each join increases $MLIFE$ at most two, we can prove the following theorem in a similar way to that of Theorem 1. Intuitively, the theorem implies that a single join spoils the efforts of at most two rounds the protocol has made.

Theorem 2. *Let E be any execution starting from an arbitrary configuration σ_0. Let $\sigma(i)$ be the last configuration of the i-th round (i.e., the first configuration*

	p_0	p_1	p_2	$\cdots$	p_{n-2}	p_{n-1}	p_n	$\cdots$	$p_{n+\#J-1}$
σ_0	0	$n-2$	$n-3$	$\cdots$	1	0			
$\sigma_{\#J}$	0	$n-2$	$n-3$	$\cdots$	1	0	0	$\cdots$ 0	0
n steps	(n)	$(n-1)$	$(n-2)$		(2)	(1)			
	1	0	$n-2$	$\cdots$	2	1	0	$\cdots$ 0	0
n steps		(n)	$(n-1)$		(3)	(2)	(1)		
	1	1	0	$\cdots$	3	2	1	$\cdots$ 0	0
$\cdots$	$\cdots$	$\cdots$	$\cdots$	$\cdots$		$\cdots$		$\cdots$	$\cdots$
$\sigma_{\#J+n(\#J+1)}$ *n steps*	1	1	1	$\cdots$	$J+2$	$J+1$	J	$\cdots$ 2	1
	(1)				$(J+3)$	$(J+2)$	$(J+1)$	(3)	(2)
	2	1	1	$\cdots$	$J+3$	$J+2$	$J+1$	$\cdots$ 3	2
n steps	(2)	(1)			$(J+4)$	$(J+3)$	$(J+2)$	(4)	(3)
	3	2	1	$\cdots$	$J+4$	$J+3$	$J+2$	$\cdots$ 4	3
$\cdots$	$\cdots$	$\cdots$	$\cdots$	$\cdots$		$\cdots$		$\cdots$	$\cdots$
	$n-2$	$n-3$	$n-4$	$\cdots$	1	1	1	$\cdots$ 0	$n-2$
n steps	$(n-2)$	$(n-3)$	$(n-4)$					(n)	$(n-1)$
$\sigma_{\#J+n(\#J+n-1)}$ *n − 1 steps*	$n-1$	$n-2$	$n-3$	$\cdots$	1	1	1	$\cdots$ 1	0
		$(n-1)$	$(n-2)$		(2)				(1)
	$n-1$	$n-1$	$n-2$	$\cdots$	2	1	1	$\cdots$ 1	1
n − 2 steps			$(n-2)$		(2)	(1)			
	$n-1$	$n-1$	$n-1$	$\cdots$	3	2	1	$\cdots$ 1	1
$\cdots$	$\cdots$	$\cdots$	$\cdots$	$\cdots$		$\cdots$		$\cdots$	$\cdots$
n − 2 steps					$(\#J+2)$	$(\#J+1)$	$(\#J)$	(2)	(1)
	$n-1$	$n-1$	$n-1$	$\cdots$	$(\#J+3)$	$(\#J+2)$	$(\#J+1)$	$\cdots$ 3	2
n − 3 steps					$(\#J+2)$	$(\#J+1)$	$(\#J)$	(2)	(1)
	$n-1$	$n-1$	$n-1$	$\cdots$	$(\#J+4)$	$(\#J+3)$	$(\#J+2)$	$\cdots$	3
$\cdots$	$\cdots$	$\cdots$	$\cdots$	$\cdots$		$\cdots$		$\cdots$	$\cdots$
3 steps								(2)	(1)
	$n-1$	$n-1$	$n-1$	$\cdots$	$n-1$	$n-1$	$n-1$	$\cdots n-2$	$n-3$
2 steps								(1)	(2)
	$n-1$	$n-1$	$n-1$	$\cdots$	$n-1$	$n-1$	$n-1$	$\cdots n-1$	$n-1$

Fig. 2. A trace of protocol execution

of the $(i+1)$-st round) in E, and $\#J(i)$ be the number of joins executed in $E[\sigma_0, \sigma(i)]$. Then, the configuration $\sigma(i)$ is safe if the following holds:

$$i \geq 2n[\sigma_0] + 2\#J(i) - 1. \qquad \square$$

The execution shown in Fig. 2 requires $2n[\sigma_0] + 2\#J[i] - 3$ rounds until it reaches a safe configuration.

Theorem 2 implies that (at most) only two rounds can be spoiled by a single join. As in the case of the step complexity, however, the single transient fault spoils all the $\#J + n - 1$ rounds between $\sigma_{\#J+1}$ and $\sigma_{\#J+n(\#J+n-1)}$.

4   Conclusions

We provided a novel observation about self-stabilization on frequently changing networks: by quantifying influence of steps of a self-stabilizing protocol and that of a topological change, efficiency of the convergence can be estimated with considering topological changes that occur during the convergence. To show the feasibility and effectiveness of the approach, we presented a simple self-stabilizing mutual exclusion protocol on a frequently changing ring. The protocol can complete the convergence from an arbitrary configuration and can continue its intended behavior on a frequently changing ring.

In this paper, we considered only the dynamic changes of a ring network. But the proposed approach can be applied to analyze execution of self-stabilizing protocols in the environment where transient faults frequently occur. One of our future work is to show the feasibility and effectiveness of the method in dealing with transient faults as well as topological changes.

References

1. Baala, H., Flauzac, O., Gaber, J., Bui, M., and El-Ghazawi, T., A self-stabilizing distributed algorithm for spanning tree construction in wireless ad hoc networks, *JPDC*, vol. 63, pp. 97–104, 2003.
2. Chen, Y. and Welch, J. L., Self-stabilizing mutual exclusion using tokens in mobile ad hoc networks, *Proc. the 6th Dial-M*, pp.34–42 (2002).
3. Dijkstra, E. W., Self-stabilizing systems in spite of distributed control, *CACM*, vol. 17, no. 11, pp. 643–644, 1974.
4. Dolev, S., Self-stabilization, *The MIT Press*, 2000.
5. Dolev, S., Schiller, E., and Welch, J., Random walk for self-stabilizing group communication in ad-hoc networks, *Proc. the 21st SRDS*, pp. 70–79, 2000.
6. Gupta, S. K. S., Bouabdallah, A., and Srimani, P. K., Self-stabilizing protocol for shortest path tree for multicast routing in mobile networks, *Proc. the 6th Euro-Par*, pp. 600–604, 2000.
7. Gupta, S. K. S., Srimani, P. K., Self-stabilizing multicast protocols for ad hoc networks, *JPDC*, vol. 63, pp. 87–96, 2003.
8. Kakugawa, H. and Yamashita, M., A dynamic reconfiguration tolerant self-stabilizing token circulation algorithm in ad-hoc networks, *Proc. the 8th OPODIS*, pp. 179–186, 2004.
9. Li, X., Misra, J., and Plaxton, C. G., Active and concurrent topology maintenance, *Proc. the 18th DISC*, pp. 320–334, 2004.
10. Li, X., Misra, J., and Plaxton, C. G., Brief announcement: Concurrent maintenance of rings, *Proc. of the 23rd PODC*, p. 376, 2004.

Towards Automatic Convergence Verification of Self-stabilizing Algorithms*

Jens Oehlerking, Abhishek Dhama, and Oliver Theel

Carl von Ossietzky University of Oldenburg,
Department of Computer Science,
D-26111 Oldenburg, Germany
oliver.theel@uni-oldenburg.de

Abstract. The verification of the self-stabilization property of a distributed algorithm is a complicated task. By exploiting certain analogies between self-stabilizing distributed algorithms and globally asymptotically stable feedback systems, techniques originally developed for the verification of feedback system stability can be adopted for the verification of self-stabilization of distributed algorithms. In this paper, we show how for a certain subclass of dynamic systems – namely piecewise affine hybrid systems – and distributed algorithms suitable to be modeled in terms of these dynamic systems, a proof of convergence can be obtain *fully automatically*. Together with some additional non-automated arguments, the complete proof of self-stabilization can be derived.

Keywords: Distributed Algorithms, Self-Stabilization, Verification, Convergence, Hybrid Systems, Piecewise Affine Systems, Lyapunov Functions.

1   Introduction

Designing and implementing a crucial application in a distributed environment by means of a self-stabilizing algorithm is highly advisable, in particular, if the application is required to be very dependable. But, unfortunately, the verification of the self-stabilization property of an algorithm is quite complicated [14]. Informally, an algorithm is self-stabilizing, if 1) it is guaranteed to return from any state of the system state space to a particular set of legal states in finite time, and 2) once in a legal state, the algorithm either remains in this state or it only switches to other legal states without ever voluntarily leaving the legal state set. The former property is called *convergence* whereas the latter one is referred to as *closure* [20]. The specification of the set of legal states depends on the algorithm and is often given via a certain state predicate. Since verification

---

* This work was partly supported by the German Research Foundation (DFG) as part of the Transregional Collaborative Research Center "Automatic Verification and Analysis of Complex Systems" (SFB/TR 14 AVACS, www.avacs.org) and the Graduate School of Trustworthy Software Systems (GRK 1076/1, www.trustsoft.org).

T. Herman and S. Tixeuil (Eds.): SSS 2005, LNCS 3764, pp. 198–213, 2005.

of self-stabilization is tedious, the research community is working towards a simplification of this important task. The ultimate vision is to provide for proofs of self-stabilization in an automatic fashion.

One possible strategy in simplifying the verification task is the exploitation of an analogy between self-stabilizing algorithms and stable feedback systems that are used, for example, in electronic engineering. Here, informally, a feedback system is *globally asymptotically stable (wrt. the equilibrium point)* if the system converges from anywhere in the system state space towards a unique *equilibrium point*. An equilibrium point is a dedicated state of the system state space which – once reached – is never voluntarily left by the feedback system [11]. Thus, a globally asymptotically stable feedback system also exhibits a certain convergence as well as a closure property.

The aim of our work presented in this paper is to exploit this analogy for more easily deriving proofs of self-stabilization. We will show how to model distributed algorithms in terms of certain feedback systems, namely, discrete-time hybrid systems. Discrete-time hybrid system are a special class of discrete-time dynamic systems [25,1]. Generally, they exhibit various *modes* of operation. In every mode, a potentially different set of *difference equations* may govern the dynamic behavior of the overall feedback system. Modes are changed if certain conditions apply. This conceptual model quite easily allows for the modeling of distributed algorithms specified by collections of guarded commands [7]. The idea is that – based on the modeling in terms of a discrete-time hybrid systems – an algorithm may basically be analyzed wrt. self-stabilization by techniques originally used for the verification of global asymptotic stability.

The exploitation of the analogy between self-stabilizing algorithms and stable feedback systems has previously been reported in literature. For example, in [23], convergence verification of algorithms that can be modeled as *linear* feedback systems has been described. Linear feedback systems are an easy subclass of piecewise affine hybrid systems used in this paper. In [22], verification of self-stabilization is achieved using the so-called "Second Method" of Lyapunov [15,13]. Although applicable to general dynamic systems, the Second Method still requires the intuition of a proof designer even for the convergence part of the proof: he or she must specify a particular function called *Lyapunov function* which serves as variant function in the convergence verification procedure. Lyapunov functions can be seen as generalized "energy functions" of the system, as they are required to monotonously decrease over time and converge to zero at an equilibrium point.

Contrary to the approaches cited above, the approach reported in this paper is able to *fully automatically derive convergence proofs* for a subclass of general dynamic systems, namely *piecewise affine hybrid systems*. The specification of a suited Lyapunov function by a human designer is no further required but automatically derived by the verification tool. Together with some additional arguments, based on local reasoning, the complete proof of self-stabilization is obtained.

The paper is structured as follows: in Section 2, we briefly introduce an example algorithm whose self-stabilization property is to be verified. In Section 3, we present the system model and describe how the example algorithm can be modeled in terms of a hybrid system. Section 4 presents the verification technique. We introduce the underlying concepts of hybrid system analysis required for the understanding of the technique and apply it to the example algorithm. Furthermore, we state additional arguments needed for completing the proof of self-stabilization. Section 5 states related work in the fields of self-stabilization and feedback systems. Finally, in Section 6, a conclusion together with an outlook onto future work is given.

2   An Example Algorithm

In this section, we present a distributed algorithm, that – although quite simplistic – is complex enough to show the overall functioning of the verification technique. We would like to emphasize that the example algorithm *per se* is not in the focus of our attention, but the automatic manner in which convergence of this algorithm towards a certain state predicate can be proven.

The example algorithm has been motivated by a self-stabilizing general graph leader election algorithm as given in [8]. The example algorithm presented here identifies in a self-stabilizing way the minimum state value among N "worker processes" and a "whiteboard process." Once self-stabilized, all processes of the distributed application adopt the minimum value as their own local state. Thus, they agree on this particular value and the minimum value is "posted on the whiteboard." This value might then be exploited by a subsequent operational phase for its own, specific purpose. Since we focus on how this minimum value is identified in a self-stabilizing manner and convergence towards it is automatically proven, subsequent exploitation of the agreed value is neither stated by the algorithm presented here nor further discussed as it is out of the scope of this paper.

We assume that the distributed application consists of $N + 1$ processes P_i, $i = 1, \ldots, N+1$. Process P_{N+1} acts as a so-called *whiteboard*. For ease of description, this process is synonymously called *whiteboard process* and is addressed as process W. The other processes are called *worker processes*. The assumed communication topology of all the processes participating in the distributed algorithm is given in Fig. 1. Here, processes are represented as circles and possible information flow between the processes is indicated by arrows. In particular, the worker processes P_i, $i = 1, \ldots, N$, may bi-directionally communicate with the whiteboard process W, but not directly among each other. Communication among worker processes must be achieved indirectly via the whiteboard process.

The process bodies of the processes of the distributed algorithm are given as collections of *guarded commands* [7]. A guarded command is comprised of a *guard* and an *assignment statement*. Guard and assignment statement are separated by an arrow. A guard is a boolean expression over the local state and/or communication variables. An assignment statement is an assignment

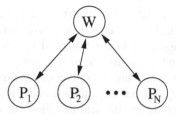

Fig. 1. Bi-directional communication topology among worker processes P_i, $i = 1, \ldots, N$, and whiteboard process W

```
process P_i
   var x_i : integer     {* local worker state *}
   com_var w     {* w is a communication variable *}
   begin
      x_i < w → w := x_i
    ‖ x_i > w → x_i := w
   end
```

Fig. 2. Process P_i, $i = 1, \ldots, N$, of the example algorithm

```
process W
   var w : integer     {* local whiteboard state *}
   begin
    {* no operation *}
   end
```

Fig. 3. Whiteboard process W

over local variables and/or communication variables. The processes' bodies are shown in Figs. 2 and 3 for worker processes and for the whiteboard process, respectively. The local state of a worker process P_i is given by the local variable x_i. After a process starts, this variable is assumed having an arbitrary value. The communication variable w represents the local state of the whiteboard, i.e., "what is currently posted on the whiteboard." Communication is achieved by the inspection and possible modification of communication variables. The whiteboard process has a local variable w and does not use any communication variable. By inspection (modification) of the communication variable w done by a worker process, the local variable of the whiteboard process is read (written). Thus, the attribute "local" in our model refers to the process where a variable is implemented whereas the declaration as a "communication variable" specifies that a variable local to some other process can locally be read or written by the process declaring it.

While the distributed algorithm executes, all the processes cyclically evaluate their guards. Guards which evaluate to "true" as well as the guarded commands they belong to are called *active*. A global entity, called *central daemon* selects

within each evaluation cycle exactly one active guarded command if one or more
guarded commands are active [7]. In other words: we assume *serial execution
semantics*. Selection is assumed being followed by an atomic execution of the
selected guarded command's assignment statement. It is also assumed that the
central daemon selects guards – one after the other – in a *fair* manner implying
that in an infinitely long execution sequence each active guarded command is
selected infinitely often. This further implies that an active guarded command
is eventually selected [16].

Worker processes' bodies consist of two guarded commands (see Fig. 2). The
first guarded command checks whether the local state value is less than the
value posted on the whiteboard. If this is the case (and the guarded command is
selected by the central daemon) then the value on the whiteboard is overwritten
by the local state value. The second guarded command functions analogously but
in "opposite direction:" if the local state value is more than the whiteboard value
then the former is overwritten by the latter. The process body of the whiteboard
process is empty (see Fig. 3). This process can be regarded as a passive entity
having a local state that is exclusively modified by the worker processes.

The $N+1$ individual processes may be subject to faults compromising their
local state. Let the *most recent initial local state* be the local state which a
particular process has adopted due to the most recent failure situation or initialization and not due to the execution of an action. Then, we can formulate
the following theorem.

Theorem 1. Let $x = [x_1, \ldots, x_N, w]^T \in \mathbb{R}^{N+1}$ be a system state and let $x^0 = [x_1^0, \ldots, x_N^0, w^0]^T$ be the system state where x_i^0 is the most recent initial local
state of process P_i and w^0 is the most recent initial local state of process W.
Then, the algorithm is self-stabilizing with respect to a state predicate $\mathcal{A}$ where
$\mathcal{A} := \{x \mid w = x_1 = \ldots = x_N = min(\{x_1^0, \ldots x_N^0, w^0\})\}$. $\qquad \square$

Theorem 1 states that in absence of newly occurring failures the processes of
the algorithm find the minimum value present in the system in a finite number
of steps. Once the processes reach a consensus then each of them exhibits the
minimum value as its local state.

In the next section, we introduce a system model that allows for the modeling of the example algorithm such that an automated convergence verification
technique can subsequently be applied.

3   System Model

To show self-stabilization of a certain class of distributed algorithms, we utilize
methods developed in the field of control theory. For feedback systems, *stability* is
of central importance [13], as it should not be possible to permanently unbalance
a feedback system through outside disturbances. We will show how the concept
of Lyapunov functions, that is widely used to prove stability of feedback systems,
can also be applied in the context of self-stabilizing distributed algorithms. In
this section, we will describe how to transform self-stabilization problems into

problems of feedback system stabilization that imply the self-stabilization property of the original system. Section 4 will then show the verification procedure wrt. global asymptotic stability for those feedback systems.

3.1 Modeling Distributed Algorithms Through Hybrid Systems

Modeling distributed algorithms in terms of feedback systems is achieved by means of difference equations. This means that the resulting feedback system works in discrete time – each selected guard represents one "time tick" and a "time tick" will also be taken if no guards are active. This ensures that the feedback system has an infinite timeline – a prerequisite for applying the verification technique. Each guarded command of every process of a distributed application is represented in the feedback system modeling by two different concepts: 1) a *difference equation* and 2) a *mode* of operation. At run-time, from "time tick" to "time tick" a particular mode (i.e. an active guarded command) is adopted (i.e. is selected by the central daemon). If a mode is selected then the particular difference equation belonging to that mode is applied (i.e. its assignment statement is atomically executed). In the feedback system community, feedback systems acting with modes, mode transitions, and particular difference equations[1] per mode are referred to as *hybrid systems* [25]: difference equations govern the dynamics, while the mode switches are defined through a relation.We adopt the concept of hybrid systems for our verification purposes, since it almost naturally allows for the modeling of distributed algorithms given as collections of guarded commands.

The following definition of a discrete-time hybrid systems uses a state vector x representing the system state at a particular time instance. Every coordinate of this vector stands for the value of a particular state variable at that time. Using this vector notation, the difference equations of the feedback system can then be represented by a single matrix equation.

Definition 1 (Discrete-time hybrid system[24]). An *(autonomous)* *discrete-time hybrid system* is given by the difference equation

$$x[k + 1] = f(x[k], m[k]) \tag{1}$$

and a relation

$$\Phi \subseteq \mathbb{R}^n \times \mathcal{M} \times \mathcal{M} \tag{2}$$

where $x[k] \in \mathbb{R}^n$ is called the *state vector* of the hybrid system at time instant k and $m[k] \in \mathcal{M} := \{1, \ldots, M\}$ is its *mode* at time instant k.[2] $\mathcal{H} = \mathbb{R}^n \times \mathcal{M}$ is called *hybrid state space* and $(x, m) \in \mathcal{H}$ is a *hybrid state*. The function $f : \mathcal{H} \to \mathbb{R}^n$ describes the possible state vector modifications from one time instant to the subsequent one. The relation Φ describes the possible mode switches, i.e.

---

[1] Or *differential* equations in case of time-continuous feedback systems.

[2] In a context where the value of k is not important, we will simplify $x[k]$ to x and $m[k]$ to m.

$(x, m, m') \in \Phi$ if a mode switch from m to m' can occur in state x. For deterministic systems, Φ reduces to a function mapping tuples from $\mathbb{R}^n \times \mathcal{M}$ to $\mathcal{M}$. An infinite sequence of hybrid states $(x[k], m[k])$, $k \in \mathbb{N}_0$, with $(x[k], m[k], m[k+1]) \in \Phi$ for all $k \in \mathbb{N}_0$ that fulfills Eq. (1) is called a *trajectory* of the system. The tuple $(x[0], m[0])$ is called the *initial hybrid state* of a trajectory.   □

Each trajectory represents one possible execution of the system – deterministic systems only allow one trajectory per initial hybrid state.

We prove stability for the class of self-stabilizing distributed algorithms that can be modelled as *piecewise affine* hybrid systems. Let A be a distributed algorithm and let $x = [x_1, \cdots, x_n]^T$ be its state vector such that the assignment statements of each guarded command can be represented as

$$x_i[k+1] = \sum_{j=1}^{n} a_i^j x_j[k] + b_i, \qquad \text{with } a_i^j, b_i \in \mathbb{R}$$

for each variable x_i. Thus, all guarded commands exhibit assignment statements of affine nature. Algorithm A can then be modelled as a piecewise affine hybrid system. In that case, each guarded command corresponds to one mode of the system. The dynamics of each mode m is then given by $x[k+1] = A_m x + b_m$ where a_i^j is the j-th entry of the i-th row of a matrix A_m and b_i is the i-th entry of a vector b_m. Additionally, a particular "liveness" mode must be added per process for the case that no guard is active. For this particular "liveness" mode l, A_l is the identity matrix and b_l the zero vector. Its guard is the negation of the disjunction of all other guards of the process. Then, the mode transition relation Φ can be stated as

$$(x, m_i, m_j) \in \Phi \text{ iff } A_{m_i} x + b_{m_i} \text{ fulfills the guard of } m_j, \qquad m_i, m_j \in \mathcal{M}. \text{ (3)}$$

We focus on self-stabilization with respect to a particular predicate, namely convergence to an equilibrium state. Such a state has one important characteristic: once such an equilibrium state has been reached by the system, no further changes to the system state occur in the absence of faults. Formally, sets of equilibrium states wrt. a distributed algorithm can be defined as follows.

Definition 2 (Set of equilibrium states). Let A be a distributed algorithm and let G be the set of all guards of A. Let $\mathcal{X}$ be the state space of A. For each guard $g \in G$, let c_g be the state change caused by the corresponding guarded command. For distributed algorithm A, define

$$\mathcal{F} := \{x \in \mathcal{X} \mid \forall g \in G : g(x) = true \Rightarrow x = c_g(x)\}.$$

$\mathcal{F}$ is then called the *set of equilibrium states* of distributed algorithm A.   □

Based on this definition, one can define a predicate that exclusively holds when an equilibrium state has been reached:

Definition 3 (Equilibrium predicate). For a distributed algorithm A with a set of equilibrium states $\mathcal{F}$, let $\mathcal{B}$ be a state predicate that holds for a system state x if and only if $x \in \mathcal{F}$. Then, $\mathcal{B}$ is called an *equilibrium predicate* wrt. the distributed algorithm A. □

Convergence with respect to an equilibrium predicate can then be shown by means of the technique demonstrated in this paper. This will be explained in detail in Section 4. In the following section, we show the re-modeling of the example algorithm in terms of the system model.

3.2 Applying the System Model to the Example Algorithm

When applying the system to the example algorithm as described above, we would obtain three modes per worker process: one for each guard (or: guarded command) and one "liveness" mode for the case that no guard is active, i.e. the case where $x_i = w$. However, the dynamics of each of the other two modes would be no different to the dynamics of the liveness mode: no state change would occur, as the assignments $w := x_i$ and $x_i := w$ have no effect. Therefore, in this particular example, we can spare the modeling of an explicit "liveness" mode. We simply merge the "liveness" mode with both of the other modes, resulting in just two modes per worker process. Assume that m_i^1 is the mode corresponding to the (new) guard $x_i \leq w$ for process P_i and that m_i^2 is the mode corresponding to the (new) guard $x_i \geq w$. We define the state vector as

$$x := [x_1, ..., x_N, w]^T,$$

Then, for a system with three worker processes, we obtain $3 \times 2 = 6$ modes. The dynamics of a particular mode m is given as $x[k+1] = A_m x[k] + b_m$ with

$$A_{m_1^1} = \begin{bmatrix} 1 & 0 & 0 & 0 \\ 0 & 1 & 0 & 0 \\ 0 & 0 & 1 & 0 \\ 1 & 0 & 0 & 0 \end{bmatrix}, \ A_{m_1^2} = \begin{bmatrix} 0 & 0 & 0 & 1 \\ 0 & 1 & 0 & 0 \\ 0 & 0 & 1 & 0 \\ 0 & 0 & 0 & 1 \end{bmatrix}, \ A_{m_2^1} = \begin{bmatrix} 1 & 0 & 0 & 0 \\ 0 & 1 & 0 & 0 \\ 0 & 0 & 1 & 0 \\ 0 & 1 & 0 & 0 \end{bmatrix},$$

$$A_{m_2^2} = \begin{bmatrix} 1 & 0 & 0 & 0 \\ 0 & 0 & 0 & 1 \\ 0 & 0 & 1 & 0 \\ 0 & 0 & 0 & 1 \end{bmatrix}, \ A_{m_3^1} = \begin{bmatrix} 1 & 0 & 0 & 0 \\ 0 & 1 & 0 & 0 \\ 0 & 0 & 1 & 0 \\ 0 & 0 & 1 & 0 \end{bmatrix}, \ A_{m_3^2} = \begin{bmatrix} 1 & 0 & 0 & 0 \\ 0 & 1 & 0 & 0 \\ 0 & 0 & 0 & 1 \\ 0 & 0 & 0 & 1 \end{bmatrix}$$

and b_m being the 4-dimensional zero vector for all modes. According to Eq. (3), for this example, the relation Φ is defined as follows:

$$(x, m_i^1, m_j^1) \in \Phi \quad \text{iff } x_j \leq x_i \tag{4}$$
$$(x, m_i^1, m_j^2) \in \Phi \quad \text{iff } x_j \geq x_i \tag{5}$$
$$(x, m_i^2, m_j^1) \in \Phi \quad \text{iff } x_j \leq w \tag{6}$$
$$(x, m_i^2, m_j^2) \in \Phi \quad \text{iff } x_j \geq w \tag{7}$$

The modes and their possible transitions are illustrated in Fig. 4. The boxes represent the modes of the system whereas the arrows represent possible mode transitions. The system may stay in each mode as long as the corresponding guard belonging to the mode is fulfilled - for this example this will at least be the case as long as this mode is not left. As long as the system is in a particular mode, its dynamics changes the system state, i.e., its assignment statement is applied. However, due to fairness, we know that each mode will eventually be left. When this occurs, a new mode whose guard evaluates to true at this point of time is chosen. With the only assumption about the daemon being fair, this implies that there are possible transitions from every mode to every other mode, as long as the guard corresponding to the "target mode" holds true. Figure

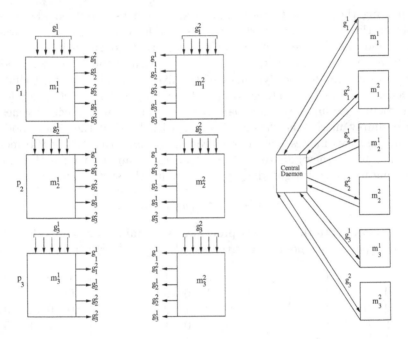

Fig. 4. Hybrid system view   **Fig. 5.** Distributed algorithm view

5 shows an alternative view of the same system which is somewhat closer to the original algorithm than to the hybrid system model. The box on the left side represents the central daemon. Every other node represents a mode of the system. Once a mode is left, control is returned to the daemon which chooses the successor mode – in this example in a non-deterministic, fair fashion.

4   Proving Self-stabilization Through Lyapunov Functions

In this section, we present control-theoretic techniques for proving stability that have been amended for the self-stabilization case. We show, how global asymptotic stability with respect to a set of equilibrium points can be proven. This result can then be used to guarantee self-stabilization wrt. an equilibrium predicate $\mathcal{B}$ for a distributed algorithm.

4.1   Global Asymptotic Stability and Lyapunov Functions

The self-stabilization property wrt. an equilibrium predicate $\mathcal{B}$ of a distributed algorithm with integer variables is equivalent to *global asymptotic stability* of the associated hybrid system, i.e. convergence of the state vector towards a set of equilibrium states. This set of equilibrium states represents the system configurations where no further changes can occur – either all guards evaluate to false or all guards that evaluate to true belong to actions that do not change the current system state.

Definition 4 (Global asymptotic stability). A discrete-time hybrid system according to Eqs. (1)–(2) is called *globally asymptotically stable* with respect to a set of equilibrium states $\mathcal{F} \subseteq \mathbb{R}^n$, iff the first coordinate $x[k]$ of all trajectories $(x[k], m[k])$ of the system converge to $\mathcal{F}$.   □

To show global asymptotic stability of hybrid systems, a variation of the so-called "Second Method" of Lyapunov [15] can be used. This method uses a function that can be interpreted as measuring the system's "energy" – if the "energy level" of the system is constantly decreasing regardless where the system starts from in the system state space and the "energy level" is converging to zero at a unique equilibrium state then global asymptotic stability is proven. The function capturing the "energy level" of the system is called *Lyapunov function*. Formally, a definition of such a classical Lyapunov function for single-mode systems is given by the following theorem.

Theorem 2 (Second Method of Lyapunov [15]). Let $x[k+1] = f(x[k])$ be a discrete-time single-mode system with $f(\underline{0}) = \underline{0}$.[3] If there exists a function $V : \mathbb{R}^n \to \mathbb{R}$, such that

(L1) $V(x)$ is positive definite, i.e. $V(\underline{0}) = 0$ and $V(x) > 0$ for all $x \neq 0$
(L2) $\dot{V}(x) := V(f(x)) - V(x)$ is negative definite, i.e. $\dot{V}(\underline{0}) = 0$ and $\dot{V}(x) < 0$
for all $x \neq 0$
(L3) $V(x) \to \infty$ for $\|x\| \to \infty$

then the system is *globally asymptotically stable* in $\underline{0}$. V is then called a *Lyapunov function* of the system.   □

As we are interested in proving convergence wrt. a *set of equilibrium points* $\mathcal{F}$ with $\underline{0} \in \mathcal{F}$ and not merely wrt. a single equilibrium point, we replace condition (L2) by (L2') as given below.

(L2') $\dot{V}(x) := V(f(x)) - V(x) < 0$ for all $x \notin \mathcal{F}$ and $\dot{V}(x) = 0$ for all $x \in \mathcal{F}$.

The Lyapunov function is only required to drop over time when the current state is not an element of $\mathcal{F}$. This means that we only require the "energy level" of a system under consideration to decrease whenever it is not already in an equilibrium state. Once an equilibrium state has been reached, it will not be left again – therefore, the Lyapunov function will remain unchanged from that point on.

---

[3] $\underline{0}$ denotes the origin of $\mathbb{R}^n$.

For multi-mode systems – such as hybrid systems – a standard approach is to search for a common Lyapunov function covering all existing modes of the system. In other words, each mode is viewed as a separate single-mode system and a Lyapunov function must be identified that fulfills conditions (L1), (L2'), and (L3) for all modes at the same time. Other possible approaches require a partitioning of the state space into disjoint regions [9,18] which can be less conservative. However, the strong non-determinism we find in self-stabilizing systems (visualized by the fully connected transition graph as given by Fig. 4 for the example) significantly reduces the gain of these methods, while still increasing computation time and risk of numerical problems. Therefore, we decided to pursue the identification of a single Lyapunov function for the entire state space.

4.2   Automatic Computation of Lyapunov Functions

If the dynamics exhibited in each mode is *affine*, i.e. in Eq. (1), we have $f(x, m) = A_m x + b_m$, where $A_m \in \mathbb{R}^{n \times n}, b_m \in \mathbb{R}^n$ for each mode m then the Lyapunov function can efficiently be computed. Systems of this class are called *piecewise affine (PWA)*. We use quadratic Lyapunov function candidates and reduce the problem of finding a Lyapunov function to *convex optimization* [4] via so-called *linear matrix inequalities (LMIs)* [3].

Definition 5 (Quadratic expressions). A function of the form

$$g(x) = x^T P x + 2p^T x + \pi, \tag{8}$$
$$P \in \mathbb{R}^{n \times n}, p \in \mathbb{R}^n, \pi \in \mathbb{R}$$

is called *quadratic expression*.   □

For convenience, the function can be rewritten as

$$g(x) = \tilde{x}^T \tilde{P} \tilde{x} \tag{9}$$

with

$$\tilde{x} := \begin{bmatrix} x \\ 1 \end{bmatrix}, \quad \tilde{P} := \begin{bmatrix} P & p \\ p^T & \pi \end{bmatrix}$$

LMI problems are of the following form.

> Find $k_i \in \mathbb{R}$, such that $x^T (F_0 + \sum_{i=1}^N k_i F_i) x \geq 0$ for all $x \in \mathbb{R}^n$

where the $F_j \in \mathbb{R}^{n \times n}, 0 \leq j \leq N$, are fixed. In short, this can also be written as

> Find $k_i \in \mathbb{R}$, such that $F_0 + \sum_{i=1}^N k_i F_i \geq 0$

where "≥ 0" denotes positive definiteness. LMI problems are convex optimization problems over a semidefinite cone. Therefore, they can be solved using standard convex optimization methods [4]. To describe the guards and the set of equilibrium points $\mathcal{F}$, we apply the so-called $\mathcal{S}$-Procedure, originally introduced in [26]. This method allows us to express local conditions as part of an LMI problem by including an additional matrix term. This term describes the region where we want the condition to hold. A detailed explanation on how to obtain these matrix terms can be found in [18]. For the sake of brevity, we just give the resulting LMI problem here. The matrix $\tilde{P}$, which is part of its solution, represents the quadratic Lyapunov function that guarantees convergence toward the equilibrium set $\mathcal{F}$.

Theorem 3 (Lyapunov function identification based on [9]). For each system mode m, find a family of matrices $\tilde{Q}_m^k \in \mathbb{R}^{n \times n}$ with $\tilde{x}^T \tilde{Q}_m^k \tilde{x} \geq 0$ for all x that fulfill the corresponding guard. Furthermore, for each mode m, find a matrix $\tilde{R}_m \in \mathbb{R}^{n \times n}$ with $\tilde{x}^T \tilde{R}_m \tilde{x} > 0$ for all x with $A_m x + b_m \neq x$ and $\tilde{x}^T \tilde{R} \tilde{x} = 0$ otherwise.

Let

$$\tilde{I} := \begin{bmatrix} I & \underline{0} \\ \underline{0}^T & 0 \end{bmatrix}, \quad \tilde{A}_m := \begin{bmatrix} A_m & b_m \\ \underline{0}^T & 0 \end{bmatrix}$$

where I is the $n \times n$ identity matrix,
Then, a PWA system

$$x[k+1] = A_m x[k] + b_m$$
$$\Phi \subseteq \mathbb{R}^n \times \mathcal{M} \times \mathcal{M}$$

is globally asymptotically stable in $\underline{0}$ if the following LMI problem has a solution:

Find $\beta \in \mathbb{R}, \alpha \geq 0, \eta_m^k \geq 0$ and $\tilde{P} \in \mathbb{R}^{n+1 \times n+1}$, such that

$$\alpha \tilde{I} \leq \tilde{P} \leq \beta \tilde{I} \text{ and} \tag{10}$$

$$\tilde{A}_m^T \tilde{P} \tilde{A}_m - \tilde{P} + \sum_{k=1}^{\kappa_m} \eta_m^k \tilde{Q}_m^k + \tilde{R}_m \leq 0 \text{ for all modes } m \tag{11}$$

$\square$

This LMI problem can easily be cast into a single standard form LMI problem. The Lyapunov function certifying stability of the system can then be obtained by $V(x) = \tilde{x}^T \tilde{P} \tilde{x}$.

Using the method outlined above, one can prove global asymptotic stability of the system with respect to the set $\mathcal{F}$ of equilibrium points. To draw the conclusion that the set $\mathcal{F}$ is indeed reached in finite time by all possible trajectories instead of being approached asymptotically, one needs to argue about the values the system variables can adopt. If there is a constant $k \in \mathbb{R}$, so that for all pairs of possible state vectors x and x', $x \neq x'$, $||x - x'|| > k$ then this implies that $\mathcal{F}$ is reached in finite time. If, for example, all possible variable values are integers then this constraint always holds.

The closedness of $\mathcal{F}$ is already implied by the fact that all its points are equilibria – no further state changes can occur in $\mathcal{F}$. Therefore, the system will remain in $\mathcal{F}$ after entering, implying self-stabilization with respect to predicate $\mathcal{B}$.

4.3   Proving Self-stabilization of the Example Algorithm

In this section, we apply the verification technique described above to the example algorithm introduced in Section 2 and modeled as a piecewise affine hybrid system as given in Section 3.2.

The example algorithm leads to an LMI problem that contains one instance of Eq. (10) and two instances of Eq. (11) per worker process resulting in a total of 7 LMI problems to be solved. The matrices $\tilde{Q}_m^k$ are obtained from the guards as described in [18–pages 103ff.]. As an example, the $\tilde{Q}_{m_1^1}^k$ matrices for mode m_1^1 representing the first guarded command of worker process P_1 in a three-worker-processes system are as follows:

$$\tilde{Q}_{m_1^1}^1 = \begin{bmatrix} -2 & 0 & 0 & 1 & 0 \\ 0 & 0 & 0 & 0 & 0 \\ 0 & 0 & 0 & 0 & 0 \\ 1 & 0 & 0 & 0 & 0 \\ 0 & 0 & 0 & 0 & 0 \end{bmatrix}, \quad \tilde{Q}_{m_1^1}^2 = \begin{bmatrix} 0 & -1 & 0 & 0 & 0 \\ -1 & 0 & 0 & 1 & 0 \\ 0 & 0 & 0 & 0 & 0 \\ 0 & 1 & 0 & 0 & 0 \\ 0 & 0 & 0 & 0 & 0 \end{bmatrix}$$

$$\tilde{Q}_{m_1^1}^3 = \begin{bmatrix} 0 & 0 & -1 & 0 & 0 \\ 0 & 0 & 0 & 0 & 0 \\ -1 & 0 & 0 & 1 & 0 \\ 0 & 0 & 1 & 0 & 0 \\ 0 & 0 & 0 & 0 & 0 \end{bmatrix}, \quad \tilde{Q}_{m_1^1}^4 = \begin{bmatrix} 0 & 0 & 0 & -1 & 0 \\ 0 & 0 & 0 & 0 & 0 \\ 0 & 0 & 0 & 0 & 0 \\ -1 & 0 & 0 & 2 & 0 \\ 0 & 0 & 0 & 0 & 0 \end{bmatrix}$$

$$\tilde{Q}_{m_1^1}^5 = \begin{bmatrix} 0 & 0 & 0 & 0 & -1 \\ 0 & 0 & 0 & 0 & 0 \\ 0 & 0 & 0 & 0 & 0 \\ 0 & 0 & 0 & 0 & 1 \\ -1 & 0 & 0 & 1 & 0 \end{bmatrix}$$

In a similar way, one can obtain the $\tilde{R}_m$ matrices, for example

$$\tilde{R}_{m_1^1} = \begin{bmatrix} 1 & 0 & 0 & -1 & 0 \\ 0 & 0 & 0 & 0 & 0 \\ 0 & 0 & 0 & 0 & 0 \\ -1 & 0 & 0 & 1 & 0 \\ 0 & 0 & 0 & 0 & 0 \end{bmatrix}$$

A solution can then be found through convex optimization and semidefinite programming software like CSDP [2]. For a three-worker-processes system, the following matrix represents a solution. The numerical values being solutions to other unknown variables occurring in the LMI problems are purely technical and not important for the description of the actual Lyapunov function. Therefore, they are omitted here.

$$\tilde{P} = \begin{bmatrix} 1 & 0 & 0 & 0 & 0 \\ 0 & 1 & 0 & 0 & 0 \\ 0 & 0 & 1 & 0 & 0 \\ 0 & 0 & 0 & 1 & 0 \\ 0 & 0 & 0 & 0 & 0 \end{bmatrix}$$

This implies that $V(x) = \tilde{x}^T \tilde{P} \tilde{x} = x_1^2 + x_2^2 + x_3^2 + w^2$ is a possible Lyapunov function, proving global asymptotic stability of the system with respect to the equilibrium set $\mathcal{F} = \{[x_1, x_2, x_3, w]^T \mid x_1 = x_2 = x_3 = w\}$. As all variables are integers, this implies that each system trajectory will eventually enter $\mathcal{F}$ (see Section 4.2). An analogous proof exists for any number of worker processes.

To complete the proof of Theorem 1, it remains to be shown that the state the system converges to is indeed given by x with $w = x_1 = \ldots = x_N = \min(\{x_1^0, \ldots, x_N^0, w\})$. So far we have only proven that the system converges to an equilibrium state with $w = x_1 = \ldots = x_N$. This can be done by the following local reasoning. Whenever a guarded command is executed then a value not being the lowest value in the system is overwritten with a lower value. Furthermore, the algorithm never introduces new values into the system that have not been present before. Therefore, $\min(\{x_1^0, \ldots, x_N^0, w\})$ will always be the value of at least one variable of the system. This means the system will always converge towards state x with $w = x_1 = \ldots = x_N = \min(\{x_1^0, \ldots, x_N^0, w\})$ – all other variable values are eventually eliminated.

5   Related Work

Traditionally, automatic verification methods for self-stabilizing algorithms have been logic-based. Temporal logic was used to provide a framework and proof rules for analysis of stabilizing systems in [21]. An extension of programming logic UNITY [6] along with theorem prover HOL [10] was used to support computer-aided verification of self-stabilizing algorithms [19]. Both these approaches require considerable assistance from the algorithm designer in order to derive the proofs. Other proof methods include *variant functions, scheduler-luck* games and the *convergence stairs* method [8]. But these methods can not be automated and proofs must be drawn "by hand."

In [12] and [18], the construction of piecewise quadratic Lyapunov functions for continuous-time systems is discussed. These approaches allow for a partitioning of the state space into regions, each with a separate quadratic function. Branicky [5] gives an overview of the use of multiple Lyapunov functions for a single feedback system. In [9], it is shown that this approach can also be used for the discrete-time domain. However, in the context of self-stabilization, these state space partitionings – unfortunately – offer little advantage, as the severe non-determinism leads to strong dependencies among the various the "local Lyapunov functions." If a specific, deterministic implementation of a daemon is assumed, this disadvantage vanishes. In such a case, there is a higher degree of freedom in the choice of Lyapunov function, enlarging the class of systems for which stability can be proven.

In [17], the authors consider certain higher-degree polynomial Lyapunov functions that can also be found through an LMI approach. This approach can also be used in conjunction with a partitioning into regions with separate Lyapunov functions. However, the increased complexity and the higher risk of running into numerical problems makes this approach less successful than the one presented in this paper.

6 Conclusion and Future Work

In this paper, we have presented a technique for automatically proving convergence of distributed algorithms with respect to set of equilibrium states. To achieve this, we modelled the distributed algorithm as a piecewise affine discrete-time feedback system and subsequently used Lyapunov functions to prove global asymptotic stability with respect to those equilibrium states. For systems with integer variables representing local states, global asymptotic stability implies convergence with respect to the set of equilibrium states. Closure of this set is given implicitly since no equilibrium state can be left once it has been entered. Based on an example, we have demonstrated the viability of the proposed verification technique for self-stabilizing distributed algorithms by employing convex optimization software.

Future work will include the extension of the approach to self-stabilizing distributed algorithms that cannot be expressed by piecewise affine dynamics: in those cases, a certain "embedding of the system" by two piecewise affine systems may yield a Lyapunov function able to prove global asymptotic stability of the system under consideration [18]. Furthermore, in some cases, it might be advantageous to exploit the piecewise quadratic Lyapunov function approach as given in [9] and [12] or the sums-of-squares approach proposed in [17], especially for systems with complex processes. Our goal is to integrate these technique into a single automatic verification tool: this tool will 1) classify the self-stabilizing distributed algorithm under consideration in order to determine the most promising verification approach and 2) apply the technique.

References

1. R. Alur, T. A. Henzinger, G. Lafferiere, and G. J. Pappas. Discrete Abstractions of Hybrid Systems. *Proceedings of the IEEE*, 88(7):971–984, 2000.
2. B. Borchers. CSDP, a C library for semidefinite programming. *Optimization Methods and Software*, 10:613–623, 1999.
3. Stephen Boyd, Laurent El Ghaoui, Eric Feron, and Venkataramanan Balakrishnan. *Linear Matrix Inequalities in System and Control Theory*. SIAM, 1994.
4. Stephen Boyd and Lieven Vandenberghe. *Convex Optimization*. Cambridge University Press, 2004.
5. Michael S. Branicky. Multiple Lyapunov functions and other analysis tools for switched and hybrid systems. *IEEE Transactions on Automatic Control*, 43(4), April 1998.
6. K. Mani Chandy and Jayadev Misra. *Parallel Program Design : A Foundation*. Addison-Wesley Publishing Company, 1988.
7. Edsger W. Dijkstra. Guarded commands, nondeterminancy, and formal derivation of programs. *Communications of Association for Computing Machinery*, 18:453–457, 1975.
8. Shlomi Dolev. *Self-stabilization*. MIT Press, 2000.
9. Gang Feng. Stability analysis of piecewise discrete-time linear systems. *IEEE Transactions on Automatic Control*, 47(7):1108–1112, 2002.

10. Mike J.C. Gordon and Tom F. Melham. *Introduction to HOL*. Cambridge University Press, 1993.
11. W. Hahn. *Stability of Motion*. Springer-Verlag, 1967.
12. Mikael Johansson and Anders Rantzer. Computation of piecewise quadratic Lyapunov functions for hybrid systems. *IEEE Transactions on Automatic Control*, 43, 1998.
13. R. E. Kalman and J. E. Bertram. Control System Analysis and Design Via the "Second Method" of Lyapunov. *Transactions of the ASME, Journal of Basic Engineering*, pages 371–400, 1960.
14. J. L. W. Kessels. An Exercise in Proving Self-Stabilization with a Variant Function. *Information Processing Letters*, 29:39–42, 1988.
15. M. A. Lyapunov. Problème général de la stabilité du movement. *Ann. Fac. Sci. Toulouse*, 9:203–474, 1907. (Translation of a paper published in Comm. Soc. math. Kharkow, 1893, reprinted in Ann. math. Studies No. 17, Princeton University Press, 1949).
16. Nancy A. Lynch. *Distributed Algorithms*. Morgan Kaufmann Publishers, Inc., 1996.
17. Antonis Papachristodoulou and Stephen Prajna. On the construction of Lyapunov functions using the sums of squares decomposition. In *Proceedings of IEEE Conference on Decision and Control*, 2002.
18. Stefan Pettersson. *Analysis and Design of Hybrid Systems*. PhD thesis, Chalmers University of Technology, Gothenburg, 1999.
19. I.S.W.B. Prasetya. *Mechanically Supported Design of Self-stabilizing Algorithms*. PhD thesis, Inst. of Information and Comp. Science, Utrecht Univ., 1995.
20. Marco Schneider. Self-stabilization. *ACM Computing Surveys*, 25(1):45–67, 1993.
21. Michael Siegel. *Phased Design and Verification of Stabilizing Systems*. PhD thesis, University of Kiel, 1996.
22. Oliver Theel. Exploitation of Ljapunov Theory for Verifying Self-Stabilizing Algorithms. In Maurice Herlihy, editor, *Proc. of the 14th Symposium on Distributed Computing (DISC'00), Toledo, Spain, LNCS Vol. 1914*, Lecture Notes in Computer Science, pages 209–222. Springer-Verlag, October 2000.
23. Oliver Theel and Felix C. Gärtner. An Exercise in Proving Convergence through Transfer Functions. In *Proc. of the 4th Workshop on Self-Stabilizing Systems (WSS'99), being part of the 19th International Conference on Distributed Computer Systems (ICDCS'99), Austin, TX, U.S.A.*, pages 41–47. IEEE, June 1999.
24. Fabio Danilo Torrisi and Alberto Bemporad. Discrete-time hybrid modeling and verification. In *Proc. of the 40th IEEE Conference on Decision and Control*, December 2001.
25. H. S. Witsenhausen. A Class of Hybrid-State Continuous Dynamical Systems. *IEEE Trans. on Automatic Control*, 11(2):161–167, 1966.
26. V. Yakubovich. S-procedure in nonlinear control theory. *Vestnik Leningrad Univ.*, 4:73–93, 1977.

About the Self-stabilization of a Virtual Topology for Self-organization in Ad Hoc Networks

Fabrice Theoleyre and Fabrice Valois

CITI, INRIA ARES, INSA Lyon,
21 av Jean Capelle, 69621 Villeurbanne Cedex, France
{fabrice.theoleyre, fabrice.valois}@insa-lyon.fr

Abstract. Ad hoc networks are spontaneous wireless networks without any wired infrastructure, composed of mobile terminals. We assume that nodes must collaborate to set up an efficient network, such a collaboration requiring a self-organization in the network. We proposed a virtual structure to organize the network: the backbone is a connected structure helping to optimize the control traffic flooding. Clusters form services area, hierarchizing the network, electing one leader per cluster. Since the ad hoc topology is volatile, the self-stabilization of the algorithms is vital. The algorithms for both the construction and the maintenance are analytically studied to prove the self-stabilization of the proposed self-organization. Thus, the virtual structure is efficient and very scalable, a local topology change impacting only locally the virtual structure. Finally, simulations investigate the behavior and the performances of the virtual structure.

1 Introduction

MANet (Mobile Ad hoc NETworks) are spontaneous topologies of mobile nodes where each of them collaborate in order to give services like routing, localization, etc. It can be used to offer a spontaneous network infrastructure. Each terminal can communicate via wireless links without preconditioned fixed infrastructure. The network must function autonomously, without any human intervention. To send packets from a source to a destination, either the destination is in the radio range of the source or intermediaries nodes must help to forward the packets. To reach such a goal, the nodes must collaborate and exchange control information to set up routes in the network. Indeed, each node is both client and router. Because of the nodes mobility, radio links are created and deleted continuously leading to topology changes. And finally, routes are volatile. So, self-adaptation of the network to the dynamicity is a major issue of MANet. Ad hoc networks can be connected to the Internet, via a dedicated device, the wireless access point (AP), gateway from the ad hoc network to the wired world. Such networks are often called *hybrid networks* constituting *wireless multihops cellular networks*.

In our point of view, self-organization can answer to the above key problems. Self-organization deals with virtual topologies in order to simplify ad hoc

T. Herman and S. Tixeuil (Eds.): SSS 2005, LNCS 3764, pp. 214–228, 2005.

topologies. For example, virtual topologies can be constituted by a backbone [10], or a combination of a backbone and clusters [8]. The goal is to offer control on the MANet. According to us, virtual topologies allow scalability (in creating a hierarchy useful for example for routing protocols), facilitate integration of MANET in wired or cellular networks (with a virtual backbone), hide topology changes (in creating a stable macroscopic view), take heterogeneity into account (in distributing unfairly the load in the network). The mobility represents a key challenge in MANet. As each node is mobile, many radio links appear and disappear, occurring many topology changes. Virtual structures must remain efficient along the time. Hence, it must be continuously maintained, such that structural constraints hold. The structure must reconstruct or repair itself with a minimal delay. Such a property conduct to the self-stabilization properties.

In this paper, we focus on the demonstration of self-stabilization properties of the virtual structure described in [8]. This article makes two main contributions to the understanding of ad hoc self-organized virtual structures. First, it proves theoretically self-stabilized properties of the virtual structure. Secondly, it proposes an evaluation of convergence time of the algorithms through simulations.

Next, we will expose related work about self-organized virtual structures in ad hoc networks. Section 3 presents the distributed algorithm of the studied virtual structure. Section 4 presents the notations and complexity results. Section 5 presents an analytical study of the self-stabilized properties for the backbone, and section 6 is dedicated to the clusters. Results of simulations are given in section 7. Finally, we conclude this work and give some perspectives.

2   Related Work

Clusters. Clustering consists in grouping nodes geographically close. A clusterhead is often elected per cluster, managing its services area. Each node must be $k_{cluster}$ hops far at most from its clusterhead. Let $N_k(u)$ be the k-neighborhood of u, i.e. the set of nodes at most k hops far from u.

[6] is the most used algorithm to construct clusters. In the first step, each node initiates a neighborhood discovering. According to this information, each node decides to become clusterhead or not. The decision is propagated in the neighborhood so that each node which has not chosen any clusterhead yet takes the source as its new clusterhead. The decision could be based on several metrics (node identifier (id), mobility, location...). The authors propose to reconstruct the cluster if the diameter constraint of 3 hops is violated.

Backbones. A backbone could be well modeled with a *Minimum Connected Dominating Set* (MCDS): each node must be neighbor of at least one node of the MCDS which is a connected structure with a minimal cardinality. The construction of an MCDS is a NP-hard problem.

Many articles propose to construct a CDS in 2 steps. First, a dominating set (DS) is created, where each node is neighbor of a node in the DS. Secondly, the DS is interconnected to form a connected structure. Usually, 4 nodes states exist: dominator(in the CDS)/dominatee(not in the CDS)/active(in election)/idle(waits for the construction). In [2,3,1], a leader declares itself dominator and broadcasts its decision: its neighbors become its dominatees. The neighbor of dominatees become active. The active nodes with the highest weight in their neighborhood become dominators, and the process keeps on. Then, the DS must be interconnected. [3] proposes an iterative exploration requiring an important overhead and delay. [1] proposes a best effort approach, sending `invite` packets.

To the best of our knowledge, only [10] proposes a localized algorithm. A node is elected as a CDS member if it has 2 disconnected neighbors. Rules for a redundancy elimination are proposed: *a node with a set of 2 connected neighbors of higher id which cover its whole neighborhood becomes dominatee, else it becomes dominator.* This rule could be extended as: *a node with a set of neighbors of higher id forming a CDS and covering its whole neighborhood becomes dominatee, else it becomes dominator.* These rules create a CDS.

Self-stabilization. Self stabilization was first defined by Dijkstra [4]: a system is self-stabilizing when "regardless of its initial state, it is guaranteed to arrive at a legitimate state in a finite number of steps." [7] presents bases of the self-stabilization in the fault tolerance domain. In ad hoc networks, topology changes occur frequently, and could be modeled as temporary faults. In consequence, the self-stabilization properties of an algorithm are essential in the ad hoc networks. Recently, [5] studied a multicast protocol in ad hoc networks. To the best of our knowledge, no prior work was done to study the self-stabilization properties of the Connected Dominating Sets structures in ad hoc networks.

3   The Virtual Topology for Self-organization

We proposed in [8] a virtual topology for self-organization. This topology helps to structure the network, to optimize floodings, to create a hierarchy... It is constituted by a backbone and clusters. First, a k-neighborhood discovering is initiated. Then, the algorithm constructs a k_{cds}-CDS. Finally, some dominators are elected as clusterheads such than $k_{cluster}$-clusters are formed.

3.1   Backbone

Construction. The following nodes states exist: dominator / dominatee / active (in election) / idle (initial state). The Access Point (AP) acts as leader and becomes the first dominator. It propagates its new state k_{cds} hops far using an `hello` packet. The following rules are applied when a node receives an `hello` to construct a k_{cds}-Dominating Set:

1. An active or idle node which receives an `hello` from a dominator D, k_{cds} hops far, becomes dominatee and chooses D as parent
2. An idle node which receives an `hello` from a dominatee D, k_{cds} hops far, becomes active and triggers a timer of $\Delta_{election}$ seconds. $\Delta_{election}$ is the maximal round-trip-time to a farthest k_{cds}-neighbor.

3. After the timer expiration, a node which owns the highest weight among its active k_{cds}-neighbors becomes dominator. We can remark that a dominator has no parent during this phase.

The interconnection is inspired from [1]: the leader sends a cds-invite, with a TTL $2 \cdot k_{cds} + 1$. A dominator without parent chooses the source as new parent and sends a cds-join along the inverse route. Each intermediary dominatee becomes dominator and sets its parent as the next hop in the route. A dominator which sent a cds-join can send a cds-invite for other dominators in its $(2k_{cds} + 1)$-neighborhood. The dominators form finally a k_{cds}-CDS structure.

Maintenance. A node sends periodically hellos containing its id, weight, cds-state, parent in the CDS and ids of its 1-neighbors. hellos being forwarded k_{cds} hops along, each node has a complete knowledge of its k_{cds}-neighborhood. Hence, each dominatee can verify that its parent is still valid: it is at most k_{cds} hops far, is dominator, and there exists a dominatee neighbor having the same parent and being nearer of this parent (to force connectivity of the cds-dominance area).

The backbone must remain connected. Hence, the AP sends periodically ap-hellos, forwarded only by dominators. If a node misses several ap-hellos from its parent in the backbone, it considers itself disconnected and engages a backbone reconnection. It sends a cds-request in broadcast with a TTL of $2k_{cds}+1$. At least one connected dominator is at most $2k_{cds}+1$ hops far. It will reply with a cds-reply following the inverse route. Finally, the disconnected dominator sends a cds-accept to force intermediaries to become dominators.

To avoid a constant growth in the size of the backbone, we propose a mechanism to eliminate redundancy. A dominator is *useless* if it has no dominatee at exactly k_{cds} hops and no dominator for which it is a parent. An useless dominators sends a useless-advertisement forcing all its children in the backbone to choose its parent as new parent.

If many reconnections occur in the backbone, the load on the radio medium could be important. Hence, many collisions occur, disturbing the reconnection process. A dominator which tries many unsuccessful cds-reconnect sends a break in broadcast and takes the *idle* state. When a node receives a break from its parent, it becomes *idle* and forwards the message. Finally, the whole branch becomes *idle*. A connected dominator neighbor of the idle area will trigger the reconstruction, acting like the construction.

3.2 Clusters

Construction. As the backbone was constructed during the first phase, we use naturally it for the cluster construction. Only dominators participate to the election, reducing the overhead. Moreover, a clusterhead is forced to be dominator: a clusterhead will use further the backbone to optimize the floodings.

During the construction, each dominator begins to send periodically cluster-hellos when all its neighborhood has either the dominator or the dominatee state. cluster-hellos contain the address of the source and its weight. Theses packets are forwarded $k_{cluster} - k_{cds}$ hops along, uniquely by virtual neighbors. A virtual neighbor of N is either a parent of N in the CDS, or a child (a node for which N is a parent). A `cluster-hello` is forwarded only if it comes from a parent or a child in the CDS. A node is elected clusterhead if it has the highest weight among all its $k_{cluster} - k_{cds}$-virtual neighbors without clusterhead. An elected clusterhead sends a gratuitous `cluster-hello` to advertise its decision. A dominator without clusterhead chooses the source of the `cluster-hello` as clusterhead if the previous hop has also chosen this clusterhead, and if the clusterhead is at most $k_{cluster} - k_{cds}$ hops far. Such a condition forces the construction of connected clusters. Since dominatees are at most k_{cds} hops far from their parent, the algorithm constructs clusters of radius $k_{cluster}$.

Maintenance. `cluster-hellos` are not yet required for the maintenance. However, each node adds in its `hellos` its clusterhead, the relay and the distance toward it. Hence, each dominator can easily verify that its clusterhead is valid, i.e. a virtual neighbor has the same clusterhead and is at most $k_{cluster} - k_{cds} - 1$ hops far from its clusterhead.

If a node A loses its clusterhead C_{old}, i.e. C_{old} is no more valid, it searches a new candidate: a node is a virtual neighbors and announces a clusterhead at most $k_{cluster} - k_{cds} - 1$ hops far. When a node changes its clusterhead, it sends immediately a gratuitous `hello` to force other nodes to change potentially their own clusterhead. In this way, the convergence delay is reduced.

We propose a procedure to eliminate redundancy. If a clusterhead has no virtual neighbor having chosen it as clusterhead, the node is an useless clusterhead. Since a cluster is connected, no other node has a fortiori chosen it as clusterhead. A useless clusterhead tries to find a new valid clusterhead and become client.

4   Preliminaries

To study the ad hoc networks, we use the graph theory: a node in the network is represented by a vertex, and there exists one edge from one vertex to another iff there exists a radio link between the two nodes. Since we use only bidirectional links, we study undirected graphs. We note G(V,E) the graph, V being the set of vertices and E the set of edges. We assume that the graph is connected. We use the following notations:

- n: the cardinality of the network $(= |V|)$
- D: the set of dominators: $|D|$ is the CDS cardinality
- $N_k(u)$: the k-neighborhood of u
- $\Delta_k(u)$: the number of k-neighbors $(\Delta_k(u) = |N_k(u)|)$, i.e. the number of nodes at most k hops far. By convention, $\Delta_1(u) = \Delta(u)$
- $\Delta'_k(u)$: the number of k-virtual-neighbors. A virtual neighbor of N is either the parent or the child of N the CDS. We can remark that $\Delta'_k(u) \leq \Delta_k(u)$
- $w(u)$: the weight of the node u
- $d(u,v)$: the distance in hops from u to v
- h_T: the maximal distance from one node to the root of T (the *height* of T)

- $dominator(u)$: is the parent of a dominatee u. $dominator(u) \in N_{k_{cds}}(u)$
- $parent(u)$: is the parent of a dominator u. $parent(u) \in N(u)$

5   Backbone Self-stabilization

Ad hoc networks presenting a volatile topology, the virtual structure must adapt itself to changes. We present here and in the following section results about self-stabilization of the virtual structure presented in section 3. The construction algorithms converge in a finite time. In the same way, the maintenance algorithms form a valid virtual structure if the number of topology changes (edge/vertex addition or deletion) is finite and sufficiently inter-spaced. We assume that the graph associated to the ad hoc network is connected. If during the construction, not enough time is sufficient to let the structure converge because of unknown reason, the algorithm will converge during the maintenance step. More details are given in the long version of this article[9].

Hypothesis 1. *We assume that the radio topology is stable after a list of changes, constituted by a sum of elementary topology change (vertex/edge deletion/addition). The inter-changes time is sufficient to let the algorithm converge.*

We propose here to demonstrate that the construction algorithm provides a k_{cds}-Connected Dominating Set (CDS). We prove first that the backbone forms a k_{cds}-Dominating Set (DS), then a connected structure, being moreover a tree. Same proofs are given for the maintenance.

5.1   Construction

Creation of a k_{cds}-Dominating Set

Theorem 1. *The algorithm of the first phase terminates and forms a k_{cds}-DS.*

Lemma 1. *Every vertex has either the dominator or the dominatee state at the end of the first step.*

Proof. Let separate the problem in 2 cases:

- Let assume that an idle vertex I exists, and that there exists another not-idle vertex N in the connected component including N. Let $c = \langle I, c_1, c_2, ..., c_k, N \rangle$ be a path from I to N. All the k_{cds}-neighbors of I are idle, else I would have change its state. Thus, $\{c_j\}_{j \in [1..k_{cds}]}$ are idle. In the same way, the recurrence formula is: $\forall i, \{c_{i \cdot k_{cds} + j}\}_{j \in [1..k_{cds}]}$ *idle* $\Rightarrow \{c_{(i+1) \cdot k_{cds} + j}\}_{j \in [1..k_{cds}]}$ *idle*. In consequence, N must be idle. The connected component is only constituted by idle vertices. However, at least the leader is not idle. This leads to a contradiction.
- Let assume that a vertex N is active. If a k_{cds}-neighbor is dominator, N would be dominatee. In the same way, if all the k_{cds}-neighbors are dominatees, N would be dominator. If N is the active node of highest weight in its k_{cds}-neighborhood, then N is elected dominator after $\Delta_{election}$ time at most. So, there exists A_1, active, at most k_{cds} hops far and with an higher weight than N.

Let A_k be the graph so that its vertices are the active vertices of G during the kth round, and so that there exists an edge from a vertex a_i to a vertex a_j if and only if $w(a_i) < w(a_j)$. A_k is acyclic and has a finite cardinality, inferior or equal to n. The second property is trivial, let demonstrate the first property. Let $c = \langle c_0, c_1, ..., c_k \rangle$ be a cycle in A_k. An edge exists from c_i to c_{i+1}, i.e. $w(c_i) < w(c_{i+1})$ with $i \in [1..k-1]$. Transitively, $w(c_0) < w(c_k)$. However, c is a cycle: the edge (c_k, c_0) exists and $w(c_k) < w(c_0)$, this leads to a contradiction.

The graph A_k contains at least a sink a_k, i.e. a vertex has a null outer degree. After $\Delta_{election}$ seconds, a_k will be elected and become dominator, its k_{cds}-neighbors becoming its dominatees. Let I_k be the set of idle vertices in G during the kth round. During the round k, at least one vertex a_k becomes dominator. So, $a_k \notin A_{k+1} \cup I_{k+1}$. The k_{cds}-neighbors of a_k in $A_k \cup I_k$ become its dominatees. Simultaneously, some vertices are extracted from I_k and added to A_{k+1}. So $|I_k| + |A_k| \geq |I_{k+1}| + |A_{k+1}| + |\{a_k\}|$. In consequence: $|A_n| = |I_n| = 0$. In consequence, the algorithm will converge at the end of the first phase to a graph with no active vertex.

Lemma 2. *Every vertex is at most k_{cds} hops far from a dominator, or is itself a dominator, i.e. the graph of dominators forms a k_{cds}-DS.*

Proof. The proof comes directly from the lemma 1: at the end of the first phase, only dominatees and dominators exist: a dominatee changes its state because a dominator is at most k_{cds} hops far (by construction) and a vertex elected dominator remains dominator.

Formation of a k_{cds}-CDS

Theorem 2. *The set of dominators forms at the end of the construction a connected set of k_{cds}-dominating, i.e. a k_{cds}-CDS.*

Property 1. Let c be a path between 2 dominators D_1 and D_k. c follows the property 1 if it is composed by a set of i dominators, interspaced consecutively from each other by at most $2 \cdot k_{cds}$ dominatees: $\exists c = \langle D_1, d_1, ..., d_j, D_2, d_{j+1}, ..., D_i \rangle$ such that d_l are dominatees, and such that $d_c(D_i, D_{i+1}) \leq 2 \cdot k_{cds} + 1$.

Lemma 3. *A path c exists at the end of the first phase of the algorithm which follows the property 1, binding each dominator to the leader $\mathcal{L}$.*

Proof. Let D_k be the set of dominators elected during or before the k round. $D_0 = \{\mathcal{L}\}$. D_0 comprises only one dominator following trivially the property 1.

Let assume that D_k follows the property 1. At the end of the $k - 1^{th}$ round, a set S_{k-1} of vertices was elected dominators, such that $S_{k-1} \cup D_{k-1} = D_k$ and $S_{k-1} \cap D_{k-1} = \emptyset$. A node N of S_{k-1} is active during the k-1th round before being elected at the end of the round. Let $c_1 = <N, a_1, ...a_i, d>$ be the path from N to the nearest dominatee d during the round $k - 1$. N being active, by construction, $|c_1| \leq k_{cds} + 1$. The $\{a_l\}$ are by definition not dominatees, and are by construction at most k_{cds} hops far from d, a dominatee. In consequence, $\{a_l\}$

are active. Since N will be elected dominator, $\{a_l\}$ will become its dominatees at the end of the round. Let $c_2 =< d, d_1, ... d_i, D >$ be the path from the dominatee d to its parent D. By definition, $D \in D_k$, $|c_2| \leq k_{cds}$, and d_l are dominatees. Since $D \in D_k$, let $c_3 =< D, ..., \mathcal{L} >$ be the path from D to the leader. c_3 follows the property 1. Clearly, the path concatenation $c_1.c_2.c_3$ follows the property 1 at the end of the first phase of the algorithm.

Lemma 4. *If the property 1 is respected at the end of the first phase, the algorithm will construct a connected k_{cds}-DS.*

Proof. Let $\mathcal{D}_i$ be the set of dominators such that for each dominator D from $\mathcal{D}_i$, the path c from D to the leader, following the property 1 has at most i dominators. $\mathcal{D}_0 = \{\mathcal{L}\}$. $\mathcal{D}_0$ forms a trivial connected k_{cds}-DS applied to the vertices dominated by $\mathcal{D}_0$. It will send, according to the construction algorithm, a `join-invite` with a TTL$=2 \cdot k_{cds} + 1$.

Let assume that the set $\mathcal{D}_i$ forms a connected k_{cds}-DS. Let a dominator $u \in \mathcal{D}_{i+1}$, and c be the path from u to the leader $\mathcal{L}$, respecting the property 1. $c = \langle u, v_1, ..., v_k, \mathcal{L} \rangle$. From the lemma 3, there exists a dominator v_i from c, at most $2k_{cds}+1$ hops far from u since c respects the property 1. v_i has a path $c' \subset c$ respecting the property 1. Moreover, $v_i \in \mathcal{D}_i$. Thus, v_i will send a `join-invite` with a TTL$=2k_{cds}+1$. u will receive the `join-invite`, and will connect itself to $\mathcal{D}_i$. In consequence, $\mathcal{D}_{i+1}$ forms a connected k_{cds}-DS.

Formation of a Tree

Definition 1. *Let the CDS $\mathcal{G}_{CDS}$ containing all the vertices of G, and such that an edge exists from a vertex u to a vertex v iif v is the parent of u if u is a dominator, or iif v is the relay toward its dominator if u is a dominatee.*

Theorem 3. *$\mathcal{G}_{CDS}$ is a tree.*

Proof. According to the previous definition of $\mathcal{D}_i$, $\mathcal{D}_0 = \{\mathcal{L}\}$ is a trivial tree, formed by a singleton. Let assume that $\mathcal{D}_i$ forms a tree. $\mathcal{D}_i$ has $|\mathcal{D}_i - 1|$ edges. Let $u \in \mathcal{D}_{i+1}/\mathcal{D}_i$. u will interconnect itself to the CDS thanks to a `join-invite` sent by a dominator from $\mathcal{D}_i$. Let v be this dominator. The path $c = \langle u, u_1, ..., u_k, v \rangle$ has only dominatees, else u choosing the nearest dominator, will not interconnect itself to v. In consequence, dominatees will become dominators. We add to $\mathcal{D}_i$ a branch of k dominatees and one dominator, with k edges from a dominatee to its new parent, and an edge from u to its new parent. Thus, $\mathcal{D}_i \cup \{u\} \cup \{u_i\}_{i\in[1..k]}$ has $|\mathcal{D}_i| - 1 + 1 + k$ edges, i.e. $\left|\mathcal{D}_i \cup \{u\} \cup \{u_i\}_{i\in[1..k]}\right| - 1$ edges. In consequence, $\mathcal{D}_{i+1}$ is a tree.

Let d_i the set of dominatees at at most i hops from their father. When a vertex d_0 to $\mathcal{D}$, the vertex and the edge toward its parent is added. Then, $d_0 \cup \mathcal{D}$ remains a tree.

Let $d_i \cup \mathcal{D}$ be a tree. Let $u \in d_{i+1}$ be a dominatee. u chooses a parent and a relay r toward this parent. r is one hop nearer from its parent, by construction. Thus, $r \in d_i$. Only one vertex and one edge are added. $d_i \cup \mathcal{D}$ is a tree. A dominatee being at most k_{cds} hops far from its dominator, $\bigcup_{i \in [1..k_{cds}]} d_i \cup \mathcal{D} = G$. In conclusion, the CDS forms a tree.

5.2 Maintenance

Dominating Set

Theorem 4. *A dominatee has always a dominator, at most k_{cds} hops far, i.e. the CDS forms a k_{cds}-DS.*

Proof. Dominatees with a dominator neighbor choose it as parent. This dominator is valid. Let assume that the set of dominatees at most i hops far from their parent have a valid parent. A dominatee at most $i+1$ hops far from its parent has chosen it since it is at most k_{cds} hops far, through another dominatee having chosen the same dominator, but at i hops, with $i < k_{cds}$. Thus, since the parent of dominatees at most i hops far from their parent is valid, each dominatee chooses a valid parent.

A dominatee can have no dominator candidate for reconnection in its neighborhood table, i.e. no neighbor exists having chosen a dominator at most k_{cds}-1 hops far. Such a dominatee becomes active. An active vertex becomes dominatee iif it finds a valid dominator as parent. Active vertices becoming dominators execute the maintenance reserved for dominators. Thus, each dominatee has a dominator at most k_{cds} hops far, and this dominator is reachable through a dominatee with the same dominator, one hop nearer from its parent.

Connectivity

Theorem 5. *The set of dominators forms a tree.*

Lemma 5. *The set of dominators remains a (connected) tree when the radio topology is stable.*

Proof. Let assume that the topology is stable. Each dominator receives an `ap-hello`, maintaining the source as parent. Let $\mathcal{D}_i$ the set of dominators, i hops far via other dominators from the leader, the root of the CDS. $\mathcal{D}_i$ is supposed connected. The vertices of $\mathcal{D}_{i+1}/\mathcal{D}_i$ choose a parent in $\mathcal{D}_i$ since they receive the `ap-hello` from their parent, and so they are one hop farther from the leader. Thus, $\mathcal{D}_{i+1}$ is connected.

Let assume $\mathcal{D}_i$ has no cycle, E_i be the set of edges of $\mathcal{D}_i$, and V_i be the set of its vertices. We can establish that $|E_i| = |V_i - 1|$. For each vertex of $\mathcal{D}_{i+1}/\mathcal{D}_i$, we add one vertex in E_i and one edge in V_i. So :

$$|E_{i+1}| = |V_i| - 1 + [|V_{i+1}| - |V_i|] = |V_{i+1}| - 1$$

Thus $\mathcal{D}_{i+1}$ is connected, without any cycle.

Definition 2. *We consider a dominator u connected iif there exists an ascendant path directed from u to the leader $\mathcal{L}$, where the first edge is $(u, parent(u))$, and then constituted by the ascendant path $\langle parent(u), ..., \mathcal{L} \rangle$.*

Lemma 6. *When a dominator of a branch of the CDS reconnects itself, all its ascendants and descendants reconnect themselves.*

Proof. If a dominator u reconnects itself, then there exists a valid path $\langle u, ..., \mathcal{L} \rangle$ to the leader. Besides, a descendant or an ascendant v of u has by definition a path $\langle u, ..., v \rangle$. Thus, v has a path $\langle u, ..., v \rangle \cup \langle u, ..., \mathcal{L} \rangle$ to the leader. However, all dominators must perhaps change their parent to have a valid path to the leader.

Lemma 7. *When all dominator of a branch are disconnected, at least one dominator will reconnect itself.*

Proof. Every topology change could be decomposed by an elementary addition/deletion of edges. The addition of an edge in the graph cannot generate a disconnection in the CDS. Let assume that the edge (u, x) was deleted. After a finite time Δ_t, the whole branch, i.e. the descendants of u, will consider itself disconnected. A dominator considers itself disconnected when it missed all `ap-hellos` during Δ_t. Δ_t depends from the interval between two `ap-hellos` and the number of acceptable missed `ap-hellos`. Let v be a dominator descendant of u. u will not forward any `ap-hello` with an id superior to l, id of the last `ap-hello` forwarded before the edge (u, x) broke. Thus, the child of u cannot forward any `ap-hello` with an id superior to l. Recursively, v can neither receive nor forward any `ap-hello`. The dominators of the branch of root u consider themselves disconnected, and try to reconnect themselves via a dominator forwarding an `ap-hello` with an id superior to l.

At least one dominator finalizes its reconnection, and no cycle is created in the CDS, i.e. v cannot choose to reconnect itself to a descendant of u. Effectively, v asks for an `ap-hello` id higher than the last `ap-hello` forwarded by any descendant of u, as explained above. Let $\mathcal{D}$ be the set of descendant dominators of u, and their dominatees (the disconnected part). $\mathcal{D}$ is a connected component. Let $C = G/\mathcal{D}$. C is also a connected component: let $c \in L$ be a descendant of $\mathcal{L}$. $c \in C$ is by definition not descendant of u. Thus $u \notin \langle c, ..., \mathcal{L} \rangle$, in other words $\langle u, x \rangle$ and $\langle c, ..., \mathcal{L} \rangle$ are disjoint.

Let $\mathcal{N}$ be the set of vertices in C, neighbors of $\mathcal{A}$. $\mathcal{N} \neq \emptyset$: let $u \in \mathcal{D}$. The graph is assumed connected. Thus, a path $p = \langle u, u_1, ..., \mathcal{L} \rangle$ exists with $u \in \mathcal{D}$ and $\mathcal{L} \in C$. $u_i \in p$ exists such that $u_i \in C$ and $u_{i-1} \in \mathcal{D} \cap p$. By definition of $\mathcal{N}$, $u_i \in \mathcal{N}$. Moreover, $dominator(u_{i-1})$ is a dominator of the disconnected branch since u_{i-1} is in $\mathcal{D}$. $dominator(u_i)$ is connected, and is in C. $d(dominant(u_{i-1}), dominator(u_i)) \leq 2 \cdot k_{cds} + 1$. Thus, a dominator at most $2k_{cds} + 1$ hops far from a connected dominator exists in the disconnected branch.

Finally, $dominator(u_{i-1})$ will reconnect itself to $dominator(u_i)$ thanks to a `cds-reconnect` with a TTL$=2k_{cds} + 1$. According to the lemma 6, each dominator of $\mathcal{D}$ will reconnect itself and choose a new valid parent with an `ap-hello`.

In consequence, we can conclude:

Theorem 6. *When an edge deletion implicates a disconnection in the CDS, the CDS will reconstruct itself and a valid CDS will be created.*

Lemma 8. *If a break of the CDS occurs, the branch is broken and then rebuilt.*

Proof. The idle zone is a connected component of the graph. Since we consider the events as discrete, the set of not idle nodes forms also a connected component, comprising the leader $\mathcal{L}$. Let u be a vertex not idle, neighbor of the idle area. Such a vertex exists for the same reason as the lemma 7. Let i be in the idle zone, and neighbor of u. Two cases exist. If u is a dominator, it will reconnect itself in a finite time according to the theorem 6. If u is a connected dominator, it will send a `cds-invite` with a TTL=$k_{cds} + 1$. Clearly, i will receive this packet. If u is a dominatee, $dominator(u)$ will be in a finite time a connected dominator for the same reason as above. For the same reason as above, $dominator(u)$ will send a `cds-invite` with a TTL=$k_{cds} + 1$ and i will receive it.

A `cds-invite` received by the idle node i triggers the reconstruction of the idle branch. i becomes the leader of the zone. The reconstruction leader i reconnects itself to $dominator(u)$ in sending a `cds-accept`. $dominator(u)$ being by definition connected itself to the leader, i is transitively connected. Following a proof similar to theorem 2, a CDS is reconstructed.

6   Cluster Self-stabilization

6.1   Construction

Theorem 7. *The set of clusterheads constructs a $k_{cluster}$-dominating set, i.e. a $k_{cluster}$-clustering.*

Proof. If a dominator is not a clusterhead, then it chooses a dominator-clusterhead according to the process of neighborhood discovering on the CDS topology. `cluster hellos` are forwarded along the CDS-links, at most $k_{cluster} - k_{cds}$ hops far. So a dominator chooses a clusterhead at most $k_{cluster} - k_{cds} < k_{cluster}$ hops far. Moreover, a dominator chooses as clusterhead the source of a `cluster hellos` only if the previous hop chose also the source as clusterhead. Hence, the cluster is connected.

A dominatee has the same clusterhead as its dominator. Moreover, according to the lemma 2, it is at most k_{cds} hops far from its dominator, itself $k_{cluster} - k_{cds}$ hops far from its clusterhead. Transitively, a dominatee is at most $(k_{cluster} - k_{cds}) + k_{cds} = k_{cluster}$ hops far from its clusterhead. Since a dominatee is connected to its dominator through a path containing at most k_{cds} dominatees having chosen the same dominator, the cluster is connected.

According to the lemma 1, each vertex is either dominator or dominatee. In consequence, any vertex has a clusterhead, at most $k_{cluster}$ hops far.

6.2   Maintenance

Theorem 8. *The maintenance algorithm maintains a set of clusterheads forming a $k_{cluster}$-dominating set of $\mathcal{G}_{CDS}$.*

Lemma 9. *Dominators are at most $k_{cluster}$ hops far from their clusterhead.*

Proof. Let $\mathcal{G}'_{CDS}$ be the set of dominators having chosen the vertex C as clusterhead. There exists one edge in $\mathcal{G}'_{CDS}$ from u to v if v is the relay toward the clusterhead for u. We can remark that such edges and vertices own to $\mathcal{G}_{CDS}$. If v is at most H hops far from its clusterhead, u is at most $H + 1$ hops far from its own clusterhead in $\mathcal{G}'_{CDS}$ and also in $\mathcal{G}_{CDS}$.

$\mathcal{G}'_{CDS}$ is a tree, i.e. no cycle exists in $\mathcal{G}'_{CDS}$. Let assume the existence of a cycle $\langle u_1, ..., u_k \rangle$. u_i with $i \in [1..k]$ is H_i hops far from C. u_1 is the relay toward the clusterhead of u_k. So $H_k = H_1 + 1$. In the same way, u_{j+1} being the relay of u_j for $j \in [1..k-1]$, $H_j = H_{j+1} + 1 \Rightarrow H_j < H_{j+1}$. Thus, $H_k = H_1 + 1$ and $H_1 < H_k$, this leads to a contradiction. $\mathcal{G}'_{CDS}$ is a tree, a dominator chooses a relay one hop nearer of the clusterhead C.

Let D_i be the set of dominators which set the field *distance to clusterhead* to i in their `hellos`. Any dominator of D_i chooses by construction a relay in D_{i-1}. Let assume that the vertices in D_{i-1} are $i - 1$ hops far from C. Thus, the vertices of D_i are i hops far from C. Moreover, $D_0 = C$ and C is 0 hops far from itself. Finally, a dominator is allowed to choose a relay only if this relay is at most $k_{cluster} - kcds$ hops far from its clusterhead. Thus, $D_{k_{cluster} - k_{cds}} = \emptyset$. A dominator has either a clusterhead at most $k_{cluster} - k_{cds}$ hops far, or becomes its own clusterhead.

Lemma 10. *Dominatees are at most $k_{cluster}$ hops far from their clusterhead.*

Proof. This result holds for the same reasons as in the theorem 7.

7   Performance Evaluation

We simulate our solution with OPNET Modeler 8.1, using the WIFI standard model (300m radio range). The default parameters are 40 nodes and a degree of 10. The 95% confidence intervals are reported on the figures.

General Performances. Figure 1 presents the general performances of the CDS, without mobility. The cardinality is stable and scalable according to the number of nodes. The connectivity is not 100% since packet collisions may occur. However, it remains over 99.5%. Algorithms for both the CDS and the clusters seem present a good horizontal scalability, i.e. according to the cardinality.

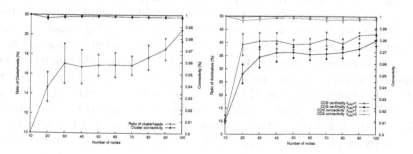

Fig. 1. Impact of the number of nodes

Convergence of the Construction Algorithm. We investigate the convergence time of the algorithm for the CDS construction. The clusters are always well-constructed before the end of the CDS construction. In consequence, the clusters are robust and don't represent the more sensitive part of the virtual structure. Thus, no simulation result about the convergence of clusters are given here, the convergence being too fast.

Approximately 5 seconds are needed to have no idle node in the networks with $k_{cds}=1$ and $k_{cluster}=2$ (fig. 2). Two supplementary seconds are necessary for the election, i.e. no active node remains in the network. Finally, less than 10 seconds are necessary to have a CDS *largely connected* or *strictly connected*. *Strictly connected* means that the tree relation (node→parent) creates a valid Connected Dominating Set. For a *largely connected* CDS, we take into account the redundant mesh structure of the CDS (edges between each backbone neighbor and each dominatee with the same parent). The construction algorithms, executed in parallel for the first and second phases seem efficient: they converge quickly, forming in a few seconds an operational and self-organized ad hoc network. Results are little higher but similar for $k_{cds}=2$ and $k_{cluster}=3$.

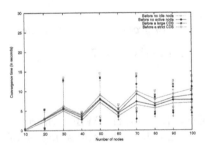

Fig. 2. Convergence Time for a CDS ($k_{cds}=1$ / $k_{cluster}=2$)

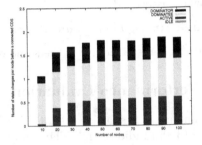

Fig. 3. Ratio of the number of cds state changes and the number of nodes before having a connected CDS ($k_{cds}=1$ / $k_{cluster}=2$)

In figure 3 is represented the number of state changes to have a valid CDS with $k_{cds}=1$ and $k_{cluster}=2$. More precisely, we measure the number of times a node changes its state before having a valid CDS. For example, with 100 nodes, 70% of the nodes become active, 80% dominatee and 35% dominators. During the first phase, among the active nodes, some nodes are elected dominators, and some other become dominatees. In the second phase, some dominatees become dominators to have a connected structure. In conclusion, a node changes its cds-state in average 2 times so that the structure becomes valid. Moreover, the number of changes per node is stable according to the number of participants.

Finally, the behavior of the structure was studied during the time (fig. 4). With a network of 50 nodes, $k_{cds}=1$ and $k_{cluster}=2$, idle and active nodes are only present during the construction part, in the very first seconds. Dominators are elected but, being redundant, they become dominatees after a few seconds.

During the maintenance, the structure is very stable: the number of dominators and dominatees is almost the same during all the simulation. Slight variations appear because of packet collisions: some `hello` or `ap-hello` packets are lost. The nodes *believe* that a topology change occurs in the neighborhood.

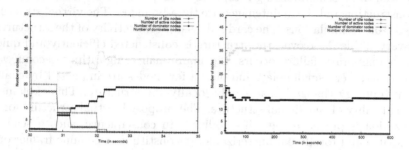

Fig. 4. Number of idle/active/dominator/dominatee nodes during a 600s simulation ($k_{cds}=1$ / $k_{cluster}=2$ / 50 nodes)

Temporary Failure. We simulate a temporary failure: a dominatee becomes arbitrarily dominator, or a dominator becomes arbitrarily dominatee (fig. 5). This simulates a node failure (after for example a power-off). We can remark that the convergence time is inferior to 3s for a dominator if the CDS is required to be strictly connected. If the CDS must be only largely connected (which is the case for flooding applications), the convergence time is inferior to 1.2 seconds. The convergence time is longer when $k_{cds}=3$ because of reconnection complexity.

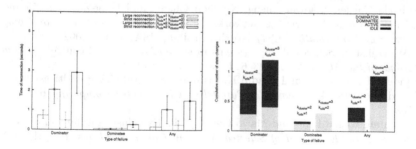

Fig. 5. Reconnection Time and number of changes after a temporary failure

8   Conclusion

In this article, we propose the construction and the maintenance of a virtual structure for the self-organization of ad hoc networks. A backbone helps to collect the traffic control and to distribute it efficiently in the network. Clusters create a hierarchical organization of the ad hoc networks, clusterheads managing their cluster, i.e. their services area. The construction algorithms are proven to construct a Connected Dominating Set and a clustering scheme in any ad hoc network. The complexity in messages is reduced, which represents a required property in wireless networks. Moreover, ad hoc networks present a very volatile topology. In consequence, maintenance is vital. The proposed algorithms are proven to be self-stabilizing if topology changes occur in the network. Both the construction and the maintenance are time-bounded. The virtual structure is studied trough simulations. The cardinality and connectivity of the structures remain very stable. Moreover, the structure is constructed efficiently and quickly. When a temporary failure occurs, the maintenance algorithms reconnect the structure in a very small delay, and only a few nodes are impacted by changes. A local topology change impacts only locally the structure. This explains the good scalability of the virtual structure. The proposed virtual structure for self-organization is proven to be self-stabilized. In consequence, such a scheme is very flexible and totally parameterizable. It constitutes a genuine framework to deploy efficiently new services in ad hoc networks: routing could be deployed on this self-organization, taking into account the natural scalability of the virtual structure.

References

1. K. Alzoubi, P-J. Wan, and O. Frieder. New distributed algorithm for connected dominating set in wireless ad hoc networks. In *Hawaii International Conference on System Sciences (HICSS)*, Big Island, USA, January 2002. IEEE.
2. Sergiy Butenko, Xiuzhen Cheng, Ding-Zhu Du, and Panos M. Pardalos. On the construction of virtual backbone for ad hoc wireless networks. In *Cooperative Control: Models, Applications and Algorithms*, pages 43–54. Kluwer Academic Publishers, 2003.
3. Mihaela Cardei, Xiaoyan Cheng, Xiuzhen Cheng, and Ding-Zhu Du. Connected domination in ad hoc wireless networks. In *International Conference on Computer Science and Informatics (CSI)*, North Carolina, USA, March 2002.
4. E.W. Dijkstra. Self-stabilizing systems in spite of distributed control. *Communications of the ACM*, 17(11):643–644, November 1974.
5. Sandeep K. S. Gupta and Pradip K. Srimani. Self-stabilizing multicast protocols for ad hoc networks. *Journal of Parallel and Distributed Computing*, 63(1):87–96, 2003.
6. Chunhung Richard Lin and Mario Gerla. Adaptive clustering for mobile wireless networks. *IEEE Journal of Selected Areas in Communications*, 15(7):1265–1275, 1997.
7. Marco Schneider. Sef-stabilization. *ACM Computing Surveys*, 25(1):45–67, March 1993.
8. Fabrice Theoleyre and Fabrice Valois. A virtual structure for mobility management in hybrid networks. In *Wireless Communications and Networking Conference (WCNC)*, volume 5 of *1*, pages 1035–1040, Atlanta, USA, March 2004. IEEE.
9. Fabrice Theoleyre and Fabrice Valois. About the self-stabilization of a virtual topology for self-organization in ad hoc networks. Research Report, INRIA, August 2005.
10. Jie Wu and Fei Dai. Distributed dominant pruning in ad hoc wireless networks. In *International Conference on Communications (ICC)*, pages 353–357, Anchorage, USA, May 2003. IEEE.

Author Index

Lecture Notes in Computer Science

For information about Vols. 1–3684

please contact your bookseller or Springer

Vol. 3729: Y. Gil, E. Motta, R.V. Benjamins, M.A. Musen (Eds.), The Semantic Web – ISWC 2005. XXIII, 1073 pages. 2005.

Vol. 3728: V. Paliouras, J. Vounckx, D. Verkest (Eds.), Integrated Circuit and System Design. XV, 753 pages. 2005.

Vol. 3726: L.T. Yang, O.F. Rana, B. Di Martino, J.J. Dongarra (Eds.), High Performance Computing and Communcations. XXVI, 1116 pages. 2005.

Vol. 3725: D. Borrione, W. Paul (Eds.), Correct Hardware Design and Verification Methods. XII, 412 pages. 2005.

Vol. 3724: P. Fraigniaud (Ed.), Distributed Computing. XIV, 520 pages. 2005.

Vol. 3723: W. Zhao, S. Gong, X. Tang (Eds.), Analysis and Modelling of Faces and Gestures. XI, 4234 pages. 2005.

Vol. 3722: D. Van Hung, M. Wirsing (Eds.), Theoretical Aspects of Computing – ICTAC 2005. XIV, 614 pages. 2005.

Vol. 3721: A. Jorge, L. Torgo, P.B. Brazdil, R. Camacho, J. Gama (Eds.), Knowledge Discovery in Databases: PKDD 2005. XXIII, 719 pages. 2005. (Subseries LNAI).

Vol. 3720: J. Gama, R. Camacho, P.B. Brazdil, A. Jorge, L. Torgo (Eds.), Machine Learning: ECML 2005. XXIII, 769 pages. 2005. (Subseries LNAI).

Vol. 3719: M. Hobbs, A.M. Goscinski, W. Zhou (Eds.), Distributed and Parallel Computing. XI, 448 pages. 2005.

Vol. 3718: V.G. Ganzha, E.W. Mayr, E.V. Vorozhtsov (Eds.), Computer Algebra in Scientific Computing. XII, 502 pages. 2005.

Vol. 3717: B. Gramlich (Ed.), Frontiers of Combining Systems. X, 321 pages. 2005. (Subseries LNAI).

Vol. 3716: L. Delcambre, C. Kop, H.C. Mayr, J. Mylopoulos, Ó. Pastor (Eds.), Conceptual Modeling – ER 2005. XVI, 498 pages. 2005.

Vol. 3715: E. Dawson, S. Vaudenay (Eds.), Progress in Cryptology – Mycrypt 2005. XI, 329 pages. 2005.

Vol. 3714: J. H. Obbink, K. Pohl (Eds.), Software Product Lines. XIII, 235 pages. 2005.

Vol. 3713: L.C. Briand, C. Williams (Eds.), Model Driven Engineering Languages and Systems. XV, 722 pages. 2005.

Vol. 3712: R. Reussner, J. Mayer, J.A. Stafford, S. Overhage, S. Becker, P.J. Schroeder (Eds.), Quality of Software Architectures and Software Quality. XIII, 289 pages. 2005.

Vol. 3711: F. Kishino, Y. Kitamura, H. Kato, N. Nagata (Eds.), Entertainment Computing - ICEC 2005. XXIV, 540 pages. 2005.

Vol. 3710: M. Barni, I. Cox, T. Kalker, H.J. Kim (Eds.), Digital Watermarking. XII, 485 pages. 2005.

Vol. 3709: P. van Beek (Ed.), Principles and Practice of Constraint Programming - CP 2005. XX, 887 pages. 2005.

Vol. 3708: J. Blanc-Talon, W. Philips, D.C. Popescu, P. Scheunders (Eds.), Advanced Concepts for Intelligent Vision Systems. XXII, 725 pages. 2005.

Vol. 3707: D.A. Peled, Y.-K. Tsay (Eds.), Automated Technology for Verification and Analysis. XII, 506 pages. 2005.

Vol. 3706: H. Fuks, S. Lukosch, A.C. Salgado (Eds.), Groupware: Design, Implementation, and Use. XII, 378 pages. 2005.

Vol. 3704: M. De Gregorio, V. Di Maio, M. Frucci, C. Musio (Eds.), Brain, Vision, and Artificial Intelligence. XV, 556 pages. 2005.

Vol. 3703: F. Fages, S. Soliman (Eds.), Principles and Practice of Semantic Web Reasoning. VIII, 163 pages. 2005.

Vol. 3702: B. Beckert (Ed.), Automated Reasoning with Analytic Tableaux and Related Methods. XIII, 343 pages. 2005. (Subseries LNAI).

Vol. 3701: M. Coppo, E. Lodi, G. M. Pinna (Eds.), Theoretical Computer Science. XI, 411 pages. 2005.

Vol. 3700: J.F. Peters, A. Skowron (Eds.), Transactions on Rough Sets IV. X, 375 pages. 2005.

Vol. 3699: C.S. Calude, M.J. Dinneen, G. Păun, M. J. Pérez-Jiménez, G. Rozenberg (Eds.), Unconventional Computation. XI, 267 pages. 2005.

Vol. 3698: U. Furbach (Ed.), KI 2005: Advances in Artificial Intelligence. XIII, 409 pages. 2005. (Subseries LNAI).

Vol. 3697: W. Duch, J. Kacprzyk, E. Oja, S. Zadrożny (Eds.), Artificial Neural Networks: Formal Models and Their Applications – ICANN 2005, Part II. XXXII, 1045 pages. 2005.

Vol. 3696: W. Duch, J. Kacprzyk, E. Oja, S. Zadrożny (Eds.), Artificial Neural Networks: Biological Inspirations – ICANN 2005, Part I. XXXI, 703 pages. 2005.

Vol. 3695: M.R. Berthold, R.C. Glen, K. Diederichs, O. Kohlbacher, I. Fischer (Eds.), Computational Life Sciences. XI, 277 pages. 2005. (Subseries LNBI).

Vol. 3694: M. Malek, E. Nett, N. Suri (Eds.), Service Availability. VIII, 213 pages. 2005.

Vol. 3693: A.G. Cohn, D.M. Mark (Eds.), Spatial Information Theory. XII, 493 pages. 2005.

Vol. 3692: R. Casadio, G. Myers (Eds.), Algorithms in Bioinformatics. X, 436 pages. 2005. (Subseries LNBI).

Vol. 3691: A. Gagalowicz, W. Philips (Eds.), Computer Analysis of Images and Patterns. XIX, 865 pages. 2005.

Vol. 3690: M. Pěchouček, P. Petta, L.Z. Varga (Eds.), Multi-Agent Systems and Applications IV. XVII, 667 pages. 2005. (Subseries LNAI).

Vol. 3689: G.G. Lee, A. Yamada, H. Meng, S.H. Myaeng (Eds.), Information Retrieval Technology. XVII, 735 pages. 2005.

Vol. 3688: R. Winther, B.A. Gran, G. Dahll (Eds.), Computer Safety, Reliability, and Security. XI, 405 pages. 2005.

Vol. 3687: S. Singh, M. Singh, C. Apte, P. Perner (Eds.), Pattern Recognition and Image Analysis, Part II. XXV, 809 pages. 2005.

Vol. 3686: S. Singh, M. Singh, C. Apte, P. Perner (Eds.), Pattern Recognition and Data Mining, Part I. XXVI, 689 pages. 2005.

Vol. 3685: V. Gorodetsky, I. Kotenko, V.A. Skormin (Eds.), Computer Network Security. XIV, 480 pages. 2005.